all recipes®
all-time favorite
best brand
recipes

California Harvest Pizza, page 69

all recipes all-time favorite
best brand recipes

Oxmoor House.

©2004 by Oxmoor House, Inc.
Book Division of Southern Progress Corporation
P. O. Box 2463, Birmingham, Alabama 35201

Allrecipes and *Allrecipes.com* are trademarks or registered trademarks of Allrecipes.com, Inc.

BABY RUTH®, BUNCHA CRUNCH®, BUTTERFINGER®, CARNATION®, CRUNCH®, GOOBERS®, JUICY JUICE®, LIBBY'S®, NESQUIK®, NESTLÉ®, RAISINETS®, SNO-CAPS®, SWEETARTS®, TOLL HOUSE®, and WONDERBALLS® are registered trademarks of Societe des Produits Nestlé S.A., Vevey, Switzerland.

ISBN: 0-8487-2830-0
Library of Congress Control Number: 2004102620
Printed in the United States of America
Second Printing 2004

To order additional publications, call 1-800-765-6400.

For more books to enrich your life, visit
oxmoorhouse.com

Cover: Key Lime Pie with Real Butter (page 258)
Back Cover: Chipotle Steak with Pineapple-Avocado Salsa (page 123); Fruit Smoothies (page 77); Chocolate Mint Layered Torte (page 300)

Allrecipes.com, Inc.
President: Bill Moore
Senior VP Development: Tim Hunt
Vice President Marketing: Esmée Williams
Production Manager: Jenni Johns
Senior Recipe Editor: Sydny Carter
Senior Food Editor: Jennifer Anderson
Recipe Editors: Emily Brune, Richard Kozel, Lesley Peterson
Creative Direction: Yann Oehl, Jeff Cummings

Allrecipes.com, Inc.
400 Mercer Street, Suite 302
Seattle, WA 98109
(206) 292-3990
www.Allrecipes.com

Oxmoor House, Inc.
Editor-in-Chief: Nancy Fitzpatrick Wyatt
Executive Editor: Susan Carlisle Payne
Art Director: Cynthia Rose Cooper
Copy Chief: Allison Long Lowery

Allrecipes All-Time Favorite Best Brand Recipes
Editor: Allison Long Lowery
Assistant Editor: McCharen Pratt
Nutrition Editor: Holley Contri Johnson, M.S., R.D.
Editorial Assistant: Shannon Friedmann
Proofreaders: Jacqueline Giovanelli, Terri Laschober
Senior Designer: Melissa Clark
Senior Photographer: Jim Bathie
Photographer: Brit Huckabay
Senior Photo Stylist: Kay E. Clarke
Photo Stylist: Ashley J. Wyatt
Director, Test Kitchens: Elizabeth Tyler Luckett
Assistant Director, Test Kitchens: Julie Christopher
Test Kitchens Staff: Kristi Carter, Nicole Lee Faber, Kathleen Royal Phillips, Jan A. Smith, Elise Weis, Kelley Wilton
Publishing Systems Administrator: Rick Tucker
Director of Production: Phillip Lee
Production Manager: Greg A. Amason
Production Assistant: Faye Porter Bonner

Contributors:
Copy Editor: Dolores Hydock
Indexer: Mary Ann Laurens
Photographer: Lee Harrelson
Test Kitchens Intern: Julie Perno

contents

dear friends:

Well, we've done it again. We've figured out a way to bring you the very best mealtime solutions. The dedicated online community of millions of home cooks at **Allrecipes.com** has put a whole new set of recipes to the test, and we've got the best of them here in this invaluable cookbook. America's most trusted brand names like Hershey's®, Tyson®, Nestlé®, and Land O'Lakes® submitted recipes on **Allrecipes.com,** the world's favorite cooking website, and put them to the test—the **Allrecipes.com** test. Online reviewers rated and reviewed the recipes after making them for their own families, and the verdict is in. We've got the best brand name recipes right here for you!

Combining trusted brand name recipes with online reviewers' savvy is not the only thing we're doing differently. To start things off, we've compiled ten **Quick & Easy Menus** to take all the guesswork out of tonight's "What's for Dinner?" dilemma. So many times, quick-and-easy means takeout or boxed dinners with no fresh ingredients involved. With these menus, you'll find recipes that pair the convenience of your favorite brand-name products with the comfort of a home-cooked meal. You'll have dinner on the table before the delivery man ever had a chance to start his engine.

You'll also find more than your typical quick-and-easy fare. Look to our **Breakfast Anytime** chapter for pancakes, egg casseroles, and other dishes that are perfect for a morning's rush out the door, a casual brunch, or a breakfast-for-dinner kind of night. In the **Entrées** chapter, you'll find recipes for elegant steak dinners, updated standbys like Chicken Pot Pie, and meatless main dishes to suit all your family's needs.

Save room for a bonus section that's sure to fulfill all your sweet cravings. In a special section of **Chocolate Fantasies,** we've gathered all the best from Hershey's®, Eagle Brand®, McCormick®, Nestlé®, and Land O'Lakes® for the ultimate in chocolate indulgence. Decadent cakes, sinful pies, stunning soufflés, and irresistible cookies and candies make being bad feel oh-so-good.

Comb through the pages, and you're sure to find what you're looking for. We've packed each page with all the information you'll need to make your time in the kitchen a pleasure. Each recipe comes with either a Test Kitchen Secret or a suggestion from online reviewers who reveal what they did when they made the dish. We've also featured tip boxes that highlight secrets or seasonal tips from our trusted brands. We hope each page will inspire you to get into your kitchen and out without any fuss!

Happy Cooking,

The Editors of Allrecipes

All About Allrecipes.com

Seven years ago, we created a place for home cooks to share their favorite recipes via the Internet. As word spread, others joined in, and in no time, **Allrecipes.com** grew into the world's largest community of home cooks—over 6 million strong—and became the number-one source for online recipes. On the website, recipes are posted for everyday home cooks to test and then rate and review them online. It's an interactive recipe swap that's helping over 6 million people get dinner on the table with confidence.

About the recipes

On **Allrecipes.com,** visitors post recipe reviews, and for this book, we've included some of the most helpful reviews alongside many of the recipes. Look for "What Other Cooks Have Done" beside recipes for these reviews that give serving suggestions and cooking tips. Look for "Test Kitchen Secrets" beside other recipes for hints on ingredients or techniques that will make you an expert.

Prep and cook times are included as a basic guide with each recipe to help you plan meals. We also include marinate, freeze, or chill times when applicable. Remember that these times are approximate. How fast you chop, the accuracy of your oven temperature, humidity, and other factors can affect your times.

Flip through the book and find banners that identify recipes that are Make-Ahead, Healthy, Kid-Friendly, Comfort Food, From the Grill, Party Pleaser, Holiday Fare, and Quick & Easy. These banners make locating recipes that suit your needs a breeze.

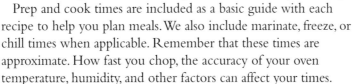

Need more information?

You'll find helpful tip boxes and test kitchen secrets throughout the book to help you with basic cooking and baking questions, and you can visit us online if you need more information. Check out the "Cooking Advice" section at **Allrecipes.com** where you can browse through articles and step-by-step cooking tutorials. You can also find information about our trusted brands on the website.

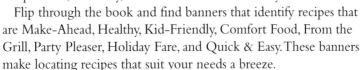

Our trusted brands

We would like to thank the following brands for submitting their best recipes for this one-of-a-kind recipe collection. Here's a complete list of all the brands that have recipes featured in the book: Boca®; Bush's Best® Beans; Cook's® Brand Ham; Dole®; Eagle Brand®; Gorton's®; Hershey's®; Hormel Foods Corporation; Kretschmer® Wheat Germ; Land O'Lakes, Inc.; Lindsay® Olives; McCormick® & Company; Near East®; Nestlé®; The Quaker® Oats Company; and Tyson®.

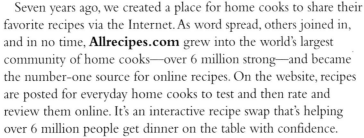

the quick & easy kitchen

Shortcut Strategies

You don't have to spend hours in the kitchen to have memorable meals. Here are some of our favorite ways to streamline preparation:

• **Read the recipe and assemble** all the ingredients and equipment before starting.

• **Chop an ingredient used in two recipes within a menu only once.** For example, if you'll need ½ cup chopped onion for 2 recipes, go ahead and chop 1 cup.

• **Purchase ingredients in their closest-to-usable form,** such as skinned and boned chicken breast halves, peeled shrimp, and shredded cheese.

• **When making a pasta dish,** put on the water to boil as soon as you start preparing the rest of the meal. Cover the pot to hold in the heat so the water will come to a boil faster.

Clean Up Fast

Neatness counts when you're preparing a quick meal. A little attention to these tips will mean less time cleaning up later.

• **Grating Parmesan cheese?** Cleanup is a breeze when you lightly brush the grater with oil or spray it with vegetable cooking spray before grating.

• **Rinse the measuring cup or spoon** with hot water before measuring honey or other sticky ingredients; the honey will then slide right out.

• **Skip the cutting board.** Kitchen shears minimize cleanup when you chop tomatoes right in the can or chop fresh herbs over a measuring cup.

• **Measure and mix ingredients with cleanup in mind.** Measure dry ingredients before wet ones, and you won't have to wash measuring utensils in between measurings.

• **Don't wash the food processor bowl between** chopping or slicing ingredients if the ingredients will later be combined.

• **Use vegetable cooking spray.** Baked food won't be as hard to clean off casserole dishes and pans if you coat them first.

• **Use disposable products when possible.** Lining baking pans with aluminum foil and crumbling crackers in zip-top plastic bags make cleanup a snap.

• **Measure ingredients** onto wax paper or paper plates for easy cleanup.

• **Nonstick cookware** and bakeware make for easy cleanup.

• **Clean up as you cook** and avoid a huge stack of dishes in the sink later.

Superfast Supermarket

Save yourself the time of going up and down every aisle at the grocery store. The list below is more than a grocery list—it's a strategic plan for shopping. We've identified the key areas of the store where you'll find convenience products so you can make selections quickly and move on. In each section, the items are listed that you'll need to keep on hand to be a superfast chef extraordinaire.

The order in which you move through the sections isn't crucial, but we do recommend that you add dairy products and frozen foods to your cart last.

One key point to keep in mind for this strategy to work: Stock up on staples. If you shop once for the staples and condiments that you use frequently, you won't have to spend time doing that each time you visit the store. Make a list of the staple foods your family loves, and keep a copy of the list for restocking.

Produce
- presliced vegetables
- packaged salad greens
- presliced fruits
- jars of fresh fruit

Canned goods
- beans
- vegetables
- fruits
- broth
- soup
- tomatoes
- tomato sauces
- pasta sauces

Pasta, rice & grains
- couscous
- dry pastas
- boil-in-bag rices
- quick-cooking rice mixes

Deli/bakery
- roasted chicken
- sliced meats
- breads/rolls
- salad bar items

Refrigerated meats
- boneless chicken tenders/breast halves
- grilled chicken slices
- premarinated meats and poultry
- roasted chicken
- precooked pot roast
- cooked beef crumbles
- ground round

Dairy
- preshredded cheese
- sliced cheese
- refrigerated pastas
- cream cheese
- sour cream
- yogurt
- milk

Freezer
- vegetables
- fruits
- chopped cooked chicken
- fish
- ice cream, sorbet, frozen yogurt

Microwave Shortcuts

Don't wait for butter to soften or take time out to toast nuts called for in a recipe.
Use your microwave to speed up these common cooking tasks.

Cooking Bacon—Cook on HIGH

Place bacon on a microwave-safe rack in a 9x13 inch baking dish; cover with paper towels. Microwave on HIGH until bacon is crisp. Drain bacon.

- 1 slice — 1 to 2 minutes
- 4 slices — 3½ to 4½ minutes
- 6 slices — 5 to 7 minutes

Melting Chocolate— Cook on MEDIUM (50% power)

Place chocolate in a small microwave-safe bowl; microwave on MEDIUM until melted, stirring once.

- 1 to 2 squares — 1½ to 2 minutes
- 4 to 5 squares — 2 to 2½ minutes
- ½ to 1 cup morsels — 2 to 3 minutes
- 1½ cups morsels — 3 to 3½ minutes

Softening Ice Cream— Cook on MEDIUM (50% power)

Microwave on MEDIUM until soft.

- ½ gallon ice cream — 30 seconds

Softening Cream Cheese— Cook on MEDIUM (50% power)

Unwrap the block, and place it on a microwave-safe plate. Microwave on MEDIUM just until softened.

- 1 (8 ounce) package cream cheese — 1 minute

Softening Butter or Margarine— Cook on LOW (10% power)

Place butter in a microwave-safe measure or bowl; microwave on LOW until softened.

- 1 to 2 tablespoons — 15 to 30 seconds
- ¼ to ½ cup — 1 to 1¼ minutes
- 1 cup — 1½ to 1¾ minutes

Toasting Nuts—Cook on HIGH

Spread nuts on a pie plate. Microwave on HIGH until toasted; stir at 2-minute intervals.

- ¼ cup chopped nuts — 3 minutes
- ½ cup chopped nuts — 3½ minutes
- 1 cup chopped nuts — 4 to 5 minutes

Thawing Whipped Topping—Cook on MEDIUM-LOW (30% power)

Microwave, uncovered, on MEDIUM-LOW until thawed.

- 1 (8 ounce) container frozen whipped topping — 1 to 1½ minutes

Freezer Friendly

Have single-serving homemade meals ready to go, make the most of extra ingredients, and keep perishable items on hand—all with the help of your freezer.

Single servings

• **Freeze single servings** of soup, stew, chili, and spaghetti sauce in microwave-safe containers.

• **Bake a double batch** of muffins, waffles, or pancakes, and freeze the leftovers up to 1 month. Reheat in the toaster oven or microwave oven.

• **Cook extra rice or pasta** and freeze in individual or family-sized portions up to 1 month. Simply microwave to thaw.

While you're at it...

• **Already shredding cheese,** chopping peppers or onions, or processing breadcrumbs or nuts for a recipe? Make extra and freeze for later use.

• **For peppers and onions,** spread a thin layer of the chopped vegetables on a baking sheet; freeze the vegetables 30 minutes or until frozen solid. Crumble them into zip-top freezer bags; freeze up to 3 months. Scoop out to measure.

Keep on hand

• **Parsley:** After snipping 1 or 2 tablespoons from a bunch of parsley for a recipe, chop the remainder. Then freeze it in an airtight freezer bag up to 2 months.

• **Fresh ginger:** Store in the freezer in a heavy-duty zip-top plastic bag; it's easy to peel and grate while frozen.

• **Browned ground chuck:** Drain browned meat, and spread in a thin layer on a baking sheet. Freeze 45 minutes. Crumble the meat into a zip-top freezer bag, label, and freeze up to 3 months. You can then quickly prepare chili, spaghetti, and casseroles.

Multitalented Tools

Make life easier by putting these versatile tools to work.

• **Swivel-bladed vegetable peeler:** Keep this handy tool for tasks other than peeling vegetables. Use it to shred a small amount of cheese, remove strings from celery stalks, or make quick chocolate curls from a milk chocolate candy bar.

• **Rolling pin:** Make cracker crumbs or cookie crumbs quickly without a food processor. Place crackers or cookies in a heavy-duty zip-top plastic bag; seal bag and roll with a rolling pin or pound gently with a meat mallet.

• **Pastry blender:** Use to mash avocados for chunky guacamole or to slice butter and hard-boiled eggs.

• **Metal colander:** Place upside down over the skillet when frying; this will prevent splatters while allowing steam to escape.

• **Pizza cutter:** Cut day-old bread into cubes for croutons using a pizza cutter—it's faster than using a knife.

**Citrus-Spiced Pork
Lo Mein, page 42**

quick & easy menus

Get a head start on **weeknight meals,** casual entertaining, and even holiday planning with these simple and **inspiring** menus. Whip up luscious selections on the grill, make elegant meals in a flash, and create **comfort food** for your whole family.

lazy gourmet

Honey-Ginger Grilled Salmon
Asian Pilaf Salad
Berry Lemon Mousse Parfaits

serves 4

5 star

submitted by: **McCormick® & Company**

Prep Time: 7 minutes
Marinate Time: 15 minutes
Cook Time: 15 minutes

What Other Cooks Have Done:

"My husband and I love this recipe. We choose to bake rather than grill. We add crushed red pepper to it for a spicy taste. I even cook a second batch of this marinade in a saucepan to pour over white rice."

Honey-Ginger Grilled Salmon

Honey and ginger provide a sweet and spicy sensation for salmon or chicken. Just substitute four boneless, skinless chicken breasts for the salmon.

1	teaspoon McCORMICK® Ground Ginger	⅓	cup orange juice
1	teaspoon McCORMICK® Garlic Powder	¼	cup honey
		1	green onion, chopped
⅓	cup soy sauce	1½	pounds salmon fillets (4 [6 ounce] fillets)

1. In a large zip-top plastic bag, combine first 6 ingredients; mix well. Place salmon in bag and seal tightly. Turn bag gently to distribute marinade.
2. Refrigerate 15 minutes or up to 30 minutes for stronger flavor. Turn bag occasionally.
3. Lightly grease cold grill rack. Preheat grill for medium heat. Remove salmon from marinade; reserve the marinade. Grill 12 to 15 minutes per inch of thickness or until fish flakes easily with a fork. Brush with reserved marinade up until the last 5 minutes of cooking time. Discard leftover marinade. **Yield:** 4 servings.

Per serving: 335 calories, 38g protein, 23g carbohydrate, 10g fat, 1g fiber, 76mg cholesterol, 1287mg sodium

Honey-Ginger Grilled Salmon and Asian Pilaf Salad, page 16

Asian Pilaf Salad *(pictured on page 15)*

quick & easy

submitted by: **Near East®**

Prep Time: 15 minutes
Cook Time: 20 minutes
Chill Time: 2 hours

Test Kitchen Secret:

If you'd like to pump up the heat in this salad, increase the crushed red pepper to taste. For another flavor boost, toast the peanuts before adding them to the salad.

This chilled rice salad has spicy undertones. Carrots, green onions, and peanuts help punctuate the salad with authentic Asian flavor.

1	(6.09 ounce) package NEAR EAST® Rice Pilaf Mix	½	cup diced carrots
1	tablespoon olive oil	¼	cup chopped peanuts
1	tablespoon soy sauce	¼	cup chopped green onions
1	clove garlic, minced	2	tablespoons diced red bell pepper
¼	teaspoon crushed red pepper flakes		Chopped peanuts (optional)

1. Prepare rice according to package directions, omitting butter or olive oil.
2. Stir in next 8 ingredients. Chill for 2 to 4 hours. Top with extra chopped peanuts right before serving, if desired. **Yield:** 4 servings.

Per serving: 267 calories, 7g protein, 39g carbohydrate, 8g fat, 2g fiber, 0mg cholesterol, 839mg sodium

Berry Lemon Mousse Parfaits

make-ahead

submitted by: **McCormick® & Company**

Prep Time: 15 minutes

What Other Cooks Have Done:

"Wow, is this ever yummy and refreshing! I added some crushed gingersnaps for a little extra punch. It's so easy to make, looks incredibly elegant, and tastes fabulous!"

Berry Lemon Mousse Parfaits make a refreshing, quick and easy, no-cook dessert. Lemon juice, lemon extract, and vanilla brighten the sweetness of fresh berries to complete this perfect summer dessert.

¾	cup heavy cream	½	teaspoon McCORMICK® Pure Vanilla Extract
¼	cup white sugar, divided		
2	tablespoons lemon juice	½	cup sliced strawberries
½	teaspoon McCORMICK® Pure Lemon Extract	½	cup fresh blueberries
		½	cup fresh raspberries

1. In a large, chilled mixing bowl, using an electric mixer, beat cream, 3 tablespoons sugar, lemon juice, and extracts until mixture mounds softly.
2. In a small bowl, add remaining sugar to berries. Mix gently.
3. Spoon layers of mousse and fruit into dessert dishes. Serve immediately or chill for several hours before serving. **Yield:** 4 servings.

Per serving: 222 calories, 1g protein, 18g carbohydrate, 17g fat, 1g fiber, 61mg cholesterol, 18mg sodium

Berry Lemon Mousse Parfait

summertime soirée

BBQ Chicken the Old Bay® Way
Summertime Coleslaw
corn on the cob
Special Dark® Picnic Cake
S'mores that Crunch!

serves 6

BBQ Chicken the Old Bay® Way

Old Bay® adds the flavor of Chesapeake Bay country to classic barbecued chicken.

1	cup ketchup	1	teaspoon Worcestershire sauce
¼	cup apple cider vinegar	1	tablespoon prepared
2	tablespoons brown sugar		horseradish
2	teaspoons OLD BAY® Seasoning	3½	pounds bone-in chicken parts Vegetable oil
1	teaspoon McCORMICK® Ground Mustard	2	teaspoons OLD BAY® Seasoning
¼	teaspoon McCORMICK® Garlic Powder		

1. Combine first 8 ingredients in a small saucepan. Simmer over low heat for 10 minutes. Remove from heat.
2. Preheat grill for high heat. Lightly brush chicken pieces with oil. Sprinkle generously with OLD BAY® Seasoning.
3. Grill chicken over hot coals for about 40 minutes, turning often. During last 10 minutes of grilling, brush chicken with barbecue sauce. Serve with additional barbecue sauce on the side. **Yield:** 6 servings.

Per serving: 627 calories, 47g protein, 17g carbohydrate, 41g fat, 1g fiber, 222mg cholesterol, 1058mg sodium

Summertime Coleslaw

**A favorite coleslaw with just the right amount of seasoning!
Add some red cabbage to brighten the color.**

make-ahead

submitted by: **McCormick® & Company**

Prep Time: 15 minutes
Chill Time: 2 hours

1	cup mayonnaise	
2	tablespoons vinegar	
2	tablespoons white sugar	
1½	teaspoons McCORMICK® SEASON-ALL® Seasoned Salt	

1 teaspoon McCORMICK® Ground Mustard
1 teaspoon McCORMICK® Celery Seed
7 cups shredded cabbage
1 cup shredded carrots

What Other Cooks Have Done:
"This is a very good coleslaw recipe. I replaced half the mayo with the reduced-fat type, and it still tasted great."

1. In a small bowl, combine mayonnaise, vinegar, sugar, seasoned salt, ground mustard, and celery seed.

2. In a large bowl, toss cabbage and carrots together. Add mayonnaise mixture and mix well.

3. Refrigerate 2 hours or until ready to serve. Stir again just before serving. **Yield:** 8 servings.

Per serving: 238 calories, 2g protein, 10g carbohydrate, 22g fat, 2g fiber, 16mg cholesterol, 403mg sodium

**BBQ Chicken the Old Bay® Way
and Summertime Coleslaw**

submitted by: HersheysKitchens.com

Prep Time: 25 minutes
Cook Time: 42 minutes

Test Kitchen Secret:

Hershey's® Special Dark® Chocolate Chips are the first "mildly sweet" chocolate chips with a deeper, darker, and richer flavor profile. In fact, these chips taste so great right out of the bag that they may not even make it into your favorite recipes. But when they do, Special Dark® Chips elevate even the best desserts to new levels of excellence.

Special Dark® Picnic Cake

A deep, dark chocolate chip cake with a rich, dark frosting, Hershey's® Special Dark® Picnic Cake is just the thing for any outdoor adventure! But don't forget, it's perfect for indoor ones, too!

1 cup HERSHEY'S® SPECIAL DARK® Chocolate Chips	½ cup sour cream
¼ cup (½ stick) butter or margarine	2 eggs
1⅓ cups boiling water	2 teaspoons baking soda
2⅓ cups all-purpose flour	1 teaspoon salt
1¼ cups white sugar	1 teaspoon vanilla extract
	SPECIAL DARK® Frosting

1. Preheat oven to 350°F. Grease and flour a 9x13 inch pan.

2. Combine chocolate chips, butter, and water in a large mixing bowl; stir with a spoon until chocolate is melted and mixture is blended. Gradually add flour, sugar, sour cream, eggs, baking soda, salt, and vanilla; beat on low speed of electric mixer until smooth. Pour batter into prepared pan.

3. Bake in the preheated oven 35 to 40 minutes or until a toothpick inserted in center of cake comes out clean. Cool completely in pan on wire rack. Frost. **Yield:** 15 servings.

Special Dark® Frosting

¼ cup (½ stick) butter or margarine	1½ cups confectioners' sugar
1 cup HERSHEY'S® SPECIAL DARK® Chocolate Chips	¼ cup milk
	½ teaspoon vanilla extract

1. Place butter and chocolate chips in a medium microwave-safe bowl. Microwave on HIGH 1 minute; stir. If necessary, microwave on HIGH 15 seconds at a time, stirring after each heating, until chocolate is melted and mixture is smooth when stirred. Gradually beat in confectioners' sugar, milk, and vanilla, beating until smooth. Refrigerate 15 to 20 minutes or until of desired spreading consistency. **Yield:** 1⅔ cups.

Per serving (includes cake and frosting): 438 calories, 5g protein, 64g carbohydrate, 19g fat, 1g fiber, 50mg cholesterol, 409mg sodium

S'mores that Crunch!

For family fun indoors or out, treat yourself and your kids to S'mores that Crunch!, an exciting version of the old campfire classic. This simple and tasty recipe combines a unique crunchy chocolate with a warm, melty marshmallow between two golden graham crackers.

6   large marshmallows
12 graham cracker squares

3   (1.55 ounce) NESTLÉ®
    CRUNCH® Candy Bars,
    cut in half

For Outdoor S'mores

1. Thread marshmallows onto skewers. Toast over flame, turning frequently, until golden. Place 1 marshmallow on each of 6 graham cracker squares. Top each marshmallow with 1 candy square and 1 graham cracker square.

For Indoor S'mores

1. Place 6 graham cracker squares on a microwave-safe plate. Top each square with 1 marshmallow.
2. Microwave on HIGH for 10 to 15 seconds or until marshmallows expand. Top each marshmallow with 1 candy bar square and 1 graham cracker square. **Yield:** 6 servings.

Per serving: 167 calories, 2g protein, 26g carbohydrate, 7g fat, 1g fiber, 3mg cholesterol, 75mg sodium

kid-friendly

submitted by: **Nestlé®**

Prep Time: 3 minutes

What Other Cooks Have Done:
"Quick, easy, and basic—these words best describe this recipe. Watch your microwave times very closely or the marshmallows will become tough and chewy. The crispy rice candy bar goes well with the marshmallows."

S'mores that Crunch!

homestyle supper

Prize-Winning Meatloaf
Squash & Tomatoes à la Old Bay®
mashed potatoes
Mini Upside Down Pineapple Cakes

serves 8

comfort food

submitted by:
The Quaker® Oats Company

Prep Time: 10 minutes
Cook Time: 1 hour

Test Kitchen Secret:
You can assemble this meatloaf the day before you want to serve it. Just combine all ingredients, press into a loaf pan, cover with plastic wrap, and refrigerate overnight. This will make your mealtime chores easier when it's time to cook!

Prize-Winning Meatloaf

Developed in the Quaker® Kitchens in the 1950s, Prize-Winning Meatloaf remains one of Quaker's® most requested recipes. Using oats in place of breadcrumbs gives this meatloaf a moist texture and adds a nutrition boost of B vitamins, protein, and fiber. Served warm, this is a deliciously hearty recipe your family will love! We glazed the top with barbecue sauce before baking.

1½	pounds lean ground beef	1	egg or 2 egg whites, lightly beaten
1	cup tomato juice or tomato sauce	¼	cup chopped onion
¾	cup QUAKER® Oats (Quick or Old Fashioned), uncooked	¼	teaspoon salt (optional)
		¼	teaspoon black pepper

1. Preheat oven to 350°F. In a large bowl, combine all ingredients, mixing lightly but thoroughly. Press into a lightly greased 4x8 inch loaf pan.
2. Bake in the preheated oven 1 hour to medium doneness (160°F) until not pink in center and juices show no pink color. Let stand 5 minutes; drain off any juices before slicing. **Yield:** 8 servings.

Per serving: 217 calories, 18g protein, 7g carbohydrate, 13g fat, 1g fiber, 76mg cholesterol, 226mg sodium

Quaker® Classic

Use Quaker's® basic recipe for meatloaf and add your family's favorite ingredients to make your own "classic."

Customize meatloaf by adding one of the following to meatloaf ingredients:

- *½ cup frozen (thawed) or canned (drained) corn*
- *½ cup chopped green or red bell pepper*
- *1 (2½ ounce) jar sliced mushrooms, drained*
- *⅓ cup grated Parmesan cheese*
- *2 tablespoons finely chopped fresh parsley or cilantro*
- *Sprinkle top of baked meatloaf with 1 cup shredded cheese. Return to oven for 3 minutes to melt cheese.*
- *You can even kick things up by spooning heated prepared spaghetti sauce, pizza sauce, barbecue sauce, or salsa over each serving.*

**Prize-Winning Meatloaf and
Squash & Tomatoes à la Old Bay®,
page 24**

submitted by: **McCormick® & Company**

Prep Time: 10 minutes
Cook Time: 15 minutes

What Other Cooks Have Done:

"Squash and tomatoes are a summer standby for our family, but I had never thought to add the Old Bay®. Yummy! We used a blend of Cheddar and Parmesan cheese, and it still turned out well."

Squash & Tomatoes à la Old Bay® *(pictured on page 23)*

A medley of summer-fresh tomatoes and zucchini are an Eastern Shore delight when seasoned with Old Bay®.

2	tablespoons olive oil	2	teaspoons OLD BAY® Seasoning
6	medium zucchini, sliced into rounds	½	teaspoon McCORMICK® Ground Black Pepper
1	medium onion, diced	1	cup shredded mozzarella cheese
4	tomatoes, cored, seeded, and chopped		

1. Heat the olive oil in a large skillet. Add the zucchini and onion and sauté a few minutes. Add the tomatoes, OLD BAY®, and pepper. Cover the skillet, reduce heat to low, and simmer for 5 minutes.
2. Sprinkle with cheese, cover, and cook 5 more minutes, or until cheese is completely melted. **Yield:** 8 servings.

Per serving: 106 calories, 6g protein, 9g carbohydrate, 6g fat, 3g fiber, 8mg cholesterol, 212mg sodium

---

party pleaser

submitted by: **Dole®**

Prep Time: 15 minutes
Cook Time: 25 minutes

Test Kitchen Secret:

Brown sugar is made by adding molasses to granulated white sugar, so the moisture content is higher. Be sure to seal brown sugar in an airtight bag to keep it soft and fresh. If the sugar does become hard, microwave it on MEDIUM-LOW until soft, usually about 1 to 2 minutes.

Mini Upside Down Pineapple Cakes

Turn old-fashioned pineapple upside down cake into a delightful mini dessert that's crowned with the traditional cherry or a red raspberry.

2	(20 ounce) cans DOLE® Pineapple Slices	1	(18.25 ounce) package yellow or pineapple-flavored cake mix
⅓	cup margarine, melted		Red raspberries or maraschino cherries
⅔	cup packed brown sugar		

1. Preheat oven to 350°F. Drain pineapple; reserve juice.
2. Stir together melted margarine and brown sugar. Evenly divide sugar mixture into 3 inch greased muffin cups. Arrange pineapple over sugar mixture.
3. Prepare cake mix according to package directions, replacing water with reserved juice. Evenly pour batter into muffin cups.
4. Bake in the preheated oven for 20 to 25 minutes or until a toothpick inserted in center of cakes comes out clean.
5. Cool 5 minutes. Loosen edges and invert onto serving platter. Place raspberries in center of pineapple slices. **Yield:** 20 servings.

Per serving: 200 calories, 1g protein, 38g carbohydrate, 7g fat, 1g fiber, 0mg cholesterol, 204mg sodium

Mini Upside Down Pineapple Cakes

warming one-dish dinner

Bush's Best® "CaribBean" One-Pot Stew
Hershey's® Hot Fudge Pudding Cake

serves 8

comfort food

submitted by: **Chef Katy Keck on behalf of Bush's Best® Beans**

Prep Time: 30 minutes
Cook Time: 50 minutes

Test Kitchen Secret:

Top this exotic stew with a spoonful of fruity relish made from 1 cup chopped pineapple, 2 sliced scallions, and 2 tablespoons chopped cilantro. The fresh flavors of the relish balance the earthy undertones of the stew.

Bush's Best® "CaribBean" One-Pot Stew

Flavorful sweet potatoes put a new twist on classic winter stew.

1	pound sweet potatoes	1	teaspoon ground cumin
2	tablespoons olive oil	½	teaspoon salt
2	tablespoons minced ginger	¼	teaspoon ground black pepper
3	cloves garlic, minced	3	(16 ounce) cans BUSH'S
¼	jalapeño pepper, minced		BEST® Dark Red Kidney
2	stalks celery, diced		Beans, rinsed and drained
1	green bell pepper, diced	1	(14.5 ounce) can diced
1	small onion, diced		tomatoes
1	pound pork loin, trimmed	1	(14.5 ounce) can chicken broth
	and cut into ½ inch pieces		Hot sauce (optional)

1. Prick sweet potatoes with a fork and microwave on HIGH for 6 to 8 minutes until tender. Set aside. When cool, peel and cut into ½ inch cubes.

2. Heat olive oil in large stockpot. Add ginger, garlic, and jalapeño; sauté until soft, about 2 minutes. Add celery, bell pepper, and onion; cook until onion is translucent, about 5 minutes.

3. Season pork with cumin, salt, and black pepper. Push vegetables to one side of stockpot and add pork, browning on all sides. Add BUSH'S BEST® Dark Red Kidney Beans, tomatoes, broth, and sweet potatoes; bring to a boil. Reduce heat and simmer, covered, for 25 to 30 minutes, or until pork is tender. Taste and adjust seasonings. Serve with hot sauce, if desired. **Yield:** 8 servings.

Per serving: 366 calories, 22g protein, 45g carbohydrate, 10g fat, 12g fiber, 27mg cholesterol, 818mg sodium

Hershey's® Hot Fudge Pudding Cake

This rich, moist chocolate cake makes its own fudge sauce while baking.

5 star

submitted by: **HersheysKitchens.com**

Prep Time: 15 minutes
Cook Time: 40 minutes
Stand Time: 15 minutes

¾ cup white sugar
1 cup all-purpose flour
¼ cup HERSHEY'S® Cocoa Powder
2 teaspoons baking powder
¼ teaspoon salt
½ cup milk
⅓ cup butter, melted
1½ teaspoons vanilla extract
½ cup white sugar
½ cup packed light brown sugar
¼ cup HERSHEY'S® Cocoa Powder
1¼ cups hot water
Whipped topping (optional)

What Other Cooks Have Done:
"My 13-year-old son made this cake for us. It should be called Magic Cake—we couldn't believe how the hot fudge sauce formed under the cake as it baked! We didn't even wait for it to cool. We served it with a scoop of vanilla ice cream...to die for!"

1. Preheat oven to 350°F. Combine ¾ cup white sugar, flour, ¼ cup cocoa, baking powder, and salt. Stir in milk, butter, and vanilla; beat until smooth.

2. Pour batter into an ungreased 9 inch square pan. Stir together ½ cup white sugar, brown sugar, and ¼ cup cocoa; sprinkle mixture evenly over batter. Pour hot water over top; do not stir.

3. Bake in the preheated oven 35 to 40 minutes or until center of cake is almost set. Remove from oven; let stand 15 minutes. Serve in dessert dishes, spooning sauce from bottom of pan over top. Garnish with whipped topping, if desired. **Yield:** 8 servings.

Per serving: 356 calories, 6g protein, 62g carbohydrate, 10g fat, 5g fiber, 22mg cholesterol, 227mg sodium

Hershey's® Hot Fudge Pudding Cake

break for brunch

Holiday Morning French Toast
Honey-Lime Fruit Toss
Quick Cinnamon Twists

serves 10 to 12

make-ahead

submitted by: **McCormick® & Company**

Prep Time: 20 minutes
Chill Time: 4 to 24 hours
Cook Time: 45 minutes

What Other Cooks Have Done:
"This is a delicious recipe and especially good for Christmas morning. The dish can be assembled the night before and baked while the family is busily opening their Christmas presents! Any leftovers reheat well."

Holiday Morning French Toast

This French toast is the perfect breakfast dish to serve your family on a special holiday morning. It can be assembled the night before and simply baked in the morning. The aroma lets your family know that they're in for a real treat.

1	cup packed brown sugar	1	loaf Italian or French bread, cut into 1 inch slices
½	cup butter, melted		
3	teaspoons McCORMICK® Ground Cinnamon, divided	6	large eggs
		1½	cups milk
3	tart apples, such as Granny Smith, peeled, cored, and thinly sliced	1	tablespoon McCORMICK® Pure Vanilla Extract
½	cup dried cranberries or raisins		Confectioners' sugar (optional)

1. Combine brown sugar, butter, and 1 teaspoon cinnamon in a 9x13 inch baking dish. Add apples and cranberries; toss to coat well. Smooth apple mixture evenly in baking dish. Arrange slices of bread on top.
2. Mix eggs, milk, vanilla, and remaining 2 teaspoons cinnamon until well blended. Pour mixture over bread, soaking bread completely. Cover and refrigerate 4 to 24 hours.
3. Bake, covered with aluminum foil, in a preheated 375°F oven for 40 minutes. Uncover and bake 5 more minutes. Remove from oven; let stand 5 minutes. Serve warm. For an eye-catching presentation, loosen edges of baking dish and invert onto a large serving platter. Sprinkle with confectioners' sugar, if desired. **Yield:** 12 servings.

Per serving: 308 calories, 7g protein, 43g carbohydrate, 12g fat, 2g fiber, 131mg cholesterol, 296mg sodium

Holiday Morning French Toast and
Honey-Lime Fruit Toss,
page 30

quick & easy

submitted by: **Dole®**

Prep Time: 10 minutes

Test Kitchen Secret:

Adjust the amount of honey you add to this simple salad based on the sweetness of your fruit. Also, feel free to add your favorite seasonal fruit to make your own combination.

Honey-Lime Fruit Toss *(pictured on page 29)*

Fresh lime juice and zest combine with honey for a tangy-sweet dressing for fruit salad that lets the fruit take center stage.

2	(20 ounce) cans DOLE® Pineapple Chunks	2	cups quartered DOLE® Strawberries
2	(11 or 15 ounce) cans DOLE® Mandarin Oranges, drained	½	teaspoon grated lime zest
2	large DOLE® Bananas, sliced	¼	cup lime juice
2	DOLE® Kiwis, peeled, halved, and sliced	2	tablespoons honey

1. Drain pineapple; reserve ½ cup juice.

2. Combine pineapple chunks, mandarin oranges, banana, kiwi, and strawberries in a bowl.

3. Stir together reserved juice, lime zest, lime juice, and honey. Pour over salad; toss to coat. **Yield:** 14 servings.

Per serving: 93 calories, 1g protein, 24g carbohydrate, 0g fat, 2g fiber, 0mg cholesterol, 3mg sodium

kid-friendly

submitted by: **McCormick® & Company**

Prep Time: 10 minutes
Cook Time: 8 minutes

Test Kitchen Secret:

When making these quick-and-easy twists, line your baking sheet with aluminum foil and spray with non-stick cooking spray for easy cleanup.

Quick Cinnamon Twists

Quick Cinnamon Twists are a wonderful, sweet-tasting snack for kids or a delicious addition to your breakfast table.

¼	cup white sugar	1	(12 ounce) can refrigerated biscuit dough
1½	teaspoons McCORMICK® Ground Cinnamon	2	tablespoons butter or margarine
½	cup finely chopped nuts		

1. Preheat oven to 475°F. Place sugar, cinnamon, and nuts on a plate and stir to combine.

2. Remove biscuits from package and pull each to about 6 inches in length.

3. Melt butter in a small pan over low heat, leave butter in pan, and remove from heat. Dip each biscuit in melted butter and roll in sugar-nut mixture. Twist and place on a greased baking sheet. Bake 8 minutes or until golden brown.

4. Remove from baking sheet and place on wire rack to cool slightly. Serve warm. **Yield:** 10 servings.

Per serving: 169 calories, 3g protein, 18g carbohydrate, 10g fat, 1g fiber, 6mg cholesterol, 333mg sodium

amazing meatless menu

California Burgers
Old Bay® Potato & Green Bean Salad
Chocolate Caramel Cheesecake Bites

serves 4

California Burgers

healthy

submitted by: **Boca®**

Prep Time: 10 minutes
Cook Time: 15 minutes

Test Kitchen Secret:
For a creamy topping to your burger, omit the avocado and spread the bun with homemade or store-bought guacamole. You can also save time by microwaving the burger as directed on the package. Top with a slice of pepper jack cheese for a truly authentic cheeseburger flavor.

Ride the waves with this surfer's special burger topped with roasted bell peppers, cucumber, and avocado.

4	frozen BOCA® Meatless Burgers (any variety)	4	slices onion
4	whole wheat buns, toasted	1	avocado, thinly sliced
8	lettuce leaves	4	slices tomato
1	cup grilled or roasted red bell peppers, sliced (optional)	¼	cup reduced-fat Ranch or your favorite salad dressing (optional)
1	cup cucumber slices		

1. Grill frozen BOCA® Meatless Burgers as directed on package.
2. Serve on a toasted whole wheat bun with lettuce. Top burgers with grilled or roasted peppers, if desired, cucumber, onion slices, avocado, and tomato. Drizzle with salad dressing, if desired. **Yield:** 4 servings.

Per serving: 240 calories, 18g protein, 31g carbohydrate, 6g fat, 7g fiber, 0mg cholesterol, 600mg sodium

California Burger and
Old Bay® Potato & Green Bean Salad,
page 34

Old Bay® Potato & Green Bean Salad *(pictured on page 33)*

Old Bay® Seasoning supplies one-step flavor while green beans and cucumber add crunch to this oil- and vinegar-dressed potato salad. Leftovers store well in the refrigerator for lunches during the week.

submitted by: **McCormick® & Company**

Prep Time: 15 minutes
Cook Time: 15 minutes
Chill Time: 1 hour

What Other Cooks Have Done:

"This is the perfect potato salad to take on picnics or to outdoor barbecues. There's no mayonnaise, so it travels well, plus it's a lot more healthy than traditional potato salad recipes. No guilt here!"

3	pounds red-skinned potatoes, cut into 1 inch cubes
½	pound fresh or frozen green beans
1	cup chopped cucumber
½	cup finely chopped onion
2	tablespoons olive oil
2	tablespoons white wine vinegar
4	teaspoons OLD BAY® Seasoning

1. Place potatoes in a 4 quart saucepan and cover with water. Bring to a boil. Cook, uncovered, 5 to 6 minutes. Add green beans and continue cooking 3 minutes; drain.
2. In a large bowl, combine potatoes and beans with remaining ingredients. Mix well. Chill at least 1 hour; stir before serving. **Yield:** 10 servings.

Per serving: 144 calories, 3g protein, 28g carbohydrate, 3g fat, 3g fiber, 0mg cholesterol, 225mg sodium

Chocolate Caramel Cheesecake Bites

You'll delight in these mini treats that pack all the flavor of a slice of cheesecake.

submitted by: **Kretschmer® Wheat Germ**

Prep Time: 15 minutes
Cook Time: 15 minutes
Cool Time: 40 minutes

Test Kitchen Secret:

Take advantage of quality convenience products to jazz up these cheesecake bites. Substitute any dessert topping, like chocolate or butterscotch, for the caramel topping. Also, substitute walnut halves or almonds for the pecan halves, if desired.

1½	tablespoons margarine, softened
¾	cup KRETSCHMER® Wheat Germ (any flavor)
2	(8 ounce) packages light cream cheese, softened
¾	cup white sugar
⅓	cup unsweetened cocoa powder
1	teaspoon vanilla extract
4	egg whites
36	small pecan halves (optional)
6	tablespoons fat-free caramel topping

1. Preheat oven to 350°F. Generously coat the inside of 36 mini muffin cups with margarine. Divide wheat germ among muffin cups; rotate cups to completely cover insides with wheat germ. Set aside.
2. Beat cream cheese on medium speed of an electric mixer until smooth. Blend in sugar, cocoa powder, and vanilla. Beat in egg whites, one at a time, until well blended. Pour into prepared muffin cups, dividing evenly.
3. Bake just until set, about 12 to 15 minutes. Let stand in pan 10 minutes. To remove from pan, run small narrow spatula between crust and edge of each cup to loosen; lift out cheesecake. Cool 30 minutes on a wire rack; cover and chill.
4. To serve, top each cheesecake with small pecan half, if desired. Microwave caramel topping on HIGH about 10 seconds until spoonable. Spoon ½ teaspoon topping over each cheesecake. Refrigerate leftovers. **Yield:** 3 dozen.

Per cheesecake: 90 calories, 2g protein, 8g carbohydrate, 6g fat, 1g fiber, 25mg cholesterol, 60mg sodium

Chocolate Caramel Cheesecake Bites

slow-cooker fare

Crock-Pot® Corned Beef & Cabbage
Kisses® Peanut Butter Pie

serves 6

comfort food

submitted by: **Cook's® Brand Corned Beef**

Prep Time: 10 minutes
Cook Time: 8 to 9 hours

Test Kitchen Secret:

Each Cook's® Brand Corned Beef Brisket is made with a specially formulated mild cure for a flavor profile enjoyed by corned beef lovers throughout the country. A separate spice packet is included with each corned beef package for those who prefer the option of a spicier brisket.

Crock-Pot® Corned Beef & Cabbage

Celebrate St. Patrick's Day in traditional style this year with a corned beef brisket that's waiting for you when you get home.

8 small red-skinned potatoes, quartered	2 cloves garlic, crushed
	4 bay leaves
1 (3 pound) COOK'S® Brand Corned Beef Flat Brisket, cut into 3 to 4 pieces	1½ teaspoons black pepper
	1 head cabbage, cored and cut into 8 wedges
1 onion, cut into wedges	
1 teaspoon OLD BAY® Seasoning	

1. Place the potatoes in the bottom of a 6 quart slow cooker. Top with the corned beef, including any juices in the package. Scatter on the onion wedges, contents of the spice packet, OLD BAY® Seasoning, garlic, bay leaves, and pepper. Add water to cover. Cover and cook on High 1 hour; reduce heat to Low and cook 5 more hours. Add the cabbage wedges and continue cooking until meat is cooked and vegetables are tender, 2 to 3 more hours.

2. Thinly slice the corned beef across the grain and serve with the vegetables. Drizzle some of the juices over all, if desired. **Yield:** 6 servings.

Per serving: 456 calories, 35g protein, 33g carbohydrate, 21g fat, 6g fiber, 101mg cholesterol, 2370mg sodium

Kisses® Peanut Butter Pie

Chocolate kisses are melted and spread on a graham cracker crust that's filled with a creamy peanut butter mélange.

5 star

submitted by: **HersheysKitchens.com**

Prep Time: 20 minutes
Chill Time: 6 hours 30 minutes

42 HERSHEY'S® KISSES®
    Milk Chocolates, divided
2   tablespoons milk
1   (6 ounce) prepared graham
    cracker crust
1   (8 ounce) package cream
    cheese, softened

¾   cup white sugar
1   cup REESE'S® Creamy
    Peanut Butter
1   (8 ounce) container frozen
    whipped topping, thawed

What Other Cooks Have Done:
"I used a chocolate graham cracker crust and topped the pie with finely chopped kisses. A tall glass of milk is a must! Next time, I think I'll try it with HERSHEY'S® HUGS® for a little something different."

1. Remove wrappers from chocolate pieces. Place 26 pieces and milk in a small microwave-safe bowl. Microwave on HIGH 1 minute; stir. Microwave 30 to 45 seconds or just until melted and smooth when stirred. Spread evenly on bottom of crust. Refrigerate for 30 minutes.

2. Beat cream cheese in a medium bowl until smooth; gradually add sugar, beating well. Beat in peanut butter. Reserve ½ cup whipped topping; fold remaining whipped topping into peanut butter mixture. Spoon into crust over chocolate. Cover; refrigerate about 6 hours or until set.

3. Garnish with reserved whipped topping and additional chocolate pieces. **Yield:** 8 servings.

Per serving: 709 calories, 14g protein, 64g carbohydrate, 48g fat, 3g fiber, 37mg cholesterol, 413mg sodium

Kisses® Peanut Butter Pie

from the grill

Summer 'n' Spice Chicken
Roasted Garlic Grilled Vegetables
Ohana Sundaes

serves 4

Summer 'n' Spice Chicken

Every backyard chef has a favorite recipe for grilled chicken. This could well become yours.

party pleaser

submitted by: **Tyson®**

Prep Time: 10 minutes
Marinate Time: 30 minutes
Cook Time: 25 minutes

Test Kitchen Secret:

You can substitute Tyson® Fresh Boneless, Skinless Chicken Breasts for the frozen breasts; this may decrease cooking time. And if you can't wait for summer, this recipe can also be prepared using an indoor grill or the oven broiler.

½   cup ReaLemon® Lemon Juice from Concentrate
¼   cup chili sauce
2   tablespoons Dijon-style mustard
1   tablespoon dried basil leaves
1   tablespoon minced fresh parsley
4   TYSON® Individually Fresh Frozen® Boneless, Skinless Chicken Breasts

1. Combine all ingredients except chicken in large zip-top plastic bag. Mix well. Rinse chicken; pat dry. Add chicken to marinade. Wash hands. Refrigerate chicken 30 minutes or longer.

2. Preheat grill for medium heat. Drain chicken and discard marinade. Grill chicken 18 to 25 minutes or until done (internal temperature of 170°F). **Yield:** 4 servings.

Per serving: 152 calories, 24g protein, 6g carbohydrate, 3g fat, 1g fiber, 64mg cholesterol, 353mg sodium

Summer 'n' Spice Chicken and
Roasted Garlic Grilled Vegetables,
page 40

submitted by: **McCormick® & Company**

Prep Time: 10 minutes
Cook Time: 15 minutes

What Other Cooks Have Done:

"This is a great recipe. I made it with whole mushrooms, quartered red onion, yellow squash, and zucchini. I put it on a baking sheet covered with foil that I sprayed with olive oil spray. I broiled it in the oven 4 inches from the heat. Not one piece was left over! I will make this again very soon."

Roasted Garlic Grilled Vegetables *(pictured on page 39)*

Grilled vegetables are the hottest food of the summer! This McCormick® Seasoning gives vegetables a robust flavor boost. It's good with any of your favorite vegetables; try it on green beans, yellow squash, shallots, or eggplant.

1½ teaspoons McCORMICK® GRILL MATES® Roasted Garlic Montreal Chicken Seasoning
1 tablespoon olive oil
1 cup zucchini, cut into 1½ inch pieces

1 cup fresh mushrooms
1 small onion, cut into wedges
1 cup green bell pepper, cut into 1½ inch pieces

1. Preheat grill for medium-high heat. Toss together Roasted Garlic Montreal Chicken Seasoning, oil, and vegetables.
2. Place vegetables in a grill basket, grill rack, or place on skewers.
3. Grill, uncovered, 12 to 15 minutes, or until vegetables are tender, turning occasionally. **Yield:** 4 servings.

Per serving: 58 calories, 1g protein, 6g carbohydrate, 4g fat, 2g fiber, 0mg cholesterol, 235mg sodium

submitted by: **Dole®**

Prep Time: 35 minutes
Cook Time: 10 minutes

Test Kitchen Secret:

If you use bamboo skewers when grilling, always soak the skewers in water at least 30 minutes prior to using so they do not burn during grilling.

Ohana Sundaes

Taste the sweet flavors of Hawaii with this simple dessert. The natural sweetness of the fruit is drawn out from the heat of a grill.

½ cup orange juice
1 (20 ounce) can DOLE® Pineapple Chunks, drained, ½ cup juice reserved
2 tablespoons lemon juice
2 tablespoons honey
¼ teaspoon ground allspice or ground cinnamon

1 tablespoon cornstarch
3 DOLE® Bananas, cut into 20 (1 inch) rounds
20 medium DOLE® Strawberries
2 DOLE® Mangos, peeled and cut into 20 (2 inch) pieces
10 (10 inch) skewers
Vanilla ice cream (optional)

1. Preheat grill for medium heat.
2. Combine orange juice, reserved pineapple juice, lemon juice, honey, allspice, and cornstarch in a small saucepan. Bring to a boil over medium heat, stirring occasionally, and cook until thickened. Remove from heat; cool slightly.
3. Thread pineapple, banana, strawberries, and mango on wooden skewers, using 2 pieces of each fruit on each skewer.
4. Grill kabobs 3 to 5 minutes per side until fruit starts to brown. Generously brush fruit with sauce while grilling.
5. Serve skewers alone or with vanilla ice cream. Pour remaining sauce over fruit and ice cream. **Yield:** 5 servings.

Per serving: 372 calories, 4g protein, 66g carbohydrate, 13g fat, 4g fiber, 68mg cholesterol, 116mg sodium

Ohana Sundae

asian fusion menu

Citrus-Spiced Pork Lo Mein
Spicy Cardamom Crisps

serves 4

quick & easy

submitted by: **Hormel Foods Corporation**

Prep Time: 15 minutes
Cook Time: 10 minutes

Test Kitchen Secret:

Bok choy is a mild-flavored Chinese cabbage with large, crunchy white stalks and tender, dark green leaves. It is available year-round in most supermarkets.

Citrus-Spiced Pork Lo Mein *(pictured on page 12)*

Pork tenderloin is quickly stir-fried with bok choy and dressed with a spicy citrus sauce for a beautiful and tasty meal in minutes.

6	ounces linguine noodles	¾	cup water
4	teaspoons HERB-OX® Chicken Flavored Bouillon Granules, divided	¼	cup orange juice
		2	tablespoons soy sauce
8	ounces pork tenderloin, halved lengthwise and cut into ¼ inch strips	2	teaspoons sesame oil
		½	teaspoon crushed red pepper flakes
2	teaspoons vegetable oil	1	(11 ounce) can mandarin oranges, drained
2	cups sliced bok choy		

1. Cook noodles according to package directions, adding 2 teaspoons of the bouillon granules to the cooking liquid. Meanwhile, in a wok or large skillet, stir-fry pork in hot oil for 3 minutes. Add bok choy and cook for 3 to 4 more minutes or until pork is cooked through and bok choy is tender-crisp. Add the water, orange juice, remaining bouillon granules, soy sauce, sesame oil, and pepper flakes to the pork mixture. Bring mixture to a boil.

2. Stir in prepared noodles and stir for 1 minute. Remove mixture from heat and gently stir in oranges. **Yield:** 4 servings.

Per serving: 303 calories, 17g protein, 40g carbohydrate, 8g fat, 3g fiber, 32mg cholesterol, 539mg sodium

Spicy Cardamom Crisps

Cardamom, an aromatic spice with an exotic, sweet flavor, enhances these flavorful cookies. A single sliced almond crowns each crisp to perfection.

1⅓	cups white sugar		1	teaspoon vanilla extract
1	cup LAND O'LAKES® Butter, softened		3	cups all-purpose flour
1	egg		1½	teaspoons baking soda
2	tablespoons dark corn syrup		2	teaspoons ground cardamom
1	tablespoon water		½	teaspoon ground cinnamon Sliced almonds

1. Combine sugar and butter in a large bowl. With an electric mixer, beat on medium until creamy, scraping bowl often. Add egg, corn syrup, water, and vanilla; beat until well mixed. Reduce speed to low; add remaining ingredients except almonds. Beat until well mixed.

2. Divide dough into thirds. Shape each third into a ½ inch thick square. Wrap each square in plastic wrap. Refrigerate until firm (1 to 2 hours).

3. Preheat oven to 375°F. Roll out dough onto a lightly floured surface, ⅓ at a time (keeping remaining dough refrigerated), to a 10x12 inch rectangle. Cut into 2 inch squares using a pastry cutter or sharp knife; cut squares diagonally in half to form triangles. Place 1 inch apart on ungreased baking sheets. Lightly press almond slices into center of each cookie. Bake 7 to 9 minutes or until edges are lightly browned and cookies are set. **Yield:** 7½ dozen.

Per cookie: 48 calories, 1g protein, 7g carbohydrate, 2g fat, 0g fiber, 8mg cholesterol, 43mg sodium

holiday fare

submitted by: **Land O'Lakes, Inc.**

Prep Time: 1 hour
Chill Time: 2 hours
Cook Time: 9 minutes

Test Kitchen Secret:
Substitute Land O'Lakes® Soft Baking Butter with Canola Oil right from the refrigerator for the butter if you don't have time to let your butter soften.

Spicy Cardamom Crisps

elegant dining

Rosemary Marinated Lamb Chops
Red-Skinned Garlic Mashed Potatoes
steamed asparagus
Golden Lemon Pound Cake
Winter Fruit Compote

serves 4

5 ⭐ star

submitted by: **McCormick® & Company**

Prep Time: 15 minutes
Cook Time: 12 minutes
Marinate Time: 1 hour

What Other Cooks Have Done:

"The best part of this recipe is how easy it is. Throw all the ingredients in a bag, shake it, and let it them marinate in the fridge for about an hour, and then cook it. What a wonderful flavor! We actually used pineapple/orange juice and it worked wonderfully! Delicious!"

Rosemary Marinated Lamb Chops

These elegant but easy loin lamb chops are marinated, then quickly sautéed. Crushed rosemary is just the right herb to complement the other savory flavors in this lamb marinade.

2 teaspoons McCORMICK® Gourmet Collection™ Crushed Rosemary Leaves	½ teaspoon salt
	1 cup finely chopped onion
1 teaspoon McCORMICK® Gourmet Collection™ Thyme Leaves	½ cup orange juice
	¼ cup dry white wine
1 teaspoon McCORMICK® Gourmet Collection™ Ground Black Pepper	3 tablespoons olive oil, divided
	8 loin lamb chops, cut 1 to 1¼ inch thickness, trimmed
1 teaspoon McCORMICK® Gourmet Collection™ Garlic Powder	

1. Mix crushed rosemary, thyme, black pepper, garlic powder, and salt in a bowl. Add onion, orange juice, white wine, and 2 tablespoons olive oil. Whisk together and reserve ½ cup marinade mixture for later use.
2. Place lamb chops in a zip-top plastic bag; add marinade. Turn to coat. Refrigerate 30 to 60 minutes. Remove lamb from marinade and blot dry with a paper towel. (Do not remove onion pieces from chops.)
3. Heat remaining oil in a heavy skillet over medium-high heat. Place lamb in skillet. Sear one side of lamb approximately 4 minutes or until well browned. Turn chops over and cook 4 more minutes or until desired doneness. Add reserved marinade and simmer 2 minutes. Remove lamb to a serving plate. Pour reduced marinade over lamb. **Yield:** 8 servings.

Per serving: 362 calories, 16g protein, 4g carbohydrate, 31g fat, 1g fiber, 70mg cholesterol, 200mg sodium

**Rosemary Marinated Lamb Chops and
Red-Skinned Garlic Mashed Potatoes, page 46**

Red-Skinned Garlic Mashed Potatoes *(pictured on page 45)*

comfort food

submitted by: **Hormel Foods Corporation**

Prep Time: 50 minutes
Cook Time: 25 minutes

Test Kitchen Secret:

To roast garlic, slice off the end of the garlic bulb. Drizzle with olive oil and wrap in aluminum foil. Roast in a 400°F oven for 45 to 50 minutes or until garlic is soft. It's great added to mashed potatoes or served on toasted baguettes.

Make your mashed potatoes memorable by mashing them with fresh roasted garlic and cream cheese. It's a delightful twist on the traditional recipe.

1¼	pounds red-skinned potatoes, washed and quartered	6	to 8 cloves roasted garlic
2½	cups water	¼	cup cream cheese, softened
3	cubes HERB-OX® Chicken Flavored Bouillon	2	tablespoons chopped fresh parsley

1. Place potatoes in a large saucepan. Add water and bouillon cubes. Bring mixture to a boil. Reduce heat, cover, and cook for 20 to 25 minutes or until potatoes are tender. Drain, reserving the cooking liquid. Mash potatoes with a potato masher or beat with an electric mixer. Add roasted garlic and cream cheese to potatoes. Gradually beat in enough reserved cooking liquid to make potatoes light and fluffy. Stir in parsley and serve immediately. **Yield:** 6 servings.

Per serving: 68 calories, 3g protein, 7g carbohydrate, 3g fat, 3g fiber, 11mg cholesterol, 588mg sodium

Golden Lemon Pound Cake

party pleaser

submitted by: **Land O'Lakes, Inc.**

Prep Time: 15 minutes
Cook Time: 65 minutes

Test Kitchen Secret:

Golden Lemon Pound Cake can be baked in loaves. Divide batter between two greased and floured (5x9 inch) loaf pans. Bake for 55 to 65 minutes or until a toothpick inserted in center comes out clean. Cool 10 minutes; remove from pan. Cool completely.

Buttery, moist, and truly a Land O'Lakes® "golden" recipe!

2	cups white sugar	½	teaspoon salt
1	cup LAND O'LAKES® Butter, softened	¾	cup buttermilk★
4	eggs	1	tablespoon grated lemon zest
3	cups all-purpose flour	1	tablespoon lemon juice
½	teaspoon baking powder	1¼	cups sifted confectioners' sugar
½	teaspoon baking soda	2	teaspoons lemon juice
		1	to 2 tablespoons milk

1. Preheat oven to 325°F. With an electric mixer, beat sugar and butter in a large bowl at medium speed until creamy, scraping bowl often. Continue beating, adding eggs, one at a time, until well mixed.
2. Combine flour, baking powder, baking soda, and salt in a medium bowl. Reduce speed to low. Beat, gradually adding flour mixture alternately with buttermilk and scraping bowl often until well mixed. Add lemon zest and 1 tablespoon lemon juice. Continue beating until well mixed.
3. Spread batter into a greased and floured 12 cup Bundt® pan or 10 inch tube pan. Bake for 55 to 65 minutes or until a toothpick inserted in center of cake comes out clean. Cool 10 minutes; remove from pan. Cool completely.
4. To make glaze, stir together confectioners' sugar, 2 teaspoons lemon juice, and enough milk for desired glazing consistency in small bowl. Drizzle over cooled cake. **Yield:** 16 servings.
★Substitute 2 teaspoons vinegar or lemon juice plus enough milk to equal ¾ cup. Let stand 10 minutes.

Per serving: 350 calories, 4g protein, 55g carbohydrate, 13g fat, 1g fiber, 80mg cholesterol, 250mg sodium

Golden Lemon Pound Cake and Winter Fruit Compote

Winter Fruit Compote

The flavors of ginger, cinnamon, and vanilla go so well with winter fruits. Cranberries, figs, and dried apricots are featured in this compote that can be served with poultry or with desserts such as pound cake or ice cream.

1	cup apple juice	½	cup dried cranberries
¼	cup packed light brown sugar	½	teaspoon McCORMICK® Ground Ginger
¼	cup water		
1	tablespoon fresh lemon juice	¼	teaspoon McCORMICK® Ground Cinnamon
½	cup dried apricot halves, quartered		
½	cup dried whole figs, sliced	1	teaspoon McCORMICK® Pure Vanilla Extract

1. Simmer apple juice, brown sugar, water, and lemon juice in a small saucepan, stirring occasionally until dissolved.
2. Add fruit and remaining ingredients; simmer 15 more minutes or until fruits are plump and liquid is slightly thick. Serve chilled. **Yield:** 4 servings.

Per serving: 234 calories, 1g protein, 58g carbohydrate, 1g fat, 6g fiber, 0mg cholesterol, 12mg sodium

make-ahead

submitted by: **McCormick® & Company**

Prep Time: 10 minutes
Cook Time: 18 minutes

What Other Cooks Have Done:
"This recipe was so delicious. I served this compote with pork and turkey. I also had it as a side dish with my morning toast."

Ham, Spinach & Pepper Wraps,
page 59

appetizers, snacks & beverages

Whether you're planning an elaborate gala or intimate gathering, look no further for last-minute **entertaining** ideas—we've got everything you need to make your next affair a hit. Savory nibbles, upscale pizzas, and **kid-friendly** snacks will keep everyone happy. And to whet your appetite, you'll find **festive** beverages and warming brews that are a snap to throw together.

Spiced Pumpkin Dip

submitted by: **McCormick® & Company**

Prep Time: 5 minutes
Chill Time: 30 minutes

Test Kitchen Secret:

Serve with apples or pears, cored and cut into ½ inch slices, leaving skin on for color. Toss fruit with a little orange juice to prevent browning.

Serve this easy pumpkin dip for any fall or winter gathering! The warmth of pumpkin pie spice and the citrus flavor from orange extract go great with pumpkin.

1   (8 ounce) package cream cheese, softened
2   cups confectioners' sugar
1   (15 ounce) can pumpkin puree
1   tablespoon McCORMICK® Pumpkin Pie Spice
1   teaspoon McCORMICK® Pure Orange Extract
½   teaspoon McCORMICK® Ground Ginger
Gingersnap cookies

1. Blend cream cheese and confectioners' sugar until smooth in a mixer or food processor. Remove cover; add pumpkin, pumpkin pie spice, orange extract, and ginger. Blend thoroughly.
2. Chill 30 minutes or until ready to serve. Serve with gingersnap cookies.
Yield: 20 servings.

Per serving: 94 calories, 1g protein, 14g carbohydrate, 4g fat, 1g fiber, 12mg cholesterol, 85mg sodium

Creamy Orange Dip

submitted by: **Eagle Brand®**

Prep Time: 5 minutes
Chill Time: 1 hour

Test Kitchen Secret:

Serve this dip anytime of year with seasonal fruit. Make a wreath of red and green pears or apples for Christmas or serve with tropical fruits such as pineapple, kiwi, and mango for a summertime treat.

Your friends will rave about this creamy orange fruit dip. Serve with strawberries, cherries, or whatever tasty fruit is in season.

1   (14 ounce) can EAGLE BRAND® Sweetened Condensed Milk (not evaporated milk)
½   cup frozen unsweetened orange juice concentrate
½   cup water
2   teaspoons grated orange zest
Assorted fresh fruit

1. In a small bowl, combine all ingredients except fruit; mix well. Chill at least 1 hour to blend flavors. Serve with fresh fruit. **Yield:** 18 servings.

Per 2 tablespoons: 85 calories, 2g protein, 16g carbohydrate, 2g fat, 0g fiber, 7mg cholesterol, 28mg sodium

Dulce de Leche

Here's a fun and foolproof way to make a delicious caramel dip. It's a perfect complement to apples in the fall or berries in the summer—it goes great with everything!

1 (14 ounce) can EAGLE BRAND® Sweetened Condensed Milk (not evaporated milk)

Assorted dippers: cookies, cake, banana chunks, apple slices, strawberries

1. Preheat oven to 425°F. Pour sweetened condensed milk into a 9 inch pie plate. Cover with foil; place pie plate in larger shallow baking pan. Pour hot water into larger pan to depth of 1 inch.
2. Bake in the preheated oven for 1 hour or until thick and caramel-colored. Beat until smooth. Cool at least 1 hour or until ready to serve. Serve as a dip with assorted dippers. Store leftovers covered in refrigerator for up to 1 week. **Yield:** 5 servings.

Per ¼ cup: 252 calories, 6g protein, 43g carbohydrate, 7g fat, 0g fiber, 27mg cholesterol, 100mg sodium

make-ahead

submitted by: **Eagle Brand®**

Prep Time: 2 minutes
Cook Time: 1 hour
Chill Time: 1 hour

Test Kitchen Secret:
If you want to trim the fat for any recipe calling for Eagle Brand® Sweetened Condensed Milk, just use Eagle Brand® Fat-Free or Low-Fat Sweetened Condensed Milk instead of the original. Remember never to heat an unopened can of Eagle Brand® milk. This is an old method that's been proven to be dangerous. See the box below for alternative cooking methods for creating caramel sauce from Eagle Brand® Sweetened Condensed Milk.

Secrets from the Eagle Brand® Kitchens

Eagle Brand® Sweetened Condensed Milk is a blend of milk and sugar that is condensed by a special vacuum process to create a foolproof "base" for a variety of recipe uses. Most recipes that use Eagle Brand® milk require no additional sugar because it contains sugar that has been thoroughly dissolved during manufacturing.

Eagle Brand® milk has a magical thickening quality. When it's combined with acidic fruit juice, such as lemon juice, it thickens—without heating—to form velvety pie fillings, puddings, and other desserts.

Making a rich caramel sauce with a single ingredient is one of the classic uses for Eagle Brand® Sweetened Condensed Milk. Caramel sauce, or "Dulce de Leche," is made by heating Eagle Brand® milk for an extended time. With only one ingredient, you'll have a caramel

topping or dip perfect to serve over ice cream or with cookies or fruit (such as apples and strawberries).

You can skip the oven and prepare the caramel sauce either in the microwave or on the stovetop.

Stovetop Method
Pour 1 can Eagle Brand® Sweetened Condensed Milk into top of double boiler; place over boiling water. Over low heat, simmer 1 to 1½ hours or until thick and caramel-colored, stirring occasionally. Beat until smooth.

Microwave Method
Pour 1 can Eagle Brand® Sweetened Condensed Milk into a 2 quart glass measuring cup. Cook on MEDIUM (50%) 4 minutes, stirring briskly every 2 minutes until smooth. Cook on MEDIUM-LOW (30%) 20 to 26 minutes or until very thick and caramel-colored, stirring briskly every 4 minutes during the first 16 minutes and every 2 minutes during the last 4 to 10 minutes.

Bush's Best® Chili Cheese Dip

Cream cheese, salsa, and chili beans topped with melted Cheddar create this warm dip that will have everyone lining up for seconds.

quick & easy

submitted by: **Bush's Best® Beans**

Prep Time: 10 minutes
Cook Time: 15 minutes

Test Kitchen Secret:

If you like a little kick to your dip, add hot salsa, pepper jack cheese, or jalapeño rings to intensify the flavors.

1 (8 ounce) package cream cheese, softened	3 tablespoons sliced green onions
½ cup chunky salsa	3 tablespoons pitted, sliced black olives (optional)
1 cup shredded Cheddar cheese, divided	Tortilla chips
1 (16 ounce) can BUSH'S BEST® Chili Beans, undrained	

1. Preheat oven to 350°F. Combine cream cheese and salsa and spread in bottom of a 9 inch pie plate. Sprinkle with ½ cup cheese. Spread BUSH'S BEST® Chili Beans over shredded cheese. Top with remaining shredded cheese, sliced green onions, and olives, if desired.

2. Bake in the preheated oven for 15 minutes until mixture is thoroughly heated and cheese is melted. Serve with tortilla chips. **Yield:** 8 servings.

Per serving: 361 calories, 11g protein, 30g carbohydrate, 23g fat, 5g fiber, 46mg cholesterol, 635mg sodium

Bush's Best® Black Bean Con Queso Dip

This spicy cheese dip is perfect for entertaining.

comfort food

submitted by: **Bush's Best® Beans**

Prep Time: 15 minutes
Cook Time: 20 minutes

Test Kitchen Secret:

You can substitute 2 (15 ounce) cans Bush's Best® Blackeye Peas, rinsed and drained, for the black beans, if desired.

¼ cup butter or margarine	1 (4.5 ounce) can chopped green chilies
1 large onion, finely chopped	1 teaspoon Worcestershire sauce
2 cloves garlic, pressed	¼ teaspoon ground red pepper
⅓ cup all-purpose flour	Tortilla or corn chips
2 cups milk	
2 (8 ounce) packages shredded Cheddar cheese	
2 (15.8 ounce) cans BUSH'S BEST® Black Beans, rinsed and drained	

1. Melt butter in a large soup pot over medium heat; add onion and sauté 8 minutes. Add garlic and sauté 2 minutes or until onion is tender. Stir in flour until smooth; cook mixture, stirring constantly, 1 minute. Gradually add milk, stirring constantly until thickened.

2. Add cheese, stirring constantly over low heat until cheese melts. Stir in BUSH'S BEST® Black Beans and next 3 ingredients, gently stirring until mixture is thoroughly heated. Serve warm with chips. **Yield:** 6 servings.

Per serving: 709 calories, 33g protein, 55g carbohydrate, 42g fat, 11g fiber, 106mg cholesterol, 1522mg sodium

Celebrate the Seasons with Land O'Lakes®

This will be a hit at your next gathering—holidays or not! You can make it ahead and chill it until your guests arrive. Just before serving, sprinkle with extra sliced green onions for festive color.

Holiday Pepper Cheese Dip

Hot pepper cheese brings pizzazz to this great party dip.

Prep Time: 10 minutes   **Chill Time:** 2 hours

1   cup LAND O'LAKES® Light Sour Cream
1   (8 ounce) package cream cheese, softened
8   ounces (2 cups) LAND O'LAKES® Hot Pepper Monterey Jack Cheese, shredded
¼   cup chopped, pitted ripe olives
1   (2 ounce) jar diced pimiento, drained
1   tablespoon sliced green onion
Tortilla chips or crackers

1. Combine sour cream and cream cheese in a small bowl. With an electric mixer, beat at medium speed, scraping often, until smooth.

2. Stir in by hand remaining ingredients except tortilla chips. Cover; chill at least 2 hours. Serve with tortilla chips. **Yield:** 48 servings.

Per serving: 41 calories, 1g protein, 3g carbohydrate, 3g fat, 0g fiber, 7mg cholesterol, 44mg sodium

submitted by: **Chef Katy Keck for Bush's Best® Beans**

Prep Time: 10 minutes

Test Kitchen Secret:
Serve this dip chilled with breadsticks, flatbread, crostini, or fresh vegetables. Like hummus, it also makes a nice spread for pita sandwiches.

Bush's Best® Fresh Herb Bean Spread

Fresh herbs and lime juice add a flavorful twist to this ten-minute dip every guest will rave about.

3	cloves garlic	2	tablespoons fresh basil, coarsely chopped
2	(15.8 ounce) cans BUSH'S BEST® Great Northern Beans, rinsed and drained	1	tablespoon fresh thyme
3	tablespoons lime juice	1	teaspoon kosher salt
2	tablespoons olive oil	½	teaspoon ground black pepper

1. With motor running, drop garlic cloves into a food processor. Add BUSH'S BEST® Great Northern Beans, lime juice, and olive oil; puree until smooth. Add basil, thyme, salt, and pepper; pulse until incorporated and herbs are coarsely chopped. **Yield:** 4 servings.

Per serving: 258 calories, 12g protein, 33g carbohydrate, 8g fat, 12g fiber, 0mg cholesterol, 1161mg sodium

submitted by: **McCormick® & Company**

Prep Time: 10 minutes

Test Kitchen Secret:
Make this a low-fat party dip by substituting reduced-fat cream cheese, mayonnaise, and Cheddar cheese. Your guests will never know the difference!

Spicy Layered Dip

This colorful dip comes together in just ten minutes—perfect for those last-minute get-togethers.

2	(8 ounce) packages cream cheese, softened	¼	cup sliced green onions
2	tablespoons mayonnaise	1	cup shredded Cheddar cheese
1	tablespoon OLD BAY® Seasoning	¼	cup sliced black olives (about 2 ounces)
1	cup diced tomatoes		Tortilla chips or crackers

1. In a medium bowl, combine cream cheese, mayonnaise, and OLD BAY® Seasoning. Evenly spread cream cheese mixture in a 9 inch pie plate.
2. Sprinkle tomatoes, green onions, shredded cheese, and black olives in layers over cream cheese mixture. Serve with tortilla chips or assorted crackers. **Yield:** 16 servings.

Per serving: 151 calories, 5g protein, 2g carbohydrate, 14g fat, 0g fiber, 41mg cholesterol, 269mg sodium

Bush's Best® Fresh
Herb Bean Spread

Ham Pâté

Pungent horseradish and dry sherry add depth of flavor to this showstopper.

1½   cups chopped COOK'S®
      Brand Bone-In Ham, leftover
      ham, or Ham Steak
2   tablespoons mayonnaise
2   teaspoons Dijon-style mustard

1   teaspoon prepared horseradish
2   teaspoons dry sherry
     Salt and pepper to taste
     Crackers or gourmet breads

1. Heat ham per package directions or warm leftover ham. Pulse ham in food processor or blender until finely chopped. Combine ham and next 5 ingredients and mix well. Serve warm or cover and chill. Serve on crackers or gourmet breads. **Yield:** 4 servings.

Per serving: 148 calories, 12g protein, 0g carbohydrate, 10g fat, 0g fiber, 33mg cholesterol, 892mg sodium

Cheddar & Bacon Log

Form this cheese and bacon mixture into either a log or a ball for an easy appetizer during the holidays.

1   (8 ounce) package cream
     cheese, softened
3   tablespoons mayonnaise
⅛   teaspoon Worcestershire sauce
3   drops hot pepper sauce
¼   cup crumbled crisply cooked
     bacon

8   ounces LAND O'LAKES®
     Cheddar Cheese, shredded
2   tablespoons sliced green onions
1   cup chopped pecans, toasted
     Crackers

1. Combine cream cheese, mayonnaise, Worcestershire sauce, and hot pepper sauce in a large bowl. Beat at medium speed, scraping bowl often, until smooth. Stir in bacon, cheese, and green onions by hand. Cover; refrigerate at least 2 hours.
2. Form cheese mixture into log shape or cheese ball; roll in pecans to coat. Wrap in plastic wrap; chill until serving time. Serve with crackers. **Yield:** 48 servings.

Per serving: 88 calories, 2g protein, 3g carbohydrate, 8g fat, 0g fiber, 11mg cholesterol, 99mg sodium

Smoked Salmon & Dill Vegetable Bites

This delicately flavored salmon dip makes a beautiful presentation for any holiday party when piped in or on multicolored vegetables.

1   (8 ounce) package whipped cream cheese
3   ounces sliced smoked salmon, finely chopped
2   teaspoons lemon juice
1½   teaspoons McCORMICK® Dill Weed
1½   teaspoons McCORMICK® Minced Onion

1   teaspoon McCORMICK® Parsley Flakes
     Cherry tomatoes, hollowed out
     Red and green bell pepper pieces
     Cucumber slices
     Celery pieces

make-ahead

submitted by: **McCormick® & Company**

Prep Time: 10 minutes
Chill Time: 2 hours

Test Kitchen Secret:
One (8 ounce) container salmon-flavored cream cheese may be used in place of smoked salmon and whipped cream cheese.

1. In a bowl, stir together all ingredients except vegetables.

2. Spoon or pipe with a pastry tube a small amount of cheese mixture into each piece of vegetable.

3. Place on serving plate; cover and chill at least 2 hours or up to 24 hours. **Yield:** 21 servings.

Per serving: 41 calories, 1g protein, 1g carbohydrate, 4g fat, 0g fiber, 14mg cholesterol, 124mg sodium

Secrets from the McCormick® Kitchens

All McCormick® recipes, like the one above, are carefully evaluated in the McCormick® test kitchens. The culinary staff's selective process ensures that consumers will get only the finest recipes from the McCormick® kitchens. Here are a few hints about cooking with spices and herbs.

• Ground spices release their flavor more quickly than whole spices. Ground spices such as ground thyme or ground cumin can be used in recipes with short cooking times or can be added near the end of cooking for longer cooking recipes.

• Whole spices need a longer time to release their flavor. They work well in longer-cooking recipes such as soups and stews.

• Robust herbs such as sage, thyme, and bay leaves stand up well in long cooking while milder herbs such as basil, marjoram, and parsley can be added at the last minute for best results.

• Rub leafy herbs in the palm of your hand to release the flavor and aroma.

• To double a recipe, increase spices and herbs by one and one-half, taste, and then add more, if necessary. In most recipes, one and one-half times the seasoning will be sufficient to provide the desired flavor.

• Spices such as fennel seed, cumin seed, sesame seed, and white peppercorns may be toasted to intensify their flavors. Simply add the spice to a dry nonstick heated skillet and heat until aromatic, stirring often.

• A small electric coffee grinder or spice mill is your best bet for grinding whole spices and seeds. A pepper mill or mortar and pestle will also do the trick.

Ham & Cheese Spirals

Transform leftover ham into a zesty party appetizer in just fifteen minutes.

party pleaser

submitted by: **Cook's® Brand Ham**

Prep Time: 15 minutes
Chill Time: 1 hour

Test Kitchen Secret:

Substitute pepper jack cheese for the Cheddar and add hot salsa to kick up the heat in this snack.

1 cup COOK'S® Brand Ham (chopped), leftover ham (shredded), or Ham Steak (chopped)	1 cup Cheddar cheese, shredded
	3 green onions, diced
	½ cup red bell pepper, chopped
	1 (24 ounce) jar salsa, divided
1 (8 ounce) package cream cheese, softened	6 soft, taco-sized flour tortillas

1. Heat ham according to package directions or warm leftover ham. Combine cooled ham, cream cheese, Cheddar cheese, green onions, bell pepper, and ½ cup salsa in a mixing bowl. Spread approximately ⅓ cup mixture over each tortilla; roll up. Wrap each roll in plastic wrap. Refrigerate for 1 hour.
2. Remove plastic wrap; slice each roll into 6 pieces. Serve with remaining salsa for dipping. **Yield:** 36 servings.

Per serving: 65 calories, 4g protein, 5g carbohydrate, 4g fat, 1g fiber, 14mg cholesterol, 166mg sodium

Confetti Bites

Chopped vegetable pieces give a colorful, confetti-like appearance to these festive canapé bites.

make-ahead

submitted by: **McCormick® & Company**

Prep Time: 15 minutes
Cook Time: 15 minutes

What Other Cooks Have Done:

"This makes a very pretty appetizer. I also serve this in larger squares as a refreshing summer meal. I sometimes drizzle a little Italian dressing over it to soak into the bread base."

2 (8 ounce) packages refrigerated crescent dinner rolls	¼ teaspoon McCORMICK® Garlic Powder
2 (8 ounce) packages cream cheese, softened	1½ cups chopped vegetables (green and red bell pepper, carrots, broccoli)
3 tablespoons mayonnaise	
½ teaspoon McCORMICK® Basil Leaves	2 tablespoons McCORMICK® Salad Supreme Seasoning

1. Preheat oven to 350°F. Press crescent rolls into a greased 10x15 inch baking sheet to form a crust. Bake in the preheated oven for 12 to 15 minutes.
2. Combine cream cheese, mayonnaise, basil leaves, and garlic powder. Spread thinly over cooled crust. Top with chopped vegetables. Sprinkle generously with salad seasoning.
3. Cover and chill from 1 hour to overnight, or serve immediately. Cut into squares to serve. **Yield:** 35 servings.

Per serving: 110 calories, 2g protein, 6g carbohydrate, 8g fat, 0g fiber, 15mg cholesterol, 182mg sodium

Ham, Spinach & Pepper Wraps *(pictured on page 48)*

Slice these wraps into bite-sized pieces for a fun appetizer or keep them wrapped for a healthy lunch.

1   (8 ounce) package cream cheese, softened
2   tablespoons Dijon-style mustard
3   green onions, chopped
6   (8 inch) flour tortillas
12 to 18 large spinach leaves, stems removed
1   (12 ounce) jar whole roasted red bell peppers, drained and patted dry
1   pound COOK'S® Brand Ham, heated and julienned or shredded

1. In a small bowl, combine cream cheese and mustard. Add green onions; mix well. Spread about ¼ cup cream cheese mixture onto each tortilla to within ½ inch of edge. Cover each with 2 or 3 spinach leaves, pressing lightly into cream cheese mixture; top with 1 or 2 bell peppers and ham. Roll up tightly; wrap each in plastic wrap.
2. Refrigerate, seam side down, for 1 hour or longer. Remove from plastic wrap and cut each into 1 inch slices. **Yield:** 48 servings.

Per serving: 65 calories, 3g protein, 4g carbohydrate, 4g fat, 0g fiber, 10mg cholesterol, 222mg sodium

make-ahead

submitted by: **Cynthia Hooper, national winner of the Cook's® Brand Ham Recipe Contest**

Prep Time: 30 minutes
Cook Time: 10 minutes
Chill Time: 1 hour

Test Kitchen Secret:
Make these wraps even healthier by using low-fat cream cheese and whole wheat tortillas.

Ham-Stuffed Eggs

Deviled eggs—a potluck classic—get a face-lift with a hearty helping of leftover ham.

½   cup COOK'S® Brand Bone-In Ham (minced), leftover ham (finely shredded), or Ham Steak (minced)
6   hard-boiled eggs, peeled, halved lengthwise, yolks reserved
3   tablespoons mayonnaise or salad dressing
1   teaspoon ground mustard
1½ teaspoons prepared horseradish, or to taste
½   teaspoon lemon juice
    Salt and black pepper to taste
    Cayenne pepper to taste

1. Heat ham per package directions or warm leftover ham. Cool ham. Mash egg yolks with fork and stir in ham, mayonnaise, mustard, horseradish, lemon juice, salt, and black pepper. Fill egg whites with mixture, heaping slightly. Sprinkle with cayenne. Cover and refrigerate for at least 1 hour before serving. **Yield:** 12 servings.

Per serving: 76 calories, 5g protein, 0g carbohydrate, 6g fat, 0g fiber, 113mg cholesterol, 56mg sodium

holiday fare

submitted by: **Cook's® Brand Ham**

Prep Time: 35 minutes
Chill Time: 1 hour

Test Kitchen Secret:
The best way to prepare the perfect hard-boiled egg is simple: Place the eggs in a single layer in a saucepan and add enough water to come to 1 inch above the eggs. Bring them to a boil and immediately cover and remove from heat. Let the eggs sit, covered, 15 minutes. Pour off the water and immediately place the eggs under cold, running water. This method will ensure they won't have that unattractive greenish ring around the yolks.

Fried Stuffed Lindsay® Olives

Lindsay® Extra-Large Black Olives are stuffed with a garlic, basil, and lemon-scented anchovy paste, lightly breaded, then fried for an impressive, mouth-watering appetizer.

2	tablespoons minced garlic	¾	cup all-purpose flour
2	tablespoons anchovy paste	2	eggs, lightly beaten
1	tablespoon grated lemon zest	¾	cup plain or seasoned dry breadcrumbs
½	teaspoon chopped fresh thyme		Olive oil for frying
½	teaspoon chopped fresh basil		
2	dozen LINDSAY® Extra-Large Black Ripe Pitted Olives, drained		

1. In a small bowl, make a paste of the garlic, anchovy paste, lemon zest, thyme, and basil. Fill a small pastry bag fitted with a small plain tip with the paste.
2. Stuff olives. Roll in flour, dip in eggs, and roll in breadcrumbs. Fry in oil at a moderate temperature (350° to 375°F) until crisp and golden brown. Drain on a paper towel-lined plate. Serve hot. **Yield:** 4 servings.

Per serving: 273 calories, 10g protein, 38g carbohydrate, 9g fat, 1g fiber, 110mg cholesterol, 1316mg sodium

Crisp Tortellini Bites

Fresh cheese tortellini is breaded and baked until crispy, then served with a side of pizza sauce for dipping.

½	cup plain dry breadcrumbs	½	cup sour cream
2	teaspoons HERB-OX® Chicken Flavored Bouillon Granules	2	tablespoons milk
¼	teaspoon garlic powder	1	(9 ounce) package refrigerated cheese-filled tortellini
¼	cup grated Parmesan cheese		Warm pizza sauce or marinara sauce for dipping

1. Preheat oven to 400°F. In bowl, combine breadcrumbs, bouillon, garlic powder, and Parmesan cheese. In another small bowl, combine sour cream and milk. Dip tortellini in sour cream mixture, then in the breadcrumbs; coat evenly. Place tortellini on lightly greased baking sheet.
2. Bake in the preheated oven for 10 to 12 minutes or until crisp and golden brown, turning once. Serve immediately with warm pizza sauce or marinara sauce. **Yield:** 8 servings.

Per serving: 145 calories, 6g protein, 17g carbohydrate, 6g fat, 1g fiber, 14mg cholesterol, 314mg sodium

Crisp Tortellini Bites

Tomato Cheese Bruschetta

Prepare these ingredients ahead and assemble this appetizer just before serving.

Prep Time: 25 minutes
Cook Time: 12 minutes

What Other Cooks Have Done:

"Instead of putting the basil, garlic, and seasonings in the olive oil, I put about 1 or 2 tablespoons of pesto in the olive oil and brushed that on the bread. I served the baguette slices as an appetizer at a Christmas party, and everyone loved them. A few of these along with a salad would make a great light lunch."

¼	cup olive oil
2	tablespoons chopped fresh basil leaves★
½	teaspoon finely chopped garlic
¼	teaspoon salt
¼	teaspoon black pepper
24	(½ inch thick) slices baguette
6	slices LAND O'LAKES® Deli American Cheese or Monterey Jack Cheese, quartered
3	Roma tomatoes, sliced into 24 (⅛ inch) slices

1. Preheat oven to 350°F. Stir together oil, basil, garlic, salt, and pepper in a small bowl. Place bread slices onto an ungreased baking sheet. Brush top of each bread slice with oil mixture.

2. Bake in the preheated oven for 8 to 10 minutes or until lightly toasted.

3. Preheat broiler. Top each bread slice with 1 piece cheese and 1 slice tomato; brush with remaining oil mixture. Broil 5 to 6 inches from heat until cheese begins to melt, about 1 to 2 minutes. **Yield:** 24 servings.

★Substitute 2 teaspoons dried basil leaves, if desired.

Per serving: 83 calories, 2g protein, 8g carbohydrate, 4g fat, 1g fiber, 5mg cholesterol, 188mg sodium

---

Secrets from the Herb-Ox® Kitchens

For more than 80 years, good cooks have included Herb-Ox® Bouillon Cubes or Granules as a staple in their pantries, much like coffee, sugar, or flour. Herb-Ox® Bouillon has been an essential ingredient in the kitchen ever since the Pure Foods Company of Mamaroneck, New York, introduced it in 1918. In 1993, Hormel Foods Corporation welcomed Herb-Ox® into their family of fine products. Still made with real dried herbs and real stock concentrate, Herb-Ox® Bouillon is truly an essential cooking ingredient.

• Be sure to use Herb-Ox® Bouillon in any recipe that calls for broth. A container of 25 Herb-Ox® cubes is the equivalent of 12 cans of broth. That's a lot of broth crowding your cupboards. With recyclable glass and plastic containers, Herb-Ox® doesn't crowd landfills, either. Those same 12 cans of broth can cost up to 4 times as much as 1 container of Herb-Ox® cubes…that's expensive water.

• For amazing flavor without any additional fat, add 1 serving of Herb-Ox® Bouillon to every cup of water you boil for your rice and pasta dishes.

• To make a great herb butter, stir in 1 serving of Herb-Ox® Bouillon (crushed), 1 tablespoon finely chopped peppers and onions, and a pinch of your favorite herbs into 1 cup softened butter.

• For really tasty burgers, mix 1 serving Herb-Ox® Bouillon into each pound of ground beef before grilling.

Seasoned Crab Cakes

Simple and quick crab patties are coated with cornflake crumbs and pan-fried. Serve with lemon wedges and tartar sauce or Dijon-style mustard.

party pleaser

submitted by: **Hormel Foods Corporation**

Prep Time: 10 minutes
Cook Time: 15 minutes

2   (6 ounce) cans crabmeat, drained and chunked
2   eggs, beaten
½   cup dry breadcrumbs
¼   cup minced green onions
¼   cup mayonnaise or salad dressing
1   tablespoon Dijon-style mustard
1   teaspoon Worcestershire sauce
2   teaspoons HERB-OX® Chicken Flavored Bouillon Granules, divided
½   cup crushed cornflake crumbs
    Vegetable oil for frying
    Lemon wedges (optional)
    Tartar sauce and Dijon-style mustard

Test Kitchen Secret:
This recipe uses canned crabmeat, but 12 ounces of fresh flaked or lump crabmeat may be substituted. When using canned crabmeat, soak it in ice water 10 minutes, then drain and pat dry. This helps it taste more like fresh crab.

1. In a bowl, combine first 7 ingredients and 1 teaspoon bouillon. Stir until blended. In another bowl, combine cornflake crumbs with remaining bouillon. Evenly shape crab mixture into 12 (2½ inch) patties. Coat patties with cornflake mixture.

2. In a large skillet, heat a small amount of oil. Place patties in skillet, in batches, and cook over medium heat, about 3 minutes on each side, until golden brown. Add additional oil to skillet and continue cooking crab cakes. If desired, garnish with lemon wedges and serve with tartar sauce and mustard. Serve crab cakes immediately. **Yield:** 12 servings.

Per serving: 93 calories, 8g protein, 7g carbohydrate, 4g fat, 0g fiber, 62mg cholesterol, 240mg sodium

Crispy Chicken Dippers

Whether you serve them for a light meal or a hearty appetizer, these crispy chicken tenders practically melt in your mouth.

party pleaser

submitted by: **Tyson®**

Prep Time: 20 minutes
Cook Time: 25 minutes

Test Kitchen Secret:

For a party, serve chicken dippers with dill dipping sauce, pickles, olives, and fresh vegetables.

¼	cup olive oil		¼	cup mayonnaise
1¼	cups finely crushed buttery crackers		¼	cup sour cream
½	cup grated Parmesan cheese		¾	teaspoon dried dill weed
¼	teaspoon garlic powder		2	tablespoons minced dill pickle
16	TYSON® Fresh Chicken Breast Tenders			

1. Preheat oven to 375°F. Line a jellyroll pan with foil; spray with nonstick cooking spray. Pour olive oil into shallow dish. In separate shallow dish, combine cracker crumbs, cheese, and garlic powder. Dip tenders one at a time into olive oil, then roll in crumb mixture. Arrange coated tenders in single layer on prepared pan. Wash hands.

2. Bake in the preheated oven for 20 to 25 minutes or until chicken is done (internal temperature of 170°F).

3. While chicken bakes, combine mayonnaise, sour cream, dill weed, and pickle in small bowl. Refrigerate until ready to serve. **Yield:** 4 servings.

Per serving: 779 calories, 36g protein, 43g carbohydrate, 51g fat, 2g fiber, 79mg cholesterol, 1058mg sodium

Cornflake Crunch Tenders

Cornflakes aren't just for breakfast! Here they make a tasty, crispy coating for tender chicken strips.

kid-friendly

submitted by: **Tyson®**

Prep Time: 15 minutes
Cook Time: 20 minutes

Test Kitchen Secret:

Serve with marinara sauce, honey mustard, or barbecue sauce for dipping. You can also substitute Tyson® Fresh Chicken Breast Tenders—just decrease the cooking time by about one-third.

2	cups finely crushed cornflakes		16	TYSON® Individually Fresh Frozen Boneless, Skinless Chicken Tenderloins
1	teaspoon Italian seasoning			
½	teaspoon salt		¼	cup butter or margarine, melted
¼	teaspoon black pepper			
1	large egg			

1. Preheat oven to 400°F. Line a jellyroll pan with foil; spray with nonstick cooking spray.

2. Combine crushed cornflakes, Italian seasoning, salt, and pepper in a shallow dish. Lightly beat egg in another shallow dish.

3. Rinse ice glaze off chicken. Pat dry. Dip chicken in egg, then in cornflakes mixture. Place on pan. Wash hands.

4. Drizzle chicken with butter. Bake in the preheated oven for 20 minutes or until done (internal temperature of 170°F). **Yield:** 4 servings.

Per serving: 601 calories, 23g protein, 67g carbohydrate, 27g fat, 3g fiber, 117mg cholesterol, 1811mg sodium

Chicken Florentine Pizza

comfort food

submitted by: **Tyson®**

Prep Time: 10 minutes
Cook Time: 25 minutes

Test Kitchen Secret:

Cut pizza into eight portions for four servings or cut into smaller, bite-sized portions to use as an appetizer.

If pizza makes you think "greasy, spicy junk food," this tasty version will make you think again!

1	pound TYSON® Fresh Chicken Tenders
1	tablespoon garlic oil
1	teaspoon Italian seasoning
1	cup ricotta cheese
½	cup shredded mozzarella cheese
1	(16 ounce) prebaked pizza crust
1	(10 ounce) package frozen chopped spinach, thawed and squeezed dry
2	tablespoons chopped dried tomatoes marinated in olive oil, drained
¼	cup grated Parmesan cheese

1. Preheat oven to 425°F. Cut chicken into 1 inch pieces. Wash hands.
2. Heat garlic oil in large skillet over medium heat. Add chicken and cook 10 minutes or until done, turning once (internal temperature of 170°F). Stir in Italian seasoning and remove from heat.
3. Combine ricotta and mozzarella; spread on prebaked pizza crust. Spread spinach over cheese mixture; add chicken and tomatoes. Sprinkle with Parmesan cheese.
4. Bake in the preheated oven for 10 to 15 minutes or until cheese is melted. **Yield:** 4 servings.

Per serving: 648 calories, 52g protein, 54g carbohydrate, 23g fat, 4g fiber, 107mg cholesterol, 930mg sodium

Crispy Chicken Dippers

Chicken & Artichoke Pizza with Fresh Tomatoes

Make a gourmet pizza at home in less time than it takes for delivery!

3	TYSON® Fresh Boneless, Skinless Chicken Breasts	1	(10 ounce) prebaked pizza crust
1	(6 ounce) jar marinated artichoke hearts, undrained	4	Roma tomatoes, thinly sliced
		½	teaspoon dried basil leaves
1	large clove garlic, minced	1½	cups (6 ounces) shredded mozzarella cheese

1. Preheat oven to 425°F. Cut chicken into ¾ inch pieces. Wash hands and cutting board. Drain artichoke hearts, reserving liquid. Coarsely chop artichoke hearts.

2. Place artichoke liquid in large nonstick skillet and bring to a boil over medium-high heat. Cook until most of liquid has evaporated, about 1 minute. Add chicken and garlic to skillet. Cook chicken 3 to 5 minutes or until done (internal temperature of 170°F). Stir in artichoke hearts. Remove from heat.

3. Place pizza crust on baking sheet; top evenly with tomato slices. Top with chicken mixture; sprinkle with basil. Top with cheese. Bake in the preheated oven for 12 to 17 minutes or until hot and cheese is melted. **Yield:** 6 servings.

Per serving: 177 calories, 21g protein, 6g carbohydrate, 8g fat, 2g fiber, 49mg cholesterol, 262mg sodium

party pleaser

submitted by: **Tyson®**

Prep Time: 15 minutes
Cook Time: 25 minutes

What Other Cooks Have Done:
"This recipe was excellent. I did change it around a little to suit my taste. I used pizza sauce, then put on the chicken and artichokes, and then cheese. Last, I topped with small, sliced, vine-ripened tomatoes and sprinkled with fresh basil. I love fresh tomatoes on pizza, but I like mine with sauce also. This was a big hit with my family."

Cheeseburger Pizza

Dish up this easy-to-assemble vegetarian pizza made with convenient Boca® Meatless Ground Burger and ingredients commonly found in your kitchen.

1	(12 inch) Italian pizza crust	1	small onion, thinly sliced
1	tablespoon vegetable oil	1	medium tomato, sliced
½	cup pizza sauce	¾	cup shredded mozzarella-Cheddar pizza cheese
¼	cup ketchup		
1	pouch (1 cup) frozen BOCA® Meatless Ground Burger, thawed		

1. Preheat oven to 425°F. Brush pizza crust with oil.

2. Mix pizza sauce, ketchup, and ground burger until well blended. Spread evenly onto crust; top with remaining ingredients.

3. Bake in the preheated oven for 10 minutes or until heated through. **Yield:** 6 servings.

Per serving: 220 calories, 11g protein, 25g carbohydrate, 8g fat, 2g fiber, 10mg cholesterol, 632mg sodium

quick & easy

submitted by: **Boca®**

Prep Time: 10 minutes
Cook Time: 10 minutes

Test Kitchen Secret:
Serve this healthy pizza with crisp carrots and celery sticks. For fun and even more cheeseburger flavor, top with sweet pickle relish.

California Harvest Pizza

California Harvest Pizza

Lindsay® Pimiento-Stuffed Olives, goat cheese, roasted peppers, and marinated artichoke hearts unite in a homemade pizza destined to land at the top of your summer menu picks.

2 (10 ounce) packages (8 inch) Italian bread shells, such as Boboli®
4 teaspoons olive oil
1 (6.5 ounce) jar marinated artichoke hearts, drained and quartered
½ cup julienned prepared roasted red bell peppers
1 (5 ounce) package goat cheese, crumbled
1 (6 ounce) jar LINDSAY® Manzanilla Olives Stuffed with Pimiento, drained
¼ cup grated Asiago cheese
¼ cup julienned fresh basil

1. Preheat oven to 400°F. Brush each bread shell with 1 teaspoon oil. Top each shell with artichoke hearts, bell peppers, goat cheese, olives, and Asiago cheese, dividing equally. Place on baking sheets.
2. Bake in the preheated oven for 8 minutes. Sprinkle each pizza with 1 tablespoon basil. **Yield:** 4 servings.

Per serving: 745 calories, 31g protein, 82g carbohydrate, 36g fat, 5g fiber, 48mg cholesterol, 2297mg sodium

quick & easy

submitted by: **Lindsay® Olives**

Prep Time: 12 minutes
Cook Time: 8 minutes

What Other Cooks Have Done:
"This recipe is very good for a nice summertime pizza. I actually modified it slightly by cooking it on the grill instead of the oven, and it came out perfect!"

Lindsay® Olive & Brie Pizza Pie

Lindsay® Black Olives and Brie, with a little help from tomatoes and grated Parmesan, manage to pull off one heck of a tasty pizza pie! Brush the crust with Dijon-style mustard before baking for additional flavor.

1 refrigerated 9 inch pie crust, at room temperature
2 tablespoons Dijon-style mustard
8 ounces Brie cheese, rind removed, cut into ½ inch pieces
3 plum tomatoes, halved crosswise, seeded, and thinly sliced
⅔ cup LINDSAY® Black Ripe Pitted Olives, drained and halved
3 tablespoons thinly sliced green onions with tops
2 teaspoons chopped fresh or ¾ teaspoon dried oregano
½ cup coarsely grated Parmesan cheese

1. Preheat oven to 400°F. Place crust on a lightly floured baking sheet. Fold in edges of crust ½ inch, pressing down to form a rim. Spread mustard over inside of crust; top with half of Brie cheese, tomatoes, olives, green onions, remaining Brie cheese, oregano, and Parmesan cheese.
2. Bake in the preheated oven for 18 to 20 minutes or until crust is crisp and golden brown. Let stand 10 minutes before serving. Serve warm or at room temperature. **Yield:** 6 servings.

Per serving: 352 calories, 14g protein, 17g carbohydrate, 26g fat, 2g fiber, 44mg cholesterol, 781mg sodium

5 star

submitted by: **Lindsay® Olives**

Prep Time: 20 minutes
Cook Time: 20 minutes

Test Kitchen Secret:
Brie cheese is a creamy cheese with a buttery-soft texture. It has a shorter shelf life than many cheeses, so use it within a few days of purchase. To store Brie and keep it fresh, wrap in parchment or wax paper and refrigerate.

Milk Chocolate Popcorn

kid-friendly

submitted by: **Nestlé® Toll House®**

Prep Time: 10 minutes
Cook Time: 30 minutes

What Other Cooks Have Done:
"I improvised with what I had in my cupboard and made two batches—one with the chocolate morsels and a second batch with a bag of butterscotch morsels. I mixed the chocolate and butterscotch popcorn in one bowl when it was finished baking for a colorful and very tasty treat. This was a nice change from standard caramel corn."

Kids of every age will love these crunchy treats! Loaded with chocolate and peanuts, they make great snacks and stocking stuffers.

12	cups popped popcorn	1	cup light corn syrup
2½	cups salted peanuts	¼	cup butter or margarine
1	(11.5 ounce) package NESTLÉ® TOLL HOUSE® Milk Chocolate Morsels		

1. Preheat oven to 300°F. Grease a large roasting pan. Line a large bowl or serving plate with wax paper.
2. Combine popcorn and nuts in prepared roasting pan. Combine morsels, corn syrup, and butter in medium, heavy-duty saucepan. Cook over medium heat, stirring constantly, until mixture boils. Pour over popcorn; toss well to coat.
3. Bake in the preheated oven for 30 to 40 minutes, stirring frequently. Cool slightly in pan; remove to prepared serving plate. Store in airtight container for up to 2 weeks. **Yield:** 15 servings.

Per serving: 393 calories, 8g protein, 41g carbohydrate, 25g fat, 4g fiber, 13mg cholesterol, 352mg sodium

Butterfinger® Caramel Apples *(pictured on page 73)*

holiday fare

submitted by: **Nestlé®**

Prep Time: 15 minutes
Chill Time: 45 minutes

Test Kitchen Secret:
If caramel becomes firm, return to microwave oven for 20 to 30 seconds or until dipping consistency. Two (1.5 ounce) Nestlé® Crunch® Candy Bars may be used in place of Butterfinger® Candy Bars.

Just a few ingredients mixed together make this an easy after-school snack.

6	tart apples, washed, dried, and stems removed	2	(2.1 ounce) NESTLÉ® BUTTERFINGER® Candy Bars, chopped
1	(14 ounce) package caramels		
2	tablespoons water		

1. Line tray or baking sheet with wax paper. Insert 1 wooden stick into stem end of each apple. You will need a total of 6 wooden sticks found in cake decorating or hobby shops.
2. Microwave caramels and water in large, microwave-safe bowl on HIGH (100%) for 2 minutes; stir. Microwave at additional 10 to 20 second intervals, stirring until smooth.
3. Dip each apple in melted caramel; scrape excess caramel from bottoms. Quickly roll bottom half of apples in chopped BUTTERFINGER®, then place on prepared tray. Refrigerate for 45 minutes or until set. Store apples in refrigerator in airtight container. Apples are best if they are served the same day they are prepared. **Yield:** 6 servings.

Per serving: 430 calories, 6g protein, 82g carbohydrate, 9g fat, 3g fiber, 4mg cholesterol, 218mg sodium

Cereal Snacking Mix

Shake up the troops with this good *and* good-for-you snack.

2	cups toasted whole grain oat cereal	1	tablespoon butter, melted
½	cup dried cranberries	1	cup (7 ounces) NESTLÉ® RAISINETS® Milk Chocolate-Covered Raisins
2	tablespoons white sugar		
½	teaspoon ground cinnamon		

1. Combine cereal, cranberries, sugar, and cinnamon in a large, zip-top plastic bag. Pour butter over cereal mixture; seal bag. Shake well to combine. Add RAISINETS®; shake well. **Yield:** 6 servings.

Per serving: 241 calories, 3g protein, 44g carbohydrate, 8g fat, 3g fiber, 6mg cholesterol, 126mg sodium

healthy

submitted by: **Nestlé®**

Prep Time: 10 minutes

What Other Cooks Have Done:
"This is the best mix to get your fix of chocolate without going overboard. I love to make this when we travel long distances and everyone wants something to snack on."

Bumps on a Log

Here's a quick, healthful snack kids are sure to love—no eating utensils needed!

1	stalk celery, washed and ends trimmed	10	NESTLÉ® RAISINETS® Milk Chocolate-Covered Raisins
2	tablespoons creamy or chunky peanut butter		

1. Fill celery with peanut butter.
2. Press RAISINETS® into peanut butter. **Yield:** 1 serving.

Per serving: 237 calories, 9g protein, 15g carbohydrate, 18g fat, 3g fiber, 0mg cholesterol, 188mg sodium

party pleaser

submitted by: **Nestlé®**

Prep Time: 5 minutes

Test Kitchen Secret:
Even the littlest hands can press Raisinets® into the log. For those who are still hungry, spread peanut butter on small round crackers and have the kids make eyes, noses, and mouths with Raisinets®.

Butterfinger® Popcorn Balls

This recipe's "hands-on" preparation is a thrill for kids and will be a smash at your next Halloween bash.

6	cups popped popcorn	¼	cup butter or margarine
3	(2.1 ounce) NESTLÉ® BUTTERFINGER® Candy Bars, chopped	3½	cups miniature marshmallows

1. Combine popcorn and chopped candy bars in a large bowl.
2. Melt butter in saucepan over low heat. Stir in marshmallows. Heat, stirring constantly, until marshmallows are melted and mixture is smooth.
3. Pour over popcorn mixture; quickly toss to coat well. Spray hands with nonstick cooking spray. Form popcorn mixture into 6 (3 inch) balls. Place on wax paper to cool. Store in airtight container. **Yield:** 6 servings.

Per serving: 333 calories, 5g protein, 49g carbohydrate, 14g fat, 2g fiber, 21mg cholesterol, 150mg sodium

holiday fare

submitted by: **Nestlé®**

Prep Time: 10 minutes
Cook Time: 5 minutes

What Other Cooks Have Done:
"I made this with the children I work with in a summer program. They absolutely loved crushing the Butterfingers® and putting the balls together. Of course, their favorite part was eating them!"

Celebrate the Seasons with Nestlé®

Kids will have fun making these little creatures for a birthday celebration or a Halloween party.
Adults can do all the cutting while the kids get creative and decorate their favorite bugs.

Tasty Bugs

No kid could resist our Tasty Bugs. They're so much fun to make and eat, they'll crawl right off the plate!

Prep Time: 1 hour

Small jar of creamy peanut butter
NESTLÉ® GOOBERS®, RAISINETS®, and SNO-CAPS®
2 red apples
1 bunch celery
1 bag shredded carrots
1 zip-top plastic bag
Safety scissors
Kitchen knife

1. Spoon peanut butter into a zip-top plastic bag. Seal bag and cut the tip off one corner of the bottom of the bag. Squeeze peanut butter into corner of the bag and use to dispense peanut butter, like frosting from a pastry bag.

Ladybug

1. Cut an apple in half lengthwise and place one half, cut side down, on a plate.
2. Using peanut butter as "glue," make a face for your ladybug using RAISINETS® and a small slice of celery.
3. Again, using peanut butter for "glue," give the ladybug SNO-CAP® spots.
4. *Parents Only:* With the tip of a knife, poke two small holes in the apple just above the ladybug's eyes. Insert one carrot shred into each hole for her antennae.

Snail

1. Cut a thick vertical slice from a whole apple, just missing the core.
2. Cut a celery stick that is about 1 inch longer than the width of the apple slice.
3. Fill the trough of the celery stick with peanut butter, and set aside.
4. Using the plastic bag filled with peanut butter, draw a spiral on both sides of the apple slice.
5. Wedge the apple slice into the filled celery stick.
6. Decorate the snail's shell (the red band of apple peel) with SNO-CAPS®.
7. Add two GOOBERS® to one end of the celery stick to make his eyes.
8. Don't forget to add two carrot shreds for antennae!

Caterpillar

1. Cut a 3 inch long piece of celery and fill the trough with peanut butter.
2. Place two RAISINETS® at one end of the celery stick with two carrot stick shreds poking out behind them for antennae.
3. Place SNO-CAPS® down the length of the celery stick on top of the peanut butter at even intervals.

Butterfly

1. Cut two 1 inch wedges from an apple and place on a plate, narrow edges together.
2. Cut a celery stick the same length as the apple wedges.
3. Place the celery stick, trough side down, between the two apple wedges on a plate.
4. With your peanut butter piping bag, draw stripes across the celery stick to decorate the butterfly's body.
5. Use GOOBERS® to make eyes for your butterfly.
6. Decorate the butterfly's wings with SNO-CAPS®.

Clockwise from top left: Butterfinger®
Caramel Apples, page 70, Caterpillar Tasty
Bugs, and Snail Tasty Bug

Pine-Orange Frosty

Make this favorite with low-fat frozen yogurt for a delicious, guilt-free frosty.

1   (20 ounce) can DOLE®
    Crushed Pineapple,
    undrained
1   cup orange sherbet or frozen
    yogurt

1½ cups ice cubes
    Orange slices (optional)

1. Combine crushed pineapple, sherbet, and ice cubes in blender or food processor. Cover; blend until smooth. Garnish with orange slices, if desired. **Yield:** 4 servings.

Per serving: 136 calories, 1g protein, 34g carbohydrate, 1g fat, 1g fiber, 2mg cholesterol, 20mg sodium

Fruity Frosty Nesquik®

Shake it up with fruit and Nesquik® in one! Fruity Frosty Nesquik® is an excellent source of vitamin C.

¾   cup fat-free milk
½   cup ice cubes
½   medium banana
¼   cup orange juice

3   tablespoons Strawberry Flavor
    NESTLÉ® NESQUIK®
    Powder

1. Place milk, ice cubes, banana, orange juice, and Nesquik® in blender; cover. Blend until smooth. Serve immediately. **Yield:** 2 servings.

Per serving: 140 calories, 4g protein, 31g carbohydrate, 0g fat, 1g fiber, 2mg cholesterol, 50mg sodium

Easy Aloha Smoothie

You'll want to break out the grass skirts and flower leis for this tropical concoction.

1   (15.25 ounce) can DOLE®
    Tropical Fruit Salad,
    undrained

1   cup vanilla low-fat yogurt
½   cup ice cubes
    Fresh mint (optional)

1. Combine tropical fruit salad, yogurt, and ice cubes in blender or food processor. Cover; blend until smooth. Garnish with fresh mint, if desired. **Yield:** 3 servings.

Per serving: 141 calories, 4g protein, 28g carbohydrate, 1g fat, 1g fiber, 5mg cholesterol, 66mg sodium

Bunny Safari Smoothie

Your kids will have a delicious adventure with this chocolatey treat that's packed with nutrients! Bunny Safari Smoothie is an excellent source of calcium and vitamin C.

1 cup fat-free milk	⅓ cup Chocolate Flavor
2 bananas	NESTLÉ® NESQUIK®
1 cup ice cubes	Powder

1. Place milk, bananas, ice cubes, and Nesquik® in blender; cover. Blend until smooth. **Yield:** 2 servings.

Per serving: 271 calories, 5g protein, 60g carbohydrate, 1g fat, 5g fiber, 2mg cholesterol, 103mg sodium

Chocolate Peanut Smoothie

Blend in 1 tablespoon creamy peanut butter. Proceed as above.

Fruit Smoothie

Blend in 1 cup strawberries or raspberries in place of bananas. Proceed as above.

kid-friendly

submitted by: **Nestlé® Nesquik®**

Prep Time: 5 minutes

Test Kitchen Secret:
Try freezing a banana or other fruit ahead. Then, when you make your Bunny Safari Smoothie, top it with a few pieces of the frozen fruit or slices of frozen banana.

Chocolate Peanut Bunny Shake

Shake it up, Bunny! You can feel good about giving this protein-packed treat to your kids anytime.

2 cups fat-free milk	¼ cup Chocolate Flavor
2 large scoops vanilla fat-free	NESTLÉ® NESQUIK®
frozen yogurt or fat-free	Powder
ice cream	¼ cup creamy peanut butter

1. Place milk, frozen yogurt, Nesquik®, and peanut butter in blender; cover. Blend until smooth. Divide between 4 chilled glasses. **Yield:** 4 servings.

Per serving: 308 calories, 13g protein, 45g carbohydrate, 9g fat, 1g fiber, 2mg cholesterol, 253mg sodium

5 star

submitted by: **Nestlé® Nesquik®**

Prep Time: 5 minutes

Test Kitchen Secret:
Try topping this tasty shake with a spoonful of chopped peanuts for extra crunch.

Fruit Smoothies

Fruit Smoothies

Fresh or frozen fruit, ice, and Eagle Brand® milk are all it takes to make awesome smoothies.

1   (14 ounce) can EAGLE BRAND® Sweetened Condensed Milk (not evaporated milk), chilled
1   (8 ounce) carton plain yogurt
1   small banana, cut up
1   cup frozen or fresh whole strawberries

1   (8 ounce) can crushed pineapple packed with juice, chilled
2   tablespoons lemon juice from concentrate
1   cup ice cubes
    Halved fresh strawberries (optional)

1. In blender container, combine chilled sweetened condensed milk, yogurt, banana, whole strawberries, pineapple with its juice, and lemon juice; cover and blend until smooth. With blender running, gradually add ice cubes, blending until smooth. Garnish with halved strawberries, if desired. Serve immediately. **Yield:** 5 servings.

Per serving: 341 calories, 10g protein, 61g carbohydrate, 8g fat, 3g fiber, 29mg cholesterol, 139mg sodium

Peach Smoothies

Omit strawberries and pineapple. Add 2 cups frozen or fresh sliced peaches. Proceed as above.

Key Lime Smoothies

Omit strawberries, pineapple, and lemon juice. Add ⅓ cup Key lime juice. Proceed as above. Tint with green food coloring, if desired. Garnish with lime slices, if desired.

healthy

submitted by: **Eagle Brand®**

Prep Time: 5 minutes

Test Kitchen Secret:
Sprinkle the smoothies with toasted sliced almonds or pecans and make the most out of your on-the-go breakfast.

Orange-Pineapple Punch

This fruity ice cream refresher has a great flavor for anytime of year. Top your punch bowl with mint leaves or fresh cut orange slices for a pretty presentation.

party pleaser

submitted by: **Eagle Brand®**

Prep Time: 5 minutes

Test Kitchen Secret:
Pour leftover punch into ice cube trays and freeze. Flavored ice cubes can be chopped in a blender. Spoon mixture into ice cream bowls and serve immediately.

1   (14 ounce) can EAGLE BRAND® Sweetened Condensed Milk (not evaporated milk)
1   (46 ounce) can pineapple juice, chilled

1   (2 liter) bottle orange soda, chilled
Orange sherbet (optional)

1. In punch bowl, stir together sweetened condensed milk and pineapple juice; add orange soda. Top with sherbet or serve over ice. Refrigerate leftovers. **Yield:** 12 servings.

Per serving: 252 calories, 3g protein, 54g carbohydrate, 3g fat, 0g fiber, 12mg cholesterol, 55mg sodium

Orange-Pineapple Punch

Creamy Soda Freeze

A simple recipe that makes enough shakes, frozen pops, or ice cream to feed a crowd on a hot summer day.

2	(14 ounce) cans EAGLE BRAND® Sweetened Condensed Milk (not evaporated milk)
1	(2 liter) bottle carbonated beverage, any flavor

1. In electric ice cream freezer container, combine ingredients; mix well. Freeze according to manufacturer's instructions. Store leftovers in freezer. **Yield:** 16 servings.

Per serving: 208 calories, 4g protein, 40g carbohydrate, 4g fat, 0g fiber, 17mg cholesterol, 67mg sodium

Shakes

In blender container, combine ½ (14 ounce) can sweetened condensed milk, 1 (12 ounce) can carbonated beverage, and 3 cups ice. Blend until smooth. Repeat for additional shakes. Store leftovers in freezer. **Yield:** 1 or 2 quarts.

Frozen Pops

Combine 1 (14 ounce) can sweetened condensed milk with 2 (12 ounce) cans carbonated beverage; mix well. Pour equal portions into 8 (5 ounce) paper cold-drink cups. Cover each cup with aluminum foil; make a small hole in center of each. Insert a wooden stick into each cup. Freeze 6 hours or until firm. **Yield:** 8 servings.

make-ahead

submitted by: **Eagle Brand®**

Prep Time: 5 minutes

Test Kitchen Secret:
Turn this into a guilt-free treat by using reduced-fat or fat-free Eagle Brand® Sweetened Condensed Milk and a diet beverage.

Peanut Butter S'mores Cocoa

This peanut buttery cocoa is a twist on the traditional s'mores recipe. For an extra-special treat, sprinkle chocolate graham cracker crumbs over the top just before serving.

4	tablespoons (2 envelopes) Rich Chocolate NESTLÉ® CARNATION® Hot Cocoa Mix
2	tablespoons creamy peanut butter
2	cups hot milk
6	tablespoons marshmallow cream
4	chocolate graham crackers (optional)

1. Place cocoa mix and peanut butter in small, ovenproof container. Stir in milk until peanut butter is dissolved. Divide between 2 mugs; top each with 3 tablespoons marshmallow cream. Serve immediately with chocolate graham crackers, if desired. **Yield:** 2 servings.

Per serving: 120 calories, 14g protein, 60g carbohydrate, 15g fat, 2g fiber, 21mg cholesterol, 402mg sodium

kid-friendly

submitted by: **Nestlé®**

Prep Time: 5 minutes

Test Kitchen Secret:
Try using Milk Chocolate Flavor Nestlé® Carnation® Hot Cocoa Mix.

submitted by: **Eagle Brand**®

Prep Time: 10 minutes
Cook Time: 10 minutes

Test Kitchen Secret:

To prepare in the microwave: Combine all ingredients except marshmallows in a 2 quart glass measure. Microwave on HIGH (100%) 8 to 10 minutes, stirring every 3 minutes. Top with marshmallows, if desired. Store covered in refrigerator. Hot chocolate can be stored in refrigerator up to five days. Mix well and reheat before serving.

Creamy Hot Chocolate

Keep some condensed milk on hand and whip up a batch of this rich hot chocolate to warm your loved ones on cold days.

1   (14 ounce) can EAGLE BRAND® Sweetened Condensed Milk (not evaporated milk)
½   cup unsweetened cocoa powder
1½ teaspoons vanilla extract
⅛   teaspoon salt
6½ cups hot water
    Marshmallows (optional)

1. In a large saucepan over medium heat, combine sweetened condensed milk, cocoa, vanilla, and salt; mix well. Slowly stir in water. Heat through, stirring occasionally. Do not boil. Top with marshmallows, if desired. Store covered in refrigerator. **Yield:** 8 servings.

Per serving: 194 calories, 5g protein, 35g carbohydrate, 5g fat, 2g fiber, 17mg cholesterol, 109mg sodium

Creamy Hot Chocolate

Holiday Eggnog

Eggnog is a wonderful drink for celebrating the winter holidays. Try your hand at this delicious recipe and impress your guests!

4	pasteurized eggs	½	teaspoon vanilla extract
1	(14 ounce) can EAGLE BRAND® Sweetened Condensed Milk (not evaporated milk)		Dash salt
		½	cup bourbon or brandy (optional)
3	cups milk		Nutmeg

1. In large mixer bowl, beat eggs. Gradually beat in next 4 ingredients. Chill. Garnish with nutmeg. Refrigerate leftovers. **Yield:** 8 servings.

Per serving: 280 calories, 10g protein, 32g carbohydrate, 9g fat, 0g fiber, 130mg cholesterol, 188mg sodium

party pleaser

submitted by: **Eagle Brand®**

Prep Time: 10 minutes

Test Kitchen Secret:
Since the eggs aren't cooked in this recipe, we've called for pasteurized eggs, which are heat-treated to destroy any bacteria that might be present. Pasteurized eggs are especially suitable for recipes like this where the eggs aren't cooked, but may also be used for other recipes, including baked goods. Remember to keep eggnog well chilled.

Homemade Irish Cream Liqueur

Luxurious Homemade Irish Cream Liqueur is a brisk winter drink, and it makes an excellent hostess gift for parties.

1¾	cups Irish whiskey, brandy, rum, bourbon, Scotch, or rye whiskey	2	cups whipping cream or coffee cream
1	(14 ounce) can EAGLE BRAND® Sweetened Condensed Milk (not evaporated milk)	2	tablespoons chocolate-flavored syrup
		2	teaspoons instant coffee
		1	teaspoon vanilla extract
		½	teaspoon almond extract

1. In blender container, combine all ingredients; blend until smooth. Serve over ice. Store tightly covered in refrigerator. Stir before serving. **Yield:** 7 servings.

Per serving: 536 calories, 6g protein, 36g carbohydrate, 30g fat, 0g fiber, 112mg cholesterol, 101mg sodium

Homemade Cream Liqueur

Omit Irish whiskey, chocolate-flavored syrup, coffee, and extracts. Add 1¾ cups flavored liqueur (almond, coffee, orange, or mint) to EAGLE BRAND® milk and cream. Proceed as above.

holiday fare

submitted by: **Eagle Brand®**

Prep Time: 10 minutes

Test Kitchen Secret:
For more blended flavor, store in refrigerator several hours before serving.

Libby's® Pumpkin Cranberry Bread,
page 94

breads

Quick breads **warm** from the oven define home-cooked **comfort** food. Make your next meal or breakfast-on-the-go something to remember with simple berry muffins, chocolate scones, fruit and nut loaves, and **down-home** cornbread.

Banana-Orange Muffins

healthy

submitted by:
The Quaker® Oats Company

Prep Time: 10 minutes
Cook Time: 22 minutes

What Other Cooks Have Done:
"These are very tasty, wholesome muffins! It was rainy out this morning and I wanted some home-baked warmth for breakfast, and these were perfect! I used vanilla yogurt instead of plain, and I think it added a subtle yet tasty flavor. The hint of orange works well with the muffins."

Bake a batch of warm, wholesome Banana-Orange Muffins on the weekend and freeze in individual zip-top bags for portable weekday breakfasts. They'll defrost in seconds in the microwave oven.

1½ cups QUAKER® Oats (Quick or Old Fashioned), uncooked	1 (8 ounce) carton plain non-fat yogurt or ¾ cup low-fat buttermilk
1 cup all-purpose flour	¾ cup mashed ripe banana (about 2 medium)
⅓ cup packed brown sugar	
1 teaspoon baking powder	2 egg whites or 1 egg, lightly beaten
½ teaspoon baking soda	
½ teaspoon ground cinnamon	2 tablespoons vegetable oil
¼ teaspoon salt (optional)	1½ teaspoons grated orange zest
⅓ cup chopped dates or raisins (optional)	

1. Preheat oven to 400°F. Line 12 medium-sized muffin cups with paper baking cups or lightly spray bottoms only with nonstick cooking spray.
2. In large bowl, combine oats, flour, brown sugar, baking powder, baking soda, cinnamon, and salt and dates, if desired; mix well. In medium bowl, combine yogurt, banana, egg whites, oil, and orange zest; blend well. Add to dry ingredients all at once; stir just until dry ingredients are moistened. (Do not overmix.) Fill prepared muffin cups almost full.
3. Bake in the preheated oven for 20 to 22 minutes or until golden brown. Cool muffins in pan on wire rack 5 minutes; remove from pan.
Yield: 12 servings.

Per serving: 161 calories, 5g protein, 29g carbohydrate, 3g fat, 2g fiber, 0mg cholesterol, 150mg sodium

Cinnamon Chip Muffins

5 star

submitted by: **HersheysKitchens.com**

Prep Time: 15 minutes
Cook Time: 18 minutes

What Other Cooks Have Done:
"Wow—these are great! I topped half of them with chopped walnuts before putting them in the oven. These are very light and fluffy and will be good with milk chocolate and peanut butter chips, too. I used the reduced-fat baking mix with great results."

Treat your family to these quick-and-easy cinnamon chip muffins made with baking mix.

2 cups all-purpose baking mix	1 cup HERSHEY'S® Cinnamon Chips
⅓ cup white sugar	
2 tablespoons vegetable oil	⅔ cup milk
1 egg, lightly beaten	

1. Preheat oven to 400°F. Line 12 (2½ inch) muffin cups with paper baking cups or lightly grease.
2. Stir together baking mix, sugar, vegetable oil, egg, cinnamon chips, and milk in medium bowl just until moistened. Divide batter evenly into prepared muffin cups.
3. Bake in the preheated oven for 15 to 18 minutes or just until browned. Cool slightly; remove from pan. **Yield:** 12 servings.

Per serving: 249 calories, 4g protein, 32g carbohydrate, 12g fat, 0g fiber, 20mg cholesterol, 310mg sodium

Raspberry White Chocolate Muffins

Serve these muffins at a weekend brunch or as a midmorning snack any day of the week.

1	cup milk	1	teaspoon salt
½	cup LAND O'LAKES® Butter, melted	1	cup fresh or frozen (do not thaw) raspberries
1	egg, lightly beaten	½	cup white baking chips★
2	cups all-purpose flour	¼	cup LAND O'LAKES® Butter, melted
⅓	cup white sugar	¼	cup white sugar
1	tablespoon baking powder		

holiday fare

submitted by: **Land O'Lakes, Inc.**

Prep Time: 15 minutes
Cook Time: 28 minutes

Test Kitchen Secret:
Store muffins, covered, at room temperature up to three days or freeze in airtight containers up to three months.

1. Preheat oven to 400°F. Grease a 12 cup muffin pan.
2. Combine milk, ½ cup butter, and egg in a large bowl. Stir in flour, ⅓ cup sugar, baking powder, and salt just until flour is moistened. Gently stir in raspberries and white baking chips. Spoon into prepared muffin pan.
3. Bake in the preheated oven for 24 to 28 minutes or until golden brown. Cool slightly; remove from pan.
4. Dip top of each muffin in ¼ cup melted butter, then in sugar. **Yield:** 12 servings.
★Substitute 3 ounces coarsely chopped white chocolate baking bar, if desired.

Per serving: 294 calories, 4g protein, 35g carbohydrate, 16g fat, 1g fiber, 51mg cholesterol, 408mg sodium

Raspberry White Chocolate Coffee Cake:

Preheat oven to 375°F. Spread batter into a greased 9 inch square pan. Drizzle with 2 tablespoons melted butter; sprinkle with 2 tablespoons white sugar. Bake in the preheated oven for 40 to 45 minutes or until light golden brown and wooden pick inserted in center comes out clean. Cool 10 minutes; cut into squares.

Blueberry White Chip Muffins

Breakfast or dessert? These blueberry muffins with white chocolate chips are the perfect treat anytime.

kid-friendly

submitted by: **Nestlé® Toll House®**

Prep Time: 20 minutes
Cook Time: 26 minutes

What Other Cooks Have Done:
"I did not use extra chips for drizzling on top—the streusel was the perfect topping for me. I have also substituted dried cranberries for blueberries, and they were equally good!"

2   cups all-purpose flour
½   cup white sugar
¼   cup packed brown sugar
2½   teaspoons baking powder
½   teaspoon salt
¾   cup milk
1   large egg, lightly beaten
¼   cup butter or margarine, melted
½   teaspoon grated lemon zest
1   (12 ounce) package NESTLÉ® TOLL HOUSE® Premier White Morsels, divided

1½   cups fresh or frozen blueberries

Streusel Topping

⅓   cup white sugar
¼   cup all-purpose flour
¼   teaspoon ground cinnamon
3   tablespoons butter or margarine

1. Preheat oven to 375°F. Line 18 muffin cups with paper baking cups.
2. Combine flour, white sugar, brown sugar, baking powder, and salt in large bowl. Stir in milk, egg, butter, and lemon zest. Stir in 1½ cups white morsels and blueberries. Spoon into prepared muffin cups, filling almost full.
3. For topping, combine ⅓ cup white sugar, ¼ cup all-purpose flour, and ¼ teaspoon ground cinnamon in small bowl. Cut in 3 tablespoons butter or margarine with pastry blender or 2 knives until mixture resembles coarse crumbs. Sprinkle over muffin batter.
4. Bake in the preheated oven for 22 to 25 minutes or until wooden pick inserted in center comes out clean. Cool in pans for 5 minutes; remove to wire racks to cool slightly.
5. If desired, place remaining morsels in small, heavy-duty plastic bag. Microwave on MEDIUM-HIGH (70%) power for 30 seconds; knead. Microwave at 10 to 20 second intervals, kneading until smooth. Cut tiny corner from bag; squeeze to drizzle over muffins. Serve warm. **Yield:** 18 servings.

Per serving: 267 calories, 4g protein, 39g carbohydrate, 11g fat, 1g fiber, 25mg cholesterol, 215mg sodium

Blueberry White Chip Muffins

submitted by:
Kretschmer® Wheat Germ

Prep Time: 15 minutes
Cook Time: 26 minutes

Test Kitchen Secret:

Substitute Kretschmer® Wheat Germ for up to ½ cup of flour in any recipe for cookies, muffins, coffee cakes, biscuits, or quick breads.

Raspberry Sour Cream Muffins

These melt-in-your-mouth muffins have a crunchy streusel and lemony glaze—they're perfect for any occasion.

Topping

2   tablespoons chopped pecans
2   tablespoons white sugar
1   tablespoon KRETSCHMER® Wheat Germ, any flavor

Muffins

1¼ cups all-purpose flour
½   cup KRETSCHMER® Wheat Germ, any flavor
½   cup white sugar
2   teaspoons baking powder
1   teaspoon ground cinnamon
¼   teaspoon salt (optional)
1   cup light sour cream
½   cup fat-free milk
1   egg or 2 egg whites, lightly beaten
1   cup fresh raspberries, rinsed and patted dry

Glaze

½   cup confectioners' sugar
1   tablespoon fresh lemon juice

1. Preheat oven to 375°F. Line 12 medium-sized muffin cups with paper baking cups.

2. For topping, combine pecans, 2 tablespoons sugar, and 1 tablespoon wheat germ in a small bowl; set aside.

3. For muffins, combine flour, ½ cup wheat germ, ½ cup sugar, baking powder, cinnamon, and salt, if desired, in large bowl; mix well. In medium bowl, combine sour cream, milk, and egg; blend well. Add all at once to dry ingredients; mix just until dry ingredients are moistened. (Do not overmix.) Gently fold in raspberries. Fill muffin cups almost full. Sprinkle with topping, patting gently.

4. Bake in the preheated oven 23 to 26 minutes or until wooden pick inserted in center of muffin without touching a berry comes out clean. Cool muffins in pan on wire rack 5 minutes; remove from pan.

5. For glaze, combine confectioners' sugar and lemon juice in small bowl; mix until smooth. Drizzle over muffins. Serve warm. **Yield:** 12 servings.

Per serving: 170 calories, 5g protein, 33g carbohydrate, 2g fat, 2g fiber, 18mg cholesterol, 122mg sodium

Apple Cranberry Wheat Muffins

The whole family will enjoy these delicious apple cranberry muffins for breakfast or Sunday brunch!

1¼	cups all-purpose flour	⅓	cup Apple Flavor LIBBY'S® JUICY JUICE® 100% Juice
½	cup whole wheat flour	¼	cup vegetable oil
½	cup white sugar	1	large egg
¼	cup toasted wheat germ	1¼	cups baking apple, finely chopped
2	teaspoons baking powder		
1	teaspoon ground cinnamon	¾	cup dried, sweetened cranberries
⅔	cup NESTLÉ® CARNATION® Evaporated Fat-Free Milk	1	tablespoon cinnamon sugar

1. Preheat oven to 400°F. Line 12 muffin cups with paper baking cups or lightly grease.
2. Combine all-purpose flour, whole wheat flour, white sugar, wheat germ, baking powder, and cinnamon in medium bowl.
3. Beat evaporated milk, apple juice, vegetable oil, and egg in small bowl until blended. Add to flour mixture; stir just until moistened. Fold in apple and cranberries. Spoon batter into prepared muffin cups, filling ¾ full. Sprinkle with cinnamon sugar.
4. Bake in the preheated oven for 14 to 16 minutes or until wooden pick inserted in center comes out clean. Cool in pan on wire rack for 2 minutes. Remove to wire rack to cool slightly. Serve warm. **Yield:** 12 servings.

Per serving: 203 calories, 4g protein, 35g carbohydrate, 6g fat, 2g fiber, 18mg cholesterol, 64mg sodium

holiday fare

submitted by: **Libby's® Juicy Juice®**

Prep Time: 10 minutes
Cook Time: 16 minutes

Test Kitchen Secret:
For this recipe, use good baking apple varieties such as Rome, York, or Baldwin. If you want to add a tart flavor, use Granny Smith to perk things up.

Red Hot Biscuits

These cheese biscuits are quick and easy to make. Crushed red pepper gives them a zesty bite.

quick & easy

submitted by: **McCormick® & Company**

Prep Time: 10 minutes
Cook Time: 12 minutes

Test Kitchen Secret:
Serve these spicy little biscuits with a bowl of warm soup or chili or alongside a salad for lunch. Substitute whatever shredded cheese you have on hand and adjust the seasonings to your taste. If you like things a little more "red hot," then bump up the crushed red pepper.

2¾ cups all-purpose baking mix
 ½ teaspoon McCORMICK®
       Crushed Red Pepper
 ¾ teaspoon McCORMICK®
       Garlic Powder, divided

1 cup milk
1 cup shredded Cheddar cheese
2 tablespoons butter, melted

1. Preheat oven to 425°F. Combine baking mix, crushed red pepper, and ½ teaspoon garlic powder. With a fork, stir in milk and cheese until mixture forms a soft dough. Drop dough by ¼ cupfuls onto greased baking sheet.
2. Combine butter and remaining garlic powder; brush on top of dough. Bake in the preheated oven for 10 to 12 minutes or until golden brown.
Yield: 12 servings.

Per serving: 186 calories, 6g protein, 18g carbohydrate, 10g fat, 1g fiber, 19mg cholesterol, 447mg sodium

Red Hot Biscuits

Cinnamon Bun Scones

A cinnamon-pecan swirl and creamy glaze impart the flavors of a bake-shop cinnamon bun to these easy-to-make oat scones.

2	cups all-purpose flour	¾	cup whole or 2% milk
1	cup QUAKER® Oats (Quick or Old Fashioned), uncooked	1	egg, lightly beaten
¼	cup plus 2 tablespoons white sugar	1	teaspoon vanilla extract
		½	cup toasted chopped pecans
1	tablespoon baking powder	2	teaspoons ground cinnamon
¼	teaspoon salt	¾	cup confectioners' sugar
½	cup butter or margarine, chilled and cut into pieces	3	to 4 teaspoons orange juice or milk

1. Preheat oven to 425°F. Spray baking sheet with nonstick cooking spray.
2. In large bowl, combine flour, oats, ¼ cup white sugar, baking powder, and salt; mix well. Cut in butter with pastry blender or 2 knives until mixture resembles coarse crumbs. In small bowl, combine milk, egg, and vanilla; blend well. Add to dry ingredients all at once; stir with fork or rubber spatula until dry ingredients are moistened. In small bowl, combine remaining 2 tablespoons white sugar with the pecans and cinnamon; mix well. Sprinkle evenly over dough in bowl; gently stir batter to swirl in cinnamon mixture (do not blend completely). Drop dough by ¼ cupfuls 2 inches apart on baking sheet.
3. Bake in the preheated oven for 11 to 13 minutes or until golden brown. Remove to wire rack; cool 5 minutes.
4. In small bowl, combine confectioners' sugar and enough orange juice for desired consistency; mix until smooth. Drizzle over warm scones. Serve warm. **Yield:** 12 servings.

Per serving: 293 calories, 5g protein, 41g carbohydrate, 13g fat, 2g fiber, 41mg cholesterol, 198mg sodium

holiday fare

submitted by:
The Quaker® Oats Company

Prep Time: 15 minutes
Cook Time: 13 minutes

What Other Cooks Have Done:
"I just love scones and oatmeal adds a nice flavor to these. A pot of hot tea or coffee along with them sounds just right."

Special Dark® Chocolate Chip Scones

Special Dark® Chocolate Chip Scones

"Knead" a little morning pick-me-up? Bake away those gray mornings with homemade dark chocolate chip-studded scones!

3¼ cups all-purpose flour
½ cup white sugar
1 tablespoon plus 1 teaspoon baking powder
¼ teaspoon salt
2 cups HERSHEY'S® SPECIAL DARK® Chocolate Chips
½ cup chopped nuts (optional)
2 cups chilled whipping cream
2 tablespoons butter, melted
Additional white sugar
Confectioners' sugar (optional)

1. Preheat oven to 375°F. Lightly grease 2 baking sheets.

2. Stir together flour, ½ cup sugar, baking powder, and salt in large bowl. Stir in chocolate chips and nuts, if desired.

3. Stir whipping cream into flour mixture, stirring just until ingredients are moistened.

4. Turn mixture out onto lightly floured surface. Knead gently until soft dough forms (about 2 minutes). Pat dough into 2 (6½ inch) circles. Cut each circle into 6 wedges. Transfer wedges to prepared baking sheets, spacing 2 inches apart. Brush with melted butter and sprinkle with additional white sugar.

5. Bake in the preheated oven 20 to 25 minutes or until lightly browned. Sprinkle with confectioners' sugar, if desired. Serve warm. **Yield:** 12 scones.

Per scone: 279 calories, 4g protein, 30g carbohydrate, 17g fat, 1g fiber, 30mg cholesterol, 123mg sodium

party pleaser

submitted by: HersheysKitchens.com

Prep Time: 15 minutes
Cook Time: 25 minutes

Test Kitchen Secret:
Make smaller scones by patting the dough into a 4½ x 16 inch rectangle. Divide rectangle into 12 smaller rectangles measuring 1½ x 4 inches. Cut each rectangle diagonally, forming a total of 24 triangles. Bake at 375°F for 15 to 20 minutes.

Prep Time: 10 minutes

Cook Time: 1 hour 10 minutes

What Other Cooks Have Done:

"This was a Thanksgiving favorite! I am going to make small loaves to give out for Christmas. I just tweaked the recipe a little by substituting 1½ cups whole wheat flour and 1½ cups all-purpose flour, and ¾ cup brown sugar and 2 cups white sugar. I used ½ cup apple sauce and ½ cup vegetable oil to reduce the fat, which made it so moist and flavorful. I also added ½ cup chopped walnuts and doubled the amount of cranberries. It was very easy to make, and the house smelled wonderful!"

make-ahead

submitted by: **McCormick® & Company**

Prep Time: 25 minutes

Cook Time: 1 hour

Cool Time: 2 hours

Test Kitchen Secret:

If using dried cranberries, boil 2 cups water in a small saucepan. Remove from heat and add 1 cup dried cranberries; cover and let stand 15 minutes. Drain but do not rinse. Substitute for fresh cranberries in Step 2. If using frozen cranberries, do not thaw. Toss with dry ingredients in Step 1.

Libby's® Pumpkin Cranberry Bread *(pictured on page 82)*

Try this festive recipe for a delicious holiday treat!

3 cups all-purpose flour	4 eggs
5 teaspoons pumpkin pie spice	1 cup vegetable oil
2 teaspoons baking soda	½ cup orange juice
1½ teaspoons salt	1 cup fresh or frozen cranberries
3 cups white sugar	
1 (15 ounce) can LIBBY'S® 100% Pure Pumpkin	

1. Preheat oven to 350°F. Grease and flour 2 (5x9 inch) loaf pans.
2. Combine flour, pumpkin pie spice, baking soda, and salt in large bowl. Combine sugar, pumpkin, eggs, vegetable oil, and orange juice in large mixer bowl; beat until just blended. Add pumpkin mixture to flour mixture; stir just until moistened. Fold in cranberries. Spoon batter into prepared loaf pans.
3. Bake in the preheated oven for 1 hour 10 minutes or until wooden pick inserted in center comes out clean. Cool in pans on wire racks for 10 minutes; remove to wire racks to cool completely. **Yield:** 24 servings.

Per serving: 258 calories, 3g protein, 40g carbohydrate, 10g fat, 1g fiber, 35mg cholesterol, 262mg sodium

Cranberry Orange Almond Bread

Enjoy the tartness of cranberries with a refreshing orange flavor in a tantalizing breakfast bread that makes a terrific gift, too.

2 cups all-purpose flour	1 teaspoon McCORMICK® Pure Vanilla Extract
1½ teaspoons baking powder	2 teaspoons freshly grated orange zest
½ teaspoon baking soda	
½ teaspoon salt	2 eggs
1 teaspoon McCORMICK® Ground Ginger	½ cup orange juice
¼ teaspoon McCORMICK® Ground Nutmeg	1 cup coarsely chopped fresh cranberries
⅓ cup butter, softened	½ cup slivered almonds
1 cup white sugar	

1. Preheat oven to 350°F. In large bowl, combine first 6 ingredients. Set aside.
2. In a bowl, cream butter with sugar and vanilla. Add orange zest, eggs, and orange juice until well combined. Gradually add orange mixture to dry ingredients. Mix until just moistened. Fold in cranberries and almonds. Pour batter into a well-greased 5x9 inch loaf pan.
3. Bake in the preheated oven 55 to 60 minutes, or, for mini loaves, use 3 (3x5½ inch) mini loaf pans and bake 35 minutes, or until wooden toothpick inserted in center comes out clean. Cool 10 minutes before removing from pan. Cool at least 2 hours before cutting. **Yield:** 16 servings.

Per serving: 183 calories, 4g protein, 27g carbohydrate, 7g fat, 1g fiber, 37mg cholesterol, 183mg sodium

Cranberry Orange Almond Bread

Boca® Sausage Apple Strudel

The delicious mingling of warm apple, cinnamon, and sausage makes this simple strudel perfect for breakfast or for lunch.

healthy

submitted by: **Boca®**

Prep Time: 15 minutes
Cook Time: 15 minutes

Test Kitchen Secret:
Remove breakfast links from freezer about 5 to 10 minutes before chopping, or thaw slightly in microwave before chopping. You can substitute three Boca® Meatless Breakfast Patties for the links.

1   (10 ounce) can refrigerated pizza crust
2   tablespoons plus 1 teaspoon cinnamon sugar, divided
1   tart apple, such as Granny Smith or McIntosh, thinly sliced
5   frozen BOCA® Meatless Breakfast Links, chopped

1. Preheat oven to 400°F. Spray 10x15 inch pan with nonstick cooking spray.
2. Place pizza crust in pan; pat out dough to completely cover bottom of pan. Sprinkle with 2 tablespoons of the cinnamon sugar.
3. Arrange apples in a lengthwise row down center of dough; top with chopped links. Fold over long sides of dough to cover filling, slightly overlapping edges of dough in center. Pinch ends of dough together to seal. Sprinkle top with remaining 1 teaspoon cinnamon sugar.
4. Bake in the preheated oven for 15 minutes or until golden brown.
Yield: 8 servings.

Per serving: 170 calories, 9g protein, 25g carbohydrate, 4g fat, 4g fiber, 0mg cholesterol, 400mg sodium

Italian Cream Cheese Pinwheels

An Italian herb blend delivers a special taste for Italian Cream Cheese Pinwheels. Perfect as a bread for dinner and as an appetizer, too.

party pleaser

submitted by: **McCormick® & Company**

Prep Time: 15 minutes
Cook Time: 15 minutes

Test Kitchen Secret:
Serve with your favorite Italian meal or as an appetizer. They are great served with warm marinara sauce on the side.

1   (3 ounce) package cream cheese, softened
1   tablespoon grated Parmesan cheese
2   teaspoons McCORMICK® Italian Seasoning
1   teaspoon McCORMICK® Onion Powder
¼   teaspoon McCORMICK® Garlic Powder
1   (8 ounce) can refrigerated crescent dinner rolls
    Grated Parmesan cheese (optional)

1. Preheat oven to 375°F. In a bowl, combine first 5 ingredients; mix until smooth.
2. Unroll crescent dough into a rectangle on a smooth surface. Gently press together perforations. Spread cream cheese mixture over dough to within ¼ inch of the edge.

3. Starting with the short end, roll into a log. Cut into 12 slices and place on ungreased baking sheet. Bake in the preheated oven for 12 to 15 minutes. Sprinkle with extra Parmesan cheese, if desired. **Yield:** 12 servings.

Per serving: 101 calories, 2g protein, 8g carbohydrate, 7g fat, 0g fiber, 8mg cholesterol, 176mg sodium

Reuben Cheese Roll

All the flavors of a classic Reuben sandwich come together in a fun spiraled presentation. Serve the rolls with soup or salad or as an appetizer.

1 (10 ounce) can refrigerated pizza dough	1 cup sauerkraut, rinsed and well drained
¼ cup Thousand Island dressing	¼ pound thinly sliced or shredded Swiss cheese
1 cup cooked COOK'S® Brand Corned Beef, chopped finely or shredded	

1. Preheat oven to 375°F. Unroll pizza dough onto a rimmed baking sheet. Flatten it and shape into a rectangle. Spread crust with Thousand Island dressing, leaving a ½ inch margin of dough uncovered. Top with corned beef, distributing it evenly. Spread sauerkraut evenly over the meat. Top with Swiss cheese. Roll up dough, jellyroll style, starting with the long side. Pinch seams to seal and place the seam side down. Pinch both ends of the roll to seal.
2. Bake in the preheated oven for 25 to 30 minutes or until the roll is golden brown. Cut into slices to serve. **Yield:** 4 servings.

Per serving: 410 calories, 19g protein, 39g carbohydrate, 20g fat, 2g fiber, 49mg cholesterol, 1280mg sodium

comfort food

submitted by: **Cook's® Brand Ham**

Prep Time: 15 minutes
Cook Time: 30 minutes

Test Kitchen Secret:
Serve these rolls as an appetizer with extra Thousand Island dressing for dipping.

Country Sausage Cornbread

Ham, Pineapple & Cheese Roll

Leftover ham from a holiday feast or a Sunday supper is transformed into a salty-sweet treat the whole family will love.

2 (10 ounce) cans refrigerated pizza dough	3 cups COOK'S® Brand Bone-In Ham (diced), leftover ham (shredded), or Ham Steak (diced)
1 (20 ounce) can crushed pineapple, drained, juice reserved	½ pound Havarti cheese, sliced thinly
1 cup packed brown sugar	

1. Preheat oven to 375°F. Unroll each can of pizza dough onto a rimmed, greased baking sheet. Flatten and shape into a rectangle.

2. Mix reserved pineapple juice and brown sugar together until mixed well. Brush pizza dough with thin coating of mixture. Spread ½ of ham evenly on each pizza dough; add ½ of pineapple and cheese evenly over ham. Then drizzle desired amount of juice mixture over all. Roll up dough, jellyroll style, starting with the long side. Pinch seams to seal and place the seam side down. Pinch both ends of the roll to seal.

3. Bake in the preheated oven for 25 to 30 minutes or until golden brown. Cut into slices to serve. **Yield:** 8 servings.

Per serving: 531 calories, 25g protein, 72g carbohydrate, 16g fat, 2g fiber, 58mg cholesterol, 1430mg sodium

kid-friendly

submitted by: **Cook's® Brand Ham**

Prep Time: 10 minutes
Cook Time: 30 minutes

Test Kitchen Secret:
Havarti cheese is a mild and buttery cheese that's slightly sweet and has a smooth texture. For this recipe, you can substitute another semi-soft cheese such as Gouda or provolone, if desired.

Country Sausage Cornbread

A wonderful twist on classic cornbread, this recipe makes a satisfying and easy addition to breakfast.

1 (8.5 ounce) box corn muffin mix	½ cup chopped celery
1 cup 2% milk	½ cup chopped onion
1 (8 ounce) package frozen BOCA® Meatless Breakfast Links, chopped	¼ cup egg substitute or 1 egg, lightly beaten

1. Preheat oven to 425°F.

2. Mix all ingredients until blended. Pour into a 9 inch pie plate sprayed with nonstick cooking spray.

3. Bake in the preheated oven for 25 minutes or until golden brown. **Yield:** 8 servings.

Per serving: 210 calories, 10g protein, 28g carbohydrate, 7g fat, 5g fiber, 5mg cholesterol, 440mg sodium

comfort food

submitted by: **Boca®**

Prep Time: 10 minutes
Cook Time: 25 minutes

Test Kitchen Secret:
Remove links from freezer 5 to 10 minutes before chopping, or thaw slightly in microwave before chopping. Serve cornbread with seasonal fresh fruit.

Breakfast Sausage Casserole, page 105

breakfast anytime

Nothing spells **comfort** more than a home-cooked breakfast. Whether it's a fruit smoothie as you run out the door in the morning, a stack of **warm pancakes** for a special occasion, or a **cozy** breakfast-for-dinner casserole, you'll find just the right recipe waiting for you.

submitted by: **Nestlé® Carnation®**

Prep Time: 15 minutes
Cook Time: 30 minutes

Test Kitchen Secret:
Quiche fits a variety of meal occasions from brunch to dinner and also makes an outstanding appetizer. You can prepare the quiche two to four hours in advance of baking, and chill it until you are ready to bake.

Carnation® Quiche Lorraine

This classic quiche makes a delicious brunch, lunch, or dinner served with a fresh fruit salad.

6 slices bacon	3 large eggs
½ cup chopped onion	¼ teaspoon salt
1½ cups shredded Swiss cheese	⅛ teaspoon ground black pepper
1 (9 inch) unbaked (4 cup volume) deep-dish pie crust	⅛ teaspoon ground nutmeg
1 (12 ounce) can NESTLÉ® CARNATION® Evaporated Milk	

1. Preheat oven to 350°F.
2. Cook bacon in large skillet over medium heat. When bacon starts to turn brown, add onion. Cook until bacon is crisp; drain and crumble bacon. Sprinkle cheese into bottom of pie crust. Top with bacon and onion. Combine evaporated milk, eggs, salt, pepper, and nutmeg in small bowl until blended. Pour into pie crust.
3. Bake in the preheated oven for 25 to 30 minutes or until knife inserted halfway between center and edge comes out clean. Cool for 5 minutes on wire rack before serving. **Yield:** 8 servings.

Per serving: 398 calories, 14g protein, 17g carbohydrate, 30g fat, 0g fiber, 125mg cholesterol, 494mg sodium

submitted by: **Boca®**

Prep Time: 10 minutes
Cook Time: 45 minutes

Test Kitchen Secret:
Asparagus spears snap off naturally where they are tough. Simply bend the spear near the bottom end, and it will break off at the right point.

Crustless Quiche

Tasty asparagus and smoky sausage make this simple quiche easy and elegant.

2 cups cholesterol-free egg product★	½ cup low-fat cottage cheese
2 frozen BOCA® Meatless Smoked Sausages, cut into ½ inch thick slices	½ cup shredded Swiss cheese
	¼ cup finely chopped onion
6 fresh asparagus spears, trimmed, sliced into ½ inch pieces	1 tablespoon Dijon-style mustard

1. Preheat oven to 350°F.
2. Spray 9 inch pie plate with nonstick cooking spray.
3. Mix all ingredients until well blended; pour into prepared pie plate.
4. Bake in the preheated oven for 40 to 45 minutes or until center is puffy and golden brown. **Yield:** 6 servings.
★Substitute 8 lightly beaten eggs for the egg product.

Per serving: 160 calories, 19g protein, 5g carbohydrate, 7g fat, 1g fiber, 10mg cholesterol, 510mg sodium

Carnation® Quiche Lorraine

Secrets from the Boca® Kitchens

Boca® has been bringing its customers quality meatless burgers for years, but they have now expanded their product line to include crispy Chik'n® Nuggets and patties, savory sausages, and breakfast links and patties. All their products have a fraction of the fat content of real meat products and almost none of the cholesterol. Boca® products are soy-based and delicately flavored with herbs and spices to satisfy even the most serious meat-lover.

According to the FDA, 25 grams of soy protein a day as part of a diet low in saturated fat and cholesterol may reduce the risk of heart disease. Boca® products give you a head start on getting beneficial soy into your diet.

Boca® Breakfast Frittata

This open-faced Italian omelet is a hearty meal in itself with potatoes, sausage, and vegetables.

Prep Time: 10 minutes   Cook Time: 50 minutes

1½   cups egg substitute★
¾   cup fat-free milk
1   tablespoon vegetable oil
½   cup chopped onion
½   cup chopped green bell pepper
2   cups cubed, cooked red-skinned potatoes
1   (8 ounce) package frozen BOCA® Meatless Breakfast Patties or Links, chopped
1   tablespoon chopped fresh rosemary or 1 teaspoon dried rosemary, crushed
¼   teaspoon black pepper
¼   teaspoon salt
1   cup shredded reduced-fat mozzarella cheese

1. Preheat oven to 350°F.
2. Mix egg substitute and milk; set aside.
3. Heat oil in 10 inch oven-proof skillet over medium-high heat. Add onion and green pepper; cook 2 minutes, stirring occasionally. Add potatoes, chopped patties, and seasonings; stir. Cook 3 minutes, stirring occasionally. Remove from heat; sprinkle with cheese. Pour egg substitute mixture into skillet.
4. Bake in the preheated oven for 45 minutes or until center is set.

★You can substitute 6 large eggs or 10 large egg whites for the egg substitute, if desired.
Note: Recipe can be baked in 10 inch quiche dish or pie plate sprayed with nonstick cooking spray. Cook vegetables in large skillet as directed. Spoon into prepared quiche dish; sprinkle with cheese. Pour in egg substitute mixture. Bake as directed. **Yield:** 6 servings.

Per serving: 240 calories, 19g protein, 19g carbohydrate, 10g fat, 4g fiber, 10mg cholesterol, 560mg sodium

Breakfast Sausage Casserole *(pictured on page 100)*

Prepare this delicious egg, cheese, and sausage casserole the night before. Place it in the oven early on a weekend morning, and the whole family can wake up to this special treat!

4	cups cubed, day-old bread	1	teaspoon powdered mustard
2	cups shredded sharp Cheddar cheese	¼	teaspoon onion powder
2	(12 ounce) cans NESTLÉ® CARNATION® Evaporated Milk		Ground black pepper to taste
10	large eggs, lightly beaten	1	(12 ounce) package fresh breakfast sausage, cooked, drained, and crumbled

1. Grease a 9x13 inch baking dish. Place bread in prepared baking dish. Sprinkle with cheese. Combine evaporated milk, eggs, powdered mustard, onion powder, and pepper in medium bowl. Pour evenly over bread and cheese. Sprinkle with sausage. Cover; refrigerate overnight.
2. Preheat oven to 325°F.
3. Bake in the preheated oven for 55 to 60 minutes or until cheese is golden brown. Cover with foil if top browns too quickly. **Yield:** 8 servings.

Per serving: 551 calories, 32g protein, 19g carbohydrate, 38g fat, 0g fiber, 362mg cholesterol, 1027mg sodium

make-ahead

submitted by: **Nestlé® Carnation®**

Prep Time: 15 minutes
Chill Time: 8 hours
Cook Time: 1 hour

What Other Cooks Have Done:
"We love this recipe and make it often. It can be easily adjusted for variety. Use seasoned bread or croutons, hot sausage, or pepper jack cheese. I've also added sautéed mushrooms and green onions to the dish."

Boca® Breakfast Biscuits & Gravy

Start your day off warm and wonderful with this down-home, easy country breakfast.

4	frozen BOCA® Meatless Breakfast Patties	4	baked biscuits, split, or English muffins, toasted
1	(2.64 ounce) package country gravy mix		

1. Microwave patties as directed on package.
2. Meanwhile, prepare gravy mix in medium saucepan as directed on package. Crumble patties into gravy; mix well.
3. Place 2 biscuit halves on each plate; top evenly with gravy mixture. **Yield:** 4 servings.

Per serving: 198 calories, 11g protein, 30g carbohydrate, 5g fat, 2g fiber, 0mg cholesterol, 528mg sodium

comfort food

submitted by: **Boca®**

Prep Time: 5 minutes
Cook Time: 15 minutes

Test Kitchen Secret:
Substitute 1 (1.8 ounce) package white sauce mix for country gravy. Season generously with freshly ground black pepper.

Ham Steak Eggs Benedict

For your next brunch, serve your guests classic Eggs Benedict topped with a secret Hollandaise sauce. The secret here is how easy it is—three seconds in a blender, and you're ready to serve!

1 COOK'S® Brand Bone-In Ham Steak, cut into 6 pieces	6 eggs, poached Blender Hollandaise Sauce (prepackaged or homemade)
3 English muffins, split	

1. Heat ham steak in skillet according to package directions. Toast 6 English muffin halves. Cover each with a hot piece of ham. Top each with a poached egg. Serve hot, covered with Blender Hollandaise Sauce. **Yield:** 3 servings.

Blender Hollandaise Sauce

½ cup egg substitute	¼ teaspoon salt
2 tablespoons lemon juice Pinch cayenne pepper	½ cup butter

1. Have egg substitute, lemon juice, cayenne, and salt ready in blender. Heat butter to bubbling stage, but do not brown. Cover blender and process on high. After 3 seconds, while still processing, add butter in a steady stream. Serve at once or keep warm in a bowl over warm water. **Yield:** 1 cup.

Per serving (includes Eggs Benedict and Hollandaise Sauce): 721 calories, 46g protein, 30g carbohydrate, 46g fat, 2g fiber, 584mg cholesterol, 3130mg sodium

Simple Sausage Potato Pancakes

These potato pancakes will be ready in a flash when you use your blender.

2 large red-skinned potatoes, peeled and quartered	½ teaspoon salt
½ small onion	2 frozen BOCA® Meatless Breakfast Patties, quartered
¼ cup egg substitute or 1 egg	2 teaspoons vegetable oil, divided
1 tablespoon all-purpose flour	

1. Place potatoes, onion, egg substitute, flour, and salt into blender container; cover. Blend until smooth. Add breakfast patties; cover. Blend 5 to 10 more seconds.
2. Heat 1 teaspoon oil in a large nonstick skillet over medium heat. Add potato mixture to hot skillet to form 8 pancakes, using ¼ cup of the potato mixture for each pancake.
3. Cook 3 minutes on each side or until golden brown on both sides, adding remaining oil as necessary. **Yield:** 4 servings.

Per serving: 150 calories, 7g protein, 21g carbohydrate, 5g fat, 2g fiber, 0mg cholesterol, 460mg sodium

Ham Steak Eggs Benedict

Cornmeal Pancakes with Ham Steak Rounds

Pair savory ham steak with maple-drenched cornmeal pancakes for a salty-sweet brunch duo.

comfort food

submitted by: **Cook's® Brand Ham**

Prep Time: 10 minutes
Cook Time: 30 minutes

Test Kitchen Secret:
Save ham steak scraps to use in salads, omelets, or casseroles.

¾	cup yellow cornmeal (stone-ground preferred)	1⅓	cups buttermilk
¾	cup all-purpose flour	1½	tablespoons butter, melted
1½	teaspoons baking powder	1	COOK'S® Brand Bone-In Thick Cut Ham Steak (about 2 pounds)
¼	teaspoon salt		Pure maple syrup
2	large eggs		

1. Mix cornmeal, flour, baking powder, and salt in mixing bowl. In separate bowl, beat eggs, buttermilk, and butter together; add to cornmeal mixture. Whisk until batter is smoothly blended.

2. Heat flat griddle pan or cast iron skillet over medium heat. Spray surface with nonstick cooking spray. For each pancake, ladle 2 tablespoons batter into hot pan. Cook, in batches, until bubbles appear on surface, then flip cakes over to cook until golden on bottom, 2 to 3 minutes each side. Transfer pancakes to platter; keep warm in low oven while remaining pancakes are cooking.

3. Using 3 inch round cookie cutter, punch out 6 (3 inch) rounds from ham steak. Pan-fry ham steak rounds over medium heat 2 minutes each side until lightly browned.

4. Portion 3 pancakes with each ham steak round on plates. Serve with pure maple syrup. **Yield:** 6 servings.

Per serving: 445 calories, 32g protein, 56g carbohydrate, 11g fat, 2g fiber, 160mg cholesterol, 2307mg sodium

Wild Berry Pancakes

Pancakes bubbling with fresh berries make a delicious start to the morning, made extra special with a nutrition boost from wheat germ.

kid-friendly

submitted by: **Kretschmer® Wheat Germ**

Prep Time: 10 minutes
Cook Time: 20 minutes

Test Kitchen Secret:
Get the kids involved with this healthy breakfast. Pour batter into a bulb baster and let the kids get creative making shaped pancakes.

1	cup all-purpose flour	2	tablespoons vegetable oil
½	cup KRETSCHMER® Wheat Germ, any flavor	½	cup reduced-calorie pancake syrup
1	tablespoon white sugar	2	cups fresh blueberries, raspberries, or blackberries
1	tablespoon baking powder		Additional wheat germ (optional)
½	teaspoon salt (optional)		
1½	cups fat-free milk		
¼	cup egg substitute or 1 egg, lightly beaten		

1. Heat nonstick skillet or griddle over medium heat or electric griddle to 375°F. Skillet is ready when drops of water sizzle, then evaporate.

2. For pancakes, combine first 4 ingredients and salt, if desired, in a large bowl. In a medium bowl, combine milk, egg substitute, and oil. Mix milk mixture into dry ingredients just until moistened. Batter may have small lumps, which will disappear during cooking.

3. Pour about ¼ cup batter for each pancake onto skillet. Turn and cook other side when tops of pancakes bubble and edges appear cooked. Turn only once.

4. Combine syrup and fruit in small saucepan. Bring to a boil. Remove from heat; serve fruit mixture over pancakes. Sprinkle pancakes with more wheat germ, if desired. **Yield:** 4 servings.

Per serving: 342 calories, 13g protein, 51g carbohydrate, 10g fat, 4g fiber, 2mg cholesterol, 595mg sodium

Hearty Banana Oat Flapjacks

A healthy boost to a breakfast classic! Banana Oat Flapjacks feature oats in a basic pancake batter that is ladled onto a hot griddle and topped with sugar-coated bananas. The sugar caramelizes as the pancakes cook.

comfort food

submitted by:
The Quaker® Oats Company

Prep Time: 10 minutes
Cook Time: 15 minutes

2　large, ripe bananas, peeled and
　　sliced
1　tablespoon white sugar
1　cup all-purpose flour
½　cup QUAKER® Oats (Quick
　　or Old Fashioned), uncooked
1　tablespoon baking powder
¼　teaspoon ground cinnamon
¼　teaspoon salt (optional)

1　cup fat-free milk
1　egg, lightly beaten
2　tablespoons vegetable oil
　　Maple-flavored syrup, warmed
　　Additional banana slices
　　(optional)
　　Coarsely chopped walnuts or
　　pecans (optional)

Test Kitchen Secret:
Keep sliced bananas from turning brown by tossing them in a mixture of 1 tablespoon lemon juice and 1 cup water.

1. In medium bowl, combine banana slices and sugar; gently stir to coat slices with sugar. Set aside.

2. In large bowl, combine flour, oats, baking powder, cinnamon, and salt, if desired; mix well. In medium bowl, combine milk, egg, and oil; blend well. Add to dry ingredients all at once; mix just until dry ingredients are moistened. (Do not overmix.)

3. Heat griddle over medium-high heat (or heat electric skillet or griddle to 375°F). Lightly grease griddle. For each pancake, pour scant ¼ cup batter onto hot griddle. Top with 4 or 5 banana slices. Turn pancakes when tops are covered with bubbles and edges look cooked. Serve with warm syrup and, if desired, additional banana slices and nuts. **Yield:** 6 servings.

Per serving: 220 calories, 6g protein, 36g carbohydrate, 6g fat, 2g fiber, 0mg cholesterol, 730mg sodium

Pumpkin Pancakes

Pumpkin Pancakes

holiday fare

submitted by: **Libby's® Pure Pumpkin**

Prep Time: 15 minutes
Cook Time: 20 minutes

What Other Cooks Have Done:

"I've turned breakfast into dessert with this recipe by topping the pancakes with vanilla ice cream and then drizzling the pumpkin sauce on top."

Wake up to spicy Pumpkin Pancakes hot from the griddle! Serve with Pumpkin Maple Sauce and broiled grapefruit halves sprinkled with brown sugar and cinnamon for a winter treat.

2 cups all-purpose flour	1 large egg
2 tablespoons brown sugar	3 tablespoons vegetable oil,
1 tablespoon baking powder	divided
1¼ teaspoons pumpkin pie spice	Pumpkin Maple Sauce
1 teaspoon salt	Chopped pecans (optional)
1¾ cups milk	
½ cup LIBBY'S® 100% Pure Pumpkin	

1. Combine flour, brown sugar, baking powder, pumpkin pie spice, and salt in large bowl. Combine milk, pumpkin, egg, and 2 tablespoons oil in small bowl; mix well. Add to flour mixture. Stir just until moistened. Batter may be lumpy.

2. Heat griddle or skillet over medium heat; brush lightly with remaining vegetable oil. Pour ¼ cup batter onto hot griddle; cook until bubbles begin to burst. Turn and continue cooking 1 to 2 minutes. Repeat with remaining batter. Serve with Pumpkin Maple Sauce and chopped pecans, if desired. **Yield:** 8 servings.

Pumpkin Maple Sauce

1 cup maple syrup	¼ teaspoon ground cinnamon or
1¼ cups LIBBY'S® 100% Pure	pumpkin pie spice
Pumpkin	

1. Heat maple syrup, pumpkin, and ground cinnamon or pumpkin pie spice in a small saucepan until warm. **Yield:** 8 servings.

Per serving (includes Pancakes and Pumpkin Maple Sauce): 288 calories, 7g protein, 59g carbohydrate, 3g fat, 3g fiber, 31mg cholesterol, 419mg sodium

Pecan Pancakes with Spiced Syrup

This wonderful spice blend can be used to prepare a memorable Sunday morning treat or enjoyed as part of a festive gift basket.

½ cup chopped pecans	1 teaspoon McCORMICK®
1 teaspoon McCORMICK®	Pumpkin Pie Spice
Pure Vanilla Extract	2 cups pancake mix
1 teaspoon McCORMICK®	
Ground Cinnamon	

1. In a small bowl, combine pecans, vanilla, cinnamon, and pumpkin pie spice. Mix until pecans are coated with spices. Add dry pancake mix and stir to combine. Put into a decorative glass jar. Include preparation directions: *Combine mix with 1½ cups water. Lightly grease a nonstick skillet and preheat to medium. Pour ¼ cup pancake batter into skillet for each pancake. Cook until edges are dry. Turn and cook until golden. Best if used within 1 month.* **Yield:** 4 servings.

Spiced Syrup

1 cup pancake syrup	¼ teaspoon McCORMICK®
½ teaspoon McCORMICK®	Pumpkin Pie Spice
Pure Vanilla Extract	

1. Whisk together all ingredients until combined. Put into a decorative airtight container. Refrigerate. Include serving directions: *Syrup will keep in refrigerator 1 month. Warm before serving.* **Yield:** 4 servings.

Per serving (includes Pancakes and Spiced Syrup): 560 calories, 7g protein, 109g carbohydrate, 12g fat, 2g fiber, 0mg cholesterol, 1019mg sodium

make-ahead

submitted by: **McCormick® & Company**

Prep Time: 10 minutes
Cook Time: 15 minutes

What Other Cooks Have Done:
"I made these in jars as gifts for all my family and friends at Christmas, and they all loved them. Later, I gave a batch as a wedding gift, and the groom told a friend it was his favorite gift. Very tasty!"

Chocolate Brunch French Toast

What could be better than serving your friends and family this wonderful French toast topped with whipped cream, fresh raspberries, and grated chocolate?

kid-friendly

submitted by: **Nestlé®**

Prep Time: 30 minutes
Cook Time: 6 minutes

What Other Cooks Have Done:

"I love chocolate and cherries, so I substituted cherry pie filling for the raspberries. It was great! Fresh strawberries would also be good."

1	cup NESTLÉ® NESQUIK® Ready-to-Drink Chocolate Milk	8	slices white or French bread
2	large eggs		Confectioners' sugar
2	teaspoons LAND O'LAKES® Butter or Margarine		Sweetened whipped cream (optional)
			Grated chocolate (optional)
			Fresh raspberries (optional)

1. Whisk together NESQUIK® and eggs in medium bowl.

2. Melt butter in large, nonstick skillet over medium heat. Dip bread into NESQUIK® mixture to coat evenly. Cook bread in melted butter on each side for about 3 minutes or until cooked through. Dust with confectioners' sugar. Garnish with whipped cream, chocolate, and raspberries, if desired. **Yield:** 4 servings.

Per serving: 341 calories, 15g protein, 51g carbohydrate, 9g fat, 0g fiber, 119mg cholesterol, 603mg sodium

Cinnamon Chip Applesauce Coffee Cake

Moist, light, and wonderful, this coffee cake is full of warm apple cinnamony goodness!

5 star

submitted by: HersheysKitchens.com

Prep Time: 20 minutes
Cook Time: 35 minutes

What Other Cooks Have Done:

"If you like cinnamon, this is the cake for you! It's very easy to make, and it turned out moist and wonderful. I used homestyle applesauce with brown sugar and cinnamon, and it tasted great. I didn't bother with the glaze since I wanted something I could pack in my son's lunch. After tasting it, my husband declared, 'I'm so glad I married you!'"

1	cup butter, softened	½	teaspoon salt
1	cup white sugar	1⅔	cups HERSHEY'S® Cinnamon Chips
2	eggs	1	cup chopped pecans (optional)
½	teaspoon vanilla extract	¾	cup confectioners' sugar
¾	cup applesauce	1	to 2 tablespoons warm water
2½	cups all-purpose flour		
1	teaspoon baking soda		

1. Preheat oven to 350°F. Lightly grease 9x13 inch pan.

2. Beat butter and sugar in large bowl on medium speed of an electric mixer until well blended. Beat in eggs and vanilla. Mix in applesauce. Combine flour, baking soda, and salt; gradually add to butter mixture, beating until well blended. Stir in cinnamon chips and pecans, if desired. Spread into prepared pan.

3. Bake in the preheated oven for 30 to 35 minutes or until wooden pick inserted in center comes out clean. Cool completely in pan on wire rack.

4. Stir together ¾ cup confectioners' sugar and 1 to 2 tablespoons warm water. Drizzle over warm cake. **Yield:** 12 servings.

Per serving: 607 calories, 8g protein, 71g carbohydrate, 34g fat, 2g fiber, 78mg cholesterol, 450mg sodium

Cinnamon Chip Applesauce Coffee Cake

holiday fare

submitted by: **McCormick® & Company**

Prep Time: 15 minutes
Cook Time: 35 minutes

Test Kitchen Secret:
Use two knives or a pastry blender to cut in the butter for the streusel topping. Start with cold butter cut into cubes to make your job easier.

Lemon Cream Cheese Coffee Cake

Pumpkin pie spice gives the streusel topping an incredible flavor that really complements the delicate lemony essence of the cake.

½ cup butter, softened	1 teaspoon baking powder
1 (8 ounce) package cream cheese, softened	½ teaspoon baking soda
1¼ cups white sugar	¼ teaspoon salt
2 eggs	¼ cup milk
¼ teaspoon McCORMICK® Ground Mace or Nutmeg	½ cup white sugar
2 teaspoons McCORMICK® Pure Lemon Extract	¼ cup all-purpose flour
1¾ cups all-purpose flour	2 teaspoons McCORMICK® Pumpkin Pie Spice
	¼ cup butter

1. Preheat oven to 350°F. Cream together ½ cup butter and cream cheese. Gradually add 1¼ cups sugar, beating until light and fluffy. Add eggs, one at a time, mixing well. Stir in mace and lemon extract.
2. Sift flour with baking powder, baking soda, and salt. Add alternately with milk to butter mixture. Pour into a greased and floured 9x13 inch pan.
3. Combine remaining ingredients until crumbly. Sprinkle over batter. Bake in the preheated oven for 35 minutes or until done. Cool. Cut into 2x3 inch pieces. **Yield:** 18 servings.

Per serving: 248 calories, 3g protein, 31g carbohydrate, 13g fat, 0g fiber, 58mg cholesterol, 205mg sodium

quick & easy

submitted by:
The Quaker® Oats Company

Prep Time: 5 minutes
Cook Time: 10 minutes

Test Kitchen Secret:
If desired, substitute raisins, dried peaches, pears, cranberries, blueberries, apples, dates, or diced mixed dried fruit for apricots.

Apricot Honey Oatmeal

Steaming bowls of whole grain QUAKER® Oatmeal have been warming tummies and toes for more than 125 years. Tangy dried apricots, honey, and a sprinkle of cinnamon flavor the oats as they cook.

3½ cups water	¼ teaspoon salt (optional)
½ cup chopped dried apricots	2 cups QUAKER® Oats (Quick or Old Fashioned), uncooked
⅓ cup honey	
½ teaspoon ground cinnamon	

1. In a saucepan, bring water, apricots, honey, cinnamon, and salt, if desired, to a boil.
2. Stir in oats; return to a boil. Reduce heat to medium; cook about 1 minute for quick oats (or 5 minutes for old fashioned oats) or until most of liquid is absorbed, stirring occasionally.
3. Let stand until desired consistency. **Yield:** 4 servings.

Per serving: 190 calories, 4g protein, 41g carbohydrate, 4g fat, 3g fiber, 0mg cholesterol, 5mg sodium

Fruit & Honey Granola

Crunchy Fruit & Honey Granola tastes terrific served with milk or yogurt for breakfast or eaten out-of-hand as a high-energy, whole grain snack.

healthy

submitted by:
The Quaker® Oats Company

Prep Time: 10 minutes
Cook Time: 35 minutes

3½ cups QUAKER® Oats (Quick or Old Fashioned), uncooked
⅓ cup coarsely chopped pecans (optional)
½ cup honey
4 tablespoons butter or margarine, melted
1 teaspoon vanilla extract
½ teaspoon ground cinnamon
⅛ to ¼ teaspoon salt (optional)
1 (6 ounce) package diced dried mixed fruit (about 1⅓ cups)

Test Kitchen Secret:
Substitute dried cranberries, chopped dried apricots, or chopped dried peaches for dried mixed fruit.

1. Preheat oven to 350°F.

2. In large bowl, combine oats and pecans, if desired; mix well. Spread evenly in 10x15 inch jellyroll pan or on rimmed baking sheet. In small bowl, combine honey, butter, vanilla, cinnamon, and salt, if desired; mix well. Pour over oat mixture; mix well.

3. Bake in the preheated oven for 30 to 35 minutes or until golden brown, stirring every 10 minutes. Stir in dried fruit. Cool completely. Store, tightly covered, up to 1 week. **Yield:** 11 servings.

Per serving: 210 calories, 4g protein, 38g carbohydrate, 6g fat, 3g fiber, 0mg cholesterol, 50mg sodium

Fruit & Honey Granola

submitted by: **Chef Katy Keck on behalf of Bush's Best® Beans**

Prep Time: 45 minutes
Cook Time: 57 minutes

Test Kitchen Secret:
Make these bars and wrap them individually for a week's worth of energy-packed breakfasts on the go. Be sure to store them in the refrigerator.

Bush's Best® Spiced Energy Bars

These gingerbread-flavored bars taste great and will keep your energy up all day.

1	egg white	2	tablespoons molasses
¾	cup ground gingersnaps, about 13 cookies	1	tablespoon vanilla extract
1	tablespoon butter, melted	2	tablespoons dark brown sugar
1	(16 ounce) can BUSH'S BEST® Pinto Beans, rinsed and drained	1	tablespoon cornstarch
		1	teaspoon ground cinnamon
½	cup buttermilk	½	teaspoon ground ginger
2	eggs, lightly beaten	¼	teaspoon ground nutmeg
½	cup pumpkin puree	¼	teaspoon salt
		⅛	teaspoon ground cloves
		¾	cup low-fat granola

1. Preheat oven to 350°F. Cut an 8x12 inch piece of parchment paper and moisten one side with water. Press parchment paper, wet side down, into an 8x8 inch glass baking dish. Let longer sides of paper extend up sides of the baking dish to help with removal. Lightly spray the parchment paper and sides of the pan with nonstick cooking spray.

2. For crust, stir together egg white, gingersnap crumbs, and butter until combined. Press into pan, using back of a greased spoon. Bake for 10 to 12 minutes, or until firm. Remove pan from oven and cool.

3. For filling, puree BUSH'S BEST® Pinto Beans with buttermilk in a food processor until smooth. Transfer to mixing bowl and add eggs, pumpkin puree, molasses, and vanilla. Beat with hand mixer on high for 1 minute. In a small bowl, combine brown sugar, cornstarch, cinnamon, ginger, nutmeg, salt, and cloves. Sift mixture into filling and beat for 1 minute on high speed. Pour filling onto the prepared crust and sprinkle granola on top.

4. Bake in the preheated oven for 40 to 45 minutes or until knife inserted in center of pan comes out clean. Cool completely and lift from pan using the ends of the parchment paper. Cut into 12 bars, wrap individually, and store (in an airtight container) in the refrigerator. **Yield:** 12 servings.

Per serving: 135 calories, 4g protein, 21g carbohydrate, 3g fat, 3g fiber, 38mg cholesterol, 233mg sodium

Breakfast Burritos

An easy grab-and-go breakfast burrito you'll make again and again.

1	cup egg substitute	2	green onions, sliced
¼	cup fat-free milk	½	cup shredded non-fat
3	frozen BOCA® Meatless		Cheddar cheese
	Breakfast Patties, coarsely	4	(8 inch) flour tortillas, warmed
	chopped		Salsa (optional)

1. Beat egg substitute and milk in medium bowl with wire whisk until well blended. Add patty pieces and onions; mix well. Heat a nonstick or lightly greased skillet over medium heat. Pour egg mixture into skillet and cook until set, stirring frequently. Sprinkle with cheese; cover. Cook until cheese is melted.

2. Spoon a scant ½ cup egg substitute mixture onto each tortilla; fold in ends and roll up burrito style. Serve with salsa, if desired. **Yield:** 4 servings.

Per serving: 250 calories, 21g protein, 22g carbohydrate, 8g fat, 3g fiber, 5mg cholesterol, 690mg sodium

quick & easy

submitted by: **Boca®**

Prep Time: 5 minutes
Cook Time: 15 minutes

Test Kitchen Secret:
Get a terrific start to any day with this Breakfast Burrito. The egg substitute is rich in vitamin A and the cheese provides a good source of calcium. Substitute 1 tablespoon chopped onion for the green onions, if desired.

Boca® Breakfast Browns

A potato-perfect side dish to round out even the simplest of breakfasts.

1	teaspoon olive oil	2	mushrooms, chopped
1	large red-skinned potato, peeled	1	tablespoon chopped onion
	and cut into ½ inch pieces	¼	teaspoon garlic salt
2	frozen BOCA® Meatless		Ketchup
	Breakfast Patties, cut into		
	½ inch pieces		

1. Heat oil in medium nonstick skillet over medium heat. Add potato; cover. Cook 8 to 10 minutes or until tender, stirring occasionally.

2. Add remaining ingredients except ketchup; mix lightly. Cook and stir 5 minutes or until potatoes are lightly browned and mixture is heated through. Serve with ketchup. **Yield:** 2 servings.

Per serving: 130 calories, 7g protein, 12g carbohydrate, 6g fat, 3g fiber, 0mg cholesterol, 510mg sodium

comfort food

submitted by: **Boca®**

Prep Time: 5 minutes
Cook Time: 15 minutes

Test Kitchen Secret:
For best results, use red-skinned potatoes. They hold their shape and brown better than Idaho or Russet potatoes.

Chipotle Steak with Pineapple-Avocado Salsa, page 123

entrées

Plan your next meal, whether it's a simple **weeknight supper** or a holiday gathering, with this diverse and **delectable** collection of entrées. You'll have everyone begging for more with **knockout** recipes for beef, chicken, fish, and even meatless main dishes. Everyone in your family will be cleaning their plates tonight!

submitted by: **Hormel Foods Corporation**

Prep Time: 15 minutes
Cook Time: 2 hours 30 minutes

Test Kitchen Secret:

If you find it a challenge to locate a bay leaf in stews or in dishes like this pot roast, insert a wooden pick through the leaf before adding it to the dish. The pick makes it easier to remove. Always remove bay leaves before serving because they can be a choking hazard if swallowed.

Harvest Pot Roast

A succulent pork roast ready for the oven in minutes! All you have to do is relax while it bakes. Add a loaf of fresh bread and you have a complete meal.

¼ cup all-purpose flour	2 stalks celery, cut diagonally into
1 (2½ to 3 pound) boneless pork	1 inch pieces
roast	1 cup vegetable juice
1 pound medium-sized	1 tablespoon HERB-OX®
red-skinned potatoes,	Beef Flavored Bouillon
quartered	Granules
1 large onion, cut into thin	1 clove garlic, minced
wedges	1 bay leaf
1 cup baby carrots, cut in half	

1. Preheat oven to 350°F. Add flour to a large (14x20 inch) oven cooking bag; twist end of bag and shake to coat with flour. Place oven bag into a 9x13 inch baking dish. Add pork and remaining ingredients. Gently squeeze bag to blend ingredients. Close bag and secure with twist tie. Cut six (½ inch) slits in the top of the bag.
2. Bake in the preheated oven for 2 to 2½ hours or until pork has reached an internal temperature of 160°F and the vegetables are tender. Remove bay leaf and serve. **Yield:** 6 servings.

Per serving: 381 calories, 30g protein, 24g carbohydrate, 17g fat, 3g fiber, 90mg cholesterol, 575mg sodium

---

5 star

submitted by: **McCormick® & Company**

Prep Time: 5 minutes
Chill Time: 30 minutes
Cook Time: 20 minutes

What Other Cooks Have Done:

"What I love about this recipe is, of course, the quickness, but it really dresses up an inexpensive cut of meat. I have used the recipe with a marinade time of 30 minutes as well as 24 hours. Thirty minutes is very good and imparts plenty of flavor."

Montreal Peppered Steak

Give steak restaurant-quality flavor in under an hour.

½ cup olive oil	2 pounds sirloin or strip steak
¼ cup soy sauce	
4 teaspoons McCORMICK®	
GRILL MATES® Montreal	
Steak Seasoning	

1. Combine olive oil, soy sauce, and Montreal Steak Seasoning in a large zip-top plastic bag or glass dish. Add steak and seal bag or cover. Refrigerate 30 minutes or longer for extra flavor.
2. Preheat grill or broiler for medium-high heat.
3. Remove steak from marinade; discard marinade. Grill or broil steak 8 to 10 minutes per side or to desired doneness. **Yield:** 8 servings.

Per serving: 271 calories, 20g protein, 1g carbohydrate, 20g fat, 0g fiber, 60mg cholesterol, 743mg sodium

Montreal Peppered Steak

Savory Montreal Steak Rub

A zesty burst of flavor from Grill Mates® Montreal Steak Seasoning combined with sweet brown sugar will give your taste buds a reason to smile.

1 tablespoon McCORMICK® GRILL MATES® Montreal Steak Seasoning	½ teaspoon McCORMICK® Oregano Leaves
1 tablespoon light brown sugar	1 pound sirloin or New York strip steak
1 teaspoon McCORMICK® Onion Powder	

1. Preheat grill or broiler for medium-high heat.
2. Blend first 4 ingredients. Rub over surface of steak.
3. Grill or broil steak 8 to 10 minutes per side or to desired doneness.
Yield: 4 servings.

Per serving: 174 calories, 22g protein, 5g carbohydrate, 6g fat, 0g fiber, 76mg cholesterol, 428mg sodium

Bush's Best® Hawaiian Soft Tacos

Fresh pineapple adds a refreshing taste to traditional steak tacos.

1 pound (¾ to 1 inch thick) boneless top sirloin	8 medium-sized soft flour tortillas
2 cans (16 ounces each) BUSH'S BEST® Chili Beans, slightly drained	1 cup diced fresh pineapple
	½ cup chopped green onions or cilantro

1. Preheat grill and grill steak to desired doneness. Cut into ½ inch thick slices. Keep warm.
2. Heat BUSH'S BEST® Chili Beans in medium saucepan until hot. Spoon about ⅓ cup of warmed beans in middle of each tortilla. Top with some of the sliced meat, pineapple, and green onions. **Yield:** 4 servings.

Per serving: 875 calories, 42g protein, 120g carbohydrate, 23g fat, 17g fiber, 60mg cholesterol, 1572mg sodium

Chipotle Steak with Pineapple-Avocado Salsa

(pictured on page 118)

Pineapple and avocado cut the heat of chipotle peppers just enough without depriving the steak of its bite. Serve any extra salsa with lime wedges and tortilla chips.

(pictured on page 118)

1   (20 ounce) can DOLE®
    Pineapple Chunks
2   canned chipotle peppers in
    adobo sauce, seeded and
    minced
2   cloves garlic, minced
2   tablespoons honey
4   teaspoons fresh lime juice,
    divided

1½   pounds beef skirt steak
1   ripe avocado, pitted, peeled,
     and cut into ¾ inch chunks
½   cup red bell pepper cut into
     ½ inch chunks
¼   cup thinly sliced green onions
2   tablespoons snipped fresh
     parsley

1. Drain pineapple, reserving 1 tablespoon juice. In small bowl, combine reserved pineapple juice, chipotle peppers, garlic, honey, and 2 teaspoons lime juice. Reserve 2 teaspoons mixture for salsa.

2. Heat ridged grill pan over medium-high heat until very hot. Place steak in pan; brush top with ½ of chipotle mixture and cook 2 minutes. Turn steak over and brush with remaining mixture. Cook 2 to 3 more minutes for medium-rare or until desired degree of doneness. Turn steak over again and cook 30 more seconds. Transfer steak to a cutting board; keep warm.

3. For Pineapple-Avocado Salsa: In medium bowl, mix pineapple chunks, avocado, red bell pepper, green onions, parsley, reserved 2 teaspoons chipotle mixture, and remaining 2 teaspoons lime juice.

4. Thinly slice steak, and serve with Pineapple-Avocado Salsa. **Yield:** 4 servings.

Per serving: 460 calories, 51g protein, 28g carbohydrate, 16g fat, 4g fiber, 117mg cholesterol, 122mg sodium

from the grill

submitted by: **Dole®**

Prep Time: 15 minutes
Cook Time: 10 minutes

Test Kitchen Secret:
Chipotle peppers are smoked jalapeño peppers and are available dried, canned, and pickled. They're typically canned in adobo sauce, a Mexican sauce made from ground sesame seeds, chilies, herbs, and vinegar. Find canned chipotle peppers with adobo sauce in the Mexican foods section of your grocery.

**Baja Beef Soft Tacos with Lindsay®
Olive-Chipotle Salsa**

Baja Beef Soft Tacos with Lindsay® Olive-Chipotle Salsa

Seasoned ground beef, Cheddar cheese, and crisp shredded lettuce are all piled into flour tortillas and topped off with Lindsay® Olive-Chipotle Salsa for one fantastic taco! Great for a quick-and-easy summer meal to serve to guests or, better yet, let them build their own.

party pleaser

submitted by: **Lindsay® Olives**

Prep Time: 20 minutes
Cook Time: 18 minutes

Test Kitchen Secret:
If you're making these tacos for a party or for a busy weeknight meal, make the salsa ahead of time and store it in an airtight container in the refrigerator.

2 tablespoons olive oil
1 medium-sized yellow onion, chopped
2 cloves garlic, minced
1 pound lean ground beef
1 (14.5 ounce) can diced tomatoes with jalapeños, undrained
1 (4 ounce) can diced green chilies, undrained
1 (1.25 ounce) package taco seasoning mix
1 (6 ounce) jar LINDSAY® Spanish Salad Olives with Pimiento, drained and halved

1 medium tomato, chopped
⅓ cup chopped red onion
2 tablespoons minced chipotle peppers in adobo sauce
1 tablespoon lime juice
1 tablespoon chopped fresh cilantro
8 (8 inch) flour tortillas
2 cups shredded iceberg lettuce
1 cup shredded Cheddar cheese

1. Heat oil in a medium skillet over medium heat. Add yellow onion; sauté for 3 minutes. Add garlic; sauté for 1 minute. Add beef; cook, stirring occasionally, until browned completely, about 6 minutes. Stir in canned tomatoes, chilies, and seasoning. Bring to a boil, reduce heat, and simmer for 5 minutes. Set aside; keep hot.

2. To make the salsa: In a medium bowl, combine the olives, tomato, red onion, chipotle in adobo sauce, lime juice, and cilantro; set aside. For each serving, down the center of each tortilla, layer lettuce, meat mixture, cheese, and salsa. Fold over and serve. **Yield:** 4 servings.

Per serving: 831 calories, 44g protein, 76g carbohydrate, 39g fat, 7g fiber, 110mg cholesterol, 2885mg sodium

Moroccan Stuffed Bell Peppers

Bell peppers are stuffed with a seasoned lamb and rice mixture, and topped off with two kinds of cheese. Beef may be used in place of the ground lamb.

comfort food

submitted by: **Hormel Foods Corporation**

Prep Time: 15 minutes
Cook Time: 1 hour

What Other Cooks Have Done:

"This is so good that the whole dinner was gone in one night—no leftovers. I added some garlic powder and seasoned salt to the mixture for extra flavor. I used mozzarella cheese instead of the Swiss and Cheddar. Even my children loved it!"

2	large green, red, or yellow bell peppers	½	cup water
3	teaspoons HERB-OX® Beef Flavored Bouillon Granules, divided	⅓	cup uncooked long grain rice
		1	tablespoon Worcestershire sauce
¾	pound ground lamb or ground beef	½	teaspoon dried basil leaves
		¼	cup shredded Swiss cheese
⅓	cup chopped onion	¼	cup shredded Cheddar cheese
1	(14½ ounce) can tomatoes, undrained and cut up	2	tablespoons sliced natural almonds

1. Preheat oven to 375°F. Halve bell peppers lengthwise, removing seeds and membranes. Immerse peppers in boiling water (seasoned with 1 teaspoon bouillon granules) for 3 minutes. Remove peppers from water and sprinkle the insides with an additional 1 teaspoon bouillon granules. Invert onto paper towels to drain.

2. Meanwhile, in large skillet, cook lamb or beef and onion until meat is golden brown and onion is tender. Drain off fat. Stir in undrained tomatoes, water, uncooked rice, remaining 1 teaspoon beef bouillon granules, Worcestershire sauce, and basil. Bring mixture to a boil. Reduce heat and simmer, covered, for 18 to 20 minutes or until rice is tender. Stir in ½ of each of the cheeses. Fill pepper halves with meat mixture. Place peppers in 2 quart baking dish along with any extra filling. Sprinkle with remaining cheese and almonds.

3. Bake in the preheated oven for 12 to 15 minutes or until heated through. **Yield:** 4 servings.

Per serving: 383 calories, 24g protein, 24g carbohydrate, 21g fat, 3g fiber, 80mg cholesterol, 1218mg sodium

Southwestern Grilled Chicken with Lime Butter

Chef Robert Del Grande, owner and executive chef of Houston's Café Annie, captures the flair and essence of the Southwest with a combination of cinnamon, chili powder, cocoa, and pepper. A spike of lime in the butter drizzle adds refreshing zest.

from the grill

submitted by: **McCormick® & Company**

Prep Time: 15 minutes
Cook Time: 30 minutes

1	tablespoon McCORMICK® Ground Cinnamon
1	tablespoon McCORMICK® Chili Powder
1	tablespoon brown sugar
1	teaspoon cocoa powder
½	teaspoon salt
¼	teaspoon McCORMICK® Ground Black Pepper
3	tablespoons olive oil
1	tablespoon balsamic vinegar
3½	pounds bone-in chicken parts

Lime Butter

½	cup butter, melted
1	tablespoon fresh lime juice
1	serrano chili, minced
2	tablespoons finely minced white onion
¼	cup finely chopped fresh cilantro
	Pinch McCORMICK® Ground Black Pepper
	Lime wedges (optional)
	Cilantro sprigs (optional)

What Other Cooks Have Done:
"The lime butter is spicy, but you can control that with the type of chili pepper you use. I tone it down a bit and use a jalepeño instead of the serrano. An Anaheim chili makes it mild enough for my most tender-mouthed child."

1. Preheat grill for medium heat.

2. In a small bowl, combine first 8 ingredients. With a spoon or a basting brush, spread seasoning paste over the chicken.

3. Grill chicken using medium heat for a gas grill or indirect heat for a charcoal grill. Close the lid and grill until chicken reaches 180°F in the thighs and 170°F in the breast, about 30 minutes.

4. In a small bowl, combine all lime butter ingredients except lime wedges and cilantro springs. Drizzle over chicken just before serving or serve separately for dipping. Garnish with lime wedges and cilantro, if desired.

Yield: 8 servings.

Per serving: 406 calories, 28g protein, 4g carbohydrate, 31g fat, 1g fiber, 118mg cholesterol, 347mg sodium

Southwestern Grilled Chicken with Lime Butter

Herb-Roasted Chicken Dinner

comfort food

submitted by: **Tyson**®

Prep Time: 10 minutes
Cook Time: 40 minutes

Test Kitchen Secret:

Serve with a spinach salad and hot crusty rolls for a complete meal.

For extra-flavorful results, use minced fresh herbs in place of the dried.

4	TYSON® Fresh Chicken Leg Quarters	¾	teaspoon thyme leaves or ½ teaspoon ground thyme
4	small yellow potatoes (about 1¼ pounds), cut into halves	½	teaspoon garlic pepper
1	tablespoon butter, melted	½	teaspoon oregano leaves or ¼ teaspoon ground oregano
2	teaspoons fresh or dried rosemary leaves, finely crushed		

1. Preheat oven to 425°F. Line broiler pan with foil. Spray broiler pan rack with nonstick cooking spray. Place chicken and potatoes on rack. Wash hands.

2. In small bowl, mix butter, rosemary, thyme, garlic pepper, and oregano. Rub or brush mixture evenly on chicken and potatoes. Wash hands.

3. Roast chicken and potatoes in the preheated oven for 35 to 40 minutes or until potatoes are tender and chicken is done (internal temperature of 180°F). **Yield:** 4 servings.

Per serving: 389 calories, 19g protein, 17g carbohydrate, 28g fat, 2g fiber, 123mg cholesterol, 168mg sodium

Santa Fe Grilled Chicken

make-ahead

submitted by: **Tyson**®

Prep Time: 15 minutes
Cook Time: 30 minutes

Test Kitchen Secret:

When grilling chicken, use tongs to turn the pieces rather than a fork to avoid losing the juices that keep the meat moist and flavorful.

Serve this zesty chicken with a fresh fruit salad, grilled vegetables, and warm bread for a complete and healthy meal.

4	TYSON® Fresh Chicken Leg Quarters	1	tablespoon olive oil
2	tablespoons taco seasoning mix	½	teaspoon ground cumin
		2	cloves garlic, minced

1. Place chicken on a large platter. Place remaining ingredients in a small bowl; stir until smooth. Rub spice mixture evenly over chicken. Wash hands. Let chicken stand 5 to 10 minutes or cover and refrigerate up to 8 hours.

2. Preheat grill for medium heat. Place chicken on grill; cover. Cook 25 to 30 minutes or until done (internal temperature of 180°F), turning occasionally. **Yield:** 4 servings.

Per serving: 338 calories, 17g protein, 4g carbohydrate, 28g fat, 0g fiber, 115mg cholesterol, 398mg sodium

Nuevo Cubano Chicken with Lindsay® Spanish Olive Picadillo Salsa

A simple stovetop meal prepared in under an hour is just what you need for dinner tonight. Jerk-seasoned chicken is pan-seared, then simmered with tomatoes, capers, Lindsay® Spanish Olives Stuffed with Pimiento, and plump raisins for a unique olive salsa.

2	tablespoons olive oil	¾	cup LINDSAY® Spanish Olives Stuffed with Pimiento, drained and halved
4	skinless, boneless chicken breasts	½	cup golden or dark raisins
1	tablespoon Jamaican or Caribbean jerk seasoning	1	tablespoon drained capers
1	medium onion, chopped	1	tablespoon Worcestershire sauce
1	red or green bell pepper, chopped		Minced plum tomato (optional)
2	cloves garlic, minced		Chopped fresh basil (optional)
1	(10 ounce) can diced tomatoes and green chilies, (mild or regular), undrained		

1. Heat oil in a large nonstick skillet over medium heat until hot. Add chicken; sprinkle ½ of the jerk seasoning over chicken. Cook 4 minutes. Turn; sprinkle remaining jerk seasoning over chicken. Cook 4 minutes. Transfer to a plate; set aside.

2. Add onion, bell pepper, and garlic to the skillet; cook 3 minutes, stirring occasionally. Add tomatoes, olives, raisins, capers, and Worcestershire sauce. Increase heat to medium–high and simmer 5 minutes. Return chicken to skillet, turning to coat. Continue cooking until chicken is fully cooked, about 5 minutes. Transfer chicken to serving plates; top with olive mixture and serve with minced plum tomato and chopped basil, if desired. **Yield:** 4 servings.

Per serving: 334 calories, 28g protein, 28g carbohydrate, 13g fat, 3g fiber, 72mg cholesterol, 1283mg sodium

party pleaser

submitted by: **Lindsay® Olives**

Prep Time: 20 minutes
Cook Time: 25 minutes

Test Kitchen Secret:
These days, salsas are made from more than just tomatoes, onions, and peppers. Get creative with your salsas and add any combination of your favorite ingredients for a fresh accompaniment to tacos, grilled meat or fish, or your favorite party-time dippers.

Chicken-Prosciutto Bundles

Prosciutto is a fresh ham cured by salting and drying rather than by smoking. If you want the very best, look for prosciutto di Parma, which is imported from Italy.

4	TYSON® Fresh Boneless, Skinless Chicken Breasts	¼	teaspoon salt
8	fresh basil leaves	¼	teaspoon black pepper
4	(¼ inch thick) slices mozzarella	8	slices prosciutto
		1	tablespoon olive oil

1. Preheat oven to 400°F. Place chicken on cutting board. Holding sharp knife horizontal to board, cut a 3 inch deep pocket lengthwise in the thick side of each breast.
2. Place 2 basil leaves on each slice of mozzarella, then sprinkle with salt and pepper. Stuff each breast pocket with a cheese bundle. Wrap 2 slices prosciutto around each breast, anchoring with toothpicks. Wash hands.
3. Heat oil in large ovenproof nonstick skillet over medium-high heat. Add chicken and cook about 3 minutes on each side or until browned. Transfer chicken in skillet to oven; bake in the preheated oven for 12 to 15 minutes or until done (internal temperature of 170°F). **Yield:** 4 servings.

Per serving: 404 calories, 45g protein, 2g carbohydrate, 23g fat, 0g fiber, 123mg cholesterol, 1039mg sodium

---

holiday fare

submitted by: **Tyson®**

Prep Time: 15 minutes
Cook Time: 20 minutes

What Other Cooks Have Done:
"I used boneless breasts and boneless thighs. I seasoned my chicken with 1 tablespoon chopped rosemary, rubbed it with a little olive oil, and served it with freshly grated Parmesan cheese sprinkled over the top."

Baked Dijon Chicken

Dijon-style mustard and Parmesan cheese flavor this oven-fried chicken.

¼	cup Dijon-style mustard	¼	cup plain, dry breadcrumbs
¼	cup NESTLÉ® CARNATION® Evaporated Fat-Free Milk	¼	cup grated Parmesan cheese
		4	(4 ounce) skinless, boneless chicken breast halves

1. Preheat oven to 475°F. Spray a 9x13 inch baking dish with nonstick cooking spray.
2. Combine mustard and evaporated milk in shallow bowl. Combine breadcrumbs and cheese in separate shallow bowl. Dip chicken into mustard mixture, coating both sides, then into breadcrumb mixture. Place in prepared dish.
3. Bake in the preheated oven for 15 to 20 minutes or until chicken is golden brown and no longer pink in center (internal temperature of 170°F). **Yield:** 4 servings.

Per serving: 206 calories, 32g protein, 9g carbohydrate, 4g fat, 1g fiber, 70mg cholesterol, 762mg sodium

---

healthy

submitted by: **Nestlé® Carnation®**

Prep Time: 10 minutes
Cook Time: 20 minutes

What Other Cooks Have Done:
"Simply the best Dijon chicken I've had. I pounded the breasts, used panko crumbs, and made a light white sauce that included Dijon and mayo to spoon over the breasts. My dinner guests all raved!"

Jammin' Jerk Chicken

Escape to the Islands with the combination of sweet and spicy flavors in this 20-minute recipe that joins Caribbean jerk seasoning with thyme and allspice.

1	tablespoon McCORMICK® Caribbean Jerk Seasoning	¼	teaspoon McCORMICK® Ground Allspice
1	teaspoon McCORMICK® Thyme Leaves	2½	teaspoons orange juice
1	teaspoon McCORMICK® Onion Powder	4	skinless, boneless chicken breasts

1. Preheat grill for medium heat.

2. In a small bowl, combine Caribbean jerk seasoning, thyme, onion powder, allspice, and orange juice to make a spice paste.

3. Rub spice paste on both sides of chicken.

4. Grill or broil 5 to 7 minutes per side or until chicken is done (internal temperature of 170°F). **Yield:** 4 servings.

Per serving: 140 calories, 27g protein, 2g carbohydrate, 2g fat, 1g fiber, 68mg cholesterol, 274 sodium

from the grill

submitted by: **McCormick® & Company**

Prep Time: 5 minutes
Cook Time: 14 minutes

Test Kitchen Secret:
Use McCormick® Gourmet Collection™ Jamaican Jerk Seasoning in place of the Caribbean Jerk Seasoning for a more savory flavor.

Lemony Skillet Chicken & Shallots

The subtle, delicate flavors of shallots and lemon enhance this French-inspired dish.

4	TYSON® Fresh Boneless, Skinless Chicken Thigh Cutlets	1	tablespoon butter or margarine
½	teaspoon lemon-pepper seasoning	2	small shallots, sliced and divided
		3	tablespoons fresh lemon juice

1. Sprinkle chicken evenly with seasoning. Wash hands.

2. Melt butter in a medium nonstick skillet over medium heat. Add chicken and ½ of the shallots. Cover; cook 5 minutes. Turn chicken over. Cover; cook 3 more minutes. Stir in remaining shallots and lemon juice. Cover; reduce heat to medium-low, and cook 3 to 5 minutes or until shallots are tender, juice is slightly thickened, and chicken is done (internal temperature of 180°F). **Yield:** 2 servings.

Per serving: 233 calories, 26g protein, 11g carbohydrate, 10g fat, 1g fiber, 81mg cholesterol, 220mg sodium

comfort food

submitted by: **Tyson®**

Prep Time: 5 minutes
Cook Time: 15 minutes

Test Kitchen Secret:
Drizzle juices from the pan over chicken and garnish with lemon wedges. Serve with steamed broccoli and carrots. Two Tyson® Fresh Boneless, Skinless Chicken Breasts may be substituted for the thigh cutlets. Cook breasts to an internal temperature of 170°F.

Chicken Wellington

Impress your guests with this elegant dish, an updated and much-easier-to-prepare version of traditional Beef Wellington.

holiday fare

submitted by: **Tyson**®

Prep Time: 20 minutes
Cook Time: 30 minutes

Test Kitchen Secret:
Serve with steamed asparagus spears. Tyson® *Fresh Boneless, Skinless Chicken Breasts or Thin & Fancy Chicken Breasts may be substituted for the frozen breasts.*

4	TYSON® Individually Fresh Frozen® Boneless, Skinless Chicken Breasts, thawed
	Salt and pepper to taste
½	cup water
½	teaspoon TYSON® Chicken Bouillon Granules
½	cup instant rice
½	cup chopped fresh spinach
¼	cup finely chopped red bell pepper
1	(8 ounce) container refrigerated crescent rolls

1. Preheat oven to 375°F. Flatten each chicken breast to about ¼ inch by pounding between 2 sheets of wax paper. Season with salt and pepper to taste.
2. Combine water and bouillon granules in medium saucepan. Bring to a boil; add rice. Remove from heat; let stand 5 minutes. Stir in spinach and bell pepper; mix well. Place ¼ of rice mixture on each chicken breast. Roll up, tucking in edges. Wash hands.
3. Divide crescent roll dough into 4 squares. Press each square to measure 6x6 inches. Place chicken in center; fold dough to enclose chicken and press edges to seal. Place on greased baking pan, seam side down. Wash hands.
4. Bake in the preheated oven for 25 to 30 minutes or until dough is golden brown and chicken is done (internal temperature of 170°F). **Yield:** 4 servings.

Per serving: 438 calories, 39g protein, 33g carbohydrate, 16g fat, 1g fiber, 85mg cholesterol, 739mg sodium

Asian Chicken Grill

It's the "oh-so-easy" marinade that gives this dish its oh-so-remarkable flavor.

make-ahead

submitted by: **Tyson**®

Prep Time: 10 minutes
Marinate Time: 30 minutes
Cook Time: 20 minutes

What Other Cooks Have Done:
"This delicious dish can be a little spicy, so if you're not a hot-and-spicy person, go lighter on the crushed red pepper. The vegetables complement each other very well. I doubled the sauce on mine, served it over rice, and it turned out great."

4	TYSON® Individually Fresh Frozen® Boneless, Skinless Chicken Breasts, thawed
¼	cup orange juice
¼	cup teriyaki sauce
½	teaspoon crushed red pepper flakes
2	red bell peppers, cut into wedges
2	small zucchini, sliced diagonally
4	ounces button or shiitake mushroom caps
1	(6 ounce) package rice pilaf

1. Place chicken in a large zip-top plastic bag. In a small bowl, combine orange juice, teriyaki sauce, and red pepper flakes in a small bowl. Reserve ¼ cup marinade.
2. Add bell peppers, zucchini, mushrooms, and remaining marinade to zip-top plastic bag. Wash hands. Marinate chicken in refrigerator at least 30 minutes.

3. Preheat grill for medium-high heat. Grill chicken 15 to 20 minutes or until done (internal temperature of 170°F). Grill bell peppers, zucchini, and mushrooms 5 minutes or until tender-crisp, turning once.

4. While chicken is cooking, prepare rice according to package directions. Stir in reserved marinade. Keep warm. **Yield:** 4 servings.

Per serving: 248 calories, 38g protein, 17g carbohydrate, 4g fat, 3g fiber, 85mg cholesterol, 1086mg sodium

Secrets from the Allrecipes® Kitchens

Chicken is a favorite and healthy eating choice. As well as being versatile and delicious, it is also high in protein with the added bonus of being low in fat and calories. Like all fresh meats, it is perishable and needs care in its handling and preparation. To help you prepare a delectable and safe meal, we recommend the following procedures for handling chicken.

• Never leave raw or frozen chicken at room temperature. Raw chicken should be stored in the coldest part of your refrigerator and used within 2 days. Freeze any chicken that won't be used in 2 days. Frozen chicken can be stored in the freezer for up to 1 year without sacrificing quality. When thawing frozen chicken, do so slowly, ideally in your refrigerator, but if you're in a hurry, a cold water bath will be fine. In the refrigerator, it will take about 24 hours to thaw a whole roaster chicken and about 2 to 9 hours for cut-up chicken parts.

• Always rinse chickens with cold water (inside and out), then pat dry with paper towels before preparing. To prevent cross-contamination, use warm soapy water to thoroughly clean all surfaces, utensils, plates, cutting boards, knives, and hands that have come in contact with raw chicken before they come in contact with any other raw or cooked foods.
• Always cook chicken well done. The best way to tell if a chicken is cooked properly is to use a meat thermometer. The internal temperature of a whole chicken should reach 180°F, chicken breasts should be cooked to a temperature of

170°F, and ground chicken should reach 165°F. Another check for doneness is to pierce or make a slit in the thickest part of the meat to see if the juices run clear. If they're clear and not pink, the chicken is done.
• Always let the chicken marinate in the refrigerator, even if you plan on letting it soak for only 30 minutes. Do not baste the cooking chicken with marinade you've already used on the raw chicken: Either make extra marinade and set aside a portion for basting only, or boil it for 2 to 3 minutes to kill any bacteria that might be present.

Easy Chicken Curry

The sweetness of apples and raisins balances the pungency of curry powder for a dish that's sure to "curry favor" with your family and friends.

quick & easy

submitted by: **Tyson**®

Prep Time: 5 minutes
Cook Time: 30 minutes

Test Kitchen Secret:

Sprinkle with your choice of chopped peanuts, shredded coconut, or chopped cilantro.

4	TYSON® Fresh Boneless, Skinless Chicken Breasts	1	Granny Smith apple, peeled, cored, and chopped
½	teaspoon salt	⅓	cup golden raisins
4	tablespoons butter or margarine, divided	1	cup TYSON® Chicken Broth
1	medium onion, chopped	4	cups cooked white rice
1	tablespoon curry powder		Chopped cilantro (optional)
			Chopped peanuts (optional)

1. Sprinkle chicken with salt. Wash hands. Melt 2 tablespoons butter in large nonstick skillet over medium-high heat. Brown chicken on both sides, about 3 minutes per side. Transfer to plate.
2. Add onion and remaining butter to skillet, reduce heat to medium, and cook onion 5 minutes or until soft. Stir in curry powder. Cook 1 minute.
3. Return chicken to skillet; add apple, raisins, and broth. Bring to boil; cover, reduce heat to medium-low, and cook 10 to 12 minutes or until chicken is done (internal temperature of 170°F). Serve over hot cooked rice. Sprinkle with cilantro and peanuts, if desired. **Yield:** 4 servings.

Per serving: 476 calories, 30g protein, 53g carbohydrate, 16g fat, 3g fiber, 99mg cholesterol, 722mg sodium

Garlic Lime Chicken

Although this recipe calls for the chicken to be sautéed in a skillet, it is equally delicious grilled.

party pleaser

submitted by: **Tyson**®

Prep Time: 10 minutes
Marinate Time: 30 minutes
Cook Time: 12 minutes

Test Kitchen Secret:

Serve chicken with pasta and a vegetable medley. To grill chicken, cook over medium-high heat 5 to 6 minutes per side or until done.

4	TYSON® Fresh Boneless, Skinless Chicken Breasts	2	cloves garlic, minced
½	cup low-sodium soy sauce	½	teaspoon powdered mustard
¼	cup fresh lime juice	½	teaspoon coarsely ground black pepper
1	tablespoon Worcestershire sauce		

1. Place chicken in zip-top plastic bag. Mix together soy sauce, lime juice, Worcestershire sauce, garlic, and mustard. Reserve ¼ cup marinade. Pour remainder over chicken in bag. Toss to coat well. Wash hands. Marinate in refrigerator 30 minutes or up to 4 hours. Drain chicken; discard leftover marinade. Sprinkle chicken with pepper.
2. Spray large nonstick skillet with butter-flavored cooking spray and heat over medium heat. Add chicken and cook about 6 minutes on each side or until done (internal temperature of 170°F). Drizzle with reserved marinade. **Yield:** 4 servings.

Per serving: 169 calories, 27g protein, 6g carbohydrate, 4g fat, 0g fiber, 65mg cholesterol, 1145mg sodium

Easy Chicken Curry

Caribbean Chicken over Coconut Rice

from the grill

submitted by: **Hormel Foods Corporation**

Prep Time: 10 minutes
Cook Time: 45 minutes

Test Kitchen Secret:
Look for canned coconut milk in the ethnic foods sections of your local grocery. Do not confuse it with coconut cream, which is much thicker and sweeter than coconut milk.

Chicken breasts are seasoned with a delicious spicy rub, then grilled and served over a citrus-scented coconut rice.

4	skinless, boneless chicken breast halves (about 1 pound)	1½	cups water
3	teaspoons HERB-OX® Chicken Flavored Bouillon Granules, divided	½	cup coconut milk
		1	cup uncooked white rice
½	teaspoon Jamaican jerk seasoning blend	1	teaspoon grated orange zest Orange zest (optional)

1. Preheat grill for medium heat.
2. Rinse chicken breasts; pat dry. In small bowl, combine 1 teaspoon bouillon granules and jerk seasoning. Rub both sides of chicken breasts with seasoning mixture.
3. Place chicken on rack of an uncovered grill. Grill directly over medium heat for 12 to 15 minutes or until chicken is no longer pink and is cooked through, turning once.
4. Meanwhile, in saucepan, combine water, coconut milk, remaining bouillon granules, and rice. Bring mixture to a boil. Reduce heat, cover, and simmer for 25 to 30 minutes or until liquid is absorbed and rice is tender. Stir in orange zest. Serve chicken over rice. Garnish with orange zest, if desired.
Yield: 4 servings.

Per serving: 363 calories, 28g protein, 40g carbohydrate, 9g fat, 1g fiber, 65mg cholesterol, 142mg sodium

Caribbean Chicken over Coconut Rice

Athenian-Style Chicken Kabobs

Classic Greek ingredients like yogurt, lemon, and oregano create a simple marinade that keeps grilled chicken moist and delicious.

1   (8 ounce) carton plain low-fat yogurt
2   tablespoons lemon juice
1   clove garlic, minced
1   teaspoon dried oregano leaves
12   ounces skinless, boneless chicken breast halves (about 3), cut into 1 inch pieces
1   medium-sized red bell pepper, chopped into 1 inch pieces
1   medium zucchini, sliced into ¼ inch pieces
1   large red onion, cut into wedges
1   (10 ounce) package NEAR EAST® Original Plain Couscous
½   cup crumbled feta cheese
2   tablespoons chopped fresh parsley (optional)

1. Preheat grill for medium-high heat. In small bowl, combine yogurt, lemon juice, garlic, and oregano. Thread chicken, red bell pepper, zucchini, and red onion alternately onto 4 skewers; baste once with yogurt mixture. Discard yogurt mixture.

2. Grill or broil kabobs 4 to 5 inches from heat 3 to 5 minutes. Turn kabobs and grill 3 to 5 more minutes or until chicken is no longer pink inside.

3. Meanwhile, prepare couscous according to package directions. Stir in feta and parsley, if desired. Serve kabobs over a bed of couscous. **Yield:** 4 servings.

Per serving: 476 calories, 34g protein, 65g carbohydrate, 8g fat, 4g fiber, 69mg cholesterol, 305mg sodium

party pleaser

submitted by: **Near East®**

Prep Time: 20 minutes
Cook Time: 10 minutes

Test Kitchen Secret:
Keep with the Greek-inspired theme of this dish with a sprinkling of chopped Kalamata olives.

Chicken & Shrimp Jambalaya

comfort food

submitted by: **Hormel Foods Corporation**

Prep Time: 30 minutes
Cook Time: 40 minutes

Test Kitchen Secret:

Substitute 12 ounces frozen, cooked shrimp for 1 pound fresh or frozen raw shrimp, if desired.

Don't keep it all to yourself—this recipe is made for sharing! Spicy jambalaya with chicken, pork sausage, and shrimp simmers with tomatoes, peppers, and an impressive combination of herbs and spices.

1 pound fully cooked smoked sausage links, cut into ¼ inch slices	1 tablespoon HERB-OX® Chicken Flavored Bouillon Granules or 3 Bouillon Cubes
2 cups chopped onion	1½ teaspoons paprika
2 cups sliced celery	½ teaspoon dried basil leaves
2 cups chopped green bell pepper	½ teaspoon coarsely ground black pepper
¼ cup chopped jalapeño pepper	½ teaspoon dried thyme leaves
1 tablespoon minced garlic	⅛ to ¼ teaspoon cayenne pepper
1 (28 ounce) can whole tomatoes	2 bay leaves
3 cups water	1 pound fresh or frozen raw shrimp, shelled and deveined
2 cups cubed, cooked chicken	Hot pepper sauce
2 cups cubed ham	
1 cup uncooked long grain white rice	

1. In Dutch oven over medium heat, sauté sausage, onion, celery, peppers, and garlic until tender. Add remaining ingredients except shrimp and hot pepper sauce. Bring to a boil. Cover; reduce heat and simmer 20 to 25 minutes or until rice is tender. Add shrimp. Cook 2 to 3 minutes or until shrimp turn pink. Remove bay leaves. Serve with hot pepper sauce. **Yield:** 12 servings.

Per serving: 370 calories, 30g protein, 21g carbohydrate, 18g fat, 2g fiber, 124mg cholesterol, 790mg sodium

Chicken & Rice Amandine

quick & easy

submitted by: **Land O'Lakes, Inc.**

Prep Time: 10 minutes
Cook Time: 25 minutes

Test Kitchen Secret:

Amandine refers to any dish that's garnished or topped with almonds. Toasting or sautéeing the almonds before serving brings out maximum flavor and adds a nice golden topping to any casserole.

Using rice pilaf mix makes this recipe quick and easy.

2 tablespoons LAND O'LAKES® Butter	1 (6 ounce) package rice with toasted pasta pilaf mix
¼ teaspoon garlic powder	1½ cups frozen French-cut green beans
¼ cup sliced almonds	½ cup LAND O'LAKES® Sour Cream
12 ounces boneless, skinless chicken breast strips	
1¾ cups water	

1. Melt butter and garlic powder in 10 inch skillet until sizzling; add almonds. Cook over medium heat, stirring occasionally, until almonds are lightly browned (2 to 3 minutes). Remove almonds with slotted spoon. Set aside.

2. Increase heat to medium-high; add chicken strips to same skillet. Cook, stirring occasionally, until lightly browned (5 to 7 minutes). Stir in water

Chicken & Shrimp Jambalaya

and rice with seasoning packet. Continue cooking until mixture comes to a boil (3 to 5 minutes).

3. Reduce heat to medium. Cover; cook 5 minutes. Uncover; stir in green beans. Cover; continue cooking 5 minutes or until rice is tender and liquid is absorbed. Uncover; stir in sour cream. Sprinkle with almonds just before serving. **Yield:** 4 servings.

Per serving: 279 calories, 23g protein, 12g carbohydrate, 16g fat, 2g fiber, 79mg cholesterol, 132mg sodium

Deep Dish Chicken Pot Pie

comfort food

submitted by: **Hormel Foods Corporation**

Prep Time: 20 minutes
Cook Time: 50 minutes

Test Kitchen Secret:

Experiment with the top crust to make a homey pot pie for your family or friends. Cut strips of pie dough and form a lattice crust or use small cookie cutters to cut shapes from the dough.

This chicken pot pie is a breeze to make using frozen mixed vegetables and a ready-made pie crust. It is also a great way to use leftover chicken.

1	(15 ounce) package refrigerated pie crusts
½	cup chopped onion
¼	cup butter or margarine
⅓	cup all-purpose flour
1	tablespoon HERB-OX® Chicken Flavored Bouillon Granules
¼	teaspoon dried thyme leaves
⅛	teaspoon ground black pepper
2	cups water
¾	cup milk
1	(10 ounce) package frozen mixed vegetables, thawed
2½	cups diced, cooked chicken
1	(2 ounce) jar diced pimiento
2	tablespoons chopped fresh parsley

1. Preheat oven to 400°F. Place 1 pie crust into a 10 inch deep pie plate. In large saucepan, sauté onion in butter until tender. Stir in flour, bouillon granules, thyme, and pepper. Add water and milk all at once. Cook and stir until thickened and bubbly. Stir in mixed vegetables, chicken, pimiento, and parsley. Pour mixture into pie plate. Place top crust over chicken mixture. Flute edges of crust and cut slits in the top to allow the steam to escape.

2. Bake in preheated oven for 25 to 30 minutes or until pie crust is golden brown and filling is hot. **Yield:** 8 servings.

Per serving: 437 calories, 18g protein, 33g carbohydrate, 26g fat, 4g fiber, 50mg cholesterol, 382mg sodium

Chicken & Vegetable Stir-Fry

Chicken breast strips are quickly stir-fried with vegetables and served over rice with a tasty sauce. This dinner is easily adapted to whatever vegetables you happen to have on hand.

3 cups water, divided	4 cups assorted cut-up vegetables
5 teaspoons HERB-OX® Chicken Flavored Bouillon Granules, divided	(such as red bell pepper, carrots, celery, and green onions)
2 cups uncooked instant long grain white rice	2 teaspoons cornstarch
	½ teaspoon garlic powder
2 tablespoons vegetable oil, divided	¼ teaspoon ground ginger
1 pound skinless, boneless chicken breasts, cut into strips	

1. In medium saucepan, bring 2 cups water and 3 teaspoons bouillon granules to a boil. Add rice to mixture and prepare as package directs.

2. Meanwhile, in large skillet or wok over high heat, heat 1 tablespoon oil. Add chicken and stir-fry until no longer pink; remove and set aside. Add remaining oil to skillet. Add vegetables and stir-fry 5 minutes or until tender-crisp. Return chicken to skillet or wok.

3. In a bowl, combine remaining 1 cup water, 2 teaspoons bouillon granules, cornstarch, garlic powder, and ginger; pour over chicken and vegetables. Bring sauce to a boil, reduce heat, and simmer 5 minutes or until thickened. Serve over rice. **Yield:** 4 servings.

Per serving: 407 calories, 31g protein, 45g carbohydrate, 11g fat, 3g fiber, 69mg cholesterol, 113mg sodium

healthy

submitted by: **Hormel Foods Corporation**

Prep Time: 10 minutes
Cook Time: 15 minutes

What Other Cooks Have Done:
"I added shrimp and marinated it with the chicken in ginger, soy sauce, and lemon juice before beginning the cooking process. It turned out really good! This was a healthy, delicious recipe for stir-fry!"

Chicken Paprika

Here's an easy version of a traditional Hungarian recipe. Feel free to increase the amount of paprika. You really can't have too much.

comfort food

submitted by: Tyson®

Prep Time: 5 minutes
Cook Time: 40 minutes

Test Kitchen Secret:

Serve the chicken and sauce with cooked egg noodles and steamed asparagus spears. To substitute Tyson® Fresh Chicken Thighs, simply decrease the cooking time by about one-third.

4 TYSON® Individually Fresh Frozen® Boneless, Skinless Chicken Breasts
2 tablespoons paprika
1 large onion, thinly sliced
¾ teaspoon salt
¼ teaspoon black pepper
2 tablespoons olive oil
½ cup chicken broth
1 (8 ounce) container sour cream
Cooked egg noodles

1. Rinse chicken with cold water and pat dry with paper towels. Wash hands. Spray a large nonstick skillet with nonstick cooking spray; heat over medium-high heat. Add chicken and cook about 10 minutes, turning frequently; drain and discard juices.
2. Add paprika, onion, salt, pepper, and olive oil to skillet with chicken; stir to mix well. Cook over medium heat about 3 minutes or until onion is tender, stirring frequently.
3. Stir in broth; cover and cook over medium-low heat 20 to 25 minutes or until chicken is done (internal temperature of 170°F).
4. Remove from heat and stir sour cream into sauce. Serve over noodles. **Yield:** 4 servings.

Per serving: 337 calories, 29g protein, 9g carbohydrate, 22g fat, 1g fiber, 89mg cholesterol, 811mg sodium

Herb-Roasted Turkey Breast

Herb-Roasted Turkey Breast is a wonderful meal for special occasions or for a Sunday dinner that lasts for weekday lunches and quick dinners.

healthy

submitted by: McCormick® & Company

Prep Time: 10 minutes
Cook Time: 2 hours 30 minutes
Stand Time: 15 minutes

What Other Cooks Have Done:

"I grilled the turkey breast rather than roasting it. A turkey breast is the perfect size to grill without the hassle of a whole turkey. I added 3 tablespoons of olive oil to the herb mixture to add moisture to the bird. I basted with turkey broth, butter, and more of the herb mixture about every 15 to 20 minutes."

1 (5½ pound) turkey breast, fresh or frozen, thawed
4 teaspoons McCORMICK® Italian Seasoning
2 teaspoons McCORMICK® Season-All® Seasoned Salt
¾ teaspoon McCORMICK® Ground Black Pepper
1 cup water

1. Preheat oven to 350°F. Place turkey breast on rack in shallow roasting pan. Combine next 3 ingredients. Spread seasoning mixture under skin and over entire surface of turkey breast. Loosely tent with foil.
2. Roast in the preheated oven 1 hour; remove foil and add water to pan. Roast 1 to 1½ more hours or until internal temperature reaches 170°F, basting occasionally with pan juices.
3. Remove turkey breast from oven. Let stand loosely covered with foil for 15 minutes. Transfer to platter or carving board. **Yield:** 8 servings.

Per serving: 394 calories, 74g protein, 1g carbohydrate, 8g fat, 0g fiber, 219mg cholesterol, 454mg sodium

Grilled Pork Rub

Grilled Pork Rub is an exciting combination of seasonings that produces a richly flavored summertime meal. The rub is great on a pork loin roast or baby back ribs, too.

3 tablespoons brown sugar	½ teaspoon McCORMICK® Oregano Leaves
2 teaspoons McCORMICK® Garlic Powder	½ teaspoon salt
2 teaspoons McCORMICK® Chili Powder	2 pounds pork tenderloin
½ teaspoon McCORMICK® Ground Black Pepper	

1. Combine first 6 ingredients. Coat pork evenly with the rub. Refrigerate 30 minutes or up to 3 hours for stronger flavor.

2. Lightly oil cold grill rack. Preheat grill for medium heat. Grill 25 to 30 minutes or until pork registers 160°F with a meat thermometer, turning occasionally.

3. Remove from grill and cover with aluminum foil. Let stand 5 minutes before cutting into thin slices. **Yield:** 6 servings.

Per serving: 212 calories, 27g protein, 8g carbohydrate, 7g fat, 0g fiber, 84mg cholesterol, 261mg sodium

party pleaser

submitted by: **McCormick® & Company**

Prep Time: 10 minutes
Marinate Time: 30 minutes
Cook Time: 30 minutes

What Other Cooks Have Done:
"I have used this rub on country ribs, pork loin, and baby back ribs. It is great! The best were the country ribs, steamed with a little water and half an onion in a foil packet, then finished off on the grill."

Pork Chops with Burgundy Mushroom Sauce

Mustard-coated pork chops are braised in an elegant wine sauce and served with sautéed mushrooms.

2 cups sliced fresh mushrooms	½ cup red wine
3 tablespoons Dijon-style mustard	½ cup water
4 (4 ounce) boneless, center cut pork chops	2 HERB-OX® Beef Flavored Bouillon Cubes

1. Sauté mushrooms in skillet coated with cooking spray until golden; set aside. Spread mustard on each side of pork chops. In a skillet over medium heat, brown chops on each side. Add wine, water, and bouillon cubes to skillet.

2. Cover and cook 15 to 20 minutes or until chops are tender. Remove chops to serving platter. Bring cooking liquid to a boil; boil for 5 minutes. Stir in mushrooms. Spoon sauce over chops. **Yield:** 4 servings.

Per serving: 158 calories, 16g protein, 4g carbohydrate, 7g fat, 1g fiber, 35mg cholesterol, 764mg sodium

5 star

submitted by: **Hormel Foods Corporation**

Prep Time: 10 minutes
Cook Time: 35 minutes

What Other Cooks Have Done:
"I can no longer say, 'My boyfriend does not cook.' He made this recipe while I wasn't home to 'supervise' and phoned me to describe how great it turned out. I had it for lunch the next day and, indeed, it was wonderful! As for simplicity, it only took him 35 minutes start-to-finish! He used pork sirloin chops instead of regular chops, and they were as tender and delicious as any I have ever had."

Peppered Pork & Pilaf

Peppered pork chops are baked in an oven cooking bag with rice, bell peppers, and onion for a hearty one-dish meal. A fast, delicious dinner, and hardly any cleanup!

healthy

submitted by: **Hormel Foods Corporation**

Prep Time: 10 minutes
Cook Time: 40 minutes

Test Kitchen Secret:
Change the flavor of this dish by choosing another variety of pre-marinated pork chops.

2 tablespoons all-purpose flour
1 pound peppercorn-flavored pork chops
2 medium-sized green, red, and/or yellow bell peppers, cut into thin strips
1 small red onion, cut into thin wedges
1 cup uncooked instant white rice
1 (1.2 ounce) envelope brown gravy mix
2 teaspoons HERB-OX® Beef Flavored Bouillon Granules
3 cups water

1. Preheat oven to 350°F. Add flour to a large (14x20 inch) oven cooking bag; twist end of bag and shake to coat with flour. Place oven bag into a 9x13 inch baking dish. Add pork chops, bell peppers, onion, rice, gravy mix, bouillon granules, and water. Gently squeeze bag to blend ingredients. Arrange ingredients in an even layer in bag. Cut 6 (½ inch) slits in the top of the bag.
2. Bake in the preheated oven 40 minutes or until the pork is cooked through. **Yield:** 4 servings.

Per serving: 253 calories, 19g protein, 31g carbohydrate, 5g fat, 2g fiber, 40mg cholesterol, 834mg sodium

Pork Chops with Dijon-Dill Sauce

These delicately seasoned pan-fried pork chops take hardly any time at all to cook. Your loved ones will think they are eating at a restaurant.

quick & easy

submitted by: **Hormel Foods Corporation**

Prep Time: 5 minutes
Cook Time: 8 minutes

Test Kitchen Secret:
Using yogurt as a base for sauce rather than cream or sour cream is a healthy alternative.

1 pound thin pork loin chops
1 teaspoon olive oil
2 teaspoons HERB-OX® Chicken Flavored Bouillon Granules
¼ teaspoon garlic salt
⅛ teaspoon black pepper
¼ cup plain yogurt
2 teaspoons Dijon-style mustard
¼ teaspoon dried dill weed
¼ teaspoon white sugar

1. In skillet over medium heat, sauté pork chops in oil 6 to 8 minutes, or until cooked through and pork reaches an internal temperature of 155°F. Remove pork to platter; season with bouillon granules, garlic salt, and black pepper.
2. In small bowl, combine yogurt, mustard, dill weed, and sugar. Serve sauce with pork chops. **Yield:** 4 servings.

Per serving: 133 calories, 15g protein, 2g carbohydrate, 7g fat, 0g fiber, 36mg cholesterol, 228mg sodium

Pan-Asian Pork

A honey-based sauce tempers the heat of curry powder used on the pork chops. Serve with a salad to round out the meal.

1	(20 ounce) can DOLE® Pineapple Chunks
¼	cup all-purpose flour
1	teaspoon curry powder
½	teaspoon salt
6	pork chops
3	tablespoons vegetable oil
½	cup honey
½	teaspoon ground allspice
½	teaspoon ground cinnamon
2	tablespoons chopped fresh cilantro

1. Drain pineapple chunks; reserve ½ cup juice.

2. Stir together flour, curry powder, and salt in small bowl. Rub onto pork chops. Heat oil in large nonstick skillet over medium-high heat. Brown chops on both sides. Add pineapple chunks.

3. Stir together reserved pineapple juice, honey, allspice, and cinnamon in a small bowl. Add to pork, cover, and cook over low heat 30 minutes or until cooked through.

4. Place chops on serving dish. Spoon sauce over top and sprinkle with cilantro. **Yield:** 6 servings.

Per serving: 419 calories, 25g protein, 39g carbohydrate, 18g fat, 1g fiber, 70mg cholesterol, 252mg sodium

quick & easy

submitted by: **Dole®**

Prep Time: 10 minutes
Cook Time: 35 minutes

Test Kitchen Secret:

Curry powder, cinnamon, allspice, and cilantro enhance simple ingredients and give them an exotic touch. If your kids don't like cilantro or any of the other spices, feel free to leave them out.

submitted by: **Land O'Lakes, Inc.**

Prep Time: 25 minutes
Cook Time: 1 hour 30 minutes

Test Kitchen Secret:

To prepare these chops in the microwave, melt butter in a 9x13 inch baking dish on HIGH (40 to 50 seconds). Stir in garlic; add pork chops. Stir together all remaining ingredients except water, cornstarch, green bell pepper, onion, and basil in medium bowl. Pour over pork chops. Cover; microwave on HIGH, rearranging pork chops after half the time, until pork chops are no longer pink (25 to 35 minutes). Remove pork chops; keep warm. Stir together water and cornstarch in small bowl. Stir cornstarch mixture into hot liquid with wire whisk; add green bell pepper and onion. Microwave on HIGH, stirring twice, until sauce is thickened and vegetables are tender-crisp (4 to 5 minutes). Serve sauce over pork chops. Sprinkle with sliced basil, if desired.

Basil Tomato Pork Chops

These moist, tender pork chops are cooked in a fresh vegetable sauce. Serve over hot cooked spaghetti, fettucine, or rice.

2 tablespoons LAND O'LAKES® Butter	1 teaspoon salt
1 teaspoon finely chopped fresh garlic	½ teaspoon black pepper
8 (½ inch thick) pork chops	½ cup water
1 (28 ounce) can whole tomatoes, undrained and cut up	3 tablespoons cornstarch
	1 medium-sized green bell pepper, cut into rings
1 teaspoon dried basil leaves	1 medium onion, cut into rings
	Hot cooked noodles (optional)
	Sliced fresh basil (optional)

1. Melt butter in a large skillet until sizzling; stir in garlic. Cook pork chops, in batches, over medium-high heat, turning occasionally, until browned on both sides (4 to 6 minutes).

2. Return all pork chops to pan. Stir in tomatoes, basil, salt, and black pepper. Cook over medium-high heat until mixture comes to a boil (3 to 4 minutes). Reduce heat to low. Cover; cook, stirring occasionally, until pork chops are no longer pink (50 to 60 minutes). Remove pork chops; keep warm.

3. Stir together water and cornstarch in small bowl. Stir cornstarch mixture into hot tomato mixture in pan with wire whisk. Add green bell pepper and onion.

4. Increase heat to medium-high. Cook, stirring occasionally, until mixture is thickened and vegetables are tender-crisp (5 to 6 minutes). Serve sauce over pork chops and noodles, if desired. Sprinkle with sliced basil, if desired. **Yield:** 8 servings.

Per serving: 182 calories, 15g protein, 10g carbohydrate, 9g fat, 2g fiber, 45mg cholesterol, 555mg sodium

Basil Tomato Pork Chops

Raisin Chutney Glazed Ham

holiday fare

submitted by: **Cook's® Brand Ham**

Prep Time: 10 minutes
Cook Time: 2 hours 30 minutes

Test Kitchen Secret:

Serve sliced ham on homemade rolls with extra mango chutney.

This exotically spiced glazed ham will take your taste buds on a trip to the Far East regions of the world. Mango chutney, raisins, and curry powder blend to make a sweet and spicy glaze for any Cook's® Brand Ham.

1	COOK'S® Brand Bone-In Spiral Sliced Ham, Butt or Shank Portion Ham, or Half Ham	¼	cup raisins, finely minced
		1½	teaspoons white balsamic vinegar or white wine vinegar
½	cup mango chutney, large pieces chopped, if necessary	½	teaspoon curry powder
		¼	teaspoon ground ginger

1. Prepare and heat ham according to directions on package.
2. Meanwhile, to prepare glaze, combine chutney, minced raisins, vinegar, curry powder, and ginger in bowl; mix thoroughly.
3. Brush glaze on ham 30 minutes before meat is done. Heat ham uncovered for final 30 minutes. Remove ham from oven and let rest 10 to 15 minutes. Carve ham and serve. **Yield:** 20 servings.

Per serving: 112 calories, 6g protein, 7g carbohydrate, 7g fat, 0g fiber, 20mg cholesterol, 567mg sodium

Spiral Sliced Ham with Spiced Sugar Rub

comfort food

submitted by: **Cook's® Brand Ham**

Prep Time: 15 minutes
Cook Time: 2 hours 30 minutes

Test Kitchen Secret:

When zesting limes or other citrus fruits, make sure to get only the outside peel of the fruit. The white pith is much too bitter to add to your recipe.

A sweet and savory rub made from brown sugar, lime zest, mustard, spices, and chopped pecans gives a new spin on spiral sliced ham.

1	COOK'S® Brand Bone-In Spiral Sliced Ham, Butt or Shank Portion Ham, or Half Ham	1	teaspoon grated lime zest
		½	teaspoon ground ginger
		¼	teaspoon ground allspice
1	cup packed dark brown sugar	⅛	teaspoon ground cloves
1½	teaspoons powdered mustard	22	to 25 pecan halves, chopped
		1	tablespoon fresh lime juice

1. Prepare and heat ham according to package directions.
2. Meanwhile, combine brown sugar, powdered mustard, lime zest, ginger, allspice, cloves, and chopped pecans in bowl. Mix thoroughly with fork. Stir in lime juice to moisten sugar mixture evenly. Set rub aside.
3. Remove ham from oven 30 minutes before meat is done. Pat and rub sugar mixture over ham, covering top end first, then smearing mixture down the sides as evenly as possible.
4. Heat, uncovered, 30 to 45 minutes. Remove ham from roasting pan; set onto cutting board face down. Let rest 10 to 15 minutes loosely covered with aluminum foil. Carve ham and serve. **Yield:** 20 servings.

Per serving: 145 calories, 6g protein, 12g carbohydrate, 8g fat, 0g fiber, 20mg cholesterol, 470mg sodium

Celebrate the Seasons with Cook's® Brand Ham

Family-Style Honey Glazed Ham

With only ten minutes of prep for this recipe, you will have time to spend on other things while the ham bakes in the oven. The glaze of honey, mustard, and cloves really accentuates the flavor of Cook's® Brand Ham.

Prep Time: 10 minutes   **Cook Time:** 2 hours 30 minutes

1   COOK'S® Brand Bone-In Spiral Sliced Ham, Butt or Shank Portion Ham, or Half Ham
1   cup honey, warmed
1   teaspoon powdered mustard
½   teaspoon ground cloves
    Green apple slices and fresh thyme (optional)

1. Prepare and heat ham according to package directions.
2. Meanwhile, combine honey, powdered mustard, and cloves; blend thoroughly.
3. Brush glaze on ham 30 minutes before meat is done. Heat ham uncovered for final 30 minutes. Carve ham and serve. Garnish with apple and thyme, if desired. **Yield:** 20 servings.

Per serving: 280 calories, 21g protein, 20g carbohydrate, 15g fat, 0g fiber, 76mg cholesterol, 1291mg sodium

**Grilled Ham Steak with
Peach Fresca**

Deluxe Redeye Gravy with Smoked Ham

Coffee-spiked redeye gravy is a Southern favorite that finds a perfect match with Cook's® Brand Shoulder Ham.

comfort food

submitted by: **Cook's® Brand Ham**

Prep Time: 15 minutes
Cook Time: 15 minutes

3 pounds COOK'S® Brand Smoked Shoulder Ham, cut into ¼ inch thick slices
1 cup finely chopped onion
¼ cup finely chopped green bell pepper

3 tablespoons all-purpose flour
1½ cups black coffee
¾ cup water
¼ cup milk
Salt and pepper to taste

1. In a skillet over medium heat, cook ham until heated through. Reserve ¼ cup pan drippings and keep warm. Remove ham; keep warm while making gravy.
2. Add onion and green bell pepper to reserved drippings. Cook until vegetables are softened. Add flour and mix well. Cook 1 to 2 minutes, then add coffee and water. Mix well and cook until thickened, 5 to 6 minutes. Add milk, salt, and pepper, and cook 5 more minutes. Serve with warm ham. **Yield:** 6 servings.

Per serving: 350 calories, 46g protein, 6g carbohydrate, 14g fat, 1g fiber, 149mg cholesterol, 197mg sodium

Test Kitchen Secret:
Serve the ham and flavorful gravy with grits or biscuits for breakfast, lunch, or dinner. It's good any time of day!

Grilled Ham Steak with Peach Fresca

Fresh peaches are the main attraction of this spicy original. Served over grilled ham steak, they make this dish a sensational summer meal.

quick & easy

submitted by: **Chef Eddie Matney, Eddie Matney's Restaurant, Phoenix, Arizona, for Cook's® Brand Ham**

Prep Time: 20 minutes
Cook Time: 10 minutes

6 ripe peaches, diced
½ red onion, finely diced
¼ cup packed brown sugar
Juice from 1 lime
1 tablespoon olive oil
1 tablespoon chopped fresh mint

1 serrano chili, seeded and diced
Pinch Chinese Five Spice
Salt and pepper to taste
1 COOK'S® Brand Bone-In Thick Cut Ham Steak

1. Preheat charcoal or gas grill for medium heat. Combine all ingredients except ham steak in a bowl and mix well; set aside. Place ham steak on grill. Heat according to package instructions.
2. Place ham steak on platter and pour Peach Fresca over top. **Yield:** 4 servings.

Per serving: 423 calories, 29g protein, 29g carbohydrate, 22g fat, 0g fiber, 101mg cholesterol, 1203mg sodium

Test Kitchen Secret:
Chinese Five Spice is a pungent mixture of five ground spices. It usually consists of equal parts of cinnamon, cloves, fennel seed, star anise, and Szechuan peppercorns. Prepackaged five-spice powder is available in Asian markets and most supermarkets.

party pleaser

submitted by: **Chef Eddie Matney, Eddie Matney's Restaurant, Phoenix, Arizona, for Cook's® Brand Ham**

Prep Time: 20 minutes
Cook Time: 23 minutes

Test Kitchen Secret:

While you're at the grill, throw on some vegetables to go with the meal. Just brush sliced vegetables like red bell peppers, onions, zucchini, and squash with olive oil, and grill to desired tenderness.

Grilled Ham Steak with Peach Chipotle Glaze

The peach chipotle glaze elevates a grilled ham steak to new levels of excitement with minimal effort in the kitchen.

2	cloves garlic, chopped	2	tablespoons rice wine vinegar
1	shallot, chopped	3	tablespoons chipotle sauce
2	teaspoons olive oil		Salt and pepper to taste
1	(20 ounce) jar peach marmalade	1	COOK'S® Brand Bone-In Thick Cut Ham Steak
2	tablespoons Dijon-style mustard		

1. Sauté garlic and shallot in oil until soft. Add remaining ingredients except ham steak and simmer for 15 minutes. Set aside.

2. Preheat grill for medium heat. Grill ham steak 3 minutes. Turn ham steak; brush with peach chipotle glaze and grill 3 more minutes. Turn again; brush with remaining glaze. Grill 1 to 2 minutes or until ham is glazed and heated through. **Yield:** 4 servings.

Per serving: 707 calories, 29g protein, 103g carbohydrate, 22g fat, 1g fiber, 101mg cholesterol, 1436mg sodium

from the grill

submitted by: **Cook's® Brand Ham**

Prep Time: 15 minutes
Cook Time: 10 minutes

Test Kitchen Secret:

If the weather's not cooperating, bring things inside and prepare the ham on the stovetop in a skillet or grill pan.

Sweet & Sour Ham Steak

Ham steaks grilled and glazed with a sweet mustard sauce make any meal seem like a special occasion.

½	cup packed brown sugar	1	teaspoon pumpkin pie spice
⅓	cup beer or apple juice	2	COOK'S® Brand Bone-In Ham Steaks
2	tablespoons Dijon-style mustard		

1. Preheat charcoal or gas grill for medium heat.

2. In a small saucepan, combine brown sugar, beer or apple juice, mustard, and pumpkin pie spice. Cook glaze over medium-high heat, stirring several times, until it starts to bubble. Remove from heat.

3. Grill each ham steak 1 to 2 minutes on each side before applying glaze. Baste ham steaks with glaze. Grill 2 minutes. Turn and baste again; grill 2 more minutes. Serve hot. **Yield:** 6 servings.

Per serving: 488 calories, 38g protein, 27g carbohydrate, 25g fat, 0g fiber, 135mg cholesterol, 1595mg sodium

Tangy Apricot Glazed Ham Steak

Sweet apricots and hot horseradish combine for a perfectly balanced, twenty-minute dish.

½ cup apricot preserves
½ cup minced dried apricots
2 tablespoons chili sauce
2 teaspoons prepared horseradish
2 teaspoons powdered mustard
1 COOK'S® Brand Bone-In Ham Steak or Thick Cut Steak

1. Preheat charcoal or gas grill for medium heat. Meanwhile, to prepare glaze, combine all ingredients except ham steak in saucepan and heat gently.
2. Place ham steak on preheated grill and cook 3 minutes. Turn ham steak; brush with ½ of the jelly mixture and continue to grill 3 minutes. Turn again; brush with remaining ½ of jelly mixture and continue to grill 1 to 2 minutes or until ham is glazed and heated through. **Yield:** 4 servings.

Per serving: 281 calories, 20g protein, 42g carbohydrate, 4g fat, 2g fiber, 60mg cholesterol, 1762mg sodium

quick & easy

submitted by: **Cook's® Brand Ham**

Prep Time: 10 minutes
Cook Time: 10 minutes

Test Kitchen Secret:
Prepared horseradish serves as a one-ingredient miracle worker in many dishes that need a little flavor boost. Prepared horseradish begins to lose its hotness once it has been opened, so replace it after four months.

Ham Steak Stir-Fry

Ham steak cut into thick strips makes a nice addition in this healthy one-dish meal.

1 tablespoon vegetable oil
1 COOK'S® Brand Bone-In Ham Steak, cut into 1½ inch strips
1 clove garlic, crushed
4 ounces fresh snow peas, washed, ends snapped off
4 ounces fresh mushrooms, thinly sliced
1 medium carrot, thinly sliced
½ cup sliced water chestnuts
1 (15 ounce) can baby corn, drained
½ teaspoon ground ginger
1 tablespoon soy sauce
1 tablespoon dry sherry
1 tablespoon ketchup
1 teaspoon cornstarch
1 tablespoon cold water
2 green onions, thinly sliced
4 cups hot cooked rice

1. Heat oil in a wok or large skillet over medium-high heat. Add ham and garlic and stir-fry 1 minute. Add remaining ingredients except cornstarch, water, green onions, and rice; stir-fry 4 to 5 minutes or until vegetables are tender-crisp.
2. Combine cornstarch and water; add to skillet, stirring constantly, until ingredients are coated with a light, clear glaze, about 1 minute. Transfer to a platter, top with green onions, and serve immediately with hot cooked rice. **Yield:** 4 servings.

Per serving: 486 calories, 27g protein, 74g carbohydrate, 8g fat, 6g fiber, 43mg cholesterol, 2049mg sodium

healthy

submitted by: **Cook's® Brand Ham**

Prep Time: 10 minutes
Cook Time: 10 minutes

Test Kitchen Secret:
Bump up the nutrition in this dish even more by serving it over hot cooked brown rice. Serve with extra soy sauce on the side.

Ham Steak Kabobs

party pleaser

submitted by: **Cook's® Brand Ham**

Prep Time: 25 minutes

Cook Time: 15 minutes

Test Kitchen Secret:

When using wooden skewers, soak them in water at least 30 minutes beforehand to prevent the skewers from burning on the grill.

Cubed ham steak, bell peppers, pineapple, and mushrooms are laced onto skewers and grilled for a simply stunning meal. Serve with Classic Cherry Sauce for an even tastier treat.

1	COOK'S® Brand Bone-In Ham Steak, cut into 1 inch cubes	1½	cups pineapple chunks, fresh or canned
1	red bell pepper, cut into 1 inch chunks		Cherry tomatoes (optional)
1	green bell pepper, cut into 1 inch chunks	1	medium onion, chopped into ½ inch pieces (optional)
½	(8 ounce) package fresh mushrooms, halved		COOK'S® Classic Cherry Sauce

1. Preheat grill for medium heat. Skewer the ham, alternating with remaining ingredients except Cherry Sauce. Heat on grill for 3 to 4 minutes per side or until golden brown. Serve hot with COOK'S® Classic Cherry Sauce. **Yield:** 4 servings.

Per serving: 402 calories, 31g protein, 30g carbohydrate, 19g fat, 3g fiber, 101mg cholesterol, 1102mg sodium

Cook's® Classic Cherry Sauce

1	(12 ounce) jar cherry preserves	¼	teaspoon ground cinnamon
¼	cup honey	¼	teaspoon ground cloves
¼	cup red wine vinegar	¼	teaspoon salt
¼	teaspoon ground nutmeg		

1. In a small saucepan, combine all ingredients. Simmer for 5 minutes. **Yield:** 2 cups.

Per serving: 279 calories, 0g protein, 73g carbohydrate, 0g fat, 0g fiber, 0mg cholesterol, 149mg sodium

Ham Steak Kabobs and Cook's® Classic Cherry Sauce

submitted by: **Cook's® Brand Ham**

Prep Time: 20 minutes
Cook Time: 35 minutes

Test Kitchen Secret:

Depending on the cut of the potatoes, you may need to adjust the cooking times. If you prefer to cook this dish in the oven, simply place foil packet on a baking sheet in a preheated oven at 375°F. Bake for 60 minutes, or until potatoes are tender, and follow rest of recipe instructions.

Zesty Potato-Ham Casserole

This recipe makes a quick summertime supper that won't heat up your house. Potatoes, ham, and onion are grilled, and then cheese is melted on for a fun outdoor meal that doesn't even dirty any dishes.

9	medium potatoes, peeled and chopped
½	medium onion, chopped
1	medium-sized green bell pepper, chopped
1½	teaspoons black pepper
2½	cups COOK'S® Brand Bone-In Ham (cubed), leftover ham (shredded), or Ham Steak (cut into ½ inch cubes)
8	ounces sharp Cheddar cheese, grated
1	medium tomato, seeded and chopped

1. Preheat grill for medium heat. Make foil packet by placing potatoes, onion, and green bell pepper on the center of foil sheet. Sprinkle black pepper over entire mixture and stir to mix well. Bring up foil sides and double fold top and sides to seal, leaving room for heat circulation inside. Place on grill for 20 minutes or until potatoes are tender.

2. Remove from grill; add cubed ham, stirring slightly to mix. Reseal and return to grill for approximately 10 minutes. Remove from grill and sprinkle cheese and tomato over entire mixture. Return to grill, leaving the packet unsealed and the grill lid closed, and cook for approximately 5 minutes or until cheese is melted. Remove from grill and serve. **Yield:** 8 servings.

Per serving: 290 calories, 16g protein, 29g carbohydrate, 13g fat, 4g fiber, 49mg cholesterol, 391mg sodium

Ham Pie with Succotash Vegetables & Biscuit Crust

Comfort food at its best, this warming dish combines ham and hearty vegetables in a creamy white sauce with a homemade buttermilk biscuit crust.

Ham Filling

2	tablespoons unsalted butter
1	medium onion, finely chopped
3	tablespoons all-purpose flour
1½	cups chicken broth
1	teaspoon minced fresh thyme Hot sauce to taste
1	cup frozen corn kernels, thawed
1	cup frozen baby lima beans, thawed
2½	cups COOK'S® Brand Bone-In Ham (cubed), leftover ham (shredded), or Ham Steak (cut into ½ inch cubes)

Biscuit Crust

1	cup all-purpose flour
1	teaspoon baking powder
¼	teaspoon baking soda
¼	teaspoon salt
3	tablespoons cold unsalted butter, cut into small pieces
⅔	cup buttermilk

1. Preheat oven to 400°F.

2. For the filling, melt butter in saucepan over medium-low heat. Add onion; cook 5 minutes until softened. Stir in flour and cook 1 minute. Add broth; bring to simmer, stirring occasionally. Cook until sauce thickens, 3 to 5 minutes. Season with thyme and hot sauce to taste. Remove pan from heat; pour sauce into medium-sized bowl to cool.

3. Stir corn, lima beans, and ham cubes into cooled sauce. Spread filling in 1 quart casserole dish.

4. For the crust, combine flour, baking powder, baking soda, and salt in mixing bowl or food processor. Mix in cold butter until mixture is crumbly. Add buttermilk and mix until evenly moist and the consistency of thick batter.

5. With a large spoon, drop batter over filling to cover completely. Place casserole dish on baking sheet and bake in the preheated oven 35 to 40 minutes or until crust is browned and filling is bubbling hot. **Yield: 4 servings.**

Per serving: 553 calories, 31g protein, 54g carbohydrate, 24g fat, 5g fiber, 92mg cholesterol, 208mg sodium

comfort food

submitted by: **Cook's® Brand Ham**

Prep Time: 15 minutes
Cook Time: 55 minutes

Test Kitchen Secret:
Succotash *is an Indian word meaning "broken into bits." This simple dish of indigenous corn and lima beans was introduced to settlers by Indian tribes of the southern United States.*

Ham & Noodle Bake

Prep Time: 15 minutes
Cook Time: 40 minutes

Test Kitchen Secret:
Make a double batch of this casserole and freeze one for a rainy day.

A creamy casserole full of egg noodles, sour cream, onion, and ham makes for potluck heaven.

6	ounces wide egg noodles
⅓	cup chopped green bell pepper
⅓	cup chopped onion
2	tablespoons butter
1	(8 ounce) carton sour cream
⅓	cup milk
1	(10¾ ounce) can cream of chicken soup
¼	teaspoon black pepper
2½	cups COOK'S® Brand Bone-In Ham (cubed), leftover ham (shredded), or Ham Steak (cut into ½ inch cubes)

1. Preheat oven to 350°F.
2. Cook noodles for 8 to 10 minutes in 2 quarts of water. Drain and set aside. Sauté green bell pepper and onion in butter until tender. Remove from heat and add sour cream, milk, soup, black pepper, and ham. Mix well. Gently stir in noodles. Pour into 2 quart greased casserole. Bake in the preheated oven for 35 to 40 minutes. **Yield:** 6 servings.

Per serving: 360 calories, 20g protein, 25g carbohydrate, 19g fat, 1g fiber, 102mg cholesterol, 1136mg sodium

Fish Tacos

Prep Time: 15 minutes
Cook Time: 6 minutes

What Other Cooks Have Done:
"We had these on corn tortillas with lettuce, tomatoes, and a sour cream-red chili pepper sauce on top. We'll definitely make these again!"

These fish tacos are delicious and won't keep you waiting to eat. White fish fillets are basted with a Mexican-style sauce, then served on tortillas with sour cream dressing and cabbage.

1	pound fresh or frozen skinless cod, orange roughy, or other mild fish fillets
2	tablespoons butter or margarine, melted
2	teaspoons HERB-OX® Chicken Flavored Bouillon Granules
¼	teaspoon ground cumin
⅛	teaspoon garlic powder
2	tablespoons mayonnaise or salad dressing
2	tablespoons sour cream
1	teaspoon lime juice
1½	cups shredded coleslaw mix
6	(8 inch) flour tortillas, warmed Salsa (optional)

1. Preheat oven to 450°F. Thaw fish fillets, if frozen. Rinse fish and pat dry with paper towels. Cut fish fillets crosswise into 1 inch slices. Place fish in single layer in a greased shallow pan. Combine butter, bouillon granules, cumin, and garlic powder. Brush over fish.
2. Bake in the preheated oven for 4 to 6 minutes or until fish flakes easily when pierced with a fork. Meanwhile, combine mayonnaise, sour cream, and lime juice. Add coleslaw mix; toss to coat. Spoon coleslaw mixture onto each warm tortilla. Top with fish. Serve with salsa, if desired. **Yield:** 6 servings.

Per serving: 294 calories, 18g protein, 27g carbohydrate, 13g fat, 2g fiber, 49mg cholesterol, 333mg sodium

Cajun Pecan Catfish

The flavors of Louisiana bayou country come to life in McCormick®
Gourmet Collection™ Cajun Seasoning—a spicy-hot blend of
peppers, onion, garlic, and herbs. It's the easy way to spark this
pecan-topped baked fish. It's also good with snapper, grouper, or
other firm-fleshed fish fillets.

5 star

submitted by: **McCormick® & Company**

Prep Time: 10 minutes
Cook Time: 15 minutes

What Other Cooks Have Done:
*"I used sweet-and-spicy pecans I
baked in a soy sauce, Tabasco®, and
brown sugar mixture, which added
more flavor. Add a garnish of sliced
lemons and parsley, and it's worthy
of company!"*

1 pound catfish fillets	⅓ cup finely chopped pecans
2 tablespoons olive oil	2 tablespoons grated Parmesan cheese
1 tablespoon McCORMICK® Gourmet Collection™ Cajun Seasoning	1 tablespoon dry breadcrumbs
2 teaspoons lemon juice	1 tablespoon McCORMICK® Gourmet Collection™ Parsley Flakes
1 teaspoon McCORMICK® Gourmet Collection™ Thyme Leaves	Lemon wedges (optional) Parsley sprig (optional)

1. Preheat oven to 425°F. Coat a shallow baking pan with nonstick cooking spray; place fish in pan.
2. Combine oil, Cajun seasoning, lemon juice, and thyme in a small bowl.
Spoon or brush ½ of the mixture over fish.
3. Add pecans, Parmesan cheese, breadcrumbs, and parsley to remaining oil
mixture; mix well. Spoon onto fish and spread evenly. Bake in the preheated oven for 10 to 15 minutes (depending on thickness of fish), or until
fish flakes easily with a fork. Garnish with lemon wedges and parsley, if
desired. **Yield:** 4 servings.

Per serving: 303 calories, 21g protein, 5g carbohydrate, 24g fat, 2g fiber, 55mg cholesterol,
298mg sodium

Cajun Pecan Catfish

Chilled Salmon Steaks with Lemon Dill Dressing

Chilled Salmon Steaks with Lemon Dill Dressing

Poached salmon steaks are served chilled with a light and creamy lemon dill dressing.

2   pounds (1 to 1¼ inch thick) fresh or frozen salmon steaks
1½ cups water
1   tablespoon HERB-OX® Chicken Flavored Bouillon Granules
¼   cup white wine

1   lemon, thinly sliced
½   cup onion slices
10 whole black peppercorns
2   bay leaves
    Lettuce leaves
    Lemon Dill Dressing
    Lemon slices (optional)

make-ahead

submitted by: **Hormel Foods Corporation**

Prep Time: 10 minutes
Cook Time: 12 minutes
Chill Time: 2 hours

Test Kitchen Secret:
Use kitchen shears to snip fresh dill and chives for this refreshing dressing.

1. Thaw fish, if frozen. Rinse fish and pat dry with paper towels; set aside. In large skillet, combine water, bouillon granules, white wine, lemon slices, onion, peppercorns, and bay leaves. Bring mixture to a boil. Add salmon steaks. Cover and simmer for 8 to 12 minutes or until fish flakes easily when pierced with a fork. Remove fish and discard poaching liquid and seasoning. Cover and refrigerate fish until chilled, about 2 hours.

2. To serve, place chilled salmon fillets over lettuce and drizzle each serving with Lemon Dill Dressing. Garnish with lemon slices, if desired. **Yield:** 6 servings.

Per serving: 439 calories, 34g protein, 6g carbohydrate, 31g fat, 2g fiber, 84mg cholesterol, 247mg sodium

Lemon Dill Dressing

¾   cup mayonnaise
3   tablespoons buttermilk
1   tablespoon chopped fresh dill
1   tablespoon chopped fresh chives

2   teaspoons lemon juice
½   teaspoon finely shredded fresh lemon zest

1. In a small bowl, combine all ingredients. Drizzle over salmon fillets. **Yield:** about 1 cup.

Cheesy Fish Fillet Broccoli Casserole

Warm up this winter with this hearty, cheesy casserole. It combines delicious Gorton's® Fish Fillets with broccoli and a delightful combination of cheeses. Plus, it's ready to bake in only minutes!

2	(10 ounce) packages frozen chopped broccoli, thawed	3	tablespoons grated Parmesan cheese
1	cup milk	1	(11.4 ounce) package GORTON'S® Crunchy Golden Fish Fillets or Crispy Battered Fish Fillets
1	(10¾ ounce) can condensed Cheddar cheese soup		
1	cup shredded Cheddar cheese		

1. Preheat oven to 400°F. Grease a 7x11 inch baking dish.
2. Spread broccoli in dish. Mix milk and soup; pour over broccoli. Sprinkle with cheeses; top with fillets.
3. Bake, uncovered, in the preheated oven for 25 to 30 minutes or until sauce is bubbly and tops of fillets are crisp. Let stand 10 minutes before serving. **Yield:** 4 servings.

Per serving: 491 calories, 25g protein, 34g carbohydrate, 29g fat, 5g fiber, 77mg cholesterol, 1207mg sodium

Grilled Fillets with Broccoli Penne

Turn an ordinary pasta dish into something extraordinary. Just add delicious Gorton's® Grilled Fillets, broccoli, and a special seasoning to tender penne pasta. Seven flavors of Gorton's® Grilled Fillets allow for seven different twists to this dish.

2	GORTON'S® Grilled Fillets (any flavor)	4	ounces penne pasta, cooked
2	tablespoons olive or vegetable oil	2	tablespoons butter or margarine
1	small onion, thinly sliced	2	tablespoons grated Parmesan cheese
2	cloves garlic, finely chopped	2⅛	teaspoons crushed red pepper flakes
2	cups broccoli florets, blanched		Salt and pepper to taste
¼	teaspoon onion powder		
¼	teaspoon garlic powder		

1. Cook GORTON'S® Grilled Fillets according to package directions.
2. Meanwhile, in a 10 inch skillet, heat oil over low heat. Add onion and cook 3 minutes. Add garlic and cook 1 minute. Add broccoli, sprinkle with onion and garlic powders, and cook 2 more minutes. Toss with hot pasta, butter, cheese, and red pepper flakes. Add salt and pepper to taste. To serve, break hot fillets into large chunks with a fork and arrange over pasta. **Yield:** 2 servings.

Per serving: 608 calories, 32g protein, 53g carbohydrate, 32g fat, 6g fiber, 100mg cholesterol, 1092mg sodium

Tenders Taco Casserole

Crunch! Crunch! Crunch! Gorton's® Extra Crunchy Tenders team up with crisp tortilla chips and zesty taco ingredients to make this casserole fantastic! Season it to your family's spice level.

8	GORTON'S® Extra Crunchy or Battered Tenders	1	(8 ounce) container sour cream
1	(15 ounce) can chili beans, rinsed and drained	½	cup sliced green onions (with tops)
1	(8 ounce) can tomato sauce	1	medium tomato, chopped
2	tablespoons taco sauce	1	cup shredded Cheddar cheese
1	tablespoon chili powder		Shredded lettuce (optional)
1	teaspoon garlic salt		Chili peppers (optional)
2	cups coarsely broken tortilla chips		Taco sauce (optional)

1. Preheat oven to 375°F. In a saucepan, heat 8 frozen tenders, beans, tomato sauce, taco sauce, chili powder, and garlic salt to a boil. Reduce heat and simmer for 5 minutes.

2. Place chips in an ungreased 7x11 inch baking dish. Pour tenders mixture over chips. Spread with sour cream. Sprinkle with onions, tomato, and cheese.

3. Bake, uncovered, in the preheated oven for 20 to 25 minutes. Serve with shredded lettuce, chili peppers, and taco sauce, if desired. **Yield:** 8 servings.

Per serving: 309 calories, 13g protein, 29g carbohydrate, 18g fat, 4g fiber, 41mg cholesterol, 1023mg sodium

kid-friendly

submitted by: **Gorton's®**

Prep Time: 15 minutes
Cook Time: 40 minutes

Test Kitchen Secret:
Adjust the toppings to your family's taste. For the kids, give them mild taco sauce and lettuce. For the adults, kick it up with hot taco sauce and jalapeño peppers.

Grilled Fillets Jambalaya

A Gorton's® favorite! Filled with veggies, rice, spices, and grilled fillets, this meal will satisfy your taste for the South.

2	teaspoons vegetable oil	1	(14.5 ounce) can chicken or vegetable broth
1	onion, chopped	2	tablespoons dried parsley flakes
1	green bell pepper, chopped	2	bay leaves
2	stalks celery, chopped	1	tablespoon fresh thyme
3	cloves garlic, minced	¼	teaspoon black pepper
2	(7.6 ounce) packages GORTON'S® Cajun Grilled Fillets	½	teaspoon cayenne pepper
		⅛	teaspoon white pepper
1	(14.5 ounce) can diced tomatoes	½	cup chopped green onions
1	(8 ounce) can tomato sauce	4	cups hot cooked rice

1. In a deep skillet or Dutch oven, heat the oil. Add the onion, green bell pepper, celery, and garlic, and sauté until vegetables are soft, about 5 minutes. Add frozen fillets, tomatoes, tomato sauce, broth, and seasonings. Cover and simmer for 20 to 25 minutes.

2. Uncover and break fish into chunks. Remove bay leaves. Just before serving, mix in the green onions. Serve over rice. **Yield:** 6 servings.

Per serving: 270 calories, 17g protein, 40g carbohydrate, 5g fat, 3g fiber, 40mg cholesterol, 873mg sodium

Texas Hash with Fish Fillets

Turn up the heat a notch with Texas Hash with Fish Fillets! Adjust the spice level to your liking.

6	GORTON'S® Crunchy Golden or Southern Fried Fish Fillets	1	(16 ounce) can whole tomatoes, undrained
2	tablespoons vegetable oil	½	cup uncooked white rice
2	large onions, chopped	1	teaspoon salt
1	large green bell pepper, chopped	1½	teaspoons chili powder
		⅛	teaspoon black pepper

1. Cook GORTON'S® Fillets according to directions on package. Heat oil in a 10 inch skillet; add onions and bell pepper and cook until tender. Stir in tomatoes (with liquid) and the remaining ingredients. Heat to a boil; reduce heat.

2. Cover and simmer, stirring occasionally, until rice is tender and liquid is absorbed, about 25 to 30 minutes. Place fillets on hash mixture and serve. **Yield:** 6 servings.

Per serving: 278 calories, 7g protein, 35g carbohydrate, 13g fat, 3g fiber, 15mg cholesterol, 732mg sodium

Fish Fillet Florentine

Gorton's® Battered Fillets work best with this dish but if you can't find them, Crunchy Fillets taste great, too. Change it up with flavored fillets.

3	tablespoons margarine or butter	¼	teaspoon black pepper
1	medium onion, chopped	¼	teaspoon Worcestershire sauce
3	tablespoons all-purpose flour	1	(10 ounce) package frozen chopped spinach, thawed
1¾	cups milk	1	(12 ounce) package GORTON'S® Crispy Battered Fish Fillets
1	teaspoon salt		
1	teaspoon lemon juice		
¼	teaspoon garlic powder		

1. Preheat oven to 425°F. Melt margarine in 2 quart saucepan; add onion and cook until tender. Stir in flour. Cook over low heat, stirring constantly, until bubbly. Remove from heat; stir in milk. Bring to a boil; boil 1 minute, stirring constantly. Stir in remaining ingredients except fillets.

2. Place fillets, with sides touching, in an ungreased 7x11 inch baking dish; pour sauce over fillets. Bake, uncovered, in the preheated oven for 25 to 30 minutes. **Yield:** 3 servings.

Per serving: 515 calories, 18g protein, 37g carbohydrate, 34g fat, 4g fiber, 43mg cholesterol, 1871mg sodium

make-ahead

submitted by: **Gorton's®**

Prep Time: 15 minutes
Cook Time: 40 minutes

Test Kitchen Secret:
Simplify dinnertime frenzy by assembling this casserole the night before and refrigerating until ready to bake.

Fish Stick Enchiladas

Finally, an easy and delicious enchiladas recipe. Make it Mexican night tonight!

1	(10¾ ounce) can cream of mushroom soup	1	cup shredded Cheddar or Monterey Jack cheese, divided
1	small onion, chopped		
1	(4.5 ounce) can chopped green chilies	8	GORTON'S® Crunchy Golden Fish Sticks
1	(8 ounce) container sour cream	8	(8 inch) flour tortillas

1. Preheat oven to 375°F. In a large bowl, mix soup, onion, chilies, sour cream, and ½ cup cheese. Place a frozen fish stick in center of a tortilla. Place 2 tablespoons of sauce along the side of the stick, roll tortilla, and place seam down in a rectangular casserole dish. Make 8 wrapped tortillas. Spread remainder of sauce on top of tortillas.

2. Bake in the preheated oven for 20 minutes. Sprinkle remaining ½ cup cheese on top and cook 5 more minutes. **Yield:** 8 servings.

Per serving: 454 calories, 14g protein, 50g carbohydrate, 22g fat, 3g fiber, 34mg cholesterol, 983mg sodium

kid-friendly

submitted by: **Gorton's®**

Prep Time: 12 minutes
Cook Time: 25 minutes

Test Kitchen Secret:
Lighten this family-friendly meal by using reduced-fat cream of mushroom soup, light sour cream, reduced-fat cheese, and whole wheat tortillas.

Old Bay® Shrimp Fest

Prep Time: 15 minutes
Cook Time: 30 minutes

What Other Cooks Have Done:

"This was the best! So easy and so quick—I was able to entertain my guests while assembling the meal. Everyone loved it. Next time I'd also try crab legs or maybe chunks of grouper or clams."

Enjoy this one-pot shrimp fest for easy summertime entertaining! Shrimp, smoked sausage, potatoes, corn, and onions are perfectly seasoned with Old Bay®.

½ cup OLD BAY® Seasoning	2 pounds lean smoked sausage, cut into 2 inch lengths
2 tablespoons salt	8 ears fresh corn, broken in half
4 quarts water	4 pounds large shrimp in shells
1 (12 ounce) can beer (optional)	Additional OLD BAY® Seasoning (optional)
8 red-skinned potatoes, quartered	
2 large sweet onions, cut into wedges	

1. In an 8 quart pot, bring OLD BAY® Seasoning, salt, water, and beer, if desired, to a boil. Add potatoes and onions; cook over high heat for 8 minutes.

2. Add smoked sausage to potatoes and onions; continue to cook over high heat for 5 minutes. Add corn to pot; continue to boil for 7 minutes. Add shrimp in shells and cook for 4 minutes.

3. Drain cooking liquid. Pour contents of pot into several large bowls or shallow pails, or mound on a paper-covered picnic table. Sprinkle with additional OLD BAY® Seasoning, if desired. **Yield:** 8 servings.

Per serving: 758 calories, 72g protein, 58g carbohydrate, 26g fat, 6g fiber, 425mg cholesterol, 2334mg sodium

Secrets from the McCormick® Kitchens

The secret's out. Once a staple enjoyed by only a lucky few along the Chesapeake Bay, Old Bay® Seasoning is now available across the country to anyone who wishes to experience a distinctive, big, bold taste. Best known as the definitive seasoning for crab, shrimp, and other seafood dishes, today Old Bay® Seasoning is earning its stripes as the "secret" ingredient for great hamburgers, chicken, and vegetable dishes. It's easy to add the romance and flavor of the Chesapeake Bay to your meals every night of the week with this versatile seasoning.

Old Bay® Seasoning was founded more than 60 years ago: A man named Gustav Brunn arrived in the United States from Germany with a hand-held spice grinder and a dream of starting a spice business. In 1939, Brunn settled in Baltimore and developed his secret recipe, which would later become Old Bay® Seasoning. This unique blend of more than a dozen herbs and spices was created for a population passionate about steamed crabs, and has since become synonymous with the Chesapeake Bay and its locals.

Celery, bay leaves, and mustard combine with the heat of red pepper and ginger to flavor many dishes from grilled fish and steamed shrimp to fried chicken, potato salad, and vegetable dips. This unique spice blend evokes images of seaside dining, salty sea breezes, and sandy beaches. This fantastic blend is also at home adding flavor to bounty that's fresh from the farm as well as the sea.

Old Bay® Shrimp Fest

Grilled Shrimp Tacos with Pineapple Salsa

party pleaser

submitted by: **Dole**®

Prep Time: 15 minutes
Chill Time: 30 minutes
Cook Time: 6 minutes

Test Kitchen Secret:

This is an ideal dish for summertime barbecue parties or tailgates. Prepare the salsa ahead of time and keep in the cooler until the shrimp are ready. Warm the tortillas right on the grill.

In addition to making your own salsa, you can garnish these tacos as you would regular tacos—with cilantro, sour cream, tomatoes, or any other favorite topping.

1½	pounds unpeeled, large fresh shrimp
⅓	cup olive oil
4	tablespoons lime juice, divided
¾	teaspoon ground cumin
¼	teaspoon salt
1	(20 ounce) can DOLE® Crushed Pineapple
½	medium-sized red bell pepper, diced
¼	cup chopped fresh cilantro
2	cloves garlic, minced
2	tablespoons finely diced red onion
½	teaspoon crushed red pepper flakes
6	(8 inch) flour tortillas, warmed

1. Peel and devein shrimp.
2. Whisk together oil, 3 tablespoons lime juice, cumin, and salt in shallow dish. Add shrimp; cover and chill 30 minutes.
3. Drain pineapple, reserving ¼ cup juice in large bowl. Add remaining 1 tablespoon lime juice, pineapple, bell pepper, cilantro, garlic, red onion, and red pepper flakes. Toss gently. Cover; chill until ready to serve.
4. Remove shrimp from marinade; discard marinade. Place shrimp in a grill basket.
5. Preheat grill for medium-high heat. Grill shrimp, covered with grill lid, 2 to 3 minutes on each side or just until shrimp turn pink. Serve shrimp in warm tortillas with pineapple salsa. **Yield:** 6 servings.

Per serving: 239 calories, 23g protein, 15g carbohydrate, 9g fat, 2g fiber, 172mg cholesterol, 274mg sodium

Herbed Pecan-Crusted Scallops

Sea scallops are coated with a fresh herb and pecan rub, then skewered and grilled.

½	cup toasted pecan pieces	1	teaspoon fresh lemon zest
⅓	cup fresh oregano leaves	¼	teaspoon ground black pepper
¼	cup fresh thyme leaves	3	tablespoons olive oil
3	cloves garlic, chopped	1	pound sea scallops (12 to 15
2	teaspoons HERB-OX®		per pound)
	Chicken Flavored Bouillon		
	Granules		

1. Preheat grill for medium heat. In work bowl of food processor, combine pecan pieces, oregano, thyme, garlic, bouillon granules, lemon zest, and pepper. With machine running, gradually drizzle in olive oil until mixture forms a paste. Rub paste onto scallops. Thread scallops onto 4 skewers. Grill scallops for 5 to 8 minutes or until opaque. **Yield:** 4 servings.

Per serving: 304 calories, 21g protein, 7g carbohydrate, 22g fat, 2g fiber, 37mg cholesterol, 199mg sodium

quick & easy

submitted by: **Hormel Foods Corporation**

Prep Time: 20 minutes
Cook Time: 8 minutes

What Other Cooks Have Done:
"Seafood and nuts go together surprisingly well! Next time, I will coarsely chop the nuts instead of pureeing with the other ingredients to get more texture. I garnished with toasted pecans and fresh lemon zest before serving."

Easy One-Skillet Stroganoff

Turn the timeless classic into one you can eat once a week with Boca® Ground Burger—this all-in-one-skillet stroganoff is a keeper.

1	medium onion, thinly sliced	1	(8 ounce) can mushroom
1½	teaspoons vegetable oil		pieces and stems, drained
2	(1 cup) pouches frozen	3	cups medium egg noodles,
	BOCA® Meatless Ground		uncooked
	Burger	1	(8 ounce) container reduced-
¼	teaspoon garlic powder		fat sour cream
1	(14.5 ounce) can vegetable		Chopped fresh parsley
	broth		(optional)

1. Cook onion in oil in large nonstick skillet on medium-high heat until tender-crisp and lightly browned, stirring occasionally.
2. Add all remaining ingredients except sour cream and parsley; mix well. Bring to boil. Reduce heat to medium-low; cover. Simmer 10 to 12 minutes or until noodles are tender. Remove from heat.
3. Stir in sour cream. Sprinkle with parsley, if desired. **Yield:** 6 servings.

Per serving: 210 calories, 12g protein, 25g carbohydrate, 7g fat, 4g fiber, 35mg cholesterol, 570mg sodium

comfort food

submitted by: **Boca®**

Prep Time: 15 minutes
Cook Time: 20 minutes

Test Kitchen Secret:
Serve with a crisp green salad. Substitute all or some of the reduced-fat sour cream with fat-free sour cream for an even lighter meal.

Boca® Tacos

Make tacos in no time with this simple salsa method. This mixture also makes a wonderful topping for nachos or other Mexican favorites.

Prep Time: 5 minutes
Cook Time: 8 minutes

Test Kitchen Secret:

Use this recipe as a base for tacos, taco salads, or nachos. Change it up to suit your tastes. Top with fat-free or reduced-fat sour cream to tame the heat!

2	(1 cup) pouches frozen BOCA® Meatless Ground Burger	6	corn tortillas, warmed
¾	cup salsa	2	tablespoons shredded non-fat Cheddar cheese
¼	teaspoon chili powder		Shredded lettuce, chopped tomatoes, and onion (optional)
¼	teaspoon ground cumin		

1. Mix ground burger, salsa, chili powder, and cumin in nonstick skillet; cook over medium heat 6 to 8 minutes or until heated through, stirring occasionally.
2. Spoon ground burger mixture evenly onto tortillas; fold over. Top with cheese and desired toppings.
Variation: Omit chili powder and cumin. Prepare as directed, using medium or hot salsa. **Yield:** 6 servings.

Per serving: 120 calories, 10g protein, 20g carbohydrate, 1g fat, 4g fiber, 0mg cholesterol, 440mg sodium

Athenian Stuffed Peppers

With feta cheese, orzo pasta, and Boca® Meatless Ground Burger, this comforting classic will send you straight to Greece with all the flavor but less fat. Serve with a loaf of crusty bread and mixed green salad to round out your meal.

comfort food

submitted by: **Boca®**

Prep Time: 15 minutes
Cook Time: 35 minutes

Test Kitchen Secret:

Substitute cooked white or brown rice for the orzo.

1	(1 cup) pouch frozen BOCA® Meatless Ground Burger	¾	cup cooked orzo pasta
½	cup chopped mushrooms	½	cup crumbled feta cheese
1	clove garlic, minced	1	large green bell pepper, cut in half lengthwise
1	(14.5 ounce) can Italian-seasoned diced tomatoes, undrained, divided		

1. Preheat oven to 400°F.
2. Mix ground burger, mushrooms, garlic, and ½ of the tomatoes in large nonstick skillet. Cook on medium heat 5 minutes or until heated through, stirring frequently. Remove from heat. Add orzo and cheese; mix well. Spoon evenly into bell pepper halves.
3. Pour remaining tomatoes into 8 inch square baking dish. Top with filled pepper halves; cover with foil.
4. Bake in the preheated oven for 30 minutes. **Yield:** 2 servings.

Per serving: 310 calories, 21g protein, 43g carbohydrate, 7g fat, 9g fiber, 20mg cholesterol, 1240mg sodium

Grilled Italian Sausage & Peppers

A five-ingredient ticket to the taste of Italy, made with Boca® Italian Sausages and bell peppers, is sure to put a smile into every bite of this savory sandwich.

2	medium bell peppers (red, green, and/or yellow), cut into strips	4	frozen BOCA® Meatless Italian Sausages
1	small onion, sliced	4	hot dog buns or French bread rolls, partially split
¼	cup fat-free Italian-style dressing		

1. Preheat grill for medium heat. Place peppers, onion, and dressing in heavy-duty foil bag or foil pouch; close bag tightly. Grill 15 minutes or until vegetables are tender, turning bag occasionally.
2. Meanwhile, grill sausages as directed on package.
3. Fill buns with sausages; top with pepper mixture. **Yield:** 4 servings.

Per serving: 290 calories, 18g protein, 35g carbohydrate, 8g fat, 4g fiber, 0mg cholesterol, 1110mg sodium

from the grill

submitted by: **Boca**®

Prep Time: 10 minutes
Cook Time: 20 minutes

Test Kitchen Secret:
To cook pepper mixture on stovetop, place vegetables and dressing in large skillet. Cook over medium heat 5 minutes or until vegetables are tender-crisp, stirring frequently.

Taco Rice Skillet

Gather your family and friends together for a Mexican fiesta. This main dish can be made in twenty-five minutes flat.

2	(1 cup) pouches frozen BOCA® Meatless Ground Burger	1	medium tomato, chopped
2	cups uncooked instant white rice	1	(1.25 ounce) package taco seasoning mix
2	cups water	½	cup Mexican-style shredded cheese

1. Cook burger in large nonstick skillet as directed on package.
2. Add rice, water, tomato, and taco seasoning mix; stir until well blended. Bring to boil. Sprinkle with cheese; cover. Remove from heat. Let stand 5 minutes. **Yield:** 4 servings.

Per serving: 320 calories, 19g protein, 50g carbohydrate, 6g fat, 5g fiber, 15mg cholesterol, 950mg sodium

quick & easy

submitted by: **Boca**®

Prep Time: 10 minutes
Cook Time: 15 minutes

Test Kitchen Secret:
Serve with shredded lettuce, salsa, and other taco toppings.

Speedy Boca® Pasta Sauce, page 174

pasta & grains

Nothing says **homestyle** dinner like a plate of pasta smothered in sauce or a bowl of **robust** red beans and rice. Give your family meals to **look forward** to when you add macaroni and cheese, spicy couscous, or fried rice to the table.

submitted by: **Tyson®**

Prep Time: 20 minutes
Cook Time: 25 minutes

Test Kitchen Secret:
To prevent a bitter taste, toss eggplant cubes with 1 teaspoon salt and place in colander to drain for 30 minutes. Rinse and drain well before cooking.

Garden Chicken Sauté

It doesn't have to be gardening season to enjoy this tasty, healthful dish. Lucky for us, today's grocery stores carry a wide variety of fresh produce year-round.

4	TYSON® Fresh Boneless, Skinless Chicken Breasts	1	(16 ounce) can tomato wedges or 4 large fresh tomatoes, peeled and cut into wedges
¼	cup vegetable oil		
1	small eggplant, peeled, if desired, and cut into 1 inch cubes	2	teaspoons garlic salt
		1	teaspoon dried basil, crushed
2	small zucchini, thinly sliced	1	teaspoon chopped fresh parsley
1	medium-sized green bell pepper, cut into 1 inch pieces	½	teaspoon black pepper
			Hot cooked pasta
½	pound mushrooms, sliced		Freshly shredded Parmesan cheese (optional)
1	large onion, thinly sliced		

1. Cut chicken into 1 inch pieces. Wash hands.
2. Heat oil in large skillet over medium heat. Add chicken and sauté, stirring, about 2 minutes.
3. Add eggplant, zucchini, green bell pepper, mushrooms, and onion. Cook, stirring occasionally, about 15 minutes or until vegetables are tender-crisp. Add tomatoes, stirring carefully. Add garlic salt, basil, parsley, and black pepper.
4. Simmer, uncovered, about 5 minutes or until chicken is done (internal temperature of 170°F). Serve over hot cooked pasta. Sprinkle with Parmesan cheese, if desired. **Yield:** 4 servings.

Per serving: 362 calories, 30g protein, 23g carbohydrate, 19g fat, 7g fiber, 65mg cholesterol, 1120mg sodium

submitted by: **Boca®**

Prep Time: 5 minutes
Cook Time: 15 minutes

Test Kitchen Secret:
This sauce freezes well. Make several batches of sauce and store in rigid, plastic containers in the freezer. Heat frozen sauce in a saucepan over medium-low heat until heated through. You can boil spaghetti at the same time for a quick family meal.

Speedy Boca® Pasta Sauce *(pictured on page 172)*

Jazz up a jar of prepared spaghetti sauce with Boca® Meatless Ground Burger. Just add a little garlic, basil, and oregano, and the sauce is ready to blanket your favorite pasta.

1	(28 ounce) jar spaghetti sauce	1	teaspoon dried basil
2	(1 cup) pouches frozen BOCA® Meatless Ground Burger	1	teaspoon dried oregano
		1	clove garlic, minced
			Hot cooked pasta

1. Pour spaghetti sauce into large saucepan.
2. Stir in remaining ingredients except pasta.
3. Bring to boil; reduce heat to medium-low. Simmer 8 to 10 minutes or until heated through. Serve over hot cooked pasta. **Yield:** 6 servings.

Per serving: 123 calories, 9g protein, 16g carbohydrate, 3g fat, 5g fiber, 0mg cholesterol, 685mg sodium

Garden Chicken Sauté

Boca® Bolognese Pasta Sauce

Prep Time: 10 minutes
Cook Time: 15 minutes

Test Kitchen Secret:
If company's coming, add ¼ cup dry red wine to sauce with remaining ingredients. The wine will contribute an extra dimension of flavor that's sure to please.

A piquant garlic-basil tomato sauce that's perfect over your favorite pasta. Make a double batch and freeze one for when unexpected company arrives.

2	(1 cup) pouches frozen BOCA® Meatless Ground Burger
3	cloves garlic, minced
1	tablespoon olive oil
1	(28 ounce) can diced tomatoes
1	(6 ounce) can tomato paste
1	cup chopped mushrooms or zucchini (optional)
½	cup water
⅓	cup chopped fresh basil or 2 tablespoons dried basil
¼	teaspoon crushed red pepper flakes (optional)
	Hot cooked pasta

1. Cook and stir ground burger and garlic in hot oil in large saucepan over medium heat 4 to 5 minutes.
2. Stir in remaining ingredients except pasta. Heat 10 minutes or until heated through.
3. Serve over hot cooked pasta. **Yield:** 4 servings.

Per serving: 180 calories, 15g protein, 26g carbohydrate, 4g fat, 9g fiber, 0mg cholesterol, 810mg sodium

Oriental Beef & Noodle Bowl

Prep Time: 10 minutes
Cook Time: 15 minutes

What Other Cooks Have Done:
"I used beef broth for the water and seasoned it with grated ginger, teriyaki sauce, and rice vinegar to get more Oriental flavor."

McCormick® Brown Gravy Mix makes soup easy. Soy sauce and thin noodles give the soup an Oriental flair.

½	pound thin beef strips
1	(.87 ounce) package McCORMICK® Brown Gravy Mix
1½	cups sliced mushrooms
1	cup shredded carrots
¼	cup soy sauce
½	teaspoon hot sauce
4	cups water
2	ounces angel hair pasta or thin spaghetti, broken into small pieces
¼	cup chopped green onions

1. Coat a 3 quart saucepan with nonstick cooking spray. Add beef and brown over medium-high heat 3 to 4 minutes.
2. Mix in McCORMICK® Brown Gravy Mix, mushrooms, carrots, soy sauce, hot sauce, and water. Bring to a boil and simmer, uncovered, for 5 minutes.
3. Add pasta. Cook 5 more minutes. Stir in onions just before serving. **Yield:** 6 servings.

Per serving: 120 calories, 9g protein, 12g carbohydrate, 4g fat, 2g fiber, 20mg cholesterol, 905mg sodium

Asian Chicken Noodle Bowl

Ladle individual servings of this easy and authentic soup into deep bowls and garnish with thinly sliced green onions.

¾ teaspoon Asian five-spice powder	2 large cloves garlic, finely chopped
¼ teaspoon black pepper	3 (14 ounce) cans low-sodium chicken broth
⅛ teaspoon salt	1 tablespoon soy sauce
4 TYSON® Fresh Boneless, Skinless Chicken Thigh Cutlets	1 (9 ounce) package refrigerated angel hair pasta
2 teaspoons vegetable oil	1 (6 ounce) bag baby spinach

1. Combine five-spice powder, pepper, and salt. Cut chicken into 1 inch pieces. Rub spices onto chicken. Wash hands.
2. Heat oil in 2 quart stockpot over medium-high heat. Add chicken and cook about 5 minutes or until browned on all sides. Add garlic; cook 1 minute. Add chicken broth and soy sauce; cover and bring to a boil. Uncover, reduce heat to simmer, and cook 3 minutes. Add pasta; simmer 1 minute or until tender. Add spinach; cook just until wilted. **Yield:** 4 servings.

Per serving: 406 calories, 36g protein, 41g carbohydrate, 11g fat, 4g fiber, 147mg cholesterol, 624mg sodium

comfort food

submitted by: **Tyson®**

Prep Time: 10 minutes
Cook Time: 15 minutes

Test Kitchen Secret:
If you enjoy Asian cooking, you might want to make your own five-spice blend to keep on hand. Simply mix equal amounts of star anise, fennel, cinnamon, cloves, and Szechwan peppercorns, and grind to a powder.

Garden Herb Fettuccini

Everyone is sure to love this superfast pasta dish with chicken and cream sauce.

1 (9 ounce) package refrigerated fettuccini noodles	1 cup water
1 tablespoon olive oil	1 tablespoon HERB-OX® Chicken Flavored Bouillon Granules
1 medium-sized sweet yellow onion, cut into thin wedges	
⅓ cup julienne sliced dried tomatoes in oil, drained	1 (8 ounce) container fat-free, garden vegetable-flavored cream cheese
¾ pound skinless, boneless chicken breast, cooked and cut into thin strips	

1. Prepare noodles as package directs. Meanwhile, heat oil in a large skillet over medium-high heat; sauté onion and tomatoes about 5 minutes or until softened. Add cooked chicken breast strips and heat until warmed through. Add water and bouillon granules; bring mixture just to a boil.
2. Stir in cream cheese and heat about 2 minutes or until warmed through and cheese is smooth (do not bring to a boil). Place pasta in bowls and top with chicken mixture. Serve immediately. **Yield:** 6 servings.

Per serving: 366 calories, 25g protein, 29g carbohydrate, 14g fat, 2g fiber, 99mg cholesterol, 370mg sodium

quick & easy

submitted by: **Hormel Foods Corporation**

Prep Time: 10 minutes
Cook Time: 15 minutes

What Other Cooks Have Done:
"This is very good and doesn't take long to assemble at all. I added sliced mushrooms, chopped Roma tomatoes, minced garlic, and sliced green bell pepper. I used another half package of cream cheese to increase the amount of sauce to accommodate all the veggies."

Ham Linguine

Next time you serve your family a Cook's® Brand Ham, save the leftovers for this creamy pasta dish. Serve with white wine and a green salad to impress company.

4 ounces linguine noodles	1 cup sliced fresh mushrooms
4 ounces spinach linguine or egg noodles	1 (8 ounce) carton whipping cream
½ cup butter or margarine	2 pasteurized egg yolks
2½ cups COOK'S® Brand Bone-In Ham (cubed), leftover ham (shredded), or ham steak (cubed)	1 cup grated Parmesan cheese, divided

1. In a 6 quart Dutch oven, cook plain linguine and spinach linguine or egg noodles according to package directions. Drain pasta; return to Dutch oven. Add butter, ham, and mushrooms.

2. In a small bowl, combine whipping cream and egg yolks; beat well. Slowly stir the egg mixture into the linguine, mixing well. Add ¾ cup grated Parmesan cheese. Cook over medium heat until thickened, stirring gently. Spoon onto individual serving plates. Sprinkle with the remaining Parmesan cheese. **Yield:** 6 servings.

Per serving: 592 calories, 26g protein, 30g carbohydrate, 41g fat, 1g fiber, 226mg cholesterol, 1300mg sodium

Tenders Pasta Bake

Gorton's® Tenders make this pasta bake a complete meal that's so delicious your family will ask for more!

1 (7 ounce) package macaroni shells	1 (10.5 ounce) can condensed cream of chicken or cream of shrimp soup
2 tablespoons butter or margarine	⅔ cup milk
1 medium onion, chopped	1 cup frozen peas
1 medium stalk celery, chopped	1 (2 ounce) jar sliced pimiento (optional)
1 (8 ounce) package processed cheese spread, cut into cubes	
8 GORTON'S® Original Batter or Extra Crunchy Tenders	

1. Cook macaroni as directed on package. Heat butter in a 12 inch skillet; add onion and celery and sauté until soft. Add cooked pasta, cheese, GORTON'S® Tenders (frozen), soup, milk, peas, and pimiento, if desired. Stir to combine.

2. Cover and cook over medium heat for 20 to 25 minutes or until tenders are done. **Yield:** 8 servings.

Per serving: 326 calories, 13g protein, 34g carbohydrate, 16g fat, 2g fiber, 34mg cholesterol, 970mg sodium

Tex-Mex Macaroni & Cheese

A quick and easy casserole with a Southwestern flair—great for hurried weeknights.

8	ounces mostaccioli or other tube-shaped pasta
1	cup (4 ounces) shredded low-fat Monterey Jack cheese
½	cup finely chopped red or green bell pepper
2	jalapeño peppers, finely chopped
½	cup fat-free sour cream
½	cup fat-free milk
1	teaspoon onion powder
¾	teaspoon ground cumin, divided
½	teaspoon salt
1	cup chopped, seeded, Roma tomatoes
½	cup KRETSCHMER® Original Toasted Wheat Germ
2	tablespoons dry breadcrumbs
2	tablespoons 60% vegetable oil spread, melted

1. Prepare pasta according to package directions, omitting salt. Drain and set aside.

2. Preheat oven to 350°F. Lightly spray a 9 inch square baking dish with nonstick cooking spray.

3. In large bowl, combine pasta, cheese, bell pepper, and jalapeño pepper; spoon into baking dish. In same bowl, combine sour cream, milk, onion powder, ½ teaspoon cumin, and salt; mix well. Pour sauce over pasta mixture. Spoon chopped tomatoes evenly over top.

4. In small bowl, combine wheat germ, breadcrumbs, remaining ¼ teaspoon cumin, and vegetable oil spread; mix well. Sprinkle over tomatoes.

5. Bake in the preheated oven for 30 minutes or until heated through.

Yield: 5 servings.

Per serving: 355 calories, 18g protein, 48g carbohydrate, 11g fat, 4g fiber, 16mg cholesterol, 540mg sodium

healthy

submitted by: **Kretschmer® Wheat Germ**

Prep Time: 20 minutes
Cook Time: 30 minutes

What Other Cooks Have Done:
"Good taste. Double the sauce part, and you've got an easy, spicy meal without meat. Just make a nice tossed salad to go with it."

submitted by: **Boca**®

Prep Time: 20 minutes
Cook Time: 30 minutes

Test Kitchen Secret:

The spaghetti sauce in this contemporary twist on a traditional pasta bake provides a good source of vitamin A, and the mozzarella cheese is rich in calcium. For extra nutrition, add 1 (10 ounce) package frozen chopped spinach, thawed and drained, to ground burger mixture before spooning into baking dish.

Boca® Pasta Bake

A quick, easy, delicious supper that's perfect for family or friends.

8 ounces mostaccioli or penne pasta	¾ cup reduced-fat Parmesan-style grated topping, divided
1 (12 ounce) package frozen BOCA® Meatless Ground Burger	1 (8 ounce) package shredded reduced-fat mozzarella cheese
1 (28 ounce) jar spaghetti sauce	

1. Preheat oven to 375°F.
2. Cook pasta according to package directions; drain.
3. Combine ground burger, pasta, spaghetti sauce, and ½ cup grated topping.
4. Spoon into a 9x13 inch baking dish sprayed with nonstick cooking spray. Top with mozzarella cheese; sprinkle with remaining ¼ cup grated topping.
5. Bake in the preheated oven for 25 to 30 minutes or until thoroughly heated. **Yield:** 8 servings.

Per serving: 430 calories, 26g protein, 52g carbohydrate, 13g fat, 7g fiber, 25mg cholesterol, 1310mg sodium

submitted by: **Bush's Best® Beans**

Prep Time: 5 minutes
Cook Time: 55 minutes

Test Kitchen Secret:

For extra oomph, try using a flavored spaghetti sauce, such as onion and garlic or herb.

Bush's Best® Cheesy Pasta & Bean Bake

This easy-to-make family favorite will please kids and adults alike.

1 (16 ounce) package penne pasta	1 (26 ounce) jar spaghetti sauce
1 (14.5 ounce) can diced tomatoes	2 cups shredded mozzarella cheese
2 (16 ounce) cans BUSH'S BEST® Light or Dark Kidney Beans, rinsed and drained	

1. Preheat oven to 375°F. Grease a 2 quart baking dish.
2. Prepare pasta according to package directions. Drain and return to saucepan. Stir in tomatoes, BUSH'S BEST® Kidney Beans, and spaghetti sauce. Transfer to prepared dish and top with shredded mozzarella cheese.
3. Bake in the preheated oven for about 40 minutes or until cheese is melted and golden. **Yield:** 6 servings.

Per serving: 666 calories, 38g protein, 91g carbohydrate, 16g fat, 13g fiber, 43mg cholesterol, 1272mg sodium

Sunset Patio Pasta

Combine the great taste of grilled vegetables with seasoned pasta for the perfect summertime side dish.

8	ounces penne pasta
4	cups assorted vegetable pieces such as zucchini, yellow squash, bell pepper, mushrooms, and onions
4	tablespoons olive oil, divided
3	teaspoons McCORMICK® GRILL MATES® Montreal Chicken Seasoning, divided
2	tablespoons balsamic vinegar

1. Cook pasta according to package directions. Drain and set aside.
2. Toss vegetables with 1 tablespoon oil and 1 teaspoon GRILL MATES® Montreal Chicken Seasoning. Place vegetables in a grill basket or on skewers; grill until tender, about 8 to 10 minutes, turning frequently.
3. Combine balsamic vinegar, remaining oil, and remaining GRILL MATES® Montreal Chicken Seasoning in a large bowl. Add cooked pasta and vegetables and toss well. Serve warm or chilled. **Yield:** 8 servings.

Per serving: 183 calories, 5g protein, 25g carbohydrate, 8g fat, 2g fiber, 0mg cholesterol, 81mg sodium

party pleaser

submitted by: **McCormick® & Company**

Prep Time: 20 minutes
Cook Time: 10 minutes

What Other Cooks Have Done:
"This recipe was a hit! I was asked for the recipe at my book club meeting and again at a barbecue a few weeks later. The key is the grilled veggies. I also used portobello mushrooms and asparagus. The grill basket works great for this. Do not dress the salad until just before you eat. Best served at room temperature."

Grilled Chicken Caesar Pasta Salad

This pasta salad recreates the classic taste of a Caesar salad. Serve it with focaccia bread at a brunch or lunch party.

2	cups penne pasta
1	(10 ounce) package romaine salad blend
8	ounces fresh, whole-milk mozzarella cheese, diced
½	cup grated Romano cheese
½	cup pitted, oil-cured Moroccan (or Kalamata) olives, drained
1	teaspoon black pepper
4	TYSON® Fresh Boneless, Skinless Chicken Breasts
1⅓	cups bottled Caesar salad dressing, divided

1. Cook pasta according to package directions; rinse with cold water and drain well. In large bowl, combine pasta, romaine, mozzarella cheese, Romano cheese, olives, and pepper; toss to mix. Cover and chill. Meanwhile, preheat grill for medium heat.
2. Grill chicken 6 minutes; turn chicken over. Brush with 3 tablespoons salad dressing. Grill 5 to 7 more minutes or until internal juices run clear. (Or insert an instant-read meat thermometer in thickest part of chicken. Temperature should read 170°F.) Remove from grill. Brush with 3 tablespoons salad dressing.
3. Toss salad with remaining dressing; place on 4 serving plates. Slice chicken breasts and arrange evenly over salad. Refrigerate leftovers immediately. **Yield:** 4 servings.

Per serving: 827 calories, 50g protein, 33g carbohydrate, 54g fat, 3g fiber, 153mg cholesterol, 1547mg sodium

make-ahead

submitted by: **Tyson®**

Prep Time: 15 minutes
Cook Time: 15 minutes

Test Kitchen Secret:
Personalize your pasta salad using any garnish you'd normally add to a Caesar salad, such as croutons or grated Parmesan cheese.

Supreme Pasta Salad

Win compliments from all your friends with this easy, flavor-packed addition to any picnic, cook-out, or party.

make-ahead

submitted by: **McCormick® & Company**

Prep Time: 15 minutes
Cook Time: 15 minutes
Chill Time: 4 hours

Test Kitchen Secret:
When making this salad for a picnic, spoon pasta salad into disposable plastic containers for easy transport in your cooler. Bring along a colorful, large salad bowl for a pretty presentation.

16 ounces rotini, fusilli, or shell pasta
1 (8 ounce) bottle Italian- or Ranch-style salad dressing
¼ cup McCORMICK® SALAD SUPREME® Seasoning

5 cups assorted raw vegetables such as tomatoes, carrots, broccoli, and red onions

1. Cook pasta according to package directions. Rinse under cold water and drain well.
2. Place pasta in large salad bowl, add dressing and seasoning, and toss gently to coat.
3. Cut vegetables into bite-sized pieces. Add vegetables to pasta and toss gently. Cover and refrigerate at least 4 hours. **Yield:** 10 servings.

Per serving: 302 calories, 8g protein, 38g carbohydrate, 14g fat, 3g fiber, 51mg cholesterol, 419mg sodium

Pasta Salad with Ham & Peas

This easy, throw-together pasta salad is perfect for a brown bag lunch.

quick & easy

submitted by: **Cook's® Brand Ham**

Prep Time: 20 minutes
Cook Time: 10 minutes

Test Kitchen Secret:
To make quick work of the chives, just snip them with kitchen shears.

1 (16 ounce) package small shell pasta
2 cups COOK'S® Brand Bone-In Ham (cubed), leftover ham (shredded), or Ham Steak (cut into 1 inch cubes)
1 (8 ounce) carton plain low-fat yogurt

4 chives, finely sliced
Salt and freshly ground black pepper to taste
1 (10 ounce) package frozen peas, thawed
3 scallions, finely diced
2 large stalks celery, finely diced

1. Cook pasta according to package directions; drain and keep hot.
2. Heat ham according to package directions or warm leftover ham. In a large bowl, whisk together the yogurt, chives, and salt and pepper to taste. Add the ham, peas, scallions, and celery. Add hot pasta to the bowl with the rest of the ingredients. Toss gently and serve warm. **Yield:** 4 servings.

Per serving: 615 calories, 36g protein, 94g carbohydrate, 9g fat, 8g fiber, 45mg cholesterol, 1345mg sodium

Zesty Couscous Salad

This simple salad combines fresh zucchini and tomato with a lemony dressing, fresh basil, and feta cheese—a perfect use for vegetables from a summer garden.

1	(10 ounce) package NEAR EAST® Original Plain Couscous	2	large tomatoes, chopped
¼	teaspoon black pepper	1	medium zucchini, halved and thinly sliced
2	tablespoons lemon juice	½	cup fresh basil, cut into strips
3	tablespoons olive oil	⅓	cup sliced green onions
		¾	cup crumbled feta cheese

1. Prepare NEAR EAST® Couscous according to package directions, omitting butter or olive oil and adding black pepper with water.

2. In large bowl, combine prepared couscous, lemon juice, and olive oil. Add tomatoes, zucchini, basil, and green onions. Chill 4 hours or overnight.

3. Stir in cheese just before serving. **Yield:** 7 servings.

Per serving: 290 calories, 9g protein, 35g carbohydrate, 10g fat, 3g fiber, 15mg cholesterol, 190mg sodium

healthy

submitted by: **Near East®**

Prep Time: 20 minutes
Cook Time: 5 minutes
Chill Time: 4 hours

Test Kitchen Secret:
To make this salad a complete meal, just add thin slices of chicken or beef.

Classic Garden Couscous

After one bite of this fresh-tasting couscous salad, you'll make it a dinner table staple.

1	tablespoon olive oil	1	(5.9 ounce) package NEAR EAST® Parmesan Couscous Mix
2	cups diced skinless, boneless chicken breast		
1	clove garlic, minced	2	cups fresh or frozen broccoli florets, thawed and chopped
1¼	cups water	¼	cup crumbled feta cheese
2	tablespoons white cooking wine	1	cup chopped fresh tomato

1. In large skillet, heat olive oil over medium heat. Add chicken and garlic and cook for 5 to 8 minutes or until chicken is golden brown and no longer pink inside.

2. Stir in water, cooking wine, and contents of Spice Sack; bring to a boil. Stir in NEAR EAST® Couscous and broccoli; cover and remove from heat. Let stand 5 minutes. Stir in cheese and tomato just before serving. **Yield:** 6 servings.

Per serving: 220 calories, 19g protein, 23g carbohydrate, 6g fat, 2g fiber, 45mg cholesterol, 430mg sodium

quick & easy

submitted by: **Near East®**

Prep Time: 10 minutes
Cook Time: 10 minutes

Test Kitchen Secret:
To make this a vegetarian meal, substitute 1 (16 ounce) can of red kidney beans for the chicken.

Chicken with Tomato, Orange & Rosemary Couscous

Chicken served over a bed of couscous with zucchini and tomato makes for a quick and satisfying supper.

comfort food

submitted by: **Near East®**

Prep Time: 10 minutes
Cook Time: 20 minutes

Test Kitchen Secret:

The alcohol in the white wine will cook out, leaving behind just the flavor. However, you can omit the wine completely, if desired, and increase the water to 1¼ cups.

4   skinless, boneless chicken breast halves (about 1 pound)
Salt and freshly ground black pepper to taste
2   tablespoons olive oil
¼   cup dry white wine, such as Sauvignon Blanc
1   cup water
1   cup sliced zucchini, cut into ½ inch slices

1   (14.5 ounce) can chopped tomatoes, drained, or 1 cup chopped fresh tomatoes
1   teaspoon fresh or dried rosemary
1   (5.8 ounce) package NEAR EAST® Roasted Garlic & Olive Oil Couscous Mix
¾   cup peeled, seeded, and chopped orange

1. Season chicken with salt and pepper to taste. In a large skillet, heat olive oil over medium heat. Add chicken; cook 5 to 6 minutes on each side, or until no longer pink inside.

Chicken with Tomato, Orange & Rosemary Couscous

2. Meanwhile, in large saucepan over high heat, combine wine, 1 cup water, zucchini, tomatoes, and rosemary. Bring to a boil.

3. Stir in couscous and contents of Spice Sack. Remove from heat. Cover; let stand 5 minutes.

4. Fluff couscous lightly with a fork. Stir in chopped orange. Serve chicken with couscous. **Yield:** 4 servings.

Per serving: 350 calories, 27g protein, 40g carbohydrate, 9g fat, 4g fiber, 67mg cholesterol, 575mg sodium

Spicy Couscous with Orange Zest & Scallions

Wake up your senses with this spicy, orange-flavored couscous— a perfect accompaniment to chicken or fish.

1¼ cups water
2 teaspoons olive oil
1 teaspoon grated orange zest
½ teaspoon chile oil, or to taste
1 (5.8 ounce) package NEAR EAST® Roasted Garlic & Olive Oil Couscous Mix

1 scallion, sliced (green part only), about 2 tablespoons
¼ cup currants

1. In medium saucepan, bring 1¼ cups water, olive oil, orange zest, and chile oil to a boil.

2. Stir in couscous and contents of Spice Sack.

3. Cover; remove from heat. Let stand 5 minutes. Fluff with a fork.

4. Stir in scallions and currants. **Yield:** 4 servings.

Per serving: 182 calories, 5g protein, 28g carbohydrate, 4g fat, 2g fiber, 0mg cholesterol, 374mg sodium

healthy

submitted by: **Near East®**

Prep Time: 10 minutes
Cook Time: 5 minutes

Test Kitchen Secret:
Chile oil is vegetable oil that contains whole or ground bits of dried red chiles steeped in the oil to impart flavor and color. Chile oil will keep six months at room temperature but will retain its potency longer if refrigerated. Find it in Asian groceries and many supermarkets.

Apricot Ginger Couscous

A sweet and spicy side for the holiday table that's perfect with turkey, pork, and Cornish hens.

1¼ cups water
1 tablespoon butter or olive oil
1 teaspoon grated fresh ginger or ¼ teaspoon ground ginger
⅛ teaspoon ground cinnamon

1 (5.8 ounce) package NEAR EAST® Roasted Garlic & Olive Oil Couscous Mix
½ cup chopped dried apricots
½ cup raisins or ⅓ cup currants
⅓ cup sliced green onions

1. In a medium saucepan, combine 1¼ cups water, butter, ginger, cinnamon, and contents of Spice Sack; bring to a boil.

2. Stir in couscous, apricots, raisins, and green onions. Cover; remove from heat. Let stand 5 minutes. Fluff lightly with a fork. **Yield:** 4 servings.

Per serving: 270 calories, 7g protein, 55g carbohydrate, 4g fat, 2g fiber, 8mg cholesterol, 400mg sodium

holiday fare

submitted by: **Near East®**

Prep Time: 10 minutes
Cook Time: 10 minutes

Test Kitchen Secret:
If you're hosting a large dinner party, this quick side dish can easily be doubled. Just double all ingredients and prepare as directed in a large saucepan, keeping the cook time the same.

submitted by: **Cook's® Brand Ham**

Prep Time: 15 minutes
Cook Time: 15 minutes

Test Kitchen Secret:
Refrigerate this curry dish overnight to let the flavors infuse the ham, vegetables, and couscous.

Curried Ham & Vegetable Couscous

Take advantage of your grocery's salad bar, if available, and load up on the fresh veggies you'll need for this curry dish.

2½	cups COOK'S® Brand Bone-In Ham (diced), leftover ham (shredded), or Ham Steak (cut into strips or diced)
2	tablespoons butter
2	cups diced fresh vegetables such as bell peppers, broccoli florets, julienne carrots, and red onion
1½	teaspoons curry powder
⅛	teaspoon cayenne pepper (optional)
1	(14 ounce) can chicken or vegetable broth
¼	cup raisins
1	cup uncooked couscous
	Toppings: chopped apples, toasted sliced almonds, chopped cilantro, plain yogurt (optional)

1. Heat ham according to package directions or warm leftover ham.

2. Melt butter in a large saucepan over medium heat. Add vegetables; sauté 5 minutes or until vegetables are tender. Add curry powder and cayenne pepper, if desired; sauté 1 minute.

3. Add broth and raisins; bring to a boil. Stir in ham and couscous; mix well. Cover; turn off heat and let stand 5 minutes or until liquid is absorbed. Serve with toppings, if desired. **Yield:** 4 servings.

Per serving: 433 calories, 28g protein, 46g carbohydrate, 15g fat, 5g fiber, 67mg cholesterol, 1808mg sodium

Curried Ham & Vegetable Couscous

Couscous Salad with Chickpeas, Dates & Cinnamon

holiday fare

submitted by: **McCormick® & Company**

Prep Time: 20 minutes
Cook Time: 15 minutes

What Other Cooks Have Done:

"This has become a favorite for my husband and me; we eat it almost once a week! It tastes wonderful, and it is a great way to get more fiber in your diet. I like to add just a touch of rice vinegar to give it a little more tang."

Dates, carrots, and toasted pine nuts add color and complexity to this salad created by Chef Suzanne Goin of Luques in Los Angeles, California.

3	green onions	1	(10 ounce) package couscous
1	tablespoon olive oil	3	tablespoons white wine vinegar
1	(14 ounce) can chicken broth	¾	teaspoon salt, divided
1	teaspoon McCORMICK® Gourmet Collection™ Saigon Cinnamon	6	tablespoons olive oil
		1	(19 ounce) can chickpeas, rinsed and drained
½	teaspoon McCORMICK® Gourmet Collection™ Coarse Grind Black Pepper, divided	2	cups shredded carrots
		1	cup dates, pitted and roughly chopped
¼	teaspoon McCORMICK® Gourmet Collection™ Ground Cayenne Red Pepper	¼	cup pine nuts, toasted
		2	tablespoons chopped fresh cilantro (optional)

1. Finely dice white end of green onions. Slice green parts of green onions and reserve for salad. Heat olive oil in a medium saucepan, and gently cook white onion pieces 5 to 7 minutes. Stir in chicken broth, cinnamon, ¼ teaspoon black pepper, and red pepper. Bring to a boil; add couscous. Cover and remove pan from heat. Let stand 5 minutes.
2. Whisk together vinegar, ½ teaspoon salt, and olive oil in a small bowl.
3. Fluff couscous with a fork; put in a large bowl. Toss with sliced green onions, chickpeas, carrots, dates, pine nuts, remaining ¼ teaspoon black pepper, and remaining ¼ teaspoon salt; add vinaigrette and toss again. Serve right away or chill. Garnish with chopped cilantro, if desired.
Yield: 8 servings.

Per serving: 424 calories, 10g protein, 63g carbohydrate, 16g fat, 8g fiber, 0mg cholesterol, 655mg sodium

Fast Fried Rice

A great use for leftover rice, this dish easily stands alone with the addition of Boca® Meatless Ground Burger.

1	teaspoon oil	2	cups cooked rice
1	(1 cup) pouch frozen BOCA® Meatless Ground Burger	1	(6 ounce) can sliced mushrooms, drained
6	green onions with tops, chopped	2	tablespoons reduced-sodium soy sauce
1	egg, lightly beaten		

1. Heat oil in large nonstick skillet over medium-high heat.

2. Add ground burger and onions; cook and stir 3 minutes. Spoon burger mixture to one side of skillet. Add egg to other side of skillet; cook until set, stirring constantly.

3. Add remaining ingredients; mix all ingredients in skillet until well blended. Cook 5 minutes or until heated through, stirring frequently. **Yield:** 4 servings.

Per serving: 200 calories, 11g protein, 35g carbohydrate, 3g fat, 4g fiber, 55mg cholesterol, 510mg sodium

kid-friendly

submitted by: **Boca®**

Prep Time: 10 minutes
Cook Time: 10 minutes

Test Kitchen Secret:
If you don't have leftover rice for this dish, plan ahead and cook the rice the day before. Use ¼ cup egg substitute to cut cholesterol.

Bush's Best® Baja Rice & Beans

Black beans and pinto beans are spiced up with green chilies to create this Tex-Mex favorite.

1	medium green bell pepper, diced	1	(16 ounce) can BUSH'S BEST® Pinto Beans, rinsed and drained
1	medium onion, chopped	1	(10 ounce) can diced tomatoes with green chilies, undrained
2	cloves garlic, minced		
1	tablespoon olive oil	1	(10 ounce) package frozen whole kernel corn, thawed
1	(14 ounce) can chicken broth	1	tablespoon red wine vinegar
½	teaspoon ground cumin	1	cup hot cooked rice
1	(15 ounce) can BUSH'S BEST® Black Beans, rinsed and drained	6	chicken breasts, cooked

1. In large skillet, sauté green bell pepper, onion, and garlic in oil for 3 minutes. Stir in broth and cumin. Bring to a boil. Reduce heat; cover and simmer for 15 minutes. Add BUSH'S BEST® Black Beans, BUSH'S BEST® Pinto Beans, tomatoes, corn, and vinegar. Heat thoroughly. Serve over rice and top with chicken. **Yield:** 6 servings.

Per serving: 387 calories, 38g protein, 45g carbohydrate, 7g fat, 10g fiber, 73mg cholesterol, 1024mg sodium

make-ahead

submitted by: **Bush's Best® Beans**

Prep Time: 30 minutes
Cook Time: 20 minutes

Test Kitchen Secret:
This dish can be easily made a day or two ahead of time. Store the bean mixture in the refrigerator until a half hour before dinnertime. You can reheat the bean mixture in a saucepan on the stove while the chicken and rice cook.

Bush's Best® Red Beans & Rice

Bush's Best® Red Beans & Rice

This version of the traditional recipe is so easy and delicious, it's sure to become your family's favorite. Serve it with cornbread.

1   tablespoon vegetable oil
1   medium onion, diced
1   green bell pepper, diced
2   stalks celery, sliced
3   cloves garlic, minced
14 ounces fully cooked sausage (such as andouille), cut into ½ inch slices
3   (16 ounce) cans BUSH'S BEST® Kidney Beans, with liquid
2   (14.5 ounce) cans diced tomatoes with basil
1½ teaspoons ground cumin
1   (6 ounce) can tomato paste
    Hot sauce to taste
4   cups hot cooked rice, kept warm

1. Heat oil in a large soup pot over medium heat. Add onion, bell pepper, and celery, and sauté for 5 minutes. Add remaining ingredients except hot sauce and rice. Cover and simmer for 10 to 15 minutes. Add hot sauce to taste. Serve over hot cooked rice. **Yield:** 6 servings.

Per serving: 831 calories, 33g protein, 105g carbohydrate, 29g fat, 18g fiber, 68mg cholesterol, 1975mg sodium

quick & easy

submitted by: **Bush's Best® Beans**

Prep Time: 10 minutes
Cook Time: 20 minutes

What Other Cooks Have Done:
"This is an awesome recipe, but I did a little changing. I only used one can of diced tomatoes and only two cans of beans. I also used turkey kielbasa. Everything else was the same, and it was fantastic! It was tomatoey but very good. Great flavor."

Parmesan Chicken & Rice with Peas

Creamy cheese and tender-crisp peas turn the standard chicken and rice combo into something special.

1   tablespoon olive oil
4   TYSON® Individually Fresh Frozen® Boneless, Skinless Chicken Breasts
    Salt and freshly ground black pepper to taste (optional)
3   cloves garlic, minced
1½ cups converted-style rice
2   (14 ounce) cans low-sodium chicken broth
1   cup shredded Parmesan cheese
1   cup frozen peas, thawed

1. Heat oil in large skillet over medium-high heat. Add chicken and cook 5 to 7 minutes or until light brown; season with salt and pepper to taste, if desired. Add garlic; cook briefly. Stir in rice and chicken broth. Bring to a boil.
2. Cover and reduce heat; simmer 20 minutes or until chicken is done (internal temperature of 170°F). Remove from heat; stir in Parmesan cheese and peas. Cover and let stand 5 minutes before serving. **Yield:** 4 servings.

Per serving: 515 calories, 53g protein, 38g carbohydrate, 16g fat, 2g fiber, 109mg cholesterol, 916mg sodium

comfort food

submitted by: **Tyson®**

Prep Time: 10 minutes
Cook Time: 30 minutes

What Other Cooks Have Done:
"An impressive (and great-looking) dish that is exceptionally easy to make. I substituted grated Parmesan (spaghetti topping) for shredded Parmesan, and it tasted great."

Roasted Vegetable Pilaf

Rice pilaf gets dressed up with the addition of roasted vegetables in a balsamic vinaigrette.

holiday fare

submitted by: **Near East®**

Prep Time: 10 minutes
Cook Time: 20 minutes

Test Kitchen Secret:

If you're out of balsamic vinegar, you can use an equal amount of red wine vinegar instead.

2	tablespoons olive oil		2	large plum tomatoes, sliced
2	tablespoons balsamic vinegar		1	medium zucchini, cut in half and lengthwise
2	cloves garlic, minced		1	small red onion, sliced
1	teaspoon dried thyme			Fresh thyme sprig (optional)
1	(6.09 ounce) package NEAR EAST® Rice Pilaf Mix			

1. Preheat oven to 400°F.

2. In a small bowl, combine oil, vinegar, garlic, and thyme. Set aside.

3. Prepare NEAR EAST® Rice according to package directions, omitting butter or olive oil.

4. While rice cooks, place vegetables in a medium pan and drizzle with oil mixture. Bake in the preheated oven for 8 to 10 minutes or until golden brown. Stir vegetables into rice mixture. Garnish with fresh thyme sprig, if desired. **Yield:** 5 servings.

Per serving: 190 calories, 4g protein, 31g carbohydrate, 6g fat, 2g fiber, 0mg cholesterol, 510mg sodium

Santa Fe Chicken Pilaf

This spiced-up rice pilaf with corn, fresh tomato, and pieces of chicken is a simple and delicious one-dish meal.

quick & easy

submitted by: **Near East®**

Prep Time: 10 minutes
Cook Time: 20 minutes

What Other Cooks Have Done:

"I prefer to serve this as the stuffing for burritos. Spread sour cream and guacamole on tortillas, add some of the Santa Fe Chicken Pilaf, and top with cheese."

1	(6.09 ounce) package NEAR EAST® Rice Pilaf Mix		½	cup chopped fresh tomato
1	(14 ounce) can fat-free, low-sodium chicken broth		1	(8.75 ounce) can whole kernel corn
1	teaspoon ground cumin		1	cup canned black beans, rinsed and drained
1	cup canned seasoned diced tomatoes			Shredded Cheddar cheese (optional)
2	cups chicken strips, cooked and cut into 1 inch chunks			

1. Prepare NEAR EAST® Rice according to package directions, except use chicken broth instead of water and add cumin with contents of Spice Sack.

2. Stir next 5 ingredients into rice mixture. Top with Cheddar cheese, if desired. **Yield:** 6 servings.

Per serving: 270 calories, 20g protein, 38g carbohydrate, 5g fat, 4g fiber, 45mg cholesterol, 1200mg sodium

Roasted Vegetable Pilaf

Roasted Butternut Squash, Olive & Parmesan Risotto

holiday fare

submitted by: **Lindsay® Olives**

Prep Time: 15 minutes
Cook Time: 1 hour 40 minutes

What Other Cooks Have Done:
"I went to a restaurant and had a very similar dish that I loved, so I came home and was pleasantly surprised to find this recipe. I don't like onions, so I left those out, but added some mushrooms. I used Asiago cheese instead of Parmesan."

Lindsay® Olives brighten the mellow tones of roasted butternut squash and Parmesan cheese risotto for an unforgettable, flavorful combination.

1 small butternut squash, pierced with tip of a knife	1 cup grated Parmesan cheese
2 tablespoons butter	2 tablespoons chopped fresh Italian parsley
1 medium onion, chopped	Salt and freshly ground black pepper to taste (optional)
4 cloves garlic, minced	
1 cup Arborio rice	
2 cups warm chicken stock	
1 (6 ounce) jar LINDSAY® Sicilian Pitted Olives or LINDSAY® Spanish Olives Stuffed with Pimiento, drained and halved	

1. Preheat oven to 400°F.
2. Place squash on baking sheet; roast in the preheated oven for 1 hour or until tender. Cool slightly; halve lengthwise. Remove and discard seeds; scoop out flesh from skin. Chop flesh; set aside.
3. Melt butter in a large saucepan over medium heat. Add onion and garlic; sauté for 3 minutes. Add rice; stir to coat grains with butter. Stirring constantly, add stock, ½ cup at a time, adding more stock only when the previous amount has been absorbed. When the rice is cooked, about 30 minutes, stir in the squash, olives, cheese, and parsley. Cook and stir for 4 minutes until the cheese is melted and mixture is hot throughout. Season with salt and pepper to taste, if desired. **Yield:** 4 servings.

Per serving: 601 calories, 19g protein, 89g carbohydrate, 22g fat, 12g fiber, 36mg cholesterol, 2028mg sodium

Creamy Risotto Primavera

holiday fare

submitted by: **Hormel Foods Corporation**

Prep Time: 20 minutes
Cook Time: 45 minutes

Test Kitchen Secret:
To ensure a creamy texture, never rinse the rice before making risotto. Rinsing washes away the starch that's needed to create risotto's thick texture.

This luxurious risotto will match any Italian feast. Arborio rice is cooked in chicken broth, then mixed with two kinds of cheese for a sensational side dish.

2 tablespoons olive oil	½ cup sherry or white cooking wine
1½ cups sliced fresh mushrooms	1 cup shredded Fontina cheese
½ cup chopped onion	¼ cup grated Parmesan cheese
½ cup diced carrots	Chopped fresh parsley (optional)
2 cloves garlic, minced	Diced fresh tomato (optional)
1 cup Arborio rice	
3 cups water	
1 tablespoon HERB-OX® Chicken Flavored Bouillon Granules	

Roasted Butternut Squash, Olive & Parmesan Risotto

1. Heat oil in a large saucepan; sauté mushrooms, onion, carrots, and garlic until onion is tender. Add uncooked rice. Cook over medium heat, stirring constantly, 3 to 5 minutes or until rice is golden brown.
2. Meanwhile, in another saucepan, bring water, bouillon granules, and cooking wine to a boil. Slowly add 1 cup of the broth to the rice mixture, stirring constantly. Continue to cook over medium heat, stirring constantly, until liquid is absorbed. Continue to add ½ cup of broth at a time to rice mixture, stirring constantly, until all broth has been added and absorbed and the rice mixture is creamy. Add cheeses and stir until well blended. Garnish with fresh parsley and diced tomato, if desired.
Yield: 6 servings.

Per serving: 307 calories, 11g protein, 34g carbohydrate, 13g fat, 2g fiber, 29mg cholesterol, 428mg sodium

**Tomato & Olive Soup with
Basil Cream, page 198**

soups &
sandwiches

Make tonight a soup-and-sandwich kind of night with this collection of **warming** soups and stews and **quick-and-easy** sandwiches. Whether it's a light bisque and veggie wrap or a **hearty** chowder and burgers, you'll find just the recipe for dinner or lunch.

comfort food

submitted by: Lindsay® Olives

Prep Time: 15 minutes
Cook Time: 35 minutes

Test Kitchen Secret:

Two 4.25 ounce cans of Lindsay® Black Ripe Chopped Olives will yield enough for this recipe and save you the step of chopping the olives.

Tomato & Olive Soup with Basil Cream *(pictured on page 196)*

Lindsay® Black Ripe Pitted Olives and basil cream infuse this traditional slow-simmered tomato soup with unforgettable flavor. Simply prepared with ingredients usually on hand, this soup will be the mark of any memorable occasion.

2 tablespoons olive oil	1½ cups finely chopped LINDSAY® Black Ripe Pitted Olives, drained
1 small onion, chopped	
3 cloves garlic, minced	
1 teaspoon fennel seed	½ cup whipping cream
1 teaspoon dried oregano	2 tablespoons minced fresh basil
1 (28 ounce) can crushed tomatoes in tomato puree	Finely chopped LINDSAY® Black Ripe Pitted Olives (optional)
3 cups chicken broth	

1. Heat oil in a large saucepan over medium heat. Add onion, garlic, fennel, and oregano; cover and simmer 5 minutes, stirring occasionally.
2. Add tomatoes and broth; cover and simmer 15 minutes. Stir in 1½ cups olives; cover and simmer 15 more minutes. Ladle soup into serving bowls. Combine cream and basil; drizzle over soup and garnish with additional olives, if desired. **Yield:** 6 servings.

Per serving: 215 calories, 4g protein, 11g carbohydrate, 18g fat, 2g fiber, 27mg cholesterol, 654mg sodium

holiday fare

submitted by: Hormel Foods Corporation

Prep Time: 20 minutes
Cook Time: 35 minutes

What Other Cooks Have Done:

"I didn't have any half-and-half, so I just used a little milk and a dollop of cream cheese. It was so filling and creamy. I felt so healthy after eating it—it's loaded with vitamins and minerals."

Butternut Bisque

This warm, creamy soup made from butternut squash is a perfect way to embrace the start of the fall season.

2 tablespoons butter	1 cup half-and-half
1 large onion, diced	½ teaspoon ground allspice
1½ pounds butternut squash, peeled and cut into 1 inch cubes (about 4 cups)	⅛ teaspoon salt
	⅛ teaspoon ground white pepper
	Sour cream (optional)
2 cups water	
2 teaspoons HERB-OX® Chicken Flavored Bouillon Granules	

1. In a large saucepan, melt butter. Add onion and sauté until slightly softened, about 2 minutes. Add squash, water, and bouillon granules. Cover saucepan and bring mixture to a boil. Reduce heat and simmer 20 to 25 minutes or until squash is tender. Remove from heat and let cool for 15 minutes.
2. Place squash mixture into a food processor or blender (in batches, if necessary) and process until smooth. Return pureed squash to saucepan. Add half-and-half, allspice, salt, and pepper. Heat over medium heat, stirring constantly, until warmed through. Ladle soup into warm bowls and serve. If desired, place small dollops of sour cream in a circular fashion on

Butternut Bisque

top of soup. Gently run a toothpick through sour cream to create a swirled effect. **Yield:** 6 servings.

Per serving: 153 calories, 3g protein, 17g carbohydrate, 9g fat, 4g fiber, 26mg cholesterol, 172mg sodium

Bush's Best® Pasta Fagiole

Bush's Best® Pasta Fagiole

A truly classic Italian dinner made easy.

make-ahead

submitted by: **Sam Gugino** on behalf of **Bush's Best® Beans**

Prep Time: 20 minutes
Cook Time: 25 minutes

Test Kitchen Secret:
Substitute Bush's Best® Cannellini Beans for the Great Northern beans, if desired.

3 tablespoons olive oil
1 medium onion, chopped
4 cloves garlic, chopped
1 jalapeño pepper, minced
1 (14.5 ounce) can stewed tomatoes
2 (15.5 ounce) cans BUSH'S BEST® Great Northern Beans, rinsed and drained
6 cups chicken or vegetable broth
1 (8 ounce) box elbow macaroni or orzo
¼ cup chopped Italian parsley
Salt and freshly ground black pepper to taste
3 slices cooked bacon, crumbled (optional)
Crushed red pepper flakes (optional)
Shredded Parmesan cheese (optional)

1. Heat olive oil in a large sauté pan over medium heat. Add onion, garlic, and jalapeño to pan. Cook until onion is soft but not browned, 4 to 5 minutes. Coarsely puree tomatoes in food processor. Stir tomatoes, BUSH'S BEST® Great Northern Beans, and broth into onion mixture. Bring to a boil over high heat, stirring occasionally.
2. Add pasta and return to a boil over high heat. Reduce heat and simmer, stirring occasionally, 8 to 10 minutes. Add parsley and salt and pepper to taste. Serve warm in soup bowls. Top with crumbled bacon, red pepper flakes, and cheese, if desired. **Yield:** 6 servings.

Per serving: 392 calories, 16g protein, 58g carbohydrate, 10g fat, 10g fiber, 1mg cholesterol, 1718mg sodium

Bush's Best® Cajun Black Bean Soup

Cajun spices distinguish this black bean soup with superior flavor.

quick & easy

submitted by: **Bush's Best® Beans**

Prep Time: 8 minutes
Cook Time: 20 minutes

Test Kitchen Secret:
If you like your soup a little on the spicy side, increase the chili powder and top with pepper jack cheese.

2 tablespoons vegetable oil
1 onion, chopped
3 cloves garlic, chopped
1 teaspoon ground cumin
1 tablespoon chili powder
½ teaspoon dried oregano
3 (15 ounce) cans BUSH'S BEST® Black Beans
Black pepper to taste
Salsa (optional)
Shredded cheese (optional)

1. Heat oil in a large pot over medium heat. Add onion and cook 5 minutes. Stir in garlic, cumin, chili powder, and oregano.
2. Puree 1 can of BUSH'S BEST® Black Beans and add to pot. Add second can of beans (do not puree). Drain last can of beans and add to pot (do not puree). Reduce heat and simmer for 15 minutes, stirring often. Add black pepper to taste. Garnish with salsa and shredded cheese, if desired. **Yield:** 6 servings.

Per serving: 258 calories, 14g protein, 37g carbohydrate, 9g fat, 13g fiber, 9mg cholesterol, 890mg sodium

Hearty Italian
Minestrone

Hearty Italian Minestrone

comfort food

submitted by: **Hormel Foods Corporation**

Prep Time: 20 minutes
Cook Time: 45 minutes

Test Kitchen Secret:

Fill this hearty soup with your favorite seasonal vegetables. Summer squash, fresh green beans, and fresh button or portobello mushrooms add even more earthy flavors.

This filling and nutritious soup is a great meal any time of the year.

7   cups water
2½   tablespoons HERB-OX®
     Beef Flavored Bouillon
     Granules
2   cups coarsely chopped cabbage
1   (14.5 ounce) can diced
     tomatoes with basil, garlic,
     and oregano
1   medium onion, chopped
1   medium carrot, halved
     lengthwise and diagonally
     sliced
1   tablespoon Italian-style
     seasoning
1½   cups frozen French-cut green
     beans

1   zucchini, halved lengthwise
     and quartered
½   cup ditalini or small shell pasta
1   (15 ounce) can red kidney
     beans, drained
1   cup HORMEL® sliced
     pepperoni, quartered
     Garlic salt to taste
     Black pepper to taste
     Refrigerated prepared pesto
     (optional)
     Shredded Parmesan cheese
     (optional)

1. In a large stockpot, combine first 7 ingredients. Bring to a boil. Reduce heat to low and simmer, partially covered, for 20 minutes. Add green beans, zucchini, and pasta. Simmer, uncovered, for 15 more minutes or until vegetables and pasta are tender. Stir in beans and pepperoni. Heat until warmed through, about 2 minutes. Season to taste with garlic salt and pepper. If desired, serve with pesto and Parmesan cheese. **Yield:** 10 servings.

Per serving: 213 calories, 10g protein, 18g carbohydrate, 11g fat, 5g fiber, 19mg cholesterol, 1306mg sodium

Western Bean & Burger Soup

Boca® Ground Burger and black beans team up in this soup to offer an excellent source of fiber with the added bonus of being low in fat. Tomatoes with chilies, corn, garlic, and onion round out the satisfying flavor in this thirty-minute soup.

1	(15 ounce) can black beans, drained	3	cups water
1	(14.5 ounce) can diced tomatoes with green chilies, undrained	1	cup frozen whole kernel corn
		1	cup chopped onion
1	(12 ounce) package frozen BOCA® Meatless Ground Burger	3	cloves garlic, minced
		1	tablespoon ground cumin
		½	teaspoon hot pepper sauce
		½	teaspoon salt (optional)

1. Mix all ingredients in a large saucepan or Dutch oven.
2. Bring to boil over medium-high heat; cover. Reduce heat to low; simmer 15 minutes. **Yield:** 8 servings.

Per serving: 140 calories, 13g protein, 22g carbohydrate, 1g fat, 7g fiber, 0mg cholesterol, 470mg sodium

healthy

submitted by: **Boca®**

Prep Time: 10 minutes
Cook Time: 20 minutes

Test Kitchen Secret:
Mix ½ cup reduced-fat sour cream with 1 or 2 minced chipotle peppers in adobo sauce. For a great topping, add a dollop to each bowl of hot soup just before serving.

Quick Italian Meatball Soup

Made with ingredients on hand in the pantry, this soup takes the chill away on a cold winter's night.

Meatballs

1	pound ground turkey breast or lean ground beef
½	cup KRETSCHMER® Original Toasted Wheat Germ
1	egg white
¼	cup water
1½	teaspoons Italian-style seasoning
½	teaspoon salt (optional)
¼	teaspoon freshly ground black pepper

Soup

2	(14 ounce) cans low-sodium chicken broth
1	(14.5 ounce) can Italian-style diced tomatoes
½	cup (2 ounces) small soup pasta, such as tiny bow ties, ditalini, or shells
5	ounces fresh spinach leaves, coarsely chopped (3½ cups, packed)
¼	cup grated Parmesan cheese

1. Preheat oven to 425°F. Combine all meatball ingredients and shape into 1¼ inch meatballs. Place in a shallow pan sprayed with nonstick cooking spray. Bake in the preheated oven for 10 minutes.
2. Meanwhile, in a large saucepan, combine broth and tomatoes. Cover; bring to a boil. Stir in pasta. Cover and simmer 5 minutes. Add meatballs. Simmer, uncovered, 5 more minutes or until pasta is tender. Stir in spinach. Remove from heat. Let stand 2 to 3 minutes. Ladle soup into bowls. Sprinkle each serving with Parmesan cheese. **Yield:** 6 servings.

Per serving: 222 calories, 30g protein, 15g carbohydrate, 4g fat, 3g fiber, 61mg cholesterol, 518mg sodium

kid-friendly

submitted by: **Kretschmer® Wheat Germ**

Prep Time: 15 minutes
Cook Time: 15 minutes

Test Kitchen Secret:
If you get tired of dirtying up the grater when a recipe calls for only a small amount of grated cheese, then grate an entire block at a time. Use what's needed for the recipe and refrigerate or freeze the rest.

Mexican Spiced Turkey Tortilla Soup

submitted by: **Hormel Foods Corporation**

Prep Time: 15 minutes
Cook Time: 15 minutes

What Other Cooks Have Done:

"This went over well with a crowd of guys, and they finished the pot off. I added more cayenne because we like things spicy. I will be using this recipe again for leftover Thanksgiving turkey."

A sensationally spiced turkey soup with everyone's favorite Mexican flavors. Serve with a generous amount of shredded cheese and tortilla chips on top.

1	tablespoon olive oil	1	(10 ounce) can tomatoes with green chilies
1	onion, chopped		
1	(4 ounce) can chopped green chilies, drained	2	cups cooked turkey breast, cut into bite-sized pieces
1	teaspoon chili powder	1	cup frozen corn, thawed
1	tablespoon ground cumin	⅓	cup chopped fresh cilantro
1	clove garlic, minced	1⅓	cups shredded Monterey Jack cheese
½	teaspoon dried oregano		
¼	teaspoon cayenne pepper		Tortilla chips (optional)
6	cups water		
6	HERB-OX® Chicken Flavored Bouillon Cubes		

1. Heat oil in a large saucepan over medium-low heat. Add onion and cook 4 minutes. Add green chilies, chili powder, cumin, garlic, oregano, and cayenne pepper. Cook and stir 1 minute. Stir in water, bouillon cubes, and tomatoes with green chilies. Bring to a boil. Add turkey and simmer 3 minutes. Add corn and simmer 1 minute. Stir in cilantro. Ladle soup into bowls. Sprinkle each serving with cheese and chips, if desired. **Yield:** 6 servings.

Per serving: 299 calories, 24g protein, 17g carbohydrate, 15g fat, 3g fiber, 66mg cholesterol, 1760mg sodium

Potato Ham Soup

submitted by: **Cook's® Brand Ham**

Prep Time: 30 minutes
Cook Time: 30 minutes

Test Kitchen Secret:

Use any firm, waxy potato, like red-skinned, for this recipe.

Potatoes and savory ham star in this creamy, heart-warming soup.

2	cups peeled and diced potatoes	3	cups milk, divided
2	cups water	¼	cup butter, melted
½	cup diced onion	½	cup chicken broth
1	cup diced celery	2	cups COOK'S® Brand Bone-In Ham (cubed), leftover ham (shredded), or Ham Steak (cubed)
1	teaspoon salt		
½	teaspoon black pepper		
⅔	cup all-purpose flour		

1. Combine potatoes, water, onion, celery, salt, and pepper in a large saucepan. Simmer until vegetables are tender.
2. Combine flour and 1 cup milk, blending well. Add milk mixture, butter, chicken broth, ham, and remaining milk to vegetables. Simmer over medium heat for about 20 minutes. Cool soup slightly to thicken before serving. **Yield:** 6 servings.

Per serving: 317 calories, 18g protein, 29g carbohydrate, 15g fat, 2g fiber, 57mg cholesterol, 1333mg sodium

Bush's Best® Florentine Cannellini One Pot

Three types of beans are combined with bacon, dried tomatoes, and spices to create a hearty meal with the flair of Italian soup.

4	slices bacon, chopped		3	(14.5 ounce) cans chicken broth
3	cloves garlic, minced		½	cup dried tomatoes, cut into thin strips
1	medium onion, chopped		1	teaspoon sun-dried basil
1	(14 ounce) can chopped spinach, drained			Crushed red pepper flakes

4 slices bacon, chopped
3 cloves garlic, minced
1 medium onion, chopped
1 (14 ounce) can chopped spinach, drained
1 (15.5 ounce) can BUSH'S BEST® Cannellini Beans, rinsed and drained
1 (16 ounce) can BUSH'S BEST® Light Red Kidney Beans, rinsed and drained
1 (16 ounce) can BUSH'S BEST® Dark Red Kidney Beans, rinsed and drained

3 (14.5 ounce) cans chicken broth
½ cup dried tomatoes, cut into thin strips
1 teaspoon sun-dried basil
Crushed red pepper flakes
Salt
Shredded Parmesan cheese (optional)
Crispy French-fried onions (optional)

1. Cook bacon over high heat in a large stockpot. Add garlic and onion; sauté until browned. Mix in spinach and sauté 2 minutes. Add next 6 ingredients and simmer 10 minutes. Season to taste with red pepper flakes and salt.

2. Top with cheese and crispy onions, if desired. **Yield:** 8 servings.

Per serving: 285 calories, 16g protein, 35g carbohydrate, 9g fat, 11g fiber, 6mg cholesterol, 1361mg sodium

Boca® Sausage, Barley & Bean Soup

Making a hearty bowl of low-fat, cholesterol-free bean soup has never been this easy—or this delicious.

1 (10 ounce) package frozen BOCA® Meatless Smoked Sausage
4 cups water
1 (15.5 ounce) can Great Northern beans, rinsed and drained
1 (14.5 ounce) can stewed tomatoes

1 medium onion, chopped
2 stalks celery, sliced (about ½ cup)
2 medium carrots, sliced (about ½ cup)
½ cup quick-cooking barley
2 teaspoons Worcestershire sauce
½ teaspoon dried basil
Hot pepper sauce (optional)

1. Cut sausage into ¼ inch thick slices.

2. Place sausage and all remaining ingredients except hot pepper sauce in a Dutch oven or large saucepan. Cover and bring to a boil.

3. Reduce heat to medium-low; simmer 15 minutes or until vegetables are tender. Season to taste with hot pepper sauce, if desired. **Yield:** 6 servings.

Per serving: 230 calories, 16g protein, 32g carbohydrate, 5g fat, 7g fiber, 0mg cholesterol, 650mg sodium

Shortcut Minestrone Soup

Minestrone soup in thirty minutes! This healthy soup is laced with spinach, tomatoes, onions, and carrots. Serve with breadsticks and a salad for a complete meal.

quick & easy

submitted by: **Boca**®

Prep Time: 10 minutes
Cook Time: 20 minutes

Test Kitchen Secret:

Substitute elbow macaroni for the bow tie pasta. Remove sausage from freezer 5 to 10 minutes before slicing, or thaw slightly in microwave before slicing.

2	quarts water	2	medium carrots, sliced
2	(14.5 ounce) cans diced tomatoes, undrained	1	medium onion, chopped
1	(10 ounce) package frozen chopped spinach	1	cup bow tie pasta Grated Parmesan cheese (optional)
1	(10 ounce) package frozen BOCA® Meatless Italian Sausage, cut into ½ inch slices		

1. Place all ingredients except Parmesan cheese in a stock pot or large Dutch oven.

2. Bring to a boil over medium-high heat, stirring occasionally. Reduce heat to medium-low; simmer 15 minutes or until carrots are tender, stirring occasionally.

3. Serve sprinkled with Parmesan cheese, if desired. **Yield:** 8 servings.

Per serving: 150 calories, 11g protein, 22g carbohydrate, 3g fat, 4g fiber, 0mg cholesterol, 490mg sodium

Old Bay® Maryland Crab Soup

Lively and flavorful, Old Bay® Maryland Crab Soup is oh so good!

comfort food

submitted by: **McCormick**® **& Company**

Prep Time: 10 minutes
Cook Time: 20 minutes

What Other Cooks Have Done:

"I grew up in Baltimore and worked on the Eastern Shore of Maryland in a crab house for four years. This recipe is very close to what we served there. The Old Bay® is essential, and I doubled the amount because we like it spicy!"

1	(28 ounce) can whole tomatoes, cut into small pieces	1	cup frozen yellow sweet corn
3	cups water	2	tablespoons McCORMICK® Chopped Onions
2	cups beef broth	1	tablespoon OLD BAY® Seasoning
1	cup frozen lima beans	1	pound backfin blue crab meat, picked over
1	cup frozen baby carrots or sliced carrots		

1. Place all ingredients except crab meat in a 4 quart saucepan.

2. Heat to boil; cover and boil 5 minutes.

3. Reduce heat to low; add crab meat, cover, and simmer 10 minutes. **Yield:** 10 servings.

Per serving: 103 calories, 12g protein, 13g carbohydrate, 1g fat, 3g fiber, 35mg cholesterol, 593mg sodium

Slow-Cooked Caribbean Chicken & Squash

Slow-cooked chicken thighs and butternut squash simmer together in this Caribbean-flavored stew.

make-ahead

submitted by: **Tyson®**

Prep Time: 10 minutes
Cook Time: 8 hours

Test Kitchen Secret:
Serve in shallow soup bowls with hot bread and a crisp tossed salad on the side.

4	TYSON® Fresh Bone-In Chicken Thighs	1	(14.5 ounce) can diced tomatoes
1	small butternut squash, peeled, seeded, and cut into 1½ inch pieces	¼	cup water or chicken broth
		1	tablespoon hot (Madras) curry powder
1	medium onion, cut into wedges	1	teaspoon chopped ginger root
		1	teaspoon salt

1. Remove and discard skin from chicken. Wash hands. In a 3½ to 4 quart slow cooker, combine all ingredients except chicken; mix well. Place chicken on top of mixture.

2. Cook on High setting 1 hour. Reduce heat to Low setting and cook 7 hours or until squash is done and internal juices of chicken run clear and chicken is very tender. (Insert instant-read meat thermometer in thickest part of chicken. Temperature should read 180°F.) With fork, remove chicken from bones, then cut chicken into pieces. Stir into vegetable mixture. **Yield:** 4 servings.

Per serving: 399 calories, 21g protein, 36g carbohydrate, 21g fat, 10g fiber, 100mg cholesterol, 833mg sodium

Creamy Roasted Garlic & Potato Chowder

This simple, yet filling, potato chowder made with bacon and Cheddar cheese doesn't take long to prepare, so you can have it any night of the week.

holiday fare

submitted by: **Hormel Foods Corporation**

Prep Time: 10 minutes
Cook Time: 25 minutes

Test Kitchen Secret:
Use fully cooked bacon that just needs a zap in the microwave to crisp up to make this even easier.

2	cups 1% milk	1¼	cups instant mashed potato flakes
1½	cups water		
1	tablespoon HERB-OX® Chicken Flavored Bouillon Granules	¼	cup finely shredded Cheddar cheese
1	cup refrigerated diced potatoes	¼	cup sliced green onions
½	cup frozen whole kernel corn, thawed	¼	cup cooked and crumbled bacon
¼	cup roasted garlic-flavored cream cheese		

1. In a saucepan, bring milk, water, bouillon granules, and refrigerated potatoes to a boil. Reduce heat and simmer for 5 to 8 minutes or until potatoes are tender.

2. Stir in corn, cream cheese, and instant potato flakes. Heat over low heat until warmed through. Ladle chowder into bowls. Top with cheese, green onions, and bacon. **Yield:** 4 servings.

Per serving: 265 calories, 12g protein, 31g carbohydrate, 11g fat, 3g fiber, 24mg cholesterol, 344mg sodium

Bush's Best® Jamaican Black Bean Chili

A unique blend of spices and flavors creates a hearty chili garnished with Cheddar cheese and curled lime zest.

comfort food

submitted by: **Bush's Best® Beans**

Prep Time: 40 minutes
Cook Time: 40 minutes

Test Kitchen Secret:
Canned pumpkin is the secret ingredient here. It adds a slightly sweet, full flavor that balances well with the salty bacon and spicy chilies.

½ pound bacon, chopped
1 cup chopped onion
1 cup chopped red bell pepper
1 cup chopped green bell pepper
1 tablespoon minced roasted garlic
2 teaspoons cumin seed
2 teaspoons fennel seed
1 teaspoon ground allspice
2 cups pumpkin puree
2 (15 ounce) cans BUSH'S BEST® Black Beans, rinsed and drained
2 (10 ounce) cans diced tomatoes and green chilies, undrained
1 cup frozen whole kernel corn
1 cup chicken broth
1 tablespoon cocoa powder
2 cups shredded sharp Cheddar cheese
Fresh lime zest

1. In a large soup pot, sauté bacon over medium heat until cooked. Add onion, bell peppers, garlic, and spices. Sauté over medium heat for 5 minutes. Stir in pumpkin puree, BUSH'S BEST® Black Beans, tomatoes, corn, broth, and cocoa powder. Bring to a boil; reduce heat, cover, and simmer for 20 minutes.

2. Serve with shredded cheese and garnish with curled lime zest. **Yield:** 6 servings.

Per serving: 449 calories, 26g protein, 48g carbohydrate, 21g fat, 16g fiber, 50mg cholesterol, 1519mg sodium

Bush's Best® Jamaican Black Bean Chili

Celebrate the Seasons with Bush's Best® Beans

When the leaves start falling and football's in the air, it's time for some All-American Chili.
Your guests or tailgating buddies will never go hungry with this classic chili.

Bush's Best® All-American Chili

This classic, comforting meal incorporates all the necessary ingredients for a chili your family will enjoy.

Prep Time: 10 minutes   **Cook Time:** 30 minutes

1   pound lean ground beef
1   cup chopped onion
1   cup chopped green bell pepper
2   (16 ounce) cans BUSH'S BEST® Chili Beans
1   (14.5 ounce) can diced tomatoes
1   (6 ounce) can tomato paste
½   cup water
¼   teaspoon black pepper
1   teaspoon salt
1   tablespoon chili powder
2   teaspoons dried oregano
1   teaspoon white sugar
    Shredded Cheddar cheese (optional)
    Oyster crackers (optional)

1. In a large pan, cook beef, onion, and bell pepper until meat is browned. Drain excess grease. Stir in remaining ingredients except cheese and crackers. Bring to a boil. Cover, reduce heat to low, and simmer for 20 minutes.
2. Garnish with Cheddar cheese and crackers, if desired. **Yield:** 8 servings.

Per serving: 323 calories, 22g protein, 27g carbohydrate, 14g fat, 7g fiber, 55mg cholesterol, 1083mg sodium

Bush's Best® Three-Bean Chili

This hearty winter meal uses dark red kidney, pinto, and black beans. A dollop of sour cream atop each serving tames the heat.

2	pounds lean ground beef	2	(15 ounce) cans BUSH'S BEST® Black Beans
1	tablespoon chili powder	1	(14.5 ounce) can tomatoes
1	small yellow onion, chopped	1	(6 ounce) can tomato paste
1	small green bell pepper, chopped	1½	teaspoons salt
2	(16 ounce) cans BUSH'S BEST® Dark Red Kidney Beans	1	teaspoon garlic salt
		½	teaspoon ground black pepper
2	(16 ounce) cans BUSH'S BEST® Pinto Beans	½	teaspoon ground cumin
			Cinnamon to taste
			Sour cream (optional)

1. Brown ground beef in a heavy Dutch oven or soup pot. Add chili powder and mix well. Add onion and bell pepper to meat and cook for 2 minutes. Drain off excess grease. Stir in remaining ingredients except sour cream. Simmer over low heat for 10 minutes.

2. Top each serving with a dollop of sour cream, if desired. **Yield:** 8 servings.

Per serving: 474 calories, 34g protein, 61g carbohydrate, 11g fat, 19g fiber, 46mg cholesterol, 1901mg sodium

party pleaser

submitted by: **Bush's Best® Beans**

Prep Time: 15 minutes
Cook Time: 25 minutes

Test Kitchen Secret:
Try adding ground cinnamon to chili for a subtle, sweet kick. It's the secret ingredient—nobody will guess it's in there.

Classic Boca® Chili

You'll never miss the meat in this savory bowl of chili chock-full of flavorful beans, bell peppers, and green chilies.

2	medium bell peppers (red, yellow, or green), coarsely chopped	1	(15 ounce) can chili beans in sauce
1	medium onion, chopped (about ½ cup)	1	(15 ounce) can tomato sauce
2	cloves garlic, minced	1	(14.5 ounce) can diced tomatoes
2	teaspoons vegetable oil	1	(4 ounce) can chopped green chilies, drained
1	(12 ounce) package frozen BOCA® Meatless Ground Burger	1	tablespoon chili powder
1	(15 ounce) can black beans, rinsed and drained	½	teaspoon ground cumin

1. Cook bell peppers, onion, and garlic in oil in large saucepan over medium-high heat 3 minutes, stirring frequently.

2. Add remaining ingredients. Bring to a boil. Reduce heat to medium-low; simmer 30 minutes, stirring occasionally. **Yield:** 8 servings.

Per serving: 210 calories, 17g protein, 33g carbohydrate, 3g fat, 12g fiber, 0mg cholesterol, 960mg sodium

healthy

submitted by: **Boca®**

Prep Time: 10 minutes
Cook Time: 40 minutes

Test Kitchen Secret:
The vegetables in this robust, low-calorie, low-fat vegetarian chili provide a good source of vitamin A and an excellent source of vitamin C. Serve with your favorite chili toppings, like cheese, onion, and crackers.

Lindsay® Olive Tea Sandwiches

Lindsay® Olive Tea Sandwiches

This tea sandwich spread can be easily prepared in just minutes for an impressive and delicious appetizer. Lindsay® Black Ripe Pitted Olives, sun-dried tomatoes, pine nuts, and basil are combined, then spread with light cream cheese on sandwich bread and chilled while you await your guests' arrival.

party pleaser

submitted by: Lindsay® Olives

Prep Time: 15 minutes
Chill Time: 1 hour

1	(6 ounce) can LINDSAY® Black Ripe Pitted Olives, drained and finely chopped	3	tablespoons pine nuts
¼	cup light mayonnaise	⅛	teaspoon salt
3	tablespoons drained and chopped sun-dried tomatoes packed in oil	⅛	teaspoon freshly ground black pepper
3	tablespoons chopped green onion	12	slices firm white sandwich bread
3	tablespoons chopped fresh basil	6	tablespoons light cream cheese, softened
			Sliced olives for garnish (optional)

1. In a medium bowl, combine all ingredients except bread, cream cheese, and sliced olives; mix well. Cover; chill at least 1 hour or up to 24 hours before assembling sandwiches.

2. Cut crusts from bread, forming 4 inch squares; reserve crusts for another use. Spread cream cheese over bread. Spread olive mixture over 6 slices bread; close sandwiches with remaining bread, pressing lightly. Cut diagonally in half or lengthwise into rectangles. Garnish with sliced olives, if desired. **Yield:** 12 servings.

Per serving: 141 calories, 4g protein, 15g carbohydrate, 8g fat, 1g fiber, 6mg cholesterol, 349mg sodium

What Other Cooks Have Done:
"This is really a very tasty little recipe! I used regular mayo, regular onion instead of green onion, dried basil instead of fresh, no pine nuts, and instead of spreading the cream cheese on the bread separately, I mixed it right in with the olive mixture—it turned out great!"

Sausage Reuben

Complete with sauerkraut and Swiss cheese, this sandwich is a tasty, but healthy alternative to the traditional Reuben.

quick & easy

submitted by: Boca®

Prep Time: 10 minutes
Cook Time: 15 minutes

1	frozen BOCA® Meatless Smoked Sausage	1	slice rye bread, toasted
¼	cup drained sauerkraut		Mustard or reduced-fat Thousand Island dressing (optional)
1	slice Swiss cheese		

1. Cook sausage as directed on package.

2. Cut sausage in half lengthwise and brown in skillet over medium heat. Add sauerkraut and cheese; cover. Heat 2 minutes or until cheese melts.

3. Serve sausage on toast slice with mustard or reduced-fat Thousand Island dressing, if desired. **Yield:** 1 serving.

Per serving: 326 calories, 25g protein, 24g carbohydrate, 15g fat, 4g fiber, 26mg cholesterol, 1400mg sodium

Test Kitchen Secret:
Substitute Boca® Meatless Bratwurst for the Smoked Sausage, if desired.

Tasty Toaster Sandwich

Three ingredients, five minutes, and you're out the door with this speedy breakfast sandwich.

2 frozen BOCA® Meatless Breakfast Links
2 slices raisin bread, toasted
1 tablespoon reduced-fat cream cheese spread

1. Microwave links as directed on package.
2. Meanwhile, spread toast slices with cream cheese spread.
3. Cut links lengthwise in half; place on 1 of the toast slices. Top with remaining toast slice. **Yield:** 1 serving.

Per serving: 280 calories, 15g protein, 34g carbohydrate, 9g fat, 6g fiber, 10mg cholesterol, 610mg sodium

Grilled Chicken in Pita Pockets

McCormick® Grill Mates® Montreal Chicken Seasoning turns ordinary chicken into a zesty summer favorite. Try this recipe with kaiser rolls next time.

¼ cup olive oil
2 tablespoons white wine vinegar
2 teaspoons McCORMICK® GRILL MATES® Montreal Chicken Seasoning
½ teaspoon McCORMICK® Italian Seasoning
1 pound skinless, boneless chicken breasts
6 pita pockets, halved
6 slices Monterey Jack or Muenster cheese
6 lettuce leaves
6 slices tomato
½ cup shredded carrot

1. Combine first 4 ingredients in large zip-top plastic bag or glass dish. Add chicken; toss to coat. Refrigerate 30 minutes or more for added flavor. Remove meat from marinade; discard marinade.
2. Lightly grease cold grill rack. Preheat grill for medium-high heat. Grill chicken 5 to 6 minutes per side or until thoroughly cooked. Serve warm or cover and chill.
3. Thinly slice meat and layer in pita pocket halves or on rolls. Top with cheese, lettuce, tomato, and carrot. **Yield:** 6 servings.

Per serving: 449 calories, 29g protein, 37g carbohydrate, 20g fat, 2g fiber, 68mg cholesterol, 587mg sodium

Zesty Beef Pockets

Zesty Beef Pockets burst with flavor from the hot, marinated strips of steak and the cool garden vegetables and cheese.

¼	cup olive oil	6	pita pockets, halved, or kaiser rolls, split
2	tablespoons red wine vinegar	6	slices Monterey Jack or Muenster cheese
2	teaspoons McCORMICK® GRILL MATES® Montreal Steak Seasoning	6	lettuce leaves
1	teaspoon McCORMICK® Italian Seasoning	6	slices tomato
1	pound sirloin steak	½	cup shredded carrot

party pleaser

submitted by: **McCormick® & Company**

Prep Time: 5 minutes
Marinate Time: 30 minutes
Cook Time: 20 minutes

Test Kitchen Secret:
Use this marinade for any beef and slice extra steak to make these sandwiches for lunch the next day.

1. Combine first 4 ingredients in a large zip-top plastic bag or glass dish. Add steak; toss to coat. Refrigerate 30 minutes. Remove meat from marinade; discard marinade.
2. Lightly grease cold grill rack. Preheat grill for medium-high heat. Grill steak 8 to 10 minutes per side or until desired doneness. Serve warm or cover and chill.
3. Thinly slice meat and layer in pita pocket halves or on rolls. Top with cheese, lettuce, tomato, and carrot. **Yield:** 6 servings.

Per serving: 482 calories, 26g protein, 37g carbohydrate, 25g fat, 2g fiber, 66mg cholesterol, 672mg sodium

Chicken Pita Pockets

The ever-popular pita bread is one of the oldest recipes known to man. The name comes from the Greek word "pitta," which means thin, flat layers.

¾	cup Ranch-style salad dressing	1	(9 ounce) package TYSON® Frozen, Fully Cooked Chicken Breast Strips
1	teaspoon dried dill weed		
2	tablespoons vegetable oil		
1	cup sliced fresh mushrooms	4	large pita pockets, halved
1	medium onion, thinly sliced, separated into rings	1	cup shredded lettuce

quick & easy

submitted by: **Tyson®**

Prep Time: 5 minutes
Cook Time: 10 minutes

What Other Cooks Have Done:
"This is a wonderful recipe. Even my daughter, who is very picky about food, enjoyed this. For extra flavor, I added guacamole to it and left out the dill."

1. Blend salad dressing and dill weed in a small bowl. Set aside.
2. Heat oil in large nonstick skillet over medium heat. Add mushrooms and onion; cook 3 to 5 minutes or until vegetables are tender. Add chicken; cook and stir 3 to 5 minutes or until chicken is hot.
3. Stuff pita bread halves evenly with chicken mixture. Top with lettuce and dressing mixture. **Yield:** 4 servings.

Per serving: 544 calories, 23g protein, 40g carbohydrate, 33g fat, 3g fiber, 54mg cholesterol, 1105mg sodium

Bush's Best® Rockin' Moroccan Garbanzo Pita

submitted by: **Chef Katy Keck on behalf of Bush's Best® Beans**

Prep Time: 15 minutes
Cook Time: 5 minutes

Test Kitchen Secret:
Cumin adds a nutty flavor and aroma to recipes and works well with the Moroccan theme here. Olive oil, lemon, garbanzo beans, parsley, and yogurt lend an exotic touch to a lunchtime favorite.

This quick lunch or dinner includes cumin-spiced chicken and veggies served in a pita pocket. Cool off the spicy kick with sour cream or yogurt.

1 tablespoon ground cumin	3 green onions, thinly sliced
1 teaspoon chili powder	1 red bell pepper, diced
1 pound chicken breast, cut into 1 inch cubes	¼ cup chopped fresh parsley
4 tablespoons olive oil, divided	Salt and freshly ground black pepper to taste
¼ cup lemon juice	3 pita pockets, halved
2 (16 ounce) cans BUSH'S BEST® Garbanzo Beans, rinsed and drained	Plain fat-free yogurt or sour cream (optional)

1. Combine cumin and chili powder in a plastic bag. Add chicken and shake to coat.

2. Heat 1 tablespoon oil in large skillet over medium heat. Add chicken; cook 5 minutes or until chicken is no longer pink, stirring frequently. Remove from heat and set aside to cool.

3. Combine remaining 3 tablespoons of oil and next 5 ingredients, mixing well. Stir in chicken. Add salt and pepper to taste.

4. Divide chicken mixture among pita pocket halves; top with yogurt or sour cream, if desired. **Yield:** 6 servings.

Per serving: 519 calories, 33g protein, 66g carbohydrate, 13g fat, 13g fiber, 45mg cholesterol, 1382mg sodium

Holiday Leftovers Wrap

submitted by: **Gorton's®**

Prep Time: 10 minutes
Cook Time: 10 minutes

Test Kitchen Secret:
Look for flatbread near the pitas in your local supermarket.

Keep this recipe around for the holidays. It's the perfect meal solution for the day after turkey!

8 GORTON'S® Fish Sticks or Extra Crunchy Tenders	2 tablespoons mayonnaise
¼ cup cranberry sauce (whole berry or jellied)	2 flatbreads for wrap
	½ cup leftover stuffing

1. Cook 8 GORTON'S® Fish Sticks or 8 GORTON'S® Tenders according to directions.

2. Puree cranberry sauce with mayonnaise in blender.

3. Place 4 fish sticks or 4 tenders on each flatbread. Spoon ¼ cup stuffing on fish. Spread desired amount of cranberry mixture on top. Roll up and serve. **Yield:** 2 servings.

Per serving: 981 calories, 31g protein, 147g carbohydrate, 30g fat, 8g fiber, 21mg cholesterol, 1330mg sodium

Bush's Best® Rockin' Moroccan Garbanzo Pita

Warm Chicken Caesar Wrap

Warm Chicken Caesar Wraps

Caesar salad gets all wrapped up in this healthy lunchtime favorite. Legend has it that Caesar salad dressing was named after Caesar Cardini, who developed it in the 1920s for use in his restaurant in Tijuana, Mexico.

8	TYSON® Individually Fresh Frozen® Boneless, Skinless Chicken Tenderloins	8	(10 inch) flour tortillas, warmed
1	cup water	2	cups shredded lettuce
1	cup instant rice	2	medium tomatoes, chopped
¾	cup fat-free Caesar salad dressing	½	cup small seasoned croutons (optional)

1. Rinse chicken to remove ice glaze. Wash hands.

2. Spray a large nonstick skillet with nonstick cooking spray and heat over medium-high heat. Add chicken; cook 12 to 15 minutes or until lightly browned and done (internal temperature of 170°F).

3. Add water and bring to boil. Stir in rice. Cover and remove from heat; let stand 5 minutes or until liquid is absorbed. Stir in salad dressing.

4. Fill each tortilla with chicken and rice mixture, lettuce, tomatoes, and croutons, if desired. Fold in sides of tortilla and roll up. **Yield:** 4 servings.

Per serving: 651 calories, 27g protein, 107g carbohydrate, 12g fat, 7g fiber, 24mg cholesterol, 1476mg sodium

comfort food

submitted by: **Tyson®**

Prep Time: 10 minutes
Cook Time: 20 minutes

Test Kitchen Secret:
Serve with black beans and fresh fruit. To substitute Tyson® Fresh Chicken Tenderloins, simply decrease cooking time by about one-third.

Havarti-Ham Croissants

This savory-sweet combination of pineapple and ham finds a perfect match with melted Havarti cheese on a toasted croissant.

10	(2 inch) pieces leftover COOK'S® Brand Bone-In Spiral Sliced Ham	10	thin slices Havarti cheese
1	(20 ounce) can crushed pineapple	4	green onions, diced
		5	large plain croissants, sliced and toasted

1. Place ham on a large griddle or frying pan and top with pineapple. Sauté over medium heat until majority of pineapple juice is cooked off.

2. Place 1 slice cheese on each piece of ham, sprinkle with green onions, and heat until cheese melts. Place on bottom halves of croissants. Replace tops of croissants and serve. **Yield:** 5 servings.

Per serving: 550 calories, 22g protein, 45g carbohydrate, 31g fat, 3g fiber, 113mg cholesterol, 1489mg sodium

quick & easy

submitted by: **Cook's® Brand Ham**

Prep Time: 10 minutes
Cook Time: 15 minutes

Test Kitchen Secret:
Swiss cheese would be a nice substitute for the Havarti. Try serving on mini croissants as an appetizer or finger food for your next party.

Seafood Salad Sandwiches with Garlic Butter Grilled Fillets

submitted by: Gorton's®

Prep Time: 10 minutes
Cook Time: 10 minutes

Test Kitchen Secret:
Use one teaspoon dried mint in place of the fresh, if desired.

Craving seafood? This mouth-watering sandwich will hit the spot.

2	GORTON'S® Garlic Butter Grilled Fillets	¼	teaspoon garlic, chopped
1	celery stalk, chopped	¼	cup mayonnaise
1	carrot, chopped	1	tablespoon fresh mint, chopped
¼	cup onion, chopped	2	submarine rolls
			Lettuce leaves

1. Cook GORTON'S® Garlic Butter Grilled Fillets per instructions on package. Cut cooked fillets into sixths. Mix all remaining ingredients except rolls and lettuce in a bowl and add the grilled fillets. Stir until thoroughly mixed.
2. Place salad in sub rolls and with 1 to 2 lettuce leaves serve immediately. Salad may be kept in refrigerator for 1 to 2 days. **Yield:** 2 servings.

Per serving: 330 calories, 19g protein, 9g carbohydrate, 25g fat, 2g fiber, 76mg cholesterol, 456mg sodium

Puttanesca Sauce for Boca® Italian Sausage Roll

submitted by: Boca®

Prep Time: 10 minutes
Cook Time: 10 minutes

Test Kitchen Secret:
Turn this recipe into a hearty pasta dinner by cutting the cooked sausage into ½ inch thick slices. Add to tomato mixture and cook until heated through. Toss with hot cooked pasta.

It doesn't get much better than this! Zesty Puttanesca Sauce, made with tomatoes, capers, olives, and red pepper, dresses Boca® Meatless Italian Sausage for a night to remember.

1	BOCA® Meatless Italian Sausage	1	teaspoon drained capers
1	teaspoon olive oil	1	clove garlic, minced
1	plum tomato, chopped	⅛	teaspoon crushed red pepper flakes
1	tablespoon sliced, pitted ripe olives	1	sandwich roll, partially split

1. Cook sausage as directed on package. Meanwhile, heat oil in a small saucepan over medium–high heat.
2. Add tomato, olives, capers, garlic, and red pepper flakes; cook 2 minutes or until heated through, stirring occasionally.
3. Place sausage in roll; top with tomato mixture. **Yield:** 1 serving.

Per serving: 320 calories, 18g protein, 32g carbohydrate, 13g fat, 3g fiber, 0mg cholesterol, 1080mg sodium

Sloppy Joe Meatball Subs

Get the flavor of "subshop" meatball subs at home with this quick and easy recipe.

1 pound lean ground beef
1 teaspoon McCORMICK® Garlic Salt
1 teaspoon McCORMICK® Italian Seasoning, divided
¼ teaspoon McCORMICK® Ground Black Pepper
1 package McCORMICK® Sloppy Joes Seasoning
1 (6 ounce) can tomato paste
1½ cups water
4 (6 inch) submarine rolls
½ cup shredded mozzarella cheese

1. Combine ground beef, garlic salt, ¾ teaspoon Italian seasoning, and pepper. Shape into 16 (1½ inch) meatballs.
2. Brown meatballs in a large skillet 10 minutes or until done; drain. Add Sloppy Joes Seasoning, tomato paste, water, and remaining ¼ teaspoon Italian seasoning; stir until smooth. Simmer 5 minutes.
3. Place meatballs in submarine rolls. Spoon sauce over meatballs; sprinkle with cheese. **Yield:** 4 servings.

Per serving: 405 calories, 30g protein, 33g carbohydrate, 17g fat, 3g fiber, 64mg cholesterol, 1863mg sodium

kid-friendly

submitted by: **McCormick® & Company**

Prep Time: 10 minutes
Cook Time: 15 minutes

Test Kitchen Secret:
You can substitute ground chicken or turkey for the beef, if desired.

Quick Calzones

Quick Calzones are delicious anytime and are so easy. They make a great meal or snack.

1 (1.5 ounce) package McCORMICK® Italian-Style Spaghetti Sauce Mix
1 (6 ounce) can tomato paste
Water
1 tablespoon vegetable oil
2 (8 ounce) packages refrigerator crescent rolls
1 (4 ounce) package sliced pepperoni
1 (8 ounce) package shredded mozzarella cheese

1. Preheat oven to 350°F. Combine spaghetti sauce mix, tomato paste, 1 can water, and oil.
2. Unroll crescent rolls and separate into 8 rectangles. Press together perforations.
3. Spoon 1 tablespoon sauce on ½ of each rectangle. Top with sliced pepperoni and shredded mozzarella cheese. Fold dough over cheese and press to seal edges. Place on a large, lightly greased baking sheet.
4. Bake in the preheated oven for 10 minutes. **Yield:** 8 servings.

Per serving: 410 calories, 15g protein, 31g carbohydrate, 25g fat, 1g fiber, 27mg cholesterol, 1353mg sodium

comfort food

submitted by: **McCormick® & Company**

Prep Time: 15 minutes
Cook Time: 10 minutes

What Other Cooks Have Done:
"This is truly a good, quick, and easy recipe. The calzones make great appetizers and, of course, the kids will devour them. You can be as creative as you want with this. Try some ham with mozzarella cheese but leave out the sauce. If you want to be a little daring, you can even deep fry these babies."

Sizzlin' Steak Burgers

McCormick® Grill Mates® adds a bold, zesty flavor to burgers. To add another flavor twist, top burgers with a gourmet cheese, such as Gruyère, Havarti, or crumbled blue cheese.

kid-friendly

submitted by: **McCormick® & Company**

Prep Time: 5 minutes
Cook Time: 12 minutes

What Other Cooks Have Done:
"We will never have regular burgers again! What a simple, wonderful way to make the BEST burgers! Try adding some finely chopped garlic to the meat mixture."

1	teaspoon McCORMICK® GRILL MATES® Montreal Steak Seasoning	4	slices Gouda cheese (optional)
1	pound lean ground beef	4	hamburger rolls
		4	lettuce leaves (optional)
		4	tomato slices (optional)

1. Preheat grill for medium-high heat.
2. Mix steak seasoning into meat and form meat into 4 equal-size patties.
3. Grill patties 5 to 6 minutes on each side, or to desired doneness. Add a slice of cheese to each patty 1 minute before cooking is completed, if desired. Serve on rolls with lettuce and tomato, if desired. **Yield:** 4 servings.

Per serving: 320 calories, 20g protein, 22g carbohydrate, 16g fat, 1g fiber, 59mg cholesterol, 384mg sodium

Bistro Bagel Cheeseburgers

Sautéed sweet red onions and meaty portobello mushrooms splashed with balsamic vinegar elevate these Boca® Meatless Cheeseburgers onto high culinary ground.

quick & easy

submitted by: **Boca®**

Prep Time: 10 minutes
Cook Time: 15 minutes

Test Kitchen Secret:
Onions and mushrooms can be grilled in a foil pan coated with olive oil while grilling cheeseburgers.

2	frozen BOCA® Meatless Cheeseburgers	1	teaspoon balsamic vinegar
2	teaspoons olive oil, divided	2	plain bagels, split and toasted Arugula or leaf lettuce leaves Freshly ground black pepper to taste (optional)
¼	medium red onion, sliced		
1	medium portobello mushroom, sliced		

1. Cook cheeseburgers as directed on package.
2. Meanwhile, heat 1 teaspoon oil in nonstick skillet over medium-high heat; add onion and sauté until tender. Remove onion from skillet.
3. Add remaining 1 teaspoon oil and mushroom slices to skillet; cook until lightly browned, turning occasionally. Add onion and vinegar; mix lightly.
4. Place cheeseburger on bottom half of each bagel; top with arugula and mushroom mixture. Season with pepper to taste, if desired. Cover with remaining bagel halves. **Yield:** 2 servings.

Per serving: 370 calories, 21g protein, 47g carbohydrate, 11g fat, 6g fiber, 10mg cholesterol, 800mg sodium

Sizzlin' Steak Burger

submitted by: **Boca®**

Prep Time: 5 minutes
Cook Time: 6 minutes

Test Kitchen Secret:

Have some leftover hot dog buns? Serve the Sloppy Joe mixture in them instead of the hamburger buns. Serve with crisp fresh radishes, carrot sticks, and celery sticks.

Boca® Sloppy Joes

With no greasy ground beef to brown, you'll relish these sweet and tangy Sloppy Joe sandwiches.

1	teaspoon vegetable oil	½	cup barbecue sauce
¼	medium onion, finely chopped	1	tablespoon sweet pickle relish
1	pouch (1 cup) frozen BOCA® Meatless Ground Burger	2	hamburger buns, split

1. Heat oil in small nonstick skillet over medium heat; sauté onion 3 minutes or until tender.
2. Add ground burger, barbecue sauce, and relish; mix well. Cook 3 minutes or until heated through, stirring occasionally.
3. Serve on buns. **Yield:** 2 servings.

Per serving: 300 calories, 15g protein, 49g carbohydrate, 5g fat, 6g fiber, 0mg cholesterol, 1330mg sodium

submitted by: **Boca®**

Prep Time: 5 minutes
Cook Time: 5 minutes

Test Kitchen Secret:

Add chopped fresh mango to the pineapple salsa. You can also substitute Boca® Meatless Original Chik'n Patties for the burgers, if desired.

Tropical Salsa Burgers

Reflections of the Caribbean top these burgers with a spicy-sweet salsa that combines pineapple with the heat of red pepper and onion.

2	BOCA® Meatless All American Flame Grilled Burgers	4	green onions, sliced
		1	plum tomato, chopped
½	cup drained canned pineapple tidbits	½	teaspoon crushed red pepper
		2	split multi-grain buns
			Lettuce

1. Microwave BOCA® Meatless All American Flame Grilled Burgers as directed on package.
2. Mix ½ cup drained canned pineapple tidbits, green onions, tomato, and crushed red pepper until well blended. Serve burgers in split multi-grain buns with lettuce and topped with pineapple mixture. **Yield:** 2 servings.

Per serving: 260 calories, 19g protein, 33g carbohydrate, 7g fat, 7g fiber, 4mg cholesterol, 580mg sodium

submitted by: **Boca®**

Prep Time: 10 minutes
Cook Time: 15 minutes

Test Kitchen Secret:

For added color, use yellow or orange bell peppers and red onion.

Fajita Burgers

Enjoy Boca® Meatless Cheeseburgers in a new way with this south-of-the-border fajita recipe.

1	teaspoon olive oil, divided	¼	teaspoon chili powder
½	medium-sized green or red bell pepper, cut into strips	2	frozen BOCA® Meatless Cheeseburgers
1	small onion, thinly sliced	2	(8 inch) flour tortillas, warmed

1. Heat ½ teaspoon oil in a large nonstick skillet over medium heat. Add bell pepper, onion, and chili powder; cook and stir 5 minutes or until tender-crisp. Remove from pan.

2. Add remaining oil to skillet. Add cheeseburgers; cook 4 minutes. Turn burgers; top with vegetables. Cook 4 more minutes; cut in half. Place 2 burger halves on each tortilla; top with vegetables. Roll up tortillas. **Yield:** 2 servings.

Per serving: 270 calories, 16g protein, 28g carbohydrate, 11g fat, 6g fiber, 10mg cholesterol, 650mg sodium

Boca® Salsa Fresca Burgers

A refreshing, quick-and-easy salsa tops these healthy burgers.

1	medium tomato, chopped	¼	teaspoon ground cumin
2	tablespoons chopped yellow or green bell pepper		Salt and black pepper to taste (optional)
1	tablespoon chopped onion	1	(10 ounce) package frozen BOCA® Meatless Cheeseburgers
1	tablespoon chopped fresh cilantro		
1	teaspoon minced jalapeño pepper	4	hamburger buns, split

1. Mix all ingredients except burgers and buns; cover. Refrigerate until ready to use.

2. Cook burgers as directed on package. Serve in buns topped with tomato mixture. **Yield:** 4 servings.

Per serving: 260 calories, 17g protein, 30g carbohydrate, 8g fat, 5g fiber, 10mg cholesterol, 660mg sodium

healthy

submitted by: **Boca®**

Prep Time: 10 minutes
Cook Time: 15 minutes

Test Kitchen Secret:
Substitute Boca® Meatless Original or All American Flame Grilled Burgers or Boca® Meatless Original or Spicy Chik'n Patties for the cheeseburgers.

Gyro Burgers

Once you try this low-cholesterol version of a Greek favorite with Boca® Meatless Original Burgers, we're sure you'll be hooked.

1	(10 ounce) package BOCA® Meatless Original Burgers	1	clove garlic, peeled
½	cup fat-free sour cream	4	foldable pita bread rounds
¼	medium unpeeled cucumber, chopped (about ½ cup)	2	plum tomatoes, sliced
		1	cup shredded lettuce

1. Heat burgers as directed on package; cut in half.

2. Meanwhile, place sour cream, cucumber, and garlic in a blender or food processor container; cover. Blend 10 to 30 seconds or until almost smooth.

3. Top pita bread evenly with tomato and lettuce; drizzle with sour cream sauce. Top each with 2 burger halves and fold over. **Yield:** 4 servings.

Per serving: 290 calories, 21g protein, 47g carbohydrate, 3g fat, 6g fiber, 4mg cholesterol, 690mg sodium

comfort food

submitted by: **Boca®**

Prep Time: 10 minutes
Cook Time: 15 minutes

Test Kitchen Secret:
Top each sandwich with additional chopped cucumber.

Bush's Best® Silk Road Black Bean
Salad, page 236

simple salads & side dishes

Round out your meals with these **satisfying** salads and sides. Keep things light with a **fresh** garden salad, or get ready for a week's worth of lunches with a **make-ahead** bean salad. With these **top-rated** recipes, your sides will take center stage.

Ambrosia

This favorite fruit salad couldn't be easier. Use both red and white grapes for extra color, and top with whipped cream for a simple dessert.

1 (20 ounce) can DOLE® Pineapple Chunks, drained	1½ cups seedless grapes
1 (11 ounce) can DOLE® Mandarin Oranges, drained	½ cup miniature marshmallows
1 DOLE® Banana, sliced	1 cup vanilla low-fat yogurt
	¼ cup flaked coconut, toasted

1. Combine pineapple chunks, mandarin oranges, banana, grapes, and marshmallows in a medium bowl.

2. Stir yogurt into fruit mixture. Sprinkle with coconut. **Yield:** 6 servings.

Per serving: 196 calories, 3g protein, 44g carbohydrate, 2g fat, 2g fiber, 2mg cholesterol, 53mg sodium

Classic Mandarin Orange Salad

Give this easy salad an extra crunch by adding slivered almonds or pecan pieces, if desired.

½ pound spinach or mixed greens	½ cup sliced ripe olives
1 (11 ounce) can DOLE® Mandarin Oranges, drained	½ cup sliced red onion
	½ cup balsamic vinaigrette
	¼ cup crumbled feta cheese

1. Combine spinach, mandarin oranges, olives, and onion in a large serving bowl.

2. Pour vinaigrette over salad; toss to coat evenly. Top with feta cheese. **Yield:** 4 servings.

Per serving: 171 calories, 4g protein, 26g carbohydrate, 6g fat, 3g fiber, 14mg cholesterol, 872mg sodium

Dole® Tropicasian Salad

This salad has just the right mix of crunchiness and sweetness. Enjoy it alone or with your favorite stir-fry.

1	(20 ounce) can DOLE® Pineapple Chunks
1	(6 ounce) package DOLE® Baby Spinach
1	large English cucumber, sliced
1	large Granny Smith apple, cut into thin wedges
2	cups bean sprouts
⅔	cup extra crunchy peanut butter
1½	tablespoons brown sugar
2	teaspoons ground coriander
2	teaspoons soy sauce

quick & easy

submitted by: **Dole®**

Prep Time: 10 minutes

Test Kitchen Secret:
English cucumbers are longer and thinner than regular cucumbers and are seedless. Feel free to use regular cucumbers in this recipe.

1. Drain pineapple chunks; reserve ½ cup juice.
2. Arrange spinach, pineapple chunks, cucumber, apple wedges, and bean sprouts in large salad bowl.
3. Mix peanut butter, reserved pineapple juice, brown sugar, coriander, and soy sauce until well blended. Pour over salad; toss to coat and serve. **Yield:** 6 servings.

Per serving: 265 calories, 9g protein, 29g carbohydrate, 15g fat, 5g fiber, 0mg cholesterol, 274mg sodium

Bush's Best® Black Bean Salad

This colorful bean salad is dressed with a light lime vinaigrette and takes only a few minutes to prepare. Serve with tortilla chips or as a side dish.

1 red bell pepper, diced	¼ cup olive oil
1 green bell pepper, diced	¼ cup red wine vinegar
1 yellow bell pepper, diced	1 teaspoon lime juice
½ cup diced red onion	Salt and black pepper to taste
1 (15.2 ounce) can whole kernel corn, drained	1 (15 ounce) can BUSH'S BEST® Black Beans, rinsed and drained
1 clove garlic, minced	Tortilla chips
1 teaspoon chopped fresh cilantro	

1. In a small bowl, combine bell peppers, onion, corn, garlic, and cilantro. Add olive oil, vinegar, lime juice, and salt and black pepper to taste. Add BUSH'S BEST® Black Beans and toss well. Serve with tortilla chips.
Yield: 6 servings.

Per serving: 393 calories, 9g protein, 52g carbohydrate, 19g fat, 9g fiber, 0mg cholesterol, 657mg sodium

Minted Chicken Salad with Summer Fruit

A palate-pleasing and good-for-you salad of mixed greens, fruit, and crunchy-coated chicken makes a nice lunch or summertime supper.

¾ cup KRETSCHMER® Original Toasted Wheat Germ	¼ cup sliced green onions
¾ cup finely chopped toasted almonds	1 cup fresh blueberries, rinsed and patted dry
¼ teaspoon cayenne pepper	3 fresh nectarines, washed and sliced
Salt and black pepper to taste	3 tablespoons chopped fresh mint leaves
2 egg whites	½ cup prepared reduced-fat or regular raspberry vinaigrette salad dressing
1 tablespoon water	
4 skinless, boneless chicken breast halves (about 4 ounces each)	2 tablespoons sliced toasted almonds
1 (10 ounce) package European salad mix	

1. Preheat oven to 350°F. Lightly spray a large shallow pan with cooking spray.
2. In a shallow dish, combine wheat germ, almonds, cayenne pepper, and salt and black pepper to taste. In a second shallow dish, beat egg whites and water with fork until frothy. Dip chicken into egg white mixture, then into wheat germ mixture, coating completely. Dip and coat chicken again, coating thoroughly. Arrange chicken on a baking sheet; lightly spray with cooking spray.

Minted Chicken Salad with Summer Fruit

3. Bake in the preheated oven for 14 to 16 minutes or until chicken is no longer pink in the center.

4. While chicken is cooking, gently toss salad mix with green onions, blueberries, nectarines, mint leaves, and dressing. Arrange salad on serving platter; top with cooked chicken. Sprinkle with sliced almonds. **Yield:** 4 servings.

Per serving: 508 calories, 41g protein, 43g carbohydrate, 21g fat, 10g fiber, 65mg cholesterol, 154mg sodium

Southwestern Steak Salad

comfort food

submitted by: **Lindsay® Olives**

Prep Time: 20 minutes
Cook Time: 8 minutes

Test Kitchen Secret:

Balsamic vinegar is made from the juice of very sweet white grapes. It's dark brown with a delicate, sweet flavor that comes from being aged in wooden barrels for several years. This extended process makes it more expensive than other types of vinegars. Light-colored balsamic vinegar is available in most markets, and will work fine for this recipe.

Lindsay® Spanish and Black Ripe Olives and red bell pepper are the perfect accompaniment to this Southwestern-inspired strip steak salad. The steak is herb- and spice-rubbed, quickly sautéed, and served sliced over mixed greens with fresh tomato and cilantro. It makes a fabulous summer meal, easily prepared in minutes.

⅓ cup plus 2 tablespoons extra virgin olive oil, divided

2 tablespoons balsamic vinegar or lemon juice

1 teaspoon salt, divided

1 teaspoon freshly ground black pepper, divided

⅓ cup LINDSAY® Spanish Olives Stuffed with Pimiento, drained and sliced

⅓ cup LINDSAY® Large Black Ripe Pitted Olives, drained and sliced

⅓ cup finely chopped red bell pepper

½ teaspoon onion powder

½ teaspoon garlic powder

½ teaspoon dried thyme

½ teaspoon dried oregano

½ teaspoon paprika

¼ teaspoon cayenne pepper

4 well-trimmed beef strip steaks, cut about ¾ inch thick

1 (5 ounce) package or 4 cups mixed salad greens

2 medium tomatoes, cut into wedges

2 tablespoons chopped fresh cilantro

1. In a small bowl, whisk together ⅓ cup of oil, vinegar, and ½ teaspoon each of the salt and black pepper. Add olives and red bell pepper; mix well. Let stand while preparing steaks.

2. In another small bowl, combine remaining ½ teaspoon each salt and black pepper, onion powder, garlic powder, thyme, oregano, paprika, and cayenne pepper; mix well. Sprinkle over both sides of steaks.

3. Heat remaining 2 tablespoons oil in a large skillet over medium-high heat until hot. Add steaks; cook for 3 to 4 minutes per side or until well-browned and medium rare. Transfer to a carving board; tent with foil and let stand 5 minutes.

4. Arrange salad greens and tomatoes on 4 serving plates. Carve steaks crosswise into ¼ inch thick slices; arrange over greens. Spoon olive mixture over steak and greens; garnish with cilantro. **Yield:** 4 servings.

Per serving: 646 calories, 36g protein, 10g carbohydrate, 52g fat, 3g fiber, 102mg cholesterol, 978mg sodium

Waldorf Pasta Salad

Small shell pasta, apple, celery, grapes, and walnuts combine with turkey in a lightly seasoned citrus dressing.

1	(7 ounce) package small shell pasta
⅔	cup plain yogurt
⅔	cup mayonnaise or salad dressing
¼	cup frozen orange juice concentrate, thawed
2	teaspoons HERB-OX® Chicken Flavored Bouillon Granules

2	cups cubed turkey breast
1	apple, diced
1	cup sliced celery
½	cup halved grapes
½	cup chopped toasted walnuts
	Salt and black pepper to taste

1. Cook pasta according to package directions; drain and rinse under cold water. Drain well.

2. In a small bowl, combine yogurt, mayonnaise, orange juice, and bouillon granules; mix well. In a large bowl, combine pasta, turkey breast, apple, celery, grape halves, and walnuts. Add dressing; toss to coat. Season with salt and pepper to taste. **Yield:** 8 servings.

Per serving: 319 calories, 16g protein, 33g carbohydrate, 14g fat, 2g fiber, 33mg cholesterol, 273mg sodium

quick & easy

submitted by: **Hormel Foods Corporation**

Prep Time: 10 minutes
Cook Time: 10 minutes

Test Kitchen Secret:
The original Waldorf salad contained only apples, celery, and mayonnaise, and was created at the Waldorf-Astoria Hotel in New York in the 1890s.

Tortellini Pasta Fillet Salad

This easy recipe can be used as a side dish or as the entrée. It's fantastic at potlucks or picnics.

6	GORTON'S® Crunchy Golden Fillets
¼	cup olive oil
4	large cloves garlic, finely chopped
¼	cup red wine vinegar
2	(9 ounce) packages three cheese tortellini, cooked and drained

2	medium tomatoes, chopped
2	cups broccoli florets
1	large green bell pepper, chopped
½	cup grated Parmesan cheese
¼	cup grated Romano cheese

1. Cook GORTON'S® fish fillets according to directions and cut each fillet into 4 pieces.

2. Heat olive oil in small saucepan over medium-high heat. Add garlic and cook for 1 minute. Pour into a large bowl and cool. Whisk in vinegar.

3. Add pasta, tomatoes, broccoli, bell pepper, cheeses, and fish. Serve immediately. **Yield:** 8 servings.

Per serving: 428 calories, 17g protein, 44g carbohydrate, 21g fat, 3g fiber, 48mg cholesterol, 580mg sodium

comfort food

submitted by: **Gorton's®**

Prep Time: 25 minutes
Cook Time: 15 minutes

Test Kitchen Secret:
Make your prep time even less by using convenience products like pre-washed and chopped broccoli, bottled minced garlic, and pre-grated Parmesan and Romano cheeses.

Spinach Fillet Salad

Here's a crunchy twist to a classic spinach salad that's perfect for dinner or lunch.

submitted by: **Gorton's®**

Prep Time: 20 minutes
Chill Time: 5 minutes
Cook Time: 10 minutes

Test Kitchen Secret:

Baby spinach comes in bags, washed and ready to use. It has tender stems that do not need to be removed, making your time in the kitchen even shorter.

6	GORTON'S® Crunchy Golden Fillets	3	tablespoons vegetable oil
6	cups baby spinach leaves	2	tablespoons cider vinegar
1¼	cups chopped, unpeeled red apple	2	teaspoons chutney
¼	cup raisins	¾	teaspoon curry powder
2	tablespoons sliced green onions	½	teaspoon powdered mustard
		½	teaspoon salt

1. Cook GORTON'S® fish fillets according to directions and cut each fillet into 4 pieces.
2. Combine spinach, apple, raisins, and green onions in large bowl; refrigerate for 5 minutes.
3. Blend vegetable oil, vinegar, chutney, curry powder, mustard, and salt. Toss fillets, salad, and dressing. Serve immediately. **Yield:** 8 servings.

Per serving: 183 calories, 4g protein, 18g carbohydrate, 11g fat, 2g fiber, 11mg cholesterol, 333mg sodium

Grilled Salmon Caesar Salad

A classic salad topped with Gorton's® new Grilled Salmon. Healthy and delicious! If you can't find Grilled Salmon, substitute any flavor Gorton's® grilled fillets.

submitted by: **Gorton's®**

Prep Time: 10 minutes
Cook Time: 10 minutes

Test Kitchen Secret:

Use a vegetable peeler to shave pieces of Parmesan cheese over the salad.

1	(6.3 ounce) package GORTON'S® Classic Grilled Salmon Fillets	1	small red bell pepper, chopped
1	small head romaine lettuce, torn	1	small yellow bell pepper, chopped
¼	cup Caesar salad dressing		Parmesan cheese (optional)
			Sliced red onion (optional)

1. Cook GORTON'S® grilled salmon fillets according to directions and cut each fillet into chunks.
2. In a large bowl, toss lettuce, Caesar dressing, salmon, bell peppers, and cheese and onion, if desired. Serve immediately. **Yield:** 3 servings.

Per serving: 180 calories, 15g protein, 7g carbohydrate, 10g fat, 3g fiber, 55mg cholesterol, 238mg sodium

Grilled Salmon Caesar Salad

Old Bay® Shrimp Salad

submitted by: **McCormick® & Company**

Prep Time: 10 minutes
Chill Time: 1 hour

Test Kitchen Secret:
This shrimp salad is just as good served on a sandwich roll.

Try this terrific traditional shrimp salad featuring Old Bay® Seasoning.

1	pound cooked shrimp	2	teaspoons lemon juice
½	cup mayonnaise	¼	teaspoon Worcestershire sauce
⅓	cup chopped celery		Lettuce leaves
2	teaspoons OLD BAY® Seasoning		

1. Peel and devein shrimp; cut in half and place in a bowl. Set aside.
2. Combine remaining ingredients except lettuce and mix well. Pour dressing over shrimp and toss gently. Cover and refrigerate at least 1 hour.
3. Toss salad just before serving and serve on bed of lettuce. **Yield:** 4 servings.

Per serving: 290 calories, 19g protein, 2g carbohydrate, 23g fat, 0g fiber, 189mg cholesterol, 640mg sodium

Bush's Best® Silk Road Black Bean Salad

(pictured on page 226)

submitted by: **Chef Katy Keck on behalf of Bush's Best® Beans**

Prep Time: 15 minutes

Test Kitchen Secret:
Sesame oil comes in light and dark varieties. Dark sesame oil is much stronger in flavor than light, so use light sesame oil in this recipe to allow the other flavors to come through.

This light Asian salad is ready in minutes.

1	tablespoon plus 1 teaspoon lime juice	3	scallions, thinly sliced
1	tablespoon plus 1 teaspoon rice vinegar	1	red bell pepper, diced
1	tablespoon plus 1 teaspoon soy sauce	1	head Boston lettuce
2	teaspoons grated fresh ginger	2	tablespoons chopped mint
2	tablespoons sesame oil	½	pound cooked medium shrimp
2	(15 ounce) cans BUSH'S BEST® Black Beans, rinsed and drained	¼	cup chopped salted peanuts

1. Whisk together lime juice, rice vinegar, soy sauce, and ginger in a small bowl. Pour in the oil in a thin stream, mixing until incorporated. Combine BUSH'S BEST® Black Beans, scallions, and red bell pepper in a large bowl. Toss well with the dressing. Refrigerate, covered, until ready to serve.
2. Just before serving, arrange lettuce on platter. Add mint, shrimp, and peanuts to the salad and arrange on the lettuce. **Yield:** 4 servings.

Per serving: 358 calories, 27g protein, 40g carbohydrate, 13g fat, 14g fiber, 111mg cholesterol, 1263mg sodium

Black Bean Aloha Shrimp Salad

This salad, a blend of Mexican, Asian, and tropical flavors, is hearty enough to enjoy as a meal.

1 (6 ounce) package DOLE® Baby Spinach and Radicchio Salad Blend
2 (15 ounce) cans black beans, well drained
1 (20 ounce) can DOLE® Crushed Pineapple, well drained
1 pound cooked medium shrimp, shelled and deveined
½ cup finely diced DOLE® Red Onion
½ cup coarsely chopped fresh cilantro or basil
½ cup Oriental or Oriental chicken salad dressing
⅓ cup flaked coconut
2 tablespoons finely chopped fresh mint leaves
1 large fresh jalapeño pepper, finely chopped

1. Divide salad blend evenly among 6 plates.
2. Toss together beans, crushed pineapple, shrimp, onion, cilantro, salad dressing, coconut, mint, and jalapeño in large bowl. Spoon over salad. **Yield:** 6 servings.

Per serving: 347 calories, 22g protein, 38g carbohydrate, 14g fat, 7g fiber, 148mg cholesterol, 717mg sodium

party pleaser

submitted by: **Dole®**

Prep Time: 20 minutes

Test Kitchen Secret:
Add chopped, cooked chicken in place of the shrimp, if desired. Also, discard jalapeño seeds for less heat.

Firecracker Chik'n Salad

Spicy, sweet, and crunchy flavors bring this restaurant-style salad home.

2 frozen BOCA® Meatless Spicy Chik'n Patties
¼ cup reduced-fat French dressing
1 tablespoon low-sodium teriyaki sauce
2 teaspoons sesame seeds, toasted
4 cups torn leaf lettuce
½ cup canned mandarin orange segments, drained
¼ cup shredded red cabbage
2 green onions, sliced
2 tablespoons chow mein noodles

1. Heat patties as directed on package; cut into strips.
2. Mix dressing, teriyaki sauce, and sesame seeds.
3. Place lettuce on serving plates; top with Chik'n strips, oranges, cabbage, green onions, and noodles. Drizzle with dressing mixture. **Yield:** 2 servings.

Per serving: 320 calories, 17g protein, 35g carbohydrate, 14g fat, 6g fiber, 4mg cholesterol, 1410mg sodium

healthy

submitted by: **Boca®**

Prep Time: 10 minutes
Cook Time: 5 minutes

Test Kitchen Secret:
To toast sesame seeds, cook and stir in small nonstick skillet over medium heat 2 to 3 minutes or until lightly browned. You can substitute seedless grape halves for mandarin orange segments, if desired.

Tuscan Bread Salad

Tuscan Bread Salad

Lindsay® Black Ripe Pitted Olives and cannellini beans lend fabulous flavor to this delicious Tuscan tradition. Hearty grilled Italian bread, fresh summer tomatoes, and fragrant basil, tossed with balsamic vinaigrette, will bring Tuscan simplicity right into your home kitchen.

from the grill

submitted by: **Lindsay® Olives**

Prep Time: 15 minutes
Cook Time: 6 minutes

Test Kitchen Secret:
Serve sliced, grilled chicken over the salad, if desired.

4	tablespoons extra virgin olive oil, divided	1	large ripe tomato, seeded and diced
2	cloves garlic, minced and divided	1	cup canned Great Northern or cannellini beans, rinsed and drained
4	slices (½ inch thick) Italian bread, about 4 inches in diameter	2	tablespoons balsamic vinegar
1	small head romaine lettuce	½	teaspoon salt
½	cup LINDSAY® Black Ripe Pitted Olives, drained and halved	½	teaspoon freshly ground black pepper
		2	tablespoons sliced fresh basil leaves (optional)

1. Preheat grill pan or broiler. Combine 1 tablespoon olive oil and 1 clove garlic; brush over both sides of bread slices. Grill bread 2 to 3 minutes per side in a ridged grill pan or broil 1 to 2 minutes per side until lightly toasted.

2. Reserve outer leaves of lettuce. Tear or chop enough of the inner leaves to measure 6 cups. In a large bowl, combine torn lettuce, olives, tomato, and beans. Cut grilled bread into cubes; add to lettuce mixture. Combine remaining 3 tablespoons oil, remaining garlic, vinegar, salt, and pepper; mix well. Add to lettuce mixture; toss well.

3. Arrange outer leaves of lettuce on 4 serving plates; top with salad. Sprinkle basil over salads, if desired. **Yield:** 4 servings.

Per serving: 336 calories, 9g protein, 36g carbohydrate, 18g fat, 6g fiber, 0mg cholesterol, 597mg sodium

What Other Cooks Have Done:

"We made this recipe with lobster tails and it was even better than we thought it would be. The sauce did not overwhelm the asparagus, but brought out the natural flavors. The ease of the recipe was amazing."

Grilled Asparagus with Orange Wasabi Dressing

Wasabi powder and sesame oil add an Asian flair to this grilled asparagus recipe created by Chef Chris Schlesinger of The East Coast Grill in Cambridge, Massachusetts.

2	tablespoons soy sauce	2	tablespoons sesame oil
2	tablespoons orange juice	30	medium asparagus spears, trimmed
1	teaspoon white sugar		
1	teaspoon McCORMICK® Gourmet Collection™ Wasabi Powder	¼	teaspoon McCORMICK® Gourmet Collection™ Cracked Black Pepper
½	teaspoon McCORMICK® Gourmet Collection™ Ground Ginger	1½	cups shredded Napa cabbage

1. In a small bowl, whisk together soy sauce, orange juice, sugar, wasabi powder, and ginger.
2. Pour sesame oil into a shallow dish and add the asparagus. Sprinkle with pepper. Roll asparagus in oil to coat. Grill asparagus over medium heat 4 to 6 minutes, or until tender-crisp.
3. Place shredded cabbage on a serving platter. Arrange grilled asparagus on top and pour dressing over asparagus and cabbage. **Yield:** 6 servings.

Per serving: 70 calories, 2g protein, 6g carbohydrate, 5g fat, 2g fiber, 0mg cholesterol, 308mg sodium

---

quick & easy

submitted by: **Bush's Best® Beans**

Prep Time: 10 minutes
Cook Time: 15 minutes

Test Kitchen Secret:

Serve this blackeye pea dish on New Year's day with collard greens for lots of luck all year long.

Bush's Best® Savory Stewed Tomatoes

The flavors of four delicious ingredients blend together to make this quick-to-prepare, hearty side dish.

2	slices bacon, chopped	1	(14.5 ounce) can seasoned diced tomatoes, undrained
½	cup chopped onion		
1	(15.8 ounce) can BUSH'S BEST® Blackeye Peas, rinsed and drained		

1. Cook bacon in a 10 inch skillet over medium heat until crisp. Transfer bacon with a slotted spoon to a paper towel; set aside. Cook onion in drippings in skillet until tender, about 5 minutes, stirring occasionally.
2. Stir in BUSH'S BEST® Blackeye Peas and tomatoes; simmer, uncovered, 5 minutes, stirring occasionally. Top with reserved bacon and serve warm. **Yield:** 4 servings.

Per serving: 142 calories, 7g protein, 22g carbohydrate, 2g fat, 5g fiber, 4mg cholesterol, 588mg sodium

Bush's Best® Savory Stewed Tomatoes

Zesty Marinated Vegetables

make-ahead

submitted by: **McCormick® & Company**

Prep Time: 15 minutes
Marinate Time: 6 hours

What Other Cooks Have Done:
"This is a wonderful new way to eat your vegetables! I reduced the oil to ⅓ cup, and it worked out fine. I measured out 2 cups of cauliflower, but next time I'll just throw in an entire head. There would still be plenty of marinade."

A jar of cauliflower, mozzarella cheese, olives, and red bell pepper chunks marinated with garlic, basil, and oregano makes a great addition to a wine and cheese gift basket.

2	cups fresh cauliflower florets	2	teaspoons McCORMICK® Basil Leaves
8	ounces mozzarella cheese, cut into cubes	2	teaspoons McCORMICK® Thyme Leaves
1	(6 ounce) can pitted large ripe olives, drained	1	teaspoon McCORMICK® Oregano Leaves
1	large red bell pepper, cut into squares (about ¾ inch)	1	teaspoon McCORMICK® SEASON-ALL® Seasoned Salt
¾	cup vegetable oil	2	teaspoons white sugar
½	cup white wine vinegar		
1	tablespoon McCORMICK® Garlic Powder		

1. Place cauliflower, cheese, olives, and bell pepper in large bowl or zip-top plastic bag.

2. Combine remaining ingredients in a small bowl or jar; mix or shake well. Pour over vegetables. Marinate in refrigerator 6 hours or up to 5 days. **Yield:** 7 servings.

Per serving: 342 calories, 9g protein, 8g carbohydrate, 31g fat, 3g fiber, 19mg cholesterol, 548mg sodium

Easy Holiday Stuffing

This traditionally flavored savory stuffing is a breeze to make in the slow cooker. This leaves plenty of oven space for your main dish.

1	cup butter, melted	3	tablespoons HERB-OX® Chicken Flavored Bouillon Granules
2	cups chopped celery		
1	cup chopped onion	2	eggs, lightly beaten
1	teaspoon poultry seasoning	2	cups water
1	teaspoon crumbled leaf sage	12	cups breadcrumbs
½	teaspoon ground black pepper		

1. In large bowl, combine butter, celery, onion, poultry seasoning, sage, pepper, bouillon granules, eggs, and water. Add breadcrumbs and stir to blend. Place mixture in slow cooker. Cook on High for 45 minutes; reduce heat to Low and cook for 6 hours, or cook on High for 3 hours. **Yield:** 12 servings.

Per serving: 584 calories, 15g protein, 81g carbohydrate, 22g fat, 3g fiber, 77mg cholesterol, 1140mg sodium

holiday fare

submitted by: **Hormel Foods Corporation**

Prep Time: 10 minutes
Cook Time: 3 to 6 hours

Test Kitchen Secret:
For a drier top on your stuffing, remove the lid of the slow cooker during the last 45 minutes of cooking.

Fruit & Nut Stuffing

This easy cornbread stuffing recipe is great for a weeknight supper. It's enhanced with dried cranberries and toasted pecans.

1	(6 ounce) package cornbread stuffing, divided	¼	cup butter
		¼	cup dried cranberries or raisins
1⅔	cups water	¼	cup chopped toasted pecans
2	teaspoons HERB-OX® Chicken Flavored Bouillon Granules		

1. In a large saucepan, combine seasoning packet from stuffing mix, water, bouillon granules, and butter. Bring mixture to a boil. Cover, reduce heat, and simmer for 5 minutes. Stir in stuffing and cranberries. Remove from heat and let stand, covered, for 5 minutes. Add pecans and fluff stuffing with a fork. **Yield:** 6 servings.

Per serving: 228 calories, 3g protein, 26g carbohydrate, 12g fat, 5g fiber, 21mg cholesterol, 454mg sodium

comfort food

submitted by: **Hormel Foods Corporation**

Prep Time: 5 minutes
Cook Time: 10 minutes

Test Kitchen Secret:
Any combination of dried fruits, like dried cherries, golden raisins, and apricots, would be good in this stuffing.

Brown-Eyed Susan Sweet Potato Cake,
page 248

sweet treats

Satisfy any sweet tooth with **decadent** desserts that are sure to please. Treat your family to **creamy** pies and cheesecakes, or impress party guests with **rich** brownies and cookies.

Cool & Minty Party Cake

A majestic dessert creation of white cake and mint ice cream is frosted with whipped topping and served frozen.

make-ahead

submitted by: **Eagle Brand**®

Prep Time: 30 minutes
Cook Time: 30 minutes
Freeze Time: 12 hours

Test Kitchen Secret:
If your ice cream layer hangs over the edges of your cake layers, just use a metal spatula to scrape off the excess.

1   (14 ounce) can EAGLE BRAND® Sweetened Condensed Milk (not evaporated milk)
2   teaspoons peppermint extract
8   drops green food coloring (optional)
2   cups whipping cream (do not use non-dairy)
1   (18.25 ounce) package white cake mix
    Green crème de menthe liqueur
1   (8 ounce) container frozen non-dairy whipped topping, thawed

1. Line bottom and sides of a 9 inch round pan with aluminum foil. In a large bowl, combine EAGLE BRAND® Milk, peppermint extract, and food coloring, if desired. Fold in whipping cream. Pour into prepared pan; cover. Freeze at least 6 hours or until firm.
2. Meanwhile, prepare and bake cake mix as package directs for 2 (9 inch) round layers. Remove from pans; cool thoroughly on wire racks.
3. With a fork, poke holes 1 inch apart halfway through each cake layer. Spoon small amounts of crème de menthe in holes. Place 1 cake layer on serving plate; top with ice cream layer, then second cake layer. Trim ice cream layer, if necessary, to be even with edges of cake layers.
4. Frost quickly with whipped topping. Return to freezer and freeze at least 6 hours. Freeze any leftovers. **Yield:** 12 servings.

Per serving: 487 calories, 5g protein, 57g carbohydrate, 25g fat, 0g fiber, 65mg cholesterol, 339mg sodium

Rich Caramel Cake

Who can resist this caramel-filled chocolate cake topped with pecans?

holiday fare

submitted by: **Eagle Brand**®

Prep Time: 20 minutes
Cook Time: 1 hour

What Other Cooks Have Done:
"If you love 'turtle' candy, you will love this cake. The recipe is quick and easy, but the results look like you worked for hours."

1   (14 ounce) package caramels, unwrapped
½   cup butter or margarine
1   (14 ounce) can EAGLE BRAND® Sweetened Condensed Milk (not evaporated milk)
1   (18.25 ounce) package chocolate cake mix
1   cup coarsely chopped toasted pecans

1. Preheat oven to 350°F. Grease a 9x13 inch pan. In a saucepan over low heat, melt caramels and butter. Remove from heat; stir in EAGLE BRAND® Milk. Mix well; set aside.
2. Prepare cake mix as package directs. Spread 2 cups batter into prepared pan. Bake in the preheated oven 15 minutes. Spread caramel mixture over cake; spread remaining batter over caramel. Top with pecans. Bake 30 to 35 more minutes or until cake springs back when touched. **Yield:** 12 servings.

Per serving: 549 calories, 8g protein, 76g carbohydrate, 27g fat, 2g fiber, 13mg cholesterol, 565mg sodium

Cool & Minty Party Cake

Brown-Eyed Susan Sweet Potato Cake

(pictured on page 244)

A finalist in the 2000 Share The Very Best Recipe Contest, this Southern-style twist on carrot cake was submitted by Helen Conwell of Fairhope, Alabama.

Cake

2¼ cups all-purpose flour
1 tablespoon baking powder
1 teaspoon baking soda
1 teaspoon salt
1 teaspoon ground cinnamon
½ teaspoon ground ginger
1 (15 ounce) can mashed sweet potatoes or whole sweet potatoes, rinsed, drained, and mashed
1 cup white sugar
½ cup packed dark brown sugar
3 large eggs
1 cup vegetable oil
1 cup (6 ounces) NESTLÉ® TOLL HOUSE® Semi-Sweet Chocolate Morsels
½ cup chopped pecans
½ cup water

Creamy Premier White Icing

¾ cup NESTLÉ® TOLL HOUSE® Premier White Morsels
1½ tablespoons butter
½ (8 ounce) package cream cheese, softened
⅓ cup sour cream
¾ teaspoon vanilla extract
¼ teaspoon almond extract (optional)
3 to 4 cups confectioners' sugar

1. Preheat oven to 350°F. Lightly grease and flour 1 (9x13 inch) pan or 2 (9 inch) round pans.

2. Combine flour, baking powder, baking soda, salt, cinnamon, and ginger in a small bowl. Combine sweet potatoes, white sugar, and brown sugar in a large bowl. Add eggs, one at a time, beating well after each addition. Add oil; beat until well blended. Stir in chocolate morsels, pecans, and water. Stir in flour mixture; mix until blended. Pour into prepared pan(s).

3. Bake in the preheated oven for 35 to 40 minutes or until wooden pick inserted in center of cake comes out clean. Cool completely in pan(s) on wire rack(s). For layer cakes, remove from pans after 10 minutes.

4. Microwave white morsels and butter in a small, microwave-safe bowl on MEDIUM-HIGH (70%) for 1 minute; stir. Morsels may retain some of their original shape. If necessary, microwave in additional 10 to 15 second intervals, stirring until smooth. Cool to room temperature.

5. Beat cream cheese and sour cream into morsel mixture until creamy. Add vanilla and, if desired, almond extract. Gradually beat in confectioners' sugar until mixture reaches spreading consistency. Frost cake with icing. **Yield:** 12 servings.

Per serving: 787 calories, 8g protein, 110g carbohydrate, 36g fat, 3g fiber, 70mg cholesterol, 469mg sodium

Gingerbread Pudding Cake

Old-fashioned pudding cake makes a decadent comeback as gingerbread.

2½ cups all-purpose flour
1½ teaspoons baking soda
1¼ teaspoons ground ginger
1 teaspoon ground cinnamon
½ teaspoon salt
½ teaspoon ground allspice
¼ teaspoon ground nutmeg
1 cup molasses
1 cup water
½ cup LAND O'LAKES® Butter, softened★
½ cup white sugar
1 egg
¾ cup packed brown sugar
1½ cups hot water
⅓ cup LAND O'LAKES® Butter, melted
Ice cream (optional)

1. Preheat oven to 350°F. Combine flour, baking soda, ginger, cinnamon, salt, allspice, and nutmeg in a medium bowl; set aside. Combine molasses and water; set aside.

2. With an electric mixer, beat ½ cup butter and white sugar in a large bowl on medium speed until creamy. Add egg; continue beating until well mixed. Reduce speed to low. Add flour mixture alternately with molasses mixture, beating after each addition just until mixed.

3. Pour batter into an ungreased 9x13 inch pan; sprinkle with ¾ cup brown sugar.

4. Combine 1½ cups hot water and ⅓ cup melted butter in medium bowl; carefully pour over top of batter. (Do not stir.) Bake in the preheated oven for 40 to 55 minutes or until gingerbread is cracked on top and wooden pick inserted in center comes out clean. Serve warm with ice cream, if desired. **Yield:** 12 servings.

★Substitute LAND O'LAKES® Soft Baking Butter with Canola Oil right from the refrigerator.

Per serving: 372 calories, 3g protein, 61g carbohydrate, 14g fat, 1g fiber, 52mg cholesterol, 407mg sodium

holiday fare

submitted by: **Land O'Lakes, Inc.**

Prep Time: 30 minutes
Cook Time: 55 minutes

What Other Cooks Have Done:
"This was great! Very moist and flavorful. I topped it with whipped cream."

comfort food

submitted by: **Nestlé® Toll House®**

Prep Time: 25 minutes
Cook Time: 35 minutes

Toll House® Crumbcake

This sour cream crumbcake is topped with a mixture of brown sugar, butter, nuts, and mini chocolate chips—a special treat for morning, noon, or night.

Topping

⅓ cup packed brown sugar
1 tablespoon all-purpose flour
2 tablespoons butter or margarine
½ cup chopped nuts
1 (12 ounce) package (2 cups) NESTLÉ® TOLL HOUSE® Semi-Sweet Chocolate Mini Morsels, divided

Cake

1¾ cups all-purpose flour
1 teaspoon baking powder
1 teaspoon baking soda
¼ teaspoon salt
¾ cup white sugar
½ cup butter or margarine, softened
1 teaspoon vanilla extract
3 large eggs
1 cup sour cream

1. Preheat oven to 350°F. Grease and flour a 9x13 inch pan.
2. Combine brown sugar, flour, and butter in small bowl; mix with pastry blender or two knives until crumbly. Stir in nuts and ½ cup morsels.
3. Combine flour, baking powder, baking soda, and salt in small bowl. Beat white sugar, butter, and vanilla in large mixer bowl until creamy. Add eggs, one at a time, beating well after each addition. Gradually add flour mixture alternately with sour cream. Fold in remaining morsels. Spread into prepared pan; sprinkle with topping.
4. Bake in the preheated oven for 25 to 35 minutes or until wooden pick inserted in center comes out clean. Cool in pan on wire rack. **Yield:** 12 servings.

Per serving: 458 calories, 6g protein, 52g carbohydrate, 26g fat, 2g fiber, 88mg cholesterol, 310mg sodium

Nestlé® Wonderball® Clown Cake

Invite your kids to help decorate this beautiful clown cake—the fun they'll have is worth the effort.

1   (18.25 ounce) package cake
    mix, any flavor
5   drops food coloring, any color
1   (12 ounce) container prepared
    white frosting, divided
1   container candy sprinkles
2   NESTLÉ® WONDERBALLS®,
    unwrapped

19   strands red shoestring
    licorice, divided
1   fruit roll snack, any flavor
2   NESTLÉ® SWEETARTS®
2   peppermint candies
8   candy orange, lemon, or lime
    slices

1. Preheat oven according to cake mix package directions. Grease and flour 1 (8 inch) round pan and 1 (8 inch) square pan.

2. Prepare cake mix according to package directions. Divide batter between prepared pans. Bake according to package directions for round pans. Cool cakes in pans on wire racks for 10 minutes. Turn out onto racks to cool completely.

3. Cut hat shape from square cake by cutting from 2 adjacent corners to a midpoint on the opposite side of the square. Cut 2 rectangles from bases of the leftover triangle-shaped pieces to form collar. Assemble cake by placing the hat above the face (round cake); push together. Place 2 rectangle pieces of cake below the face to form 1 large rectangular collar.

4. Stir food coloring into ½ cup frosting; frost hat. Sprinkle with candy sprinkles. Use remaining frosting to frost face and collar, coloring it as desired and reserving 1 tablespoon white frosting. With a small dab of reserved frosting, place 1 WONDERBALL® at top of hat. Twist 16 strands of licorice to form clown's hair; press into frosting. Cut 2 diamond shapes from fruit roll snack. Place on face where eyes would be located; use small dab of reserved frosting to add SWEETART® candies for eyes. Twist remaining strands of licorice together and place on face as mouth. Place peppermint candies at both ends of mouth. Add candy orange slices to collar.

5. Cut a 1 inch square from center of face; lift out cake and discard. Press remaining WONDERBALL® into square to form clown nose. **Yield:** 12 servings.

Per serving: 415 calories, 3g protein, 64g carbohydrate, 15g fat, 1g fiber, 12mg cholesterol, 351mg sodium

kid-friendly

submitted by: **Nestlé®**

Prep Time: 30 minutes
Cook Time: 25 minutes

Test Kitchen Secret:
You can use 1 (9 inch) round and 1 (9 inch) square pan in place of the 8 inch round pan and 8 inch square cake pan. Nestlé® Wonderballs® are a hit at any children's party. Each Wonderball®, a hollow Nestlé® chocolate ball, is filled with sugar candies of assorted shapes and colors and special prizes like stickers or tattoos.

Luscious Buttercream Frosting

Silky, smooth, and satiny—a luscious topping for any cake.

4	cups confectioners' sugar	2	teaspoons vanilla extract
¼	cup milk		Food coloring (optional)
½	cup LAND O'LAKES® Butter, softened★		

1. Combine all ingredients except food coloring in a large bowl. With an electric mixer, beat at low speed until well mixed. Increase speed to medium and beat, scraping bowl often, until light and fluffy. Tint frosting with food coloring, if desired. **Yield:** 18 servings.
★Substitute LAND O'LAKES® Soft Baking Butter with Canola Oil right from the refrigerator.

Per serving: 157 calories, 0g protein, 28g carbohydrate, 5g fat, 0g fiber, 14mg cholesterol, 54mg sodium

Libby's® Pumpkin Roll with Cream Cheese Filling

This cake's autumn flavors make it a hit at holiday parties.

¼	cup confectioners' sugar	1	cup chopped walnuts (optional)
¾	cup all-purpose flour	1	(8 ounce) package cream cheese, softened
½	teaspoon baking powder		
½	teaspoon baking soda	1	cup confectioners' sugar, sifted
½	teaspoon ground cinnamon	6	tablespoons butter or margarine, softened
½	teaspoon ground cloves		
¼	teaspoon salt	1	teaspoon vanilla extract
3	large eggs	¼	cup confectioners' sugar (optional)
1	cup white sugar		
⅔	cup LIBBY'S® 100% Pure Pumpkin		

1. Preheat oven to 375°F. Grease a 10x15 inch jellyroll pan and line with wax paper. Grease and flour paper. Sprinkle a kitchen towel with ¼ cup confectioners' sugar.
2. Combine flour, baking powder, baking soda, cinnamon, cloves, and salt in small bowl. Beat eggs and sugar in large mixer bowl until thick. Beat in pumpkin. Stir in flour mixture. Spread evenly into prepared pan. Sprinkle with nuts, if desired.
3. Bake in the preheated oven for 13 to 15 minutes or until top of cake springs back when touched. Immediately turn cake onto prepared towel. Carefully peel off paper. Roll up cake and towel together, starting with narrow end. Cool on wire rack.

4. Beat cream cheese, 1 cup confectioners' sugar, butter, and vanilla in a small mixer bowl until smooth. Carefully unroll cake; remove towel. Spread cream cheese mixture over cake. Reroll cake. Wrap in plastic wrap and chill at least 1 hour. Sprinkle with confectioners' sugar before serving, if desired. **Yield:** 10 servings.

Per serving: 432 calories, 7g protein, 50g carbohydrate, 24g fat, 2g fiber, 107mg cholesterol, 303mg sodium

Sensational Irish Cream Cheesecake

This rich, creamy cheesecake with a touch of Irish cream and mini chocolate chips will impress everyone. You can even make it a day ahead!

Crust

1¾ cups finely crushed chocolate graham cracker crumbs

6 tablespoons LAND O'LAKES® Butter, melted

Filling

1 cup white sugar

3 (8 ounce) packages cream cheese, softened

4 eggs

⅓ cup Irish cream liqueur★

¾ cup mini real semi-sweet chocolate chips, divided

1 teaspoon all-purpose flour LAND O'LAKES® Gourmet Heavy Whipping Cream, whipped (optional)

Chocolate curls (optional)

1. Preheat oven to 375°F. Lightly grease a 9 inch springform pan. Combine graham cracker crumbs and butter in a medium bowl. Press onto bottom and 1 inch up sides of prepared pan. Set aside.

2. Combine sugar and cream cheese in large bowl. With an electric mixer, beat at medium speed, scraping bowl often, until creamy. Add eggs, one at a time, beating well after each addition. Stir in liqueur by hand.

3. Combine ½ cup chocolate chips and 1 teaspoon flour in small bowl; gently stir into cream cheese mixture. Pour batter over crust. Sprinkle remaining chocolate chips over batter.

4. Bake in the preheated oven for 40 to 45 minutes or until center is set and firm to touch. Cool 10 minutes. Loosen sides of cheesecake by running knife around inside of pan. Cool completely. Cover; refrigerate at least 3 hours.

5. Pipe whipped cream over top of cheesecake and top with chocolate curls, if desired. **Yield:** 16 servings.

★Substitute ¼ cup LAND O'LAKES® Half-and-Half or milk, 2 tablespoons cooled coffee, and 1 teaspoon almond extract.

Per serving: 370 calories, 6g protein, 27g carbohydrate, 27g fat, 1g fiber, 122mg cholesterol, 234mg sodium

make-ahead

submitted by: **Land O'Lakes, Inc.**

Prep Time: 30 minutes
Cook Time: 45 minutes
Chill Time: 3 hours

What Other Cooks Have Done:
"I love this recipe and have made it at least a dozen times. The only hint I have is to increase the Irish cream to just under ½ cup. Also, leave the cheesecake in the turned-off oven with the door ajar for about a half hour to cool. This will help it not to crack."

Prep Time: 20 minutes

Cook Time: 1 hour

Test Kitchen Secret:

To make a New York Style Cheese-cake, use 4 (8 ounce) cream cheese packages and 4 eggs. Proceed as directed, adding 2 tablespoons all-purpose flour after eggs. Bake 1 hour 10 minutes or until center is set. Omit sour cream. Serve and store as directed.

Creamy Baked Cheesecake

Eagle Brand® Sweetened Condensed Milk gives this cheesecake a creamy and smooth texture. Try it with Raspberry Topping, below, or serve it plain.

1¼ cups graham cracker crumbs
¼   cup white sugar
⅓   cup butter or margarine, melted
2   (8 ounce) packages cream cheese, softened
1   (14 ounce) can EAGLE BRAND® Sweetened Condensed Milk (not evaporated milk)

3   eggs
¼   cup lemon juice
1   (8 ounce) container sour cream at room temperature
    Raspberry Topping (optional)

1. Preheat oven to 300°F. Combine crumbs, sugar, and butter; press firmly onto bottom of an ungreased 9 inch springform pan.
2. In a large bowl, beat cream cheese until fluffy. Gradually beat in EAGLE BRAND® Milk until smooth. Add eggs and lemon juice; mix well. Pour over crust. Bake in the preheated oven 50 to 55 minutes or until set.
3. Remove from oven; top with sour cream. Bake 5 more minutes. Cool; cover and chill in refrigerator until ready to serve. Prepare Raspberry Topping, if desired, and serve with cheesecake. Store, covered, in refrigerator. **Yield:** 12 servings.

Per serving: 393 calories, 8g protein, 31g carbohydrate, 27g fat, 0g fiber, 114mg cholesterol, 290mg sodium

Raspberry Topping

1   (10 ounce) package frozen red raspberries in syrup, thawed
¼   cup red currant jelly or red raspberry jam

1   tablespoon cornstarch

1. Drain ⅔ cup syrup from raspberries. Set raspberries aside.
2. In small saucepan over medium heat, combine ⅔ cup syrup from raspberries, jelly, and cornstarch. Cook and stir until slightly thickened and clear. Cool. Stir in raspberries. Serve over slices of cheesecake. **Yield:** 12 servings.

Per serving: 44 calories, 0g protein, 11g carbohydrate, 0g fat, 1g fiber, 0mg cholesterol, 6mg sodium

Sweet Potato Pie

This sweet potato pie, with its rich texture and delicate blend of spices, is easy enough for beginners to make.

1	pound sweet potatoes, cooked and peeled	1	teaspoon grated orange zest
¼	cup butter or margarine	1	teaspoon vanilla extract
1	(14 ounce) can EAGLE BRAND® Sweetened Condensed Milk (not evaporated milk)	1	teaspoon ground cinnamon
		1	teaspoon ground nutmeg
		¼	teaspoon salt
		2	eggs
		1	(9 inch) unbaked pie shell

1. Preheat oven to 350°F. In a large mixer bowl, beat sweet potatoes with butter until smooth. Add remaining ingredients except pie shell; mix well. Pour into pie shell. Bake in the preheated oven for 30 minutes or until golden brown. Cool. **Yield:** 8 servings.

Per serving: 404 calories, 8g protein, 51g carbohydrate, 19g fat, 3g fiber, 69mg cholesterol, 341mg sodium

quick & easy

submitted by: **Eagle Brand®**

Prep Time: 10 minutes
Cook Time: 30 minutes

What Other Cooks Have Done:
"This is a wonderful pie. We used home-grown sweet potatoes and topped the pie with a mixture of 1 pint sour cream, ¼ cup sugar, and 1 teaspoon vanilla."

McCormick's® Classic Pumpkin Pie

Classic Pumpkin Pie is based on a recipe from the McCormick® *Spices of the World Cookbook*.

1	(9 inch) unbaked pie shell	½	teaspoon salt
2	eggs, well beaten	1	(15 ounce) can pumpkin
½	cup packed brown sugar	1	(12 ounce) can evaporated milk
1	tablespoon all-purpose flour		Whipped cream (optional)
2	teaspoons McCORMICK® Pumpkin Pie Spice		Pumpkin pie spice (optional)

1. Preheat oven to 425°F. Put unbaked pie shell in a 9 inch pie plate.
2. Combine eggs, brown sugar, flour, pumpkin pie spice, and salt in a medium bowl; mix well. Stir in pumpkin and gradually add evaporated milk, mixing well. Pour into pie shell.
3. Bake in the preheated oven for 15 minutes. Reduce temperature to 350°F and continue baking 40 minutes or until knife inserted in center comes out clean. Serve pie warm or cold, and garnish with whipped cream sprinkled with extra pumpkin pie spice, if desired. Store, covered, in refrigerator. **Yield:** 8 servings.

Per serving: 231 calories, 6g protein, 31g carbohydrate, 10g fat, 2g fiber, 65mg cholesterol, 316mg sodium

comfort food

submitted by: **McCormick® & Company**

Prep Time: 10 minutes
Cook Time: 55 minutes

Test Kitchen Secret:
If you prefer a spicier pumpkin pie, try increasing the Pumpkin Pie Spice to 1 tablespoon.

Celebrate the Seasons with Libby's® Pumpkin

Thanksgiving and the rush of holidays at the end of the year wouldn't be the same without a good old-fashioned pumpkin pie. Libby's® canned pumpkin makes the holidays a breeze. In just ten minutes of prep time, you can have Thanksgiving dessert without any fuss.

Libby's® Famous Pumpkin Pie

Whether you're hosting a festive party or a casual get-together with friends, Libby's® Famous Pumpkin Pie will make entertaining easy!

Prep Time: 10 minutes   **Cook Time:** 1 hour 5 minutes   **Stand Time:** 2 hours

- ¾ cup white sugar
- ½ teaspoon salt
- 1 teaspoon ground cinnamon
- ½ teaspoon ground ginger
- ¼ teaspoon ground cloves
- 2 eggs
- 1 (15 ounce) can LIBBY'S® 100% Pure Pumpkin
- 1 (12 ounce) can NESTLÉ® CARNATION® Evaporated Milk
- 1 (9 inch) unbaked deep dish pie shell
- Whipped topping, thawed (optional)

1. Preheat oven to 425°F.

2. Combine sugar, salt, cinnamon, ginger, and cloves in a small bowl. Set aside. Beat eggs lightly in large bowl. Stir in pumpkin and sugar-spice mixture. Gradually stir in evaporated milk. Pour into pie shell.

3. Bake in the preheated oven for 15 minutes. Reduce temperature to 350°F; bake for 40 to 50 minutes or until knife inserted near center comes out clean. Cool on wire rack for 2 hours. Top with whipped topping, if desired. Serve immediately or refrigerate. (Do not freeze as this will cause the shell to separate from the filling.)

Yield: 8 servings.

Per serving: 284 calories, 6g protein, 39g carbohydrate, 12g fat, 3g fiber, 65mg cholesterol, 355mg sodium

Butter Pecan Tartlets

These bite-sized pecan pie tartlets are a special addition to your cookie platter.

Tart Shells

1¾	cups all-purpose flour
½	cup LAND O'LAKES® Butter, softened★
½	cup white sugar
1	egg
1	teaspoon almond extract

Filling

1	cup confectioners' sugar
½	cup LAND O'LAKES® Butter
⅓	cup dark corn syrup
1	cup chopped pecans
36	pecan halves

1. Preheat oven to 400°F. Combine flour, ½ cup butter, white sugar, egg, and almond extract in large bowl. With an electric mixer, beat at medium speed, scraping bowl often, until mixture resembles coarse crumbs.

2. Press 1 tablespoon mixture into each cup of mini muffin pans to form 36 (1¾ to 2 inch) shells. Bake in the preheated oven for 7 to 10 minutes or until very lightly browned. Remove from oven. Reduce oven to 350°F.

3. Meanwhile, combine confectioners' sugar, ½ cup butter, and corn syrup in a 2 quart saucepan. Cook over medium heat, stirring occasionally, 4 to 5 minutes or until mixture comes to a full boil. Remove from heat; stir in chopped pecans.

4. Spoon filling into baked shells; top each tartlet with a pecan half. Bake for 5 minutes. Cool 20 minutes; remove from pans. **Yield:** 3 dozen.

★Substitute LAND O'LAKES® Soft Baking Butter with Canola Oil right from the refrigerator.

Per tartlet: 132 calories, 1g protein, 14g carbohydrate, 8g fat, 1g fiber, 20mg cholesterol, 59mg sodium

party pleaser

submitted by: **Land O'Lakes, Inc.**

Prep Time: 1 hour
Cook Time: 20 minutes

What Other Cooks Have Done:
"If you want something really quick, this is it. (I bought tart shells.) Do not serve these chilled! They'll be like hard candy wrapped in pastry."

Magic Lemon Pie

Finally, a show-stopping lemon meringue pie that's also easy to make.

quick & easy

submitted by: **Eagle Brand®**

Prep Time: 15 minutes
Cook Time: 28 minutes

Test Kitchen Secret:

If you don't want to grate lemon zest, use ¼ teaspoon lemon extract in its place.

1 (14 ounce) can EAGLE BRAND® Sweetened Condensed Milk (not evaporated milk)
½ cup lemon juice
1 teaspoon grated lemon zest
2 eggs, separated
1 (8 or 9 inch) crumb or baked pastry pie shell
¼ teaspoon cream of tartar
¼ cup white sugar

1. Preheat oven to 325°F. In a mixing bowl, combine EAGLE BRAND® Milk, lemon juice, lemon zest, and egg yolks; stir until mixture thickens. Pour into chilled crumb crust or cooled pastry shell.
2. Combine egg whites and cream of tartar in a medium bowl; beat until almost stiff enough to hold a peak. Add sugar gradually, beating until stiff and glossy but not dry. Pile lightly onto pie filling.
3. Bake in the preheated oven for 25 to 28 minutes or until meringue is lightly browned. Cool. **Yield:** 8 servings.

Per serving: 309 calories, 6g protein, 48g carbohydrate, 11g fat, 0g fiber, 70mg cholesterol, 203mg sodium

Key Lime Pie with Real Butter

A quick way to make a traditional Florida favorite. Cool, tart, and refreshing Key lime pie is delicious anytime.

make-ahead

submitted by: **Eagle Brand®**

Prep Time: 15 minutes
Cook Time: 10 minutes
Chill Time: 4 hours

Test Kitchen Secret:

If you do not own a food processor, use a blender to prepare the crust and an electric mixer to prepare the filling.

2 cups vanilla wafers (about 40 cookies)
1 cup slivered almonds
⅓ cup butter, melted
2 (3 ounce) packages cream cheese, softened
¼ cup butter, softened
⅓ cup Key lime juice
1 (14 ounce) can EAGLE BRAND® Sweetened Condensed Milk (not evaporated milk)
Key lime slices and frozen whipped topping, thawed (optional)

1. Preheat oven to 350°F. In a food processor bowl, process vanilla wafers until ground. Add almonds; process until coarsely ground. Transfer to a large bowl; add ⅓ cup melted butter and stir well. Press crumb mixture onto bottom and up sides of a 9 inch pie plate. Bake in the preheated oven for 10 minutes or until lightly browned; cool.
2. In a clean food processor bowl, add cream cheese and ¼ cup butter. Cover and process until fluffy, scraping sides of bowl as necessary. Add lime juice and EAGLE BRAND® Milk; cover and process until blended, scraping bowl as necessary.
3. Pour mixture into crust; cover with plastic wrap and refrigerate at least 4 hours. Garnish with key lime slices and whipped topping, if desired. **Yield:** 12 servings.

Per serving: 467 calories, 8g protein, 45g carbohydrate, 30g fat, 2g fiber, 51mg cholesterol, 268mg sodium

Key Lime Pie with Real Butter

Scandinavian Almond Puff

This is a variation of the traditional Scandinavian almond coffee cake.

make-ahead

submitted by: **Land O'Lakes, Inc.**

Prep Time: 40 minutes
Cook Time: 55 minutes

Test Kitchen Secret:
To make the recipe ahead of time, wrap puff in plastic wrap or aluminum foil, and refrigerate up to two days.

Pastry

1   cup all-purpose flour
½   cup LAND O'LAKES® Butter
2   tablespoons water

Topping

1   cup water
½   cup LAND O'LAKES® Butter
1   cup all-purpose flour
1   teaspoon almond extract
3   eggs

Glaze

1   cup confectioners' sugar
1   tablespoon LAND O'LAKES® Butter, softened
½   teaspoon almond extract
1   to 2 tablespoons milk
¼   cup sliced almonds

1. Preheat oven to 350°F. Place 1 cup flour in a large bowl; cut in ½ cup butter until mixture resembles coarse crumbs. Stir in 2 tablespoons water with fork until flour mixture is just moistened. Press dough into a ball. Pat dough into a 10 inch circle on an ungreased baking sheet. Set aside.

2. Combine 1 cup water and ½ cup butter in a 2 quart saucepan. Cook over medium heat until mixture comes to a full boil and butter is melted. Remove from heat; stir in 1 cup flour and 1 teaspoon almond extract. Reduce heat to low. Cook, stirring constantly, until mixture forms a ball (about 1 minute). Remove from heat. Add eggs, one at a time, beating with wire whisk or wooden spoon until smooth and glossy.

3. Spread egg mixture over pastry circle. Bake in the preheated oven for 50 to 55 minutes or until surface is crisp and golden. Cool completely. (Topping rises during baking and shrinks during cooling, forming a custard-like layer.)

4. Stir together confectioners' sugar, 1 tablespoon butter, and ½ teaspoon almond extract in a small bowl until well mixed. Add enough milk for desired glazing consistency. Drizzle glaze over puff; sprinkle with sliced almonds. **Yield:** 16 servings.

Per serving: 219 calories, 3g protein, 20g carbohydrate, 14g fat, 1g fiber, 73mg cholesterol, 138mg sodium

Apple Walnut Bread Pudding with Easy Eggnog Sauce

Chunks of apples and walnuts give this recipe its crunch, while cinnamon and vanilla add to its scrumptious flavor.

Pudding

½	loaf French bread
2	large eggs, lightly beaten
1¼	cups milk
1	tablespoon McCORMICK® Pure Vanilla Extract
½	cup white sugar
1	teaspoon McCORMICK® Ground Cinnamon
½	teaspoon McCORMICK® Ground Nutmeg
1	cup peeled, diced tart apples
¾	cup chopped walnuts, toasted
⅓	cup raisins
2	tablespoons butter or margarine

Eggnog Sauce

1	tablespoon cornstarch
2	cups eggnog
1	teaspoon McCORMICK® Imitation Rum Extract
½	teaspoon McCORMICK® Pure Vanilla Extract

1. Preheat oven to 325°F. Grease a 7x11 inch pan and set aside. Trim crust from bread and cut enough bread into ¾ inch cubes to make 3 cups. Set aside.

2. Place eggs, milk, 1 tablespoon vanilla, sugar, cinnamon, nutmeg, apples, walnuts, and raisins in a large bowl, and stir until well mixed. Add bread cubes and toss to combine. Spread mixture in prepared pan and dot with butter. Bake in the preheated oven for 35 minutes or until firm.

3. To make Eggnog Sauce, whisk cornstarch into eggnog in a small saucepan. Heat to boiling over medium-high heat, stirring constantly. Reduce heat and simmer 2 minutes. Remove from heat, add rum extract and ½ teaspoon vanilla, and cool 5 minutes. Sauce will thicken. Pour over bread pudding. **Yield:** 8 servings.

Per serving: 387 calories, 10g protein, 48g carbohydrate, 18g fat, 2g fiber, 101mg cholesterol, 273mg sodium

holiday fare

submitted by: **McCormick® & Company**

Prep Time: 15 minutes
Cook Time: 40 minutes

What Other Cooks Have Done:
"I soaked the raisins in cognac or bourbon to add a little extra flavor."

Caramel Flan

Caramel Flan

A soothing warm custard is a divine finish to any meal. A classic dessert that's loved by all, this flan is made with simple ingredients.

¾ cup white sugar	1¾ cups water
4 eggs	½ teaspoon vanilla extract
1 (14 ounce) can EAGLE BRAND® Sweetened Condensed Milk (not evaporated milk)	⅛ teaspoon salt
	Fresh raspberries and star fruit (optional)

1. Preheat oven to 350°F. In a heavy skillet over medium heat, cook sugar, stirring constantly, until melted and caramel-colored. Pour into an ungreased 9 inch round or square pan, tilting to coat bottom completely. In a medium bowl, beat eggs; stir in EAGLE BRAND® Milk, water, vanilla, and salt. Pour over caramelized sugar; set pan in larger pan (a broiler pan). Fill larger pan with 1 inch of hot water.
2. Bake in the preheated oven for 55 to 60 minutes or until knife inserted near center comes out clean. Cool. Chill. Loosen side of flan with knife; invert onto serving plate with rim. Garnish with raspberries and star fruit, if desired. Refrigerate leftovers. **Yield:** 10 servings.

Per serving: 214 calories, 6g protein, 37g carbohydrate, 5g fat, 0g fiber, 98mg cholesterol, 105mg sodium

holiday fare

submitted by: **Eagle Brand®**

Prep Time: 30 minutes
Cook Time: 60 minutes

What Other Cooks Have Done:
"This is the first time I've ever made flan from scratch, and it tastes exactly like the first time I had it in a restaurant!"

Easy Homemade Vanilla Ice Cream

Make vanilla ice cream or add your favorite flavors to vary it.

1 (14 ounce) can EAGLE BRAND® Sweetened Condensed Milk (not evaporated milk)	2 cups half-and-half
	2 cups whipping cream
	2 tablespoons vanilla extract

1. In a large bowl, combine all ingredients; mix well. Pour into ice cream freezer container. Freeze according to manufacturer's instructions. Store leftovers in freezer. **Yield:** 12 servings.

Per serving: 300 calories, 5g protein, 21g carbohydrate, 22g fat, 0g fiber, 80mg cholesterol, 73mg sodium

Fresh Fruit Ice Cream

Reduce half-and-half to 1 cup. Add 1 cup pureed or mashed fruit (bananas, peaches, strawberries, etc.) and a few drops food coloring, if desired. Proceed as above.

Refrigerator-Freezer Method

Omit half-and-half. Whip whipping cream. In a large bowl, combine sweetened condensed milk and vanilla; mix well. Fold in whipped cream. Pour into a 5x9 inch loaf pan or other 2 quart container; cover. Freeze 6 hours or until firm. Store leftovers in freezer.

kid-friendly

submitted by: **Eagle Brand®**

Prep Time: 20 minutes

What Other Cooks Have Done:
"This is a wonderful, easy recipe. I substituted whole milk for the 2 cups whipping cream to cut back on fat, and it was still very flavorful!"

Butterscotch Gingerbread Cookies

Butterscotch morsels add their sweet creaminess to this classic gingerbread cookie—the ultimate treat with a glass of cold milk.

comfort food

submitted by: **Nestlé® Toll House®**

Prep Time: 15 minutes
Cook Time: 11 minutes per batch

What Other Cooks Have Done:
"We used ½ teaspoon nutmeg instead of the ginger, dark molasses cut with corn syrup instead of the light molasses, and only ¾ of the butterscotch morsels called for. We also threw in a few handfuls of dried cranberries. The cookies were delicious."

3	cups all-purpose flour		1½	cups packed brown sugar
2	teaspoons baking soda		1	large egg
1½	teaspoons ground cinnamon		⅓	cup light molasses
1½	teaspoons ground ginger		1	(11 ounce) package (1⅔ cups)
¾	teaspoon ground cloves			NESTLÉ® TOLL HOUSE®
½	teaspoon salt			Butterscotch-Flavored
1	cup butter or margarine, softened			Morsels

1. Preheat oven to 350°F.

2. Combine flour, baking soda, cinnamon, ginger, cloves, and salt in a bowl.

3. Beat butter, sugar, egg, and molasses in large mixer bowl until creamy. Gradually beat in flour mixture until well blended. Stir in morsels. Drop by rounded tablespoonfuls onto ungreased baking sheets.

4. Bake in the preheated oven for 9 to 11 minutes or until cookies are lightly browned. Cool on baking sheets for 2 minutes; remove to wire racks to cool completely. **Yield:** 2 dozen.

Per cookie: 109 calories, 1g protein, 15g carbohydrate, 5g fat, 0g fiber, 13mg cholesterol, 112mg sodium

Pumpkin Spiced & Iced Cookies

These cookies offer the moistness of pumpkin pie with the chocolatey sweetness of chocolate chips.

kid-friendly

submitted by: **Libby's® Pumpkin**

Prep Time: 20 minutes
Cook Time: 20 minutes per batch

What Other Cooks Have Done:
"I made this recipe as a Halloween treat for the people I work with. I doubled everything and ended up with over 6 dozen cookies."

2¼	cups all-purpose flour		1	teaspoon vanilla extract
1½	teaspoons pumpkin pie spice		1	(12 ounce) package (2 cups)
1	teaspoon baking powder			NESTLÉ® TOLL HOUSE®
½	teaspoon baking soda			Semi-Sweet Chocolate
½	teaspoon salt			Morsels
1	cup butter or margarine, softened		1	cup chopped walnuts
1	cup white sugar			**Vanilla Glaze**
1	(15 ounce) can LIBBY'S® 100% Pure Pumpkin		1	to 1½ cups confectioners' sugar
2	eggs		1	tablespoon milk
			½	teaspoon vanilla extract

1. Preheat oven to 375°F. Generously grease baking sheets; set aside.

2. Combine flour, pumpkin pie spice, baking powder, baking soda, and salt in a medium bowl. Beat butter and white sugar in a large mixer bowl until creamy. Beat in pumpkin, eggs, and vanilla. Gradually beat in flour mixture. Stir in morsels and nuts. Drop by rounded tablespoonfuls onto prepared baking sheets.

3. Bake in the preheated oven for 15 to 20 minutes or until edges are lightly browned. Cool on baking sheets for 2 minutes; remove to wire racks to cool completely.

4. For Vanilla Glaze, combine 1 cup confectioners' sugar, 1 tablespoon milk, and ½ teaspoon vanilla in small bowl; mix well. Drizzle or spread cookies with Vanilla Glaze. **Yield:** 3 dozen.

Per cookie: 232 calories, 3g protein, 28g carbohydrate, 13g fat, 2g fiber, 26mg cholesterol, 113mg sodium

Introduced in 1955, Famous Oatmeal Cookies earned the distinction of having the longest run on the Quaker® Oats package. For millions of Americans, nothing brings back childhood memories like a fresh batch of oatmeal cookies.

Famous Oatmeal Cookies

These chewy cookies will delight adults and children alike. Try all the different variations and come up with your family's favorite.

Prep Time: 10 minutes   **Cook Time:** 13 minutes per batch

3	cups QUAKER® Oats (Quick or Old Fashioned), uncooked
1	cup all-purpose flour
1	teaspoon salt (optional)
½	teaspoon baking soda
1	cup packed brown sugar
¾	cup shortening
½	cup white sugar
1	egg
¼	cup water
1	teaspoon vanilla extract

1. Preheat oven to 350°F. In a large bowl, combine oats, flour, salt, if desired, and baking soda. Set aside. In a large bowl, beat brown sugar, shortening, and white sugar until creamy. Add egg, water, and vanilla; beat well. Add flour mixture to sugar mixture and mix well.
2. Drop dough by rounded teaspoonfuls onto ungreased baking sheets.
3. Bake in the preheated oven 11 to 13 minutes or until edges are golden brown. Remove to wire racks. Cool completely. Store tightly covered. **Yield:** 5 dozen.

Per cookie: 60 calories, 1g protein, 9g carbohydrate, 3g fat, 1g fiber, 3mg cholesterol, 13mg sodium

Variation

Add 1 cup of any one or a combination of any of the following ingredients to basic cookie dough: raisins, chopped nuts, chocolate chips, or shredded coconut.

Large Cookies

Drop by rounded tablespoonfuls onto ungreased baking sheets. Bake 15 to 17 minutes. **Yield:** about 2½ dozen.

Bar Cookies

Press dough onto bottom of ungreased 9x13 inch pan. Bake 30 to 35 minutes or until light golden brown. Cool completely in pan on wire rack. Cut into bars. Store tightly covered. **Yield:** 2 dozen.

Oatmeal Scotchies

Chewy-crisp cookies chock-full of butterscotch-flavored candy morsels are cookie jar classics.

1¼ cups all-purpose flour	1 teaspoon vanilla extract
1 teaspoon baking soda	3 cups QUAKER® Oats (Quick
½ teaspoon salt (optional)	or Old Fashioned), uncooked
½ pound margarine or butter, softened	1 (11 ounce) package (1⅔ cups) NESTLÉ® TOLL HOUSE®
¾ cup white sugar	Butterscotch-Flavored
¾ cup packed brown sugar	Morsels
2 eggs	

1. Preheat oven to 375°F. In a large bowl, mix flour, baking soda, and salt, if desired. Set aside. In a large bowl, beat margarine and sugars until creamy. Add eggs and vanilla; beat well. Add flour mixture to egg mixture; mix well. Add oats and butterscotch morsels; mix well.

2. Drop dough by level tablespoonfuls onto ungreased baking sheets.

3. Bake in the preheated oven for 7 to 8 minutes for a chewy cookie or 9 to 10 minutes for a crisp cookie. Cool 2 minutes on baking sheets; remove to wire racks. Cool completely. Store tightly covered. **Yield:** 4 dozen.

Per cookie: 60 calories, 1g protein, 8g carbohydrate, 3g fat, 1g fiber, 0mg cholesterol, 40mg sodium

quick & easy

submitted by:
The Quaker® Oats Company

Prep Time: 10 minutes
Cook Time: 10 minutes per batch

Test Kitchen Secret:
What's the difference between quick oats and old fashioned oats? Unlike old fashioned oats, quick oats have been cut into several pieces before being rolled flat. This doesn't change the flavor—both varieties taste great.

Oatmeal Buncha Crunch® Cookies

Crunchy bits of chocolate fill these not-so-traditional oatmeal cookies.

2¼ cups all-purpose flour	1½ teaspoons vanilla extract
1½ teaspoons baking soda	3 large eggs
¾ teaspoon salt	4½ cups quick or old fashioned
1½ cups butter or margarine, softened	oats
1¼ cups white sugar	1 (13 ounce) package NESTLÉ® BUNCHA CRUNCH®
1 cup packed brown sugar	Candy

1. Preheat oven to 375°F.

2. Combine flour, baking soda, and salt in a small bowl. Beat butter, white sugar, brown sugar, and vanilla in a large mixer bowl until creamy. Add eggs, one at a time, beating well after each addition. Gradually beat in flour mixture. Stir in oats and BUNCHA CRUNCH®. Drop by rounded tablespoonfuls onto ungreased baking sheets.

3. Bake for 8 to 10 minutes or until very lightly browned. Cool on baking sheets for 2 minutes; remove to wire racks to cool completely. **Yield:** 6 dozen.

Per cookie: 121 calories, 2g protein, 16g carbohydrate, 1g fat, 1g fiber, 20mg cholesterol, 105mg sodium

kid-friendly

submitted by: **Nestlé®**

Prep Time: 15 minutes
Cook Time: 10 minutes per batch

Test Kitchen Secret:
These cookies make great snacks to serve after school or add to lunch boxes.

Prep Time: 10 minutes
Cook Time: 10 minutes per batch

Test Kitchen Secret:

Try either of these variations the next time you bake macaroons.

For Chocolate Chip Macaroons, omit almond extract. Add 1 cup mini chocolate chips.

For Cherry Nut Macaroons, omit almond extract. Add 1 cup chopped nuts and 2 tablespoons maraschino cherry syrup. Press cherry half into center of each macaroon before baking.

Coconut Macaroons

Satisfy a sweet coconut craving with this easy recipe. You can adjust the amount of almond extract to suit your personal taste.

2 (7 ounce) packages flaked coconut (5⅓ cups)	1 egg white
1 (14 ounce) can EAGLE BRAND® Sweetened Condensed Milk (not evaporated milk)	2 teaspoons vanilla extract
	1½ teaspoons almond extract

1. Preheat oven to 325°F. Line baking sheets with foil; grease foil. Set aside.
2. In large bowl, combine coconut, EAGLE BRAND® Milk, egg white, vanilla, and almond extract; mix well. Drop by rounded teaspoonfuls onto prepared baking sheets.
3. Bake in the preheated oven for 8 to 10 minutes or until lightly browned around edges. Immediately remove from baking sheets; cool on wire racks. Store loosely covered at room temperature. **Yield:** 4 dozen.

Per macaroon: 66 calories, 1g protein, 8g carbohydrate, 3g fat, 0g fiber, 3mg cholesterol, 31mg sodium

Prep Time: 10 minutes
Chill Time: 1 hour
Cook Time: 8 minutes per batch

Test Kitchen Secret:

When making the Peanut Blossom Cooookies variation, be sure to add the chocolate candy drops as soon as you pull the cookies out of the oven.

Eagle Brand® Easy Peanut Butter Cookies

These yummy peanut butter cookies are as fun to make as they are to share.

1 (14 ounce) can EAGLE BRAND® Sweetened Condensed Milk (not evaporated milk)	1 egg
	1 teaspoon vanilla extract
	2 cups biscuit baking mix
¾ to 1 cup peanut butter	⅓ cup white sugar

1. In a large mixer bowl, beat EAGLE BRAND® Milk, peanut butter, egg, and vanilla until smooth. Add biscuit mix; mix well. Chill at least 1 hour.
2. Preheat oven to 350°F. Shape into 1 inch balls. Roll in sugar. Place 2 inches apart on ungreased baking sheets. Flatten with a fork in a criss-cross pattern.
3. Bake in the preheated oven for 6 to 8 minutes or until lightly browned around edges (do not overbake). Cool. Store tightly covered at room temperature. **Yield:** 5 dozen.

Per cookie: 85 calories, 2g protein, 11g carbohydrate, 4g fat, 0g fiber, 3mg cholesterol, 78mg sodium

Peanut Blossom Cookies

Make dough as directed above. Shape dough into 1 inch balls and roll in sugar; do not flatten. Bake as directed. Immediately after baking, press solid milk chocolate candy drops in the center of each cookie.

Lemon Oat Lacies

These chewy-crisp and oh-so-lemony cookies use on-hand ingredients like butter and oats.

2 cups butter, slightly softened
1 cup white sugar
1 tablespoon grated lemon zest
1 teaspoon vanilla extract

3 cups QUAKER® Oats (Quick or Old Fashioned), uncooked★
2 cups all-purpose flour
Confectioners' sugar (optional)

1. Beat together butter, sugar, lemon zest, and vanilla until creamy.
2. Add oats and flour; mix well. Cover; chill about 30 minutes.
3. Preheat oven to 350°F. Shape dough into 1 inch balls. Place 3 inches apart on ungreased baking sheets. Flatten with the bottom of a glass dipped in white sugar.
4. Bake in the preheated oven for 12 to 15 minutes or until edges are light golden brown. Remove from oven.
5. Cool 1 minute on baking sheets; remove to wire racks. Cool completely. If desired, sprinkle with confectioners' sugar. Store in tightly covered container. **Yield:** 4½ dozen.
★For the best flavor and most delicate cookie, we recommend using QUAKER® Quick Oats.

Per cookie: 65 calories, 2g protein, 8g carbohydrate, 7g fat, 1g fiber, 0mg cholesterol, 40mg sodium

party pleaser

submitted by:
The Quaker® Oats Company

Prep Time: 15 minutes
Chill Time: 30 minutes
Cook Time: 15 minutes per batch

Test Kitchen Secret:
A light dusting of confectioners' sugar adds an elegant touch to cookies, brownies, and other desserts. To get a nice, even sprinkle, pour confectioners' sugar into a sieve and tap the side of the sieve lightly with your hand. A gentle fall of sugar should land on your cookies.

Peanutty Crisscrosses

The ultimate peanut butter oatmeal cookie, Peanutty Crisscrosses taste even more peanutty when they're made with crunchy-style peanut butter.

3 cups QUAKER® Oats (Quick or Old Fashioned), uncooked
1½ cups all-purpose flour
½ teaspoon baking soda
1½ cups packed brown sugar
1 cup peanut butter

¾ cup butter or margarine, softened
⅓ cup water
1 egg
1 teaspoon vanilla extract
White sugar

1. In large bowl, combine oats, flour, and baking soda. Set aside. In large bowl, beat brown sugar, peanut butter, and butter until creamy. Add water, egg, and vanilla; beat well. Add flour mixture; mix well. Cover; chill about 2 hours.
2. Preheat oven to 350°F. Shape dough into 1 inch balls. Place balls 2 inches apart on ungreased baking sheets. Flatten with tines of a fork dipped in white sugar, forming crisscross pattern.
3. Bake in the preheated oven for 9 to 10 minutes or until edges are golden brown. Cool 2 minutes on baking sheets; remove to wire racks. Cool completely. Store tightly covered. **Yield:** 7 dozen.

Per cookie: 62 calories, 2g protein, 7g carbohydrate, 3g fat, 1g fiber, 3mg cholesterol, 41mg sodium

make-ahead

submitted by:
The Quaker® Oats Company

Prep Time: 20 minutes
Chill Time: 2 hours
Cook Time: 10 minutes

Test Kitchen Secret:
For best results, use regular peanut butter, either creamy or crunchy. Reduced-fat peanut butter is not recommended for baking.

Peppermint Meltaways

A pink glaze makes these delicate peppermint morsels look extra festive.

holiday fare

submitted by: **Land O'Lakes, Inc.**

Prep Time: 15 minutes
Chill Time: 1 hour
Cook Time: 15 minutes per batch

Test Kitchen Secret:

To dress these cookies up for a party, arrange them on a silver tray and garnish with fresh mint sprigs. Glass votives filled with candy canes or peppermint-striped candles are a nice touch.

Cookies

½ cup confectioners' sugar
1 cup LAND O'LAKES® Butter, softened★
½ teaspoon peppermint extract
1¼ cups all-purpose flour
½ cup cornstarch

Glaze

1½ cups confectioners' sugar
2 tablespoons LAND O'LAKES® Butter, softened★
¼ teaspoon peppermint extract
1 to 2 tablespoons milk, divided
2 drops red food coloring
Hard peppermint candy or candy canes, crushed

1. Combine ½ cup sugar, 1 cup butter, and ½ teaspoon peppermint extract in a large bowl. Beat at medium speed, scraping bowl often, until creamy. Reduce speed to low; add flour and cornstarch. Beat until well mixed. Cover; refrigerate until firm (30 to 60 minutes).

2. Preheat oven to 350°F. Shape rounded teaspoonfuls of dough into 1 inch balls. Place 2 inches apart on ungreased baking sheets. Bake in the preheated oven for 12 to 15 minutes or until edges are lightly browned. Let stand 1 minute; remove from baking sheets. Cool completely.

3. Combine 1½ cups confectioners' sugar, 2 tablespoons butter, ¼ teaspoon peppermint extract, and 1 tablespoon milk in small bowl. Stir in 1 additional tablespoon of milk, if desired, to reach proper glazing consistency. Stir in food coloring. Drizzle over cooled cookies. Immediately sprinkle with crushed candy. **Yield:** 4 dozen.

★Substitute LAND O'LAKES® Soft Baking Butter with Canola Oil right from the refrigerator.

Per cookie: 80 calories, 0g protein, 10g carbohydrate, 4g fat, 0g fiber, 12mg cholesterol, 45mg sodium

Almond Butter Cookies

Make a variety of cookies by rolling balls of dough in decorator sugars or in finely chopped nuts. Pressing halved red or green candied cherries onto cookies makes for tasty holiday treats.

1 cup LAND O'LAKES® Butter, softened★	¼ teaspoon salt White sugar
¾ cup white sugar	½ cup real semi-sweet chocolate chips
1 teaspoon almond extract	
2 cups all-purpose flour	2 teaspoons shortening
½ teaspoon baking powder	

1. Preheat oven to 400°F. Combine butter, sugar, and almond extract in a large bowl. Beat at medium speed, scraping bowl often, until creamy. Reduce speed to low; add flour, baking powder, and salt. Beat until well mixed.

2. Shape rounded teaspoonfuls of dough into 1 inch balls. Place 2 inches apart on ungreased baking sheets. Flatten balls to ¼ inch thickness with the bottom of a buttered glass dipped in sugar. Bake in the preheated oven for 6 to 8 minutes or until edges are lightly browned. Cool completely.

3. Melt chocolate chips and shortening in 1 quart saucepan over low heat, stirring occasionally, until smooth (2 to 4 minutes). Drizzle or pipe chocolate on top of cooled cookies. **Yield:** 5 dozen.

★Substitute LAND O'LAKES® Soft Baking Butter with Canola Oil right from the refrigerator.

Per cookie: 60 calories, 1g protein, 7g carbohydrate, 4g fat, 0g fiber, 8mg cholesterol, 43mg sodium

party pleaser

submitted by: **Land O'Lakes, Inc.**

Prep Time: 20 minutes
Cook Time: 8 minutes per batch

What Other Cooks Have Done:
"Very tasty cookies. I rolled mine in confectioners' sugar after they had cooled slightly instead of drizzling with chocolate. I thought it made for a great taste."

Pecan Cookie Balls

quick & easy

submitted by: **McCormick® & Company**

Prep Time: 15 minutes
Cook Time: 15 minutes per batch

What Other Cooks Have Done:
"These are delicious! A real hit with friends and family. Make sure to let the cookies cool before rolling in sugar."

This unique cookie recipe will be a holiday hit, perfect for gift giving and cookie exchanges.

1 cup butter or margarine, softened	2 teaspoons McCORMICK® Pure Vanilla Extract
2½ cups confectioners' sugar, divided	⅛ teaspoon salt
½ teaspoon McCORMICK® Ground Nutmeg	2 cups all-purpose flour
	2 cups finely chopped pecans

1. Preheat oven to 350°F.

2. Cream butter in a large mixer bowl until soft. Add ½ cup sugar, nutmeg, vanilla, and salt. Cream until thoroughly mixed. Stir in flour and pecans.

3. Shape dough into 1 inch balls and place 1 inch apart on ungreased baking sheets. Bake in the preheated oven for 15 minutes.

4. Remove from baking sheets and immediately roll hot cookies in remaining 2 cups sugar. Place sugared cookies on wire racks and set aside to cool. When cool, roll again in sugar. **Yield:** 4 dozen.

Per 2 cookies: 220 calories, 2g protein, 22g carbohydrate, 14g fat, 1g fiber, 21mg cholesterol, 91mg sodium

McCormick's® Simple Sugar Cookies

kid-friendly

submitted by: **McCormick® & Company**

Prep Time: 20 minutes
Cook Time: 10 minutes per batch

Test Kitchen Secret:
To make your own colored sugar, combine ½ cup white sugar and a small amount of McCormick® Food Coloring in a jar or resealable plastic bag. Stir until color is evenly mixed with sugar.

This fun and easy cookie can be decorated by the kids and enjoyed by the whole family.

1 cup white sugar	1 egg
1 cup butter or margarine, softened	2¼ cups all-purpose flour
1 teaspoon McCORMICK® Pure Vanilla Extract	Cinnamon sugar or colored sugar (optional)
¼ teaspoon McCORMICK® Ground Nutmeg	

1. Preheat oven to 375°F. With an electric mixer, beat 1 cup sugar, butter, vanilla, nutmeg, and egg in a large bowl until smooth. Gradually stir in flour.

2. Shape dough by teaspoonfuls into balls. Place dough balls 2 inches apart on ungreased baking sheets. Press dough gently with bottom of lightly floured, flat-bottomed glass. Cookies should be about ¼ inch thick. Sprinkle lightly with cinnamon sugar or colored sugar, if desired.

3. Bake in the preheated oven for 8 to 10 minutes or until edges are just golden brown. Cool cookies on baking sheets 1 minute, then remove to wire racks. Cool. Store in airtight container up to 1 week. **Yield:** 3½ dozen.

Per 2 cookies: 167 calories, 2g protein, 20g carbohydrate, 9g fat, 0g fiber, 34mg cholesterol, 93mg sodium

Raspberry Almond Shortbread Thumbprints

This thumbprint cookie is filled with raspberry jam and drizzled with an almond glaze.

Cookies

1	cup LAND O'LAKES® Butter, softened★
⅔	cup white sugar
½	teaspoon almond extract
2	cups all-purpose flour
¼	cup raspberry jam

Glaze

1	cup confectioners' sugar
2	to 3 teaspoons water
1½	teaspoons almond extract

1. Combine butter, white sugar, and ½ teaspoon almond extract in a large bowl. With an electric mixer, beat at medium speed, scraping bowl often, until creamy. Reduce speed to low; add flour. Beat until well mixed. Cover; refrigerate at least 1 hour.

2. Preheat oven to 350°F. Shape dough into 1 inch balls. Place balls 2 inches apart on ungreased baking sheets. Make an indentation in center of each cookie with thumb (edges may crack slightly). Fill each indentation with about ¼ teaspoon jam.

3. Bake in the preheated oven for 14 to 18 minutes or until edges are lightly browned. Cool 1 minute on baking sheets. Remove to wire racks to cool completely.

4. Meanwhile, stir together all glaze ingredients in a small bowl with wire whisk until smooth. Add an additional teaspoonful of water if necessary for drizzling consistency. Drizzle over cooled cookies. **Yield:** 3½ dozen.

★Substitute LAND O'LAKES® Soft Baking Butter with Canola Oil right from the refrigerator.

Per cookie: 95 calories, 1g protein, 13g carbohydrate, 4g fat, 0g fiber, 12mg cholesterol, 45mg sodium

holiday fare

submitted by: **Land O'Lakes, Inc.**

Prep Time: 15 minutes
Chill Time: 1 hour
Cook Time: 18 minutes per batch

What Other Cooks Have Done:
"These were very tasty and easy to make. I find that scooping the jelly with one of those little skinny metal baby spoons into the 'thumbprint' makes the process go a little faster."

Prep Time: 20 minutes
Chill Time: 2 hours
Cook Time: 9 minutes per batch

What Other Cooks Have Done:

"I used white sugar instead of brown sugar and added 1 cup of walnut pieces. Also, I sprinkled cinnamon and sugar on top of the cookies before baking instead of after. They came out great!"

Melt-in-your-Mouth Shortbread Cookies

Follow the recipe below for classic holiday shortbread. Press edges of cookies with the tines of a fork for an interesting decorative detail.

1 cup LAND O'LAKES® Butter, softened★	2¼ cups all-purpose flour
½ cup packed brown sugar	½ cup white sugar
1 teaspoon vanilla extract	1 teaspoon ground cinnamon

1. Combine butter, brown sugar, and vanilla in a large bowl. With an electric mixer, beat at medium speed, scraping bowl often, until creamy. Reduce speed to low; add flour. Beat, scraping bowl often, until mixture leaves side of bowl and forms a smooth, soft dough.
2. Divide dough in half. Shape each half into a 6 inch log. If desired, shape logs into squares or triangles. Wrap each log in plastic wrap; refrigerate at least 2 hours.
3. Preheat oven to 375°F. Cut logs into ¼ inch slices with sharp knife. Place slices 1 inch apart on ungreased baking sheets. Bake in the preheated oven for 7 to 9 minutes or until lightly browned on edges. Cool 5 minutes on baking sheets. Remove to wire racks to cool completely.
4. Stir together white sugar and cinnamon in small bowl. Roll warm cookies in cinnamon-sugar mixture. **Yield:** 3½ dozen.
★Substitute LAND O'LAKES® Soft Baking Butter with Canola Oil right from the refrigerator.

Per cookie: 83 calories, 1g protein, 10g carbohydrate, 5g fat, 0g fiber, 12mg cholesterol, 46mg sodium

Orange Spiced Gingerbread Cookies

Kids can help cut out cookies using their favorite shaped cutters. Once the baking's done, let kids ice the cookies, too.

Cookies

⅔ cup light molasses
⅓ cup packed brown sugar
⅓ cup LAND O'LAKES®
    Butter, softened★
1 egg
2 teaspoons grated orange zest
2¾ cups all-purpose flour
1 teaspoon ground ginger
½ teaspoon baking soda
½ teaspoon salt

Frosting

4 cups confectioners' sugar
½ cup LAND O'LAKES®
    Butter, softened★
2 teaspoons vanilla extract
3 to 4 tablespoons milk
    Food coloring (optional)

kid-friendly

submitted by: **Land O'Lakes, Inc.**

Prep Time: 15 minutes
Chill Time: 2 hours
Cook Time: 8 minutes per batch

Test Kitchen Secret:
Chilled dough is much easier to work with. If you don't have time for the refrigerator, freeze the dough to hurry the process, but only until it's firm enough to shape.

1. Combine molasses, brown sugar, ⅓ cup butter, egg, and orange zest in a large bowl. With an electric mixer, beat at medium speed until smooth and creamy. Reduce speed to low. Add all remaining cookie ingredients; beat until well mixed. Cover; refrigerate until firm, at least 2 hours.

2. Preheat oven to 375°F. Grease baking sheets. Roll out dough on well-floured surface, ½ at a time (keeping remaining dough refrigerated), to ¼ inch thickness. Cut with 3 to 4 inch cookie cutters. Place cookies 1 inch apart on greased baking sheets.

3. Bake in the preheated oven for 6 to 8 minutes or until no indentation remains when touched. Cool completely.

4. Combine confectioners' sugar, ½ cup butter, vanilla, and milk in small mixer bowl. Beat at low speed, adding extra milk if necessary to reach desired spreading consistency. Tint frosting with food coloring, if desired. Decorate cooled cookies with frosting. **Yield:** 3½ dozen.

★Substitute LAND O'LAKES® Soft Baking Butter with Canola Oil right from the refrigerator.

Per cookie: 114 calories, 1g protein, 20g carbohydrate, 3g fat, 0g fiber, 13mg cholesterol, 74mg sodium

party pleaser

submitted by: **Land O'Lakes, Inc.**

Prep Time: 30 minutes
Chill Time: 1 hour
Cook Time: 10 minutes per batch
Stand Time: 1 hour

Test Kitchen Secret:
You can cut out cookies using 2½ inch cookie cutters; you'll get about a dozen fewer cookies. If your cutter sticks to the dough, dip it in flour after every few cuts.

Starlight Mint Sandwich Cookies

Use star-shaped cutters and dip sandwiches in melted chocolate and candy to add sparkle to your cookie tray.

Cookies

1	cup white sugar
1	cup LAND O'LAKES® Butter, softened★
2	egg yolks
1½	teaspoons vanilla extract
½	teaspoon peppermint extract
2¼	cups all-purpose flour
½	cup finely crushed red and white mint candies
¼	teaspoon salt

Filling

6	(1 ounce) squares semi-sweet baking chocolate, melted Crushed red and white mint candies (optional)

1. Combine sugar and butter in a large bowl. With an electric mixer, beat at medium speed, scraping bowl often, until well mixed. Add egg yolks, vanilla, and peppermint extract. Continue beating, scraping bowl often, until well mixed. Reduce speed to low. Add flour, ½ cup crushed candies, and salt; beat until well mixed. Cover; refrigerate until firm, about 1 hour.
2. Preheat oven to 350°F. Grease baking sheets. Roll out dough on lightly floured surface, ½ at a time (keeping remaining dough refrigerated), to ⅛ inch thickness. Cut with assorted 1½ inch cookie cutters. Place cookies 1 inch apart on prepared baking sheets.
3. Bake in the preheated oven for 6 to 10 minutes or until edges are lightly browned. Cool 1 minute on baking sheets. Remove to wire racks to cool completely.
4. Spread about 1 teaspoon melted chocolate on top of 1 cookie; top with another cookie. Repeat procedure for remaining cookies. Decorate cookies, if desired, by dipping part of sandwich cookie in melted chocolate, then crushed candies, or drizzling top with melted chocolate, then sprinkling with crushed candies. Place on wax paper; let stand 1 hour to set. **Yield:** 2½ dozen.
★Substitute LAND O'LAKES® Soft Baking Butter with Canola Oil right from the refrigerator.

Per cookie: 171 calories, 2g protein, 23g carbohydrate, 8g fat, 1g fiber, 31mg cholesterol, 85mg sodium

Austrian Jam Wreaths

Feel free to experiment with the filling of this creative cookie—try apricot preserves or orange marmalade.

1	cup LAND O'LAKES® Butter, softened★	¾	cup finely chopped blanched almonds
¾	cup confectioners' sugar	½	cup sliced almonds
1	egg, separated	½	cup seedless raspberry or apricot preserves
1¾	cups all-purpose flour		
1	teaspoon vanilla extract		

1. Combine butter, confectioners' sugar, and egg yolk in a large mixer bowl. With an electric mixer, beat at medium speed, scraping bowl often, until creamy. Reduce speed to low. Add flour and vanilla; beat until well mixed. Stir in finely chopped almonds by hand. Cover and refrigerate until firm.

2. Preheat oven to 350°F. Grease baking sheets. Divide dough in half. Roll out dough on lightly floured surface, ½ at a time (keeping remaining dough refrigerated), to ⅛ inch thickness. Cut with 2½ inch round cookie cutters. Cut out a 1 inch hole in ½ of the cookies.

3. Place cookies 1 inch apart on prepared baking sheets. Brush cookies with holes in center with reserved egg white. Top with sliced almonds; press down lightly.

4. Bake in the preheated oven for 7 to 10 minutes or until edges are lightly browned. Cool completely.

5. Spread each cookie without a hole with 2 teaspoons preserves; top with almond-covered cookies. Press together lightly. Store in single layer. **Yield:** 2 dozen.

★Substitute LAND O'LAKES® Soft Baking Butter with Canola Oil right from the refrigerator.

Per cookie: 175 calories, 3g protein, 17g carbohydrate, 11g fat, 1g fiber, 30mg cholesterol, 84mg sodium

holiday fare

submitted by: **Land O'Lakes, Inc.**

Prep Time: 30 minutes
Chill Time: 1 hour
Cook Time: 10 minutes per batch

Test Kitchen Secret:
A set of graduated biscuit cutters is perfect for these cookies. Use the larger size to cut the cookies themselves, and the smallest size is just right for cutting out the middles of the "wreaths." Pick up a set of scalloped-edge cutters to make fancier wreaths for the holidays.

Celebrate the Seasons with Nestlé® Toll House®

Make this cookie pizza the centerpiece of your next Halloween party. The kids can help decorate their pizzas, and parents can enjoy their ghoulish treats. You can make Candy Shop Pizzas any time of the year or for any holiday. Decorate with Christmas candies for a festive treat.

Candy Shop Pizza

Leftover trick-or-treat candy really does the trick for pizza that's sure to be a hit with the whole family.

Prep Time: 15 minutes   **Cook Time:** 35 minutes

1   (18 ounce) package NESTLÉ® TOLL HOUSE® Refrigerated Chocolate Chip Cookie Bar Dough
1   cup (6 ounces) NESTLÉ® TOLL HOUSE® Semi-Sweet Chocolate Morsels
½   cup creamy or chunky peanut butter
1   cup coarsely chopped assorted candy

1. Preheat oven to 325°F. Grease baking sheet or pizza pan.
2. Place whole bar of dough, scored side down, onto prepared baking sheet or pizza pan.
3. Bake in the preheated oven for 30 to 35 minutes or until golden brown. Immediately sprinkle morsels over hot crust; drop peanut butter by spoonfuls onto crust. Let stand for 5 minutes or until morsels are shiny. Gently spread chocolate and peanut butter evenly over cookie crust.
4. Sprinkle candy in single layer over pizza. Cut into wedges; serve warm or at room temperature.
Yield: 12 servings.

Per serving: 430 calories, 7g protein, 53g carbohydrate, 23g fat, 2g fiber, 13mg cholesterol, 149mg sodium

Super Candy Bar Cookie Pops

Send your kids to cookie heaven with these sweet and yummy cookies on a stick.

1 (18 ounce) package NESTLÉ® TOLL HOUSE® Refrigerated Chocolate Chip Cookie Bar Dough

20 wooden craft sticks

½ cup NESTLÉ® TOLL HOUSE® Semi-Sweet Chocolate Morsels

1 tablespoon creamy peanut butter

2 (1.55 to 2.1 ounce) NESTLÉ® CRUNCH®, BABY RUTH®, and/or BUTTERFINGER® Candy Bars, chopped

1. Preheat oven to 350°F.

2. Break dough along pre-scored lines. Roll each square into a ball. Place 6 balls at a time on ungreased baking sheets. Insert wooden craft sticks into each ball to resemble a lollipop; flatten dough slightly.

3. Bake in the preheated oven for 10 to 12 minutes or until golden. Cool on baking sheets for 2 minutes; gently remove to wire racks to cool completely.

4. Microwave morsels and peanut butter in a small microwave-safe bowl on HIGH (100%) for 30 seconds; stir. Microwave in additional 10 second intervals, stirring until smooth.

5. Spread about 1 teaspoon chocolate mixture over each pop. Sprinkle each pop with chopped candy bars. Refrigerate for about 15 minutes or until chocolate has set. **Yield:** 20 servings.

Per serving: 167 calories, 2g protein, 22g carbohydrate, 8g fat, 1g fiber, 6mg cholesterol, 65mg sodium

kid-friendly

submitted by: **Nestlé® Toll House®**

Prep Time: 15 minutes
Cook Time: 12 minutes per batch
Chill Time: 15 minutes

Test Kitchen Secret:
Use a food processor to quickly chop candy bars. Processing two different types of bars at once results in a fun mix of flavors.

Eagle Brand® Magic Cookie Bars

comfort food

submitted by: **Eagle Brand®**

Prep Time: 10 minutes
Cook Time: 25 minutes

What Other Cooks Have Done:

"Instead of using graham cracker crumbs, I use chocolate cookie crumbs. This gets rave reviews whenever I make it!"

This bar cookie is an old-fashioned favorite. Substitute two cups plain candy-coated chocolate candies for semi-sweet chocolate morsels for a more colorful creation.

½ cup margarine or butter
1½ cups graham cracker crumbs
1 (14 ounce) can EAGLE BRAND® Sweetened Condensed Milk (not evaporated milk)

2 cups (12 ounces) semi-sweet chocolate morsels
1⅓ cups flaked coconut
1 cup chopped nuts

1. Preheat oven to 350°F (325°F for glass dish). In a 9x13 inch pan, melt margarine in oven. Sprinkle crumbs over margarine; pour EAGLE BRAND® Milk evenly over crumbs. Layer evenly with remaining ingredients; press down firmly.

2. Bake in the preheated oven for 25 minutes or until lightly browned. Cool. Chill, if desired. Cut into bars. Store loosely covered at room temperature. **Yield:** 36 servings.

Per serving: 196 calories, 3g protein, 22g carbohydrate, 12g fat, 2g fiber, 4mg cholesterol, 73mg sodium

Eagle Brand® Magic Cookie Bars

Lemony Cheesecake Bars

Get all the flavor of cheesecake in a smaller, more user-friendly size.

1½ cups graham cracker crumbs
⅓ cup finely chopped pecans
⅓ cup white sugar
⅓ cup butter or margarine, melted
2 (8 ounce) packages cream cheese, softened
1 (14 ounce) can EAGLE BRAND® Sweetened Condensed Milk (not evaporated milk)
2 eggs
½ cup lemon juice

1. Preheat oven to 325°F. In a medium mixer bowl, combine crumbs, pecans, sugar, and melted butter; mix well. Reserve ¼ cup crumb mixture; press remaining mixture into a 9x13 inch pan. Bake in the preheated oven for 6 minutes. Remove and cool on wire rack.

2. Meanwhile, in a large mixer bowl, beat cream cheese until fluffy. Gradually beat in EAGLE BRAND® Milk. Add eggs; beat until just combined. Stir in lemon juice. Carefully spoon mixture on top of crust in pan. Spoon reserved crumb mixture to make diagonal stripes on top of cheese mixture or sprinkle to cover.

3. Bake in the preheated oven about 30 minutes or until knife inserted near center comes out clean. Cool on wire rack 1 hour. Store in refrigerator. Cut into bars to serve. **Yield:** 36 servings.

Per serving: 191 calories, 4g protein, 17g carbohydrate, 13g fat, 0g fiber, 44mg cholesterol, 143mg sodium

make-ahead

submitted by: **Eagle Brand®**

Prep Time: 20 minutes
Cook Time: 36 minutes
Stand Time: 1 hour

What Other Cooks Have Done:
"I am a beginning baker and this always turns out delicious. I find you need to add a little more sugar and butter to get the crust to hold together. It's just right—not too sweet and not too tart!"

Peanut Butter Chips & Jelly Bars

The classic combination of peanut putter and jelly in a delicious bar cookie will have your kids begging for more.

1½ cups all-purpose flour
½ cup white sugar
¾ teaspoon baking powder
½ cup butter, chilled
1 egg, beaten
¾ cup grape jelly
1 (10 ounce) package REESE'S® Peanut Butter Chips, divided

1. Preheat oven to 375°F. Grease a 9 inch square pan.

2. Stir together flour, sugar, and baking powder; cut in butter with pastry blender or fork until mixture resembles coarse crumbs. Stir in beaten egg until blended.

3. Reserve ½ of mixture; press remaining mixture onto bottom of prepared pan. Stir jelly slightly; spread evenly over crust. Sprinkle 1 cup peanut butter chips over jelly. Stir remaining ⅔ cup chips into reserved crumb mixture; sprinkle over top.

4. Bake in the preheated oven for 25 to 30 minutes or until lightly browned. Cool completely in pan on wire rack. Cut into bars. **Yield:** 16 servings.

Per serving: 254 calories, 5g protein, 34g carbohydrate, 11g fat, 1g fiber, 29mg cholesterol, 112mg sodium

kid-friendly

submitted by: **HersheysKitchens.com**

Prep Time: 15 minutes
Cook Time: 30 minutes

Test Kitchen Secret:
Use your favorite jelly or jam to fill these treats.

Chunky Pecan Pie Bars

submitted by: **Nestlé® Toll House®**

Prep Time: 25 minutes
Cook Time: 45 minutes

What Other Cooks Have Done:
"My husband could not get enough of these! Just be careful not to overbake—the corn syrup gets very chewy and hard when it is overbaked (happened a bit on the edges of the pan for me)."

This rich bar cookie is even better than a slice of pecan pie.

Crust

1½   cups all-purpose flour
½   cup butter, softened
¼   cup packed brown sugar

Filling

3   large eggs
¾   cup corn syrup
¾   cup white sugar

2   tablespoons butter, melted
1   teaspoon vanilla extract
1   (11.5 ounce) package (1¾ cups) NESTLÉ® TOLL HOUSE® Semi-Sweet Chocolate Chunks
1½   cups coarsely chopped pecans

1. Preheat oven to 350°F. Grease a 9x13 inch pan.
2. With an electric mixer, beat flour, butter, and brown sugar until crumbly. Press into prepared baking pan. Bake in the preheated oven for 12 to 15 minutes or until lightly browned.
3. Beat eggs, corn syrup, white sugar, butter, and vanilla in a medium bowl with wire whisk. Stir in chunks and nuts. Pour evenly over baked crust. Bake for 25 to 30 minutes or until set. Cool in pan on wire rack. **Yield:** 36 servings.

Per serving: 259 calories, 3g protein, 32g carbohydrate, 15g fat, 2g fiber, 40mg cholesterol, 72mg sodium

Original Nestlé® Toll House® Chocolate Chip Pan Cookies

submitted by: **Nestlé® Toll House®**

Prep Time: 15 minutes
Cook Time: 25 minutes

What Other Cooks Have Done:
"The key is making sure the butter or margarine is room temperature. I once melted it to liquid and that didn't work. Also, go easy on the pan when greasing it or you will get greasy bars!"

These brownielike cookies have all the rich flavor of traditional Toll House® cookies, but are a cinch to make. Cook up a batch today!

2¼   cups all-purpose flour
1   teaspoon baking soda
1   teaspoon salt
1   cup butter, softened
¾   cup white sugar
¾   cup packed brown sugar
1   teaspoon vanilla extract

2   large eggs
1   (12 ounce) package (2 cups) NESTLÉ® TOLL HOUSE® Semi-Sweet Chocolate Morsels
1   cup chopped nuts (optional)

1. Preheat oven to 375°F. Grease a 10x15 inch jellyroll pan.
2. Combine flour, baking soda, and salt in a small bowl. Beat butter, white sugar, brown sugar, and vanilla in a large mixer bowl. Add eggs, one at a time, beating well after each addition. Gradually beat in flour mixture. Stir in morsels and, if desired, nuts. Spread into prepared pan.
3. Bake in the preheated oven for 20 to 25 minutes or until golden brown. Cool in pan on a wire rack, then cut into bars. **Yield:** 48 servings.

Per serving: 118 calories, 1g protein, 15g carbohydrate, 6g fat, 1g fiber, 19mg cholesterol, 118mg sodium

Caramel Pecan Fudge Bars

This easy-to-make cookie bar combines everyone's favorites—chocolate and caramel.

Bars

2	cups white sugar
1½	cups all-purpose flour
⅔	cup unsweetened cocoa powder
½	teaspoon salt
1	cup LAND O'LAKES® Butter, melted
3	eggs
2	teaspoons vanilla extract
36	pecan halves

Topping

⅓	cup caramel ice cream topping or caramel apple dip
⅓	cup chopped pecans
3	tablespoons hot fudge ice cream topping

party pleaser

submitted by: **Land O'Lakes, Inc.**

Prep Time: 20 minutes
Cook Time: 30 minutes

Test Kitchen Secret:
Refrigerate bars about 1 hour for easier cutting. Serve at room temperature.

1. Preheat oven to 350°F. Grease a 9x13 inch pan. Combine sugar, flour, cocoa powder, and salt in a medium bowl. Stir in butter, eggs, and vanilla; mix well.

2. Spread batter into greased 9x13 inch pan. Arrange pecan halves evenly over batter (6 rows crosswise and 6 rows down). Bake in the preheated oven for 25 to 30 minutes or until wooden pick inserted in center comes out clean.

3. Place caramel topping in small microwave-safe bowl. Microwave on HIGH until hot and bubbly (1 to 2 minutes). Stir chopped pecans into caramel topping. Spread evenly over hot bars.

4. Place fudge topping in another small microwave-safe bowl. Microwave on HIGH until heated through (about 1 minute). Drizzle fudge topping over caramel-pecan mixture. Cool completely. Cut into bars. **Yield:** 36 servings.

Per serving: 146 calories, 2g protein, 19g carbohydrate, 8g fat, 1g fiber, 32mg cholesterol, 105mg sodium

Cranberry Macadamia Bars

party pleaser

submitted by: **Land O'Lakes, Inc.**

Prep Time: 20 minutes
Cook Time: 44 minutes

Test Kitchen Secret:
Macadamia nuts have a high fat content, and they can quickly become rancid. Store them in an airtight container in the refrigerator, and use within a month.

An orange glaze complements this bar filled with dried cranberries, coconut, and macadamia nuts.

Crust

⅔	cup all-purpose flour
⅓	cup cold LAND O'LAKES® Butter, cut into pieces★
2	tablespoons white sugar

⅓	cup white sugar
2	eggs, beaten
1	teaspoon vanilla extract
½	teaspoon baking powder
¼	teaspoon salt

Filling

½	cup flaked coconut
⅔	cup coarsely chopped macadamia nuts
½	cup dried cranberries

Glaze

1	cup confectioners' sugar
1	teaspoon grated orange zest
2	to 3 tablespoons orange juice

1. Preheat oven to 350°F. Combine all crust ingredients in a small mixer bowl. Beat at low speed, scraping bowl often, until mixture resembles coarse crumbs. Press into ungreased 8 inch square pan. Bake in the preheated oven for 15 to 17 minutes or until lightly browned.
2. Meanwhile, combine all filling ingredients in a medium bowl; mix well. Carefully spread filling over hot, partially baked crust. Bake for 22 to 27 minutes or until golden brown.
3. Meanwhile, in a small bowl, combine confectioners' sugar, orange zest, and enough orange juice for desired glazing consistency. Drizzle glaze over warm bars. Cool completely. **Yield:** 25 servings.
★Substitute LAND O'LAKES® Soft Baking Butter with Canola Oil right from the refrigerator.

Per serving: 107 calories, 1g protein, 14g carbohydrate, 5g fat, 1g fiber, 24mg cholesterol, 62mg sodium

Pumpkin Cranberry Bars

holiday fare

submitted by: **McCormick® & Company**

Prep Time: 20 minutes
Cook Time: 45 minutes

What Other Cooks Have Done:
"I made this for Thanksgiving, and my family loved it! I cut it into big pieces and served it like cake with whipped topping. Very tasty! I did have to increase the cooking time to an hour because it had not cooked in the middle after 45 minutes."

Enjoy the combination of two fall flavors, pumpkin and cranberry, for a scrumptious treat.

1	(18.25 ounce) package yellow cake mix
2	cups finely chopped pecans or walnuts
½	cup butter or margarine, softened
3	teaspoons McCORMICK® Pumpkin Pie Spice, divided
1	(16 ounce) can jellied cranberry sauce

1	tablespoon orange juice or water
3	large eggs
1	(15 ounce) can pumpkin
1	(14 ounce) can sweetened condensed milk
1	tablespoon McCORMICK® Pure Vanilla Extract

1. Preheat oven to 350°F. Combine cake mix, nuts, butter, and 1 teaspoon pumpkin pie spice until crumbly. Reserve 1½ cups crumb mixture. Press remaining crumb mixture onto bottom of 9x13 inch baking dish.

2. Place cranberry sauce and orange juice in small saucepan. Cook, stirring frequently, over medium heat until smooth. Remove from heat; cool slightly. Meanwhile, in a large bowl, beat eggs. Add pumpkin, condensed milk, vanilla, and remaining 2 teaspoons pumpkin pie spice; mix well.
3. Spread cranberry mixture evenly over crust. Pour pumpkin mixture over cranberry mixture. Sprinkle with reserved crumb topping. Bake in the preheated oven for 45 minutes or until crumb topping is golden brown. Serve warm or chilled. **Yield:** 20 servings.

Per serving: 353 calories, 5g protein, 43g carbohydrate, 19g fat, 2g fiber, 51mg cholesterol, 309mg sodium

Holiday Peppermint Bark

These candies couldn't be easier to make. Whip up a batch for snacking, or give as gifts.

1 (12 ounce) package (2 cups) 24 hard peppermint candies
   NESTLÉ® TOLL HOUSE®
   Premier White Morsels

1. Line baking sheet with wax paper.
2. Microwave morsels in a medium-sized microwave-safe bowl on MEDIUM-HIGH (70%) for 1 minute; stir. Morsels may retain some of their original shape. If necessary, microwave in additional 10 to 15 second intervals, stirring until smooth.
3. Place peppermint candies in heavy-duty zip-top plastic bag. Crush candies using a rolling pin or other heavy object. While holding strainer over melted morsels, pour crushed candy into strainer. Shake to release all small candy pieces; reserve larger candy pieces. Stir morsel-peppermint mixture.
4. Spread mixture to desired thickness on prepared baking sheet. Sprinkle with reserved candy pieces; press in lightly. Let stand for about 1 hour or until firm. Break into pieces. Store in airtight container at room temperature. **Yield:** 32 servings.

Per serving: 75 calories, 1g protein, 10g carbohydrate, 3g fat, 0g fiber, 0mg cholesterol, 16mg sodium

make-ahead

submitted by: **Nestlé® Toll House®**

Prep Time: 10 minutes
Cook Time: 5 minutes
Stand Time: 1 hour

What Other Cooks Have Done:
"I just made this, and it turned out wonderfully. I added 2 teaspoons peppermint oil as well as 1 teaspoon vegetable oil to the morsels to keep the chocolate smooth. I crushed 12 candy canes and added them to the top, then drizzled melted semi-sweet chocolate chips over top. Looks and tastes great!"

Eagle Brand® Party Mints

These party mints are great for special occasions, and they can be made ahead of time for convenience. Roll into balls, or press into festive molds.

1   (14 ounce) can EAGLE BRAND® Sweetened Condensed Milk (not evaporated milk)
1   (32 ounce) package confectioners' sugar, divided

½   teaspoon peppermint extract Assorted colored sugar or crystals

1. With an electric mixer, beat EAGLE BRAND® Milk, ½ package confectioners' sugar, and peppermint extract at low speed until blended. Gradually add remaining confectioners' sugar, beating at medium speed until stiff.

2. Roll mixture into ½ inch balls; roll each ball in sugar, and place on a lightly greased cooling rack. Let stand 8 hours. **Yield:** 21 servings.

Per serving: 245 calories, 2g protein, 57g carbohydrate, 2g fat, 0g fiber, 6mg cholesterol, 24mg sodium

Peppermint Patties

Not only are these chocolate-covered peppermint patties delicious, they're a fun project to do with kids.

1   (14 ounce) can EAGLE BRAND® Sweetened Condensed Milk (not evaporated milk)
1   tablespoon peppermint extract

Green food coloring (optional)
6   cups confectioners' sugar Additional confectioners' sugar
1½   pounds chocolate-flavored candy coating★, melted

1. In a large mixer bowl, combine EAGLE BRAND® Milk, peppermint extract, and food coloring, if desired. Add 6 cups sugar; beat at low speed until smooth and well blended. Turn mixture onto surface sprinkled with confectioners' sugar. Knead lightly to form smooth ball. Shape into 1 inch balls. Place 2 inches apart on wax paper-lined baking sheets. Flatten each ball into a 1½ inch pattie. Let dry at least 1 hour; turn over and let dry at least 1 hour.

2. With fork, dip each pattie into warm candy coating (draw fork lightly across rim of pan to remove excess coating). Invert onto wax paper-lined baking sheets; let stand until firm. Store, covered, at room temperature or in refrigerator. **Yield:** 96 servings.

★Also called confectioners' or summer coating.

Per serving: 81 calories, 1g protein, 14g carbohydrate, 3g fat, 0g fiber, 3mg cholesterol, 12mg sodium

Fruit Bon Bons

A fruity twist on the French confection, this recipe is as easy as can be. Fill a trifle bowl with different colors and flavors for a tasty centerpiece.

1 (14 ounce) can EAGLE BRAND® Sweetened Condensed Milk (not evaporated milk)	1 (8 serving size) package fruit flavor gelatin, any flavor, divided
2 (7 ounce) packages flaked coconut (5⅓ cups)	1 cup ground blanched almonds
	1 teaspoon almond extract
	Food coloring (optional)

1. In a large mixing bowl, combine EAGLE BRAND® Milk, coconut, ⅓ cup gelatin, almonds, almond extract, and food coloring, if desired. Chill 1 hour or until firm enough to handle. Shape into 1 inch balls, using about ½ tablespoon mixture for each. Sprinkle remaining gelatin onto wax paper; roll each ball in gelatin to coat. Place on wax paper–lined baking sheets; chill. Store, covered, at room temperature or in refrigerator. **Yield:** 5 dozen.

Per serving: 75 calories, 1g protein, 8g carbohydrate, 4g fat, 1g fiber, 2mg cholesterol, 27mg sodium

make-ahead

submitted by: **Eagle Brand®**

Prep Time: 20 minutes
Chill Time: 1 hour

Test Kitchen Secret:
If you accidentally chill the gelatin mixture too long and it's too firm to handle, just place the bowl of gelatin in hot water. Stir the mixture frequently to melt it slightly, then chill again to desired firmness.

Magic Rum Balls

Give these no-bake treats in a patterned cellophane bag tied with raffia to the hostess of any Christmas party, but don't forget to keep some for yourself!

3 cups finely crushed vanilla wafers	⅓ cup rum
1 cup finely chopped walnuts	Confectioners' sugar or colored sprinkles
1 (14 ounce) can EAGLE BRAND® Sweetened Condensed Milk (not evaporated milk)	

1. Combine wafer crumbs and walnuts. Add EAGLE BRAND® Milk and rum; blend well. Chill about 1 hour. Dip palms of hands into sugar. Shape rum mixture by teaspoonfuls into small balls. Roll balls in confectioners' sugar or colored sprinkles. Store in covered container in refrigerator. Candies stay moist and fresh for several weeks. **Yield:** 4 dozen.

Per serving: 69 calories, 1g protein, 9g carbohydrate, 3g fat, 0g fiber, 3mg cholesterol, 27mg sodium

holiday fare

submitted by: **Eagle Brand®**

Prep Time: 20 minutes
Chill Time: 1 hour

Test Kitchen Secret:
Rum balls may be dipped wholly or partially in melted semi-sweet chocolate.

Chocolate Mint Layered Torte, page 300

chocolate fantasies

Chocolate treats to **dazzle** your family fill this special bonus chapter. Find cakes, **heavenly** fudge, and everything in between to tempt your family. No comfort food is more **enticing** than rich, velvety chocolate.

Mocha Shakes

Easy mocha milk shakes made with cocoa, instant coffee, milk, and ice cream will satisfy anyone's sweet tooth.

quick & easy

submitted by: HersheysKitchens.com

Prep Time: 10 minutes

What Other Cooks Have Done:

"This was great for an afternoon 'pick-me-up.' I added 1½ tablespoons of espresso powder for extra coffee flavor. We really enjoyed this."

¼	cup warm water	2	teaspoons instant coffee granules
2	tablespoons HERSHEY'S® Cocoa	½	cup milk
1	tablespoon white sugar	2	cups vanilla ice cream

1. Place water, cocoa, sugar, and instant coffee granules in blender container. Cover; blend briefly on low speed. Add milk. Cover; blend on high speed until thoroughly blended. Add ice cream. Cover; blend until smooth. Serve immediately. **Yield:** 3 servings.

Per serving: 258 calories, 7g protein, 33g carbohydrate, 12g fat, 3g fiber, 42mg cholesterol, 93mg sodium

Perfectly Chocolate Hot Cocoa

This hot cocoa is just as easy as any powdered mix, but ten times more flavorful.

comfort food

submitted by: HersheysKitchens.com

Prep Time: 10 minutes
Cook Time: 1½ minutes

What Other Cooks Have Done:

"Definitely comforting on a cold night! To avoid problems with cocoa that didn't dissolve, I simply sifted my cocoa after measuring it out—no more lumps."

2	tablespoons white sugar		Pinch salt
2	teaspoons HERSHEY'S® Cocoa	1	cup milk
		¼	teaspoon vanilla extract

1. Mix sugar, cocoa, and salt in large mug. Heat milk in microwave on HIGH (100%) 1 to 1½ minutes or until hot. Gradually add hot milk to cocoa mixture in mug, stirring until well blended. Stir in vanilla. **Yield:** 1 serving.

Per serving: 265 calories, 11g protein, 43g carbohydrate, 6g fat, 3g fiber, 20mg cholesterol, 511mg sodium

Mocha Shakes

Easy Peppermint Pattie Cappuccino

You don't need to go out for a fancy flavored coffee drink; this beverage is easy, rich, and delicious.

1	small (1½ inch) YORK® Peppermint Pattie, unwrapped and quartered	2	teaspoons milk
		1	cup hot brewed coffee
			Whipped cream (optional)

1. In large microwave-safe mug, place peppermint pattie pieces and milk.
2. Microwave on HIGH (100%) 30 seconds or until candy is melted and smooth when stirred. Stir in hot coffee until mug is almost full.
3. Top with whipped cream, if desired. Serve immediately. **Yield:** 1 serving.

Per serving: 64 calories, 1g protein, 12g carbohydrate, 1g fat, 0g fiber, 1mg cholesterol, 13mg sodium

Hugs & Kisses Crescents

Chocolate kisses wrapped in crescent roll dough satisfy your sweet tooth after dinner or for breakfast. Reheat leftovers in the microwave for a few seconds.

1	(8 ounce) package refrigerated crescent roll dough	½	cup confectioners' sugar (for dusting)
24	HERSHEY'S® KISSES® Milk Chocolates or HERSHEY'S® HUGS® Chocolates		

1. Preheat oven to 375°F. Separate dough into 8 triangles. Remove wrappers from chocolate pieces.
2. Place 2 chocolates at wide end of each triangle; place an additional chocolate on top of other two chocolates. Starting at wide end, roll to opposite point; pinch edges to seal. Place rolls, pointed side down, on ungreased baking sheet. Curve into crescent shape.
3. Bake in the preheated oven for 10 minutes or until lightly browned. Cool slightly; sift confectioners' sugar over crescents. Serve warm. **Yield:** 8 servings.

Per serving: 213 calories, 3g protein, 27g carbohydrate, 10g fat, 1g fiber, 3mg cholesterol, 232mg sodium

Cinnamon Chocolate Cake

No time to bake a great dessert from scratch? Embellish a chocolate cake mix and get scrumptious results.

1	(18.25 ounce) package devil's food cake mix	1	teaspoon McCORMICK® Pure Vanilla Extract
3	eggs	1	teaspoon McCORMICK® Ground Cinnamon
1	cup water	1	(16 ounce) container canned chocolate frosting
½	cup sour cream		
⅓	cup vegetable oil		

1. Preheat oven to 350°F. Grease sides and bottom of 2 (8 inch) round pans. Flour lightly.

2. With an electric mixer, blend cake mix, eggs, water, sour cream, oil, vanilla, and cinnamon in large mixer bowl at low speed 30 seconds or until moistened. Beat at medium speed for 2 minutes. Pour batter into prepared pans.

3. Bake in the preheated oven for 35 to 38 minutes or until wooden pick inserted in center of cake comes out clean.

4. Cool in pans on wire racks for 15 minutes. Remove from pans. Cool completely before frosting. **Yield:** 12 servings.

Per serving: 427 calories, 5g protein, 56g carbohydrate, 23g fat, 1g fiber, 57mg cholesterol, 445mg sodium

make-ahead

submitted by: **McCormick® & Company**

Prep Time: 20 minutes
Cook Time: 38 minutes

Test Kitchen Secret:
If your cake comes out of the pans in pieces, don't despair. Pull out your parfait glasses, cut the cake into cubes, and layer it with whipped cream and sliced fruit.

Glazed English Toffee Cake

party pleaser

submitted by: HersheysKitchens.com

Prep Time: 25 minutes
Cook Time: 30 minutes

Test Kitchen Secret:

Dutch processed cocoa has a more mellow flavor than other types of cocoa. Use it to dust cakes and candies for an extra chocolate fix.

Fill two layers of chocolate buttermilk cake with whipped topping and toffee bits, then glaze and sprinkle with more toffee bits.

2	eggs, separated	½	teaspoon salt
½	cup white sugar	½	cup vegetable oil
1¼	cups all-purpose flour	1	cup buttermilk
1	cup white sugar	1½	cups frozen whipped topping, thawed
½	cup HERSHEY'S® Dutch Processed Cocoa	1	cup SKOR® English Toffee Bits
¾	teaspoon baking soda		Chocolate Glaze

1. Preheat oven to 350°F. Grease and flour 2 (9 inch) round pans. Beat egg whites in small bowl until foamy; gradually add ½ cup sugar, beating until stiff peaks form.
2. Combine flour, 1 cup sugar, ½ cup cocoa, baking soda, and salt in large bowl. Add oil, buttermilk, and egg yolks; beat until smooth. Gently fold egg whites into batter. Pour into prepared pans.
3. Bake in the preheated oven for 25 to 30 minutes or until cake springs back when touched lightly in center. Cool 5 minutes; remove from pans to wire racks. Cool completely.
4. Place 1 cake layer on serving plate; spread whipped topping over top. Sprinkle with ½ of toffee bits. Top with other cake layer. Spoon Chocolate Glaze over top of cake, allowing glaze to drip down sides. Sprinkle with remaining toffee. Store covered in refrigerator. **Yield:** 10 servings.

Chocolate Glaze

½	cup white sugar	3	tablespoons light cream
¼	cup HERSHEY'S® Dutch Processed Cocoa	5	tablespoons butter

1. Combine ½ cup sugar and ¼ cup HERSHEY'S® Dutch Processed Cocoa in small saucepan. Stir in 3 tablespoons light cream and 5 tablespoons butter. Cook over medium heat, stirring constantly, until mixture comes to a boil. Boil 1 minute. Cool to room temperature, stirring occasionally. **Yield:** ¾ cup.

Per serving: 582 calories, 5g protein, 74g carbohydrate, 30g fat, 2g fiber, 42mg cholesterol, 429mg sodium

Deep Dark Chocolate Cake

A lovely chocolate cake with chocolate buttercream frosting.

2	cups white sugar		2	eggs
1¾	cups all-purpose flour		1	cup milk
¾	cup HERSHEY'S® Cocoa		½	cup vegetable oil
1½	teaspoons baking powder		2	teaspoons vanilla extract
1½	teaspoons baking soda		1	cup boiling water
1	teaspoon salt			Buttercream Frosting

1. Preheat oven to 350°F. Grease and flour 2 (9 inch) round pans or 1 (9x13 inch) pan.

2. Stir together sugar, flour, cocoa, baking powder, baking soda, and salt in a large bowl. Add eggs, milk, oil, and vanilla; with an electric mixer, beat at medium speed for 2 minutes. Stir in boiling water (batter will be thin). Pour batter into prepared pans.

3. Bake in the preheated oven for 30 to 35 minutes for round pans, 35 to 40 minutes for rectangular pan, or until wooden pick inserted in center of cake comes out clean. Cool 10 minutes; remove from pans to wire racks. Cool completely. (Cake may be left in rectangular pan, if desired.) Frost cake with Buttercream Frosting. **Yield:** 10 servings.

Buttercream Frosting

6	tablespoons butter, softened		⅓	cup milk
2⅔	cups confectioners' sugar		1	teaspoon vanilla extract
½	cup HERSHEY'S® Cocoa			

1. Beat butter in medium bowl. Add confectioners' sugar and cocoa alternately with milk, beating until spreading consistency is reached (additional milk may be needed). Stir in vanilla. **Yield:** about 2 cups.

Per serving: 682 calories, 13g protein, 108g carbohydrate, 23g fat, 10g fiber, 64mg cholesterol, 563mg sodium

comfort food

submitted by: **HersheysKitchens.com**

Prep Time: 30 minutes
Cook Time: 35 minutes

What Other Cooks Have Done:
"This is the best cake I've ever made or tasted. One thing I do is sift all of the dry ingredients. I've found this helps make the cake not as dense. I also don't use as much milk in the frosting as the recipe calls for."

Hershey's® "Perfectly Chocolate"
Chocolate Cake

Hershey's® "Perfectly Chocolate" Chocolate Cake

Attain chocolate perfection with this layer cake.

2	cups white sugar	2	eggs
1¾	cups all-purpose flour	1	cup milk
¾	cup HERSHEY'S® Cocoa	½	cup vegetable oil
1½	teaspoons baking powder	2	teaspoons vanilla extract
1½	teaspoons baking soda	1	cup boiling water
1	teaspoon salt		"Perfectly Chocolate" Frosting

1. Preheat oven to 350°F. Grease and flour 2 (9 inch) round pans. Stir together sugar, flour, cocoa, baking powder, baking soda, and salt in large bowl. Add eggs, milk, oil, and vanilla; with an electric mixer, beat at medium speed for 2 minutes. Stir in boiling water (batter will be thin). Pour batter into prepared pans.

2. Bake in the preheated oven for 30 to 35 minutes or until wooden pick inserted in center comes out clean. Cool 10 minutes; remove from pans to wire racks. Cool completely. Frost cake with "Perfectly Chocolate" Frosting. **Yield:** 12 servings.

"Perfectly Chocolate" Frosting

½	cup butter	⅓	cup milk
⅔	cup HERSHEY'S® Cocoa	1	teaspoon vanilla extract
3	cups confectioners' sugar		

1. Melt butter. Stir in cocoa. Alternately add confectioners' sugar and milk, beating until spreading consistency is reached. Add small amount of additional milk, if needed. Stir in vanilla. **Yield:** about 3 cups.

Per serving: 613 calories, 12g protein, 95g carbohydrate, 21g fat, 9g fiber, 58mg cholesterol, 489mg sodium

comfort food

submitted by: HersheysKitchens.com

Prep Time: 20 minutes
Cook Time: 35 minutes

What Other Cooks Have Done:
"Always comes out perfect! I microwave 1 cup of water on HIGH for 3 to 4 minutes instead of boiling it, and I use parchment rounds on the bottoms of pans before greasing and flouring to reduce sticking. For firmer frosting, soften butter instead of melting it."

All-Chocolate Boston Cream Pie

The traditional Boston Cream Pie gets a chocolatey twist you'll love.

comfort food

submitted by: **HersheysKitchens.com**

Prep Time: 45 minutes
Cook Time: 35 minutes

What Other Cooks Have Done:

"I used a piece of sewing thread to cut the cake. Just get enough thread to go around the cake, and long enough to grab at the ends, make sure it's in the middle of the cake, then cross the end strings and pull to get an even cut."

1 cup all-purpose flour	1½ cups half-and-half
1 cup white sugar	1 tablespoon butter
⅓ cup HERSHEY'S® Cocoa	1 teaspoon vanilla extract
½ teaspoon baking soda	2 tablespoons water
6 tablespoons butter, softened	1 tablespoon butter
1 cup milk	1 tablespoon corn syrup
1 egg	2 tablespoons HERSHEY'S® Cocoa
1 teaspoon vanilla extract	
½ cup white sugar	¾ cup confectioners' sugar
¼ cup HERSHEY'S® Cocoa	½ teaspoon vanilla extract
2 tablespoons cornstarch	

1. Preheat oven to 350°F. Grease and flour 1 (9 inch) round pan.

2. Stir together flour, 1 cup white sugar, ⅓ cup cocoa, and baking soda in large bowl. Add 6 tablespoons butter, milk, egg, and 1 teaspoon vanilla. With an electric mixer, beat at low speed until all ingredients are moistened. Beat at medium speed 2 minutes. Pour batter into prepared pan.

3. Bake in the preheated oven for 30 to 35 minutes or until wooden pick inserted in center comes out clean. Cool 10 minutes; remove from pan to wire rack. Cool completely.

4. Stir together ½ cup white sugar, ¼ cup cocoa, and cornstarch in a medium saucepan; gradually stir in half-and-half. Cook over medium heat, stirring constantly, until mixture thickens and begins to boil. Boil 1 minute, stirring constantly; remove from heat. Stir in 1 tablespoon butter and 1 teaspoon vanilla. Press plastic wrap directly onto surface. Cool completely. Cut cake into two thin layers. Place 1 layer on serving plate, cut side up; spread filling over layer. Top with remaining layer, cut side down.

5. Heat water, 1 tablespoon butter, and corn syrup in small saucepan to boiling. Remove from heat; immediately stir in 2 tablespoons cocoa. With whisk, gradually beat in confectioners' sugar and ½ teaspoon vanilla until smooth; cool slightly. Pour onto top of cake, allowing some to drizzle down sides. Refrigerate until serving time. Cover; refrigerate leftover cake.
Yield: 8 servings.

Per serving: 573 calories, 11g protein, 80g carbohydrate, 24g fat, 7g fiber, 90mg cholesterol, 244mg sodium

All-Chocolate Boston Cream Pie

make-ahead

submitted by: **Land O'Lakes, Inc.**

Prep Time: 1 hour 30 minutes
Cook Time: 40 minutes
Chill Time: 1 hour

Test Kitchen Secret:

When greasing cake pans, use shortening. Oil, butter, or margarine may cause cakes to stick or burn.

Chocolate Mint Layered Torte *(pictured on page 288)*

This elegant four-layer torte can be easily made ahead.

2	cups all-purpose flour
1½	cups white sugar
1	cup water
½	cup unsweetened cocoa powder
½	cup LAND O'LAKES® Butter, softened★
3	eggs
1¼	teaspoons baking powder
1	teaspoon baking soda
1	teaspoon vanilla extract
1	pint chilled LAND O'LAKES® Gourmet Heavy Whipping Cream

1½	teaspoons mint extract
2	tablespoons white sugar
2	tablespoons LAND O'LAKES® Butter
½	cup semi-sweet chocolate chips
2	tablespoons light corn syrup
¼	teaspoon mint extract
	Mint leaves and raspberries (optional)

1. Preheat oven to 350°F. Grease 2 (9 inch) round pans. Line each pan with waxed paper; grease waxed paper. Set aside.

2. Combine flour, 1½ cups sugar, water, cocoa, ½ cup butter, eggs, baking powder, baking soda, and vanilla in large bowl. Beat at medium speed, scraping bowl often, until smooth.

3. Pour batter into prepared pans. Bake in the preheated oven for 20 to 25 minutes or until wooden pick inserted in center comes out clean. Cool 10 minutes; remove from pans. Remove waxed paper. Cool completely.

4. Combine chilled whipping cream and 1½ teaspoons mint extract in small bowl. With an electric mixer, beat at high speed, scraping bowl often, until soft peaks form. Beat, gradually adding 2 tablespoons sugar, until stiff peaks form. Reserve ½ cup filling for garnish; refrigerate.

5. Cut each cake layer horizontally in half. Place 1 split cake layer on serving plate; spread with ⅓ of filling. Repeat with remaining cake layers and filling, ending with cake layer. Refrigerate at least 1 hour.

6. Melt 2 tablespoons butter in a 1 quart saucepan; stir in chocolate chips and corn syrup. Cook over low heat, stirring constantly, until chocolate chips are melted (2 to 3 minutes). Remove from heat; stir in ¼ teaspoon mint extract. Spread glaze over top of torte, allowing glaze to drip down sides. Garnish with reserved ½ cup filling, mint leaves, and raspberries, if desired. Refrigerate until serving time. **Yield:** 16 servings.

★Substitute LAND O'LAKES® Soft Baking Butter with Canola Oil right from the refrigerator.

Per serving: 480 calories, 6g protein, 52g carbohydrate, 29g fat, 0g fiber, 150mg cholesterol, 290mg sodium

Celebrate the Seasons with Hershey's®

Surprise your someone special with a heart-shaped cake that's perfect for Valentine's Day or any special occasion. Get your kids involved and let them decorate the cakes with colored icing and sprinkles.

Hershey's® Red Velvet Cake

Make this cake into heart-shaped treats or serve in traditional squares—either way, it makes an ideal ending to a romantic dinner.

Prep Time: 30 minutes   **Cook Time:** 35 minutes

½   cup butter, softened
1½ cups white sugar
2   eggs
1   teaspoon vanilla extract
1   cup buttermilk
2   tablespoons liquid red food coloring
2   cups all-purpose flour
⅓   cup HERSHEY'S® Cocoa
1   teaspoon salt
1½ teaspoons baking soda
1   tablespoon white vinegar
1   (16 ounce) can vanilla frosting
1   (12 ounce) package (2 cups) HERSHEY'S® Mini Chips™ Semi-Sweet Chocolate Chips (optional)

1. Preheat oven to 350°F. Grease and flour a 9x13 inch pan.

2. Beat butter and sugar in a large bowl; add eggs and vanilla, beating well. Stir together buttermilk and food coloring. Stir together flour, cocoa, and salt; add alternately to butter mixture with buttermilk mixture, mixing well. Stir in baking soda and vinegar. Pour into prepared pan.

3. Bake in the preheated oven for 30 to 35 minutes or until wooden pick inserted in center comes out clean. Cool completely in pan on a wire rack. Frost; garnish with chocolate chips, if desired. **Yield:** 15 servings.

Per serving: 473 calories, 5g protein, 72g carbohydrate, 19g fat, 2g fiber, 46mg cholesterol, 397mg sodium

Variation

To make heart-shaped cakes, freeze baked cake at least 4 hours. Remove from freezer and let stand 20 minutes. Using a 3 inch heart-shaped cookie cutter, cut cake into 6 hearts. Stack layers to make 2-layer cakes, if desired. Frost with vanilla and strawberry-flavored icing.

Rich Chocolate Pound Cake

Rich Chocolate Pound Cake

Classic pound cake gets a chocolate boost in this rich dessert that's finished with a decorative drizzle of melted chocolate.

1　(12 ounce) package (2 cups) NESTLÉ® TOLL HOUSE® Semi-Sweet Chocolate Morsels, divided
3　cups all-purpose flour
1　tablespoon baking powder
½　teaspoon salt

2　cups packed light brown sugar
1　cup butter, softened
1　tablespoon vanilla extract
4　large eggs at room temperature
½　cup milk

1. Preheat oven to 350°F. Grease a 10 inch Bundt® pan. Microwave 1½ cups morsels in a medium microwave-safe bowl on HIGH (100%) for 1 minute; stir. Morsels may retain some of their original shape. If necessary, microwave in additional 10 to 15 second intervals, stirring until smooth; cool to room temperature. Combine flour, baking powder, and salt in a medium bowl.

2. Beat sugar, butter, and vanilla in a large mixer bowl until creamy. Add eggs, one at a time, beating well after each addition. Beat in melted chocolate. Gradually beat in flour mixture alternately with milk. Spoon into prepared pan.

3. Bake in the preheated oven for 55 to 65 minutes or until a wooden pick inserted near center of cake comes out clean. Cool in pan for 30 minutes. Invert cake onto wire rack to cool completely.

4. Microwave remaining morsels in an unsealed heavy-duty zip-top plastic bag on HIGH (100%) for 30 seconds; knead bag to mix. Microwave in additional 10 to 20 second intervals, kneading until smooth. Cut a small hole in corner of bag; squeeze to drizzle chocolate over cake. **Yield:** 24 servings.

Per serving: 281 calories, 4g protein, 39g carbohydrate, 13g fat, 1g fiber, 57mg cholesterol, 208mg sodium

holiday fare

submitted by: **Nestlé® Toll House®**

Prep Time: 15 minutes
Cook Time: 1 hour 7 minutes
Cool Time: 30 minutes

What Other Cooks Have Done:
"I substituted white sugar for the brown sugar, and added 1 cup sour cream and a 3.5 ounce package instant chocolate pudding. Then I baked the cake for less time than called for in the recipe."

Hershey's® Gridiron Cake

kid-friendly

submitted by: HersheysKitchens.com

Prep Time: 50 minutes
Cook Time: 30 minutes

What Other Cooks Have Done:

"I have the secret on how to bend the goal post. Put the licorice in the microwave 6 to 8 seconds. The licorice will be soft. If you microwave too long the licorice will be really hard. Form the goal posts and let them set for 10 to 15 minutes."

Let the kids help decorate this chocolate sheet cake to look like a football field.

1	cup water
1	cup butter
½	cup HERSHEY'S® Cocoa
2	cups white sugar
1¾	cups all-purpose flour
1	teaspoon baking soda
½	teaspoon salt
3	eggs
¾	cup sour cream
1	tablespoon HERSHEY'S® Cocoa
1	(16 ounce) can vanilla frosting
1	drop red food coloring
2	drops yellow food coloring
3	drops green food coloring
1	(10 ounce) package HERSHEY'S® Premier White Chips
1	(8 ounce) package REESE'S PIECES® Candies
11	HERSHEY'S® KISSES® Milk Chocolates
11	REESE'S® Peanut Butter Cup Miniatures
3	HERSHEY'S® HUGS® Chocolates
6	HERSHEY'S® ROLO® Chocolate and Caramel Candies
2	TWIZZLERS® Strawberry Licorice Twists

1. Preheat oven to 350°F. Grease and flour a 10½x15½ inch disposable foil pan or jellyroll pan.

2. Combine water, butter, and ½ cup cocoa in medium saucepan. Cook over medium heat, stirring occasionally, until mixture boils. Boil 1 minute. Remove from heat; set aside.

3. Stir together sugar, flour, baking soda, and salt in large bowl. Add eggs and sour cream; beat until blended. Add cocoa mixture; beat just until blended (batter will be thin). Pour into prepared pan.

4. Bake in the preheated oven for 25 to 30 minutes or until wooden pick inserted in center comes out clean. Cool cake in pan on wire rack.

5. For chocolate frosting, stir 1 tablespoon cocoa into ⅓ cup frosting; stir until smooth. Tint another ⅓ cup frosting orange with 1 drop red food coloring and 2 drops yellow food coloring; stir until blended. Tint remaining frosting green with 2 or 3 drops green food coloring; stir until blended.

6. Mark "end zones," 2 inches wide at each end of cake, using wooden picks; frost one end zone with chocolate frosting and the other end zone with orange frosting. Frost the area between end zones with green frosting; mark 5 yard lines with wooden picks. Place white chips all across cake on yard lines. Remove wooden picks.

7. Use white chips to spell out "HERSHEY'S" on chocolate end zone; use brown REESE'S PIECES® on the goal line. Use yellow REESE'S PIECES® to spell out "REESE'S" on orange end zone. Use orange REESE'S PIECES® on the goal line.

8. Remove wrappers from KISSES®, peanut butter cups, and HUGS®. Arrange teams on cake playing field, using KISSES® as one team and peanut butter cups as second team. Place HUGS® as referee officials on the field.

9. Unwrap ROLO® candies; for goal posts, stack 3 ROLO® candies in the middle of each goal line on each side of field. Shape strawberry twists into "U" shapes for goal posts. "Glue" with frosting to top of each stack of ROLO® candies. **Yield:** 18 servings.

Per serving: 585 calories, 9g protein, 76g carbohydrate, 28g fat, 3g fiber, 69mg cholesterol, 351mg sodium

Eagle Brand® Chocolate Sheet Cake

A hint of cinnamon and a rich chocolate glaze take basic chocolate sheet cake to a new level of flavor.

quick & easy

submitted by: **Eagle Brand®**

Prep Time: 15 minutes
Cook Time: 15 minutes

Test Kitchen Secret:

For Chocolate Mocha Sheet Cake, add 1 tablespoon instant coffee granules with cocoa to cake, and 1 tablespoon instant coffee granules with cocoa to frosting.

1¼	cups butter or margarine, divided	½	teaspoon salt
½	cup unsweetened cocoa powder, divided	1	(14 ounce) can EAGLE BRAND® Sweetened Condensed Milk (not evaporated milk), divided
1	cup water		
2	cups all-purpose flour	2	eggs
1½	cups packed brown sugar	1	teaspoon vanilla extract
1	teaspoon baking soda	1	cup confectioners' sugar
1	teaspoon ground cinnamon	1	cup coarsely chopped nuts

1. Preheat oven to 350°F. Grease a 10x15 inch jellyroll pan.

2. In small saucepan, melt 1 cup butter; stir in ¼ cup cocoa and water. Bring to a boil; remove from heat. In large mixer bowl, combine flour, brown sugar, baking soda, cinnamon, and salt. Add cocoa mixture; beat well. Stir in ⅓ cup EAGLE BRAND® Milk, eggs, and vanilla. Pour into prepared pan.

3. Bake in the preheated oven for 15 minutes or until cake springs back when lightly touched. In small saucepan, melt remaining ¼ cup butter; add remaining ¼ cup cocoa and remaining EAGLE BRAND® Milk. Stir in confectioners' sugar and nuts. Spread on warm cake. **Yield:** 12 servings.

Per serving: 545 calories, 9g protein, 67g carbohydrate, 29g fat, 3g fiber, 46mg cholesterol, 558mg sodium

submitted by: **Nestlé®**

Prep Time: 20 minutes
Cook Time: 46 minutes

Test Kitchen Secret:

To chop Butterfinger® bars easily, seal them in a zip-top plastic bag and mash bag several times with a mallet, rolling pin, or other heavy object.

Crumble-Topped Chocolate Peanut Butter Cake

Looking for a new family-friendly dessert? This cake has the perfect combination of peanut butter, chocolate, and crunchy candy.

1 (11 ounce) package (1⅔ cups) NESTLÉ® TOLL HOUSE® Peanut Butter & Milk Chocolate Morsels, divided
½ cup NESTLÉ® TOLL HOUSE® Semi-Sweet Chocolate Morsels
2¼ cups all-purpose flour
1 teaspoon baking soda
½ teaspoon salt
1½ cups white sugar
¾ cup butter or margarine, softened
1 teaspoon vanilla extract
3 large eggs
1 cup water
2 (2.1 ounce) NESTLÉ® BUTTERFINGER® Candy Bars, coarsely chopped

1. Preheat oven to 325°F. Grease a 9x13 inch pan.

2. Microwave 1 cup peanut butter and milk chocolate morsels and ½ cup semi-sweet morsels in a medium microwave-safe bowl, uncovered, on MEDIUM-HIGH (70%) for 1 minute; stir. The morsels may retain some of their original shape. If necessary, microwave in additional 10 to 15 second intervals, stirring just until melted. Set aside.

3. Combine flour, baking soda, and salt in small bowl. Beat sugar, butter, and vanilla in large mixer bowl until creamy. Add eggs, one at a time, to butter mixture, beating well after each addition. Beat in melted morsels. Gradually beat in flour mixture alternately with water until smooth. Spread into prepared pan.

4. Bake in the preheated oven for 40 to 45 minutes or until wooden pick inserted in center comes out clean. Immediately sprinkle remaining peanut butter and milk chocolate morsels over cake. Let stand 5 minutes or until morsels are shiny; spread evenly. Sprinkle with BUTTERFINGER® pieces. Cool completely in pan on wire rack. **Yield:** 15 servings.

Per serving: 325 calories, 5g protein, 45g carbohydrate, 15g fat, 1g fiber, 67mg cholesterol, 290mg sodium

Crumble-Topped Chocolate Peanut Butter Cake

Hershey's® Special Dark® Snack Cake Medley

party pleaser

submitted by: HersheysKitchens.com

Prep Time: 20 minutes
Cook Time: 56 minutes

What Other Cooks Have Done:
"We prefer milk chocolate chips, so we made that substitution. We also traded the nuts for SKOR® chips."

A study in light and dark, this recipe is perfect for everyday snacking or for special occasions.

½ cup HERSHEY'S® SPECIAL DARK® Chocolate Chips
1 (8 ounce) package cream cheese, softened
⅓ cup white sugar
1 egg
½ teaspoon vanilla extract
3 cups all-purpose flour
2 cups white sugar
⅔ cup HERSHEY'S® Cocoa
2 teaspoons baking soda
1 teaspoon salt
2 cups water
⅔ cup vegetable oil
2 eggs
2 tablespoons white vinegar
2 teaspoons vanilla extract
½ cup HERSHEY'S® SPECIAL DARK® Chocolate Chips
½ cup MOUNDS® Sweetened Coconut Flakes
½ cup chopped nuts

1. Preheat oven to 350°F. Grease and flour a 9x13 inch pan.

2. Place ½ cup chocolate chips in small microwave-safe bowl. Microwave on HIGH (100%) 1 minute; stir. If necessary, microwave in additional 15 second intervals, stirring after each heating, until chips are melted and

**Hershey's® Special Dark®
Snack Cake Medley**

smooth when stirred. Beat cream cheese and ⅓ cup sugar in medium bowl until well blended. Beat in 1 egg and ½ teaspoon vanilla. Add melted chocolate, beating until well blended. Set aside.

3. Stir together flour, 2 cups sugar, cocoa, baking soda, and salt in large bowl. Add water, oil, 2 eggs, vinegar, and 2 teaspoons vanilla; with an electric mixer, beat at medium speed for 2 minutes or until well blended. Pour 3 cups batter into prepared pan. Gently drop cream cheese filling onto batter by heaping teaspoonfuls. Carefully spoon remaining batter over filling. Combine ½ cup chocolate chips, coconut, and nuts; sprinkle over top of batter.

4. Bake in the preheated oven for 50 to 55 minutes or until wooden pick inserted in center of cake comes out almost clean and cake starts to crack slightly. Cool completely in pan on wire rack. Cover; store leftover cake in refrigerator. **Yield:** 16 servings.

Per serving: 509 calories, 9g protein, 65g carbohydrate, 25g fat, 4g fiber, 55mg cholesterol, 360mg sodium

Black Forest Cake

Chocolate and cherries are a magical combination. This cake is so moist and yummy, it doesn't need icing.

make-ahead

submitted by: **McCormick® & Company**

Prep Time: 10 minutes
Cook Time: 45 minutes

Test Kitchen Secret:
Black Forest cake traditionally contains kirsch, a cherry liqueur. Add a splash to some whipped cream to top squares of cake.

1	(18.25 ounce) package chocolate cake mix		1	teaspoon McCORMICK® Pure Vanilla Extract
2	eggs		1	(6 ounce) package semi-sweet chocolate morsels
1	(21 ounce) can cherry pie filling			
1	teaspoon McCORMICK® Pure Almond Extract			

1. Preheat oven to 350°F. Grease and flour a 9x13 inch pan.
2. Pour cake mix into mixer bowl. Add eggs, pie filling, almond extract, and vanilla. Stir until combined. With an electric mixer, beat at medium speed for 2 minutes. Fold in chocolate morsels.
3. Pour batter into prepared pan. Bake in the preheated oven for 40 to 45 minutes or until wooden pick inserted in center of cake comes out clean.
4. Cool in pan on wire rack 15 minutes. Remove from pan and cool completely on wire rack. Place on flat surface and cut into squares. **Yield:** 15 servings.

Per serving: 259 calories, 4g protein, 44g carbohydrate, 9g fat, 2g fiber, 28mg cholesterol, 301mg sodium

make-ahead

submitted by: **Nestlé® Toll House®**

Prep Time: 1 hour
Cook Time: 25 minutes
Chill Time: 4 hours

What Other Cooks Have Done:

"I made twice as much of the chocolate syrup/coating—I hate having to spread a thick mixture. Definitely make this at least a day ahead of time."

Chocolate Rhapsody

This dessert will be music to your taste buds. Garnish with whipped cream and fresh raspberries.

Cake Layer

⅔ cup all-purpose flour
½ teaspoon baking powder
¼ teaspoon salt
6 tablespoons butter or margarine, softened
½ cup white sugar
1 large egg
1 teaspoon vanilla extract
¼ cup milk

Chocolate Layer

1 (12 ounce) package (2 cups) NESTLÉ® TOLL HOUSE® Semi-Sweet Chocolate Morsels
¾ cup heavy whipping cream

Raspberry Mousse Layer

⅓ cup white sugar
2 tablespoons water
1 teaspoon cornstarch
2 cups (8 ounces) frozen raspberries, thawed
1 (6 ounce) box (3 bars) NESTLÉ® TOLL HOUSE® Premier White Baking Bars, broken into pieces
1¾ cups heavy whipping cream, divided
1 teaspoon vanilla extract
Sweetened whipped cream (optional)
Fresh raspberries (optional)

1. For Cake Layer: Preheat oven to 350°F. Grease a 9 inch springform pan.
2. Combine flour, baking powder, and salt in small bowl. With an electric mixer, beat butter and sugar until creamy. Beat in egg and vanilla. Alternately beat in flour mixture and milk. Spread into springform pan.
3. Bake in the preheated oven for 15 to 20 minutes or until lightly browned. Cool completely in pan on wire rack.
4. For Chocolate Layer: Microwave morsels and cream in a microwave-safe bowl on HIGH (100%) for 1 minute; stir. Morsels may retain some of their original shape. If necessary, microwave in additional 10 to 15 second intervals, stirring until smooth. Cool completely.
5. For Raspberry Mousse Layer: Combine sugar, water, and cornstarch in a medium saucepan; stir in raspberries. Bring mixture to a boil. Boil, stirring constantly, for 1 minute. Cool completely.
6. Microwave baking bars and ½ cup cream in a microwave-safe bowl on MEDIUM-HIGH (70%) for 1 minute; stir. Bars may retain some of their shape. If necessary, microwave in additional 10 to 15 second intervals, stirring until smooth. Cool completely. Stir into raspberry mixture.
7. With an electric mixer, beat remaining cream and vanilla until stiff peaks form. Fold raspberry mixture into whipped cream.
8. Remove side of springform pan; dust off crumbs. Grease inside of pan; reattach side. Spread ½ cup chocolate mixture over cake layer; freeze for 5 minutes. Spoon raspberry mousse over chocolate; freeze for 10 minutes. Carefully spread remaining chocolate mixture over raspberry mousse. Refrigerate for at least 4 hours or until firm. Carefully remove side of springform pan. Garnish with whipped cream and raspberries, if desired.
Yield: 12 servings.

Per serving: 573 calories, 6g protein, 58g carbohydrate, 38g fat, 4g fiber, 105mg cholesterol, 164mg sodium

Chocolate Rhapsody

submitted by: **HersheysKitchens.com**

Prep Time: 40 minutes
Cook Time: 58 minutes
Chill Time: 2 hours

What Other Cooks Have Done:

"I used the food processor for the crust. Be sure not to overbake, and remove cake from the oven while the center is still jiggly—it will set up, and you'll have no cracks."

Hershey's® Special Dark® Chocolate Layered Cheesecake

Dark, darker, darkest! This three-layered chocolate cheesecake is a masterpiece in consistency and taste. You'll never buy another chocolate cheesecake again.

1½	cups vanilla wafer crumbs (about 45 wafers)
½	cup confectioners' sugar
¼	cup HERSHEY'S® Cocoa
¼	cup melted butter or margarine
3	(8 ounce) packages cream cheese, softened
¾	cup white sugar
4	eggs
¼	cup heavy cream
2	teaspoons vanilla extract
¼	teaspoon salt
1	(12 ounce) package (2 cups) HERSHEY'S® SPECIAL DARK® Chocolate Chips, divided
½	teaspoon shortening (do not use butter, margarine, spreads, or oil)

1. Preheat oven to 350°F. To prepare crust: Stir together vanilla wafer crumbs, ½ cup confectioners' sugar, and cocoa; stir in melted butter. Press mixture onto bottom and 1½ inches up sides of a 9 inch springform pan.

2. Beat cream cheese and white sugar in a large bowl until smooth. Gradually beat in eggs, heavy cream, vanilla, and salt, beating until well blended.

3. Reserve 2 tablespoons chocolate chips. Place remaining chips in a large microwave-safe bowl. Microwave on HIGH (100%) 1½ minutes; stir. If necessary, microwave on HIGH in additional 15 second intervals, stirring after each heating, until chocolate is melted when stirred.

4. Gradually blend 1½ cups cheesecake batter into melted chocolate. Remove 2 cups chocolate mixture; spread in bottom of prepared crust.

5. Blend 2 cups cheesecake filling into remaining chocolate mixture; spread 2 cups mixture over first layer in pan. Stir remaining cheesecake batter into remaining chocolate mixture; spread over second layer.

6. Bake in the preheated oven for 50 to 55 minutes or until center is almost set. Remove to a wire rack. With knife, immediately loosen cake from side of pan. Cool to room temperature.

7. Place reserved chocolate chips and shortening in a small microwave-safe bowl. Microwave on HIGH 30 seconds or until chocolate is melted and smooth when stirred. Drizzle over top of cheesecake. Cover; refrigerate several hours until cold. Refrigerate leftovers. **Yield:** 12 servings.

Per serving: 685 calories, 12g protein, 63g carbohydrate, 45g fat, 2g fiber, 150mg cholesterol, 346mg sodium

Black Forest Mini Cheesecakes

Make these mini chocolate cheesecakes in muffin cups.

24	vanilla wafer cookies	1	(8 ounce) container sour cream
2	(8 ounce) packages cream cheese, softened	½	teaspoon almond extract
1¼	cups white sugar	1	(8 ounce) container sour cream
⅓	cup HERSHEY'S® Cocoa	2	tablespoons white sugar
2	tablespoons all-purpose flour	1	teaspoon vanilla extract
3	eggs	1	(21 ounce) can cherry pie filling, chilled

1. Preheat oven to 325°F. Line 24 muffin cups (2½ inches in diameter) with foil bake cups. Place 1 vanilla wafer (flat-side down) in bottom of each cup.

2. With an electric mixer, beat cream cheese in large bowl until smooth. Add 1¼ cups sugar, cocoa, and flour; blend well. Add eggs; beat well. Stir in 1 container sour cream and almond extract. Fill each muffin cup almost full with batter. Bake in the preheated oven for 20 to 25 minutes or until set. Remove from oven; cool 5 to 10 minutes.

3. To make topping: Stir together 1 container sour cream, 2 tablespoons sugar, and 1 teaspoon vanilla in small bowl until sugar is dissolved.

4. Spread heaping teaspoon sour cream topping on each cup. Cool completely in pan on wire rack; refrigerate. Just before serving, garnish with cherry pie filling. Cover; refrigerate leftover cheesecakes. **Yield:** 24 servings.

Per serving: 234 calories, 4g protein, 27g carbohydrate, 13g fat, 1g fiber, 55mg cholesterol, 97mg sodium

party pleaser

submitted by: **HersheysKitchens.com**

Prep Time: 30 minutes
Cook Time: 25 minutes

What Other Cooks Have Done:
"For the crust, I used peanut butter cookie dough (that I bought) and used about ½ tablespoon smashed down to fit into the bottom of each cup. Then I baked them for about 10 minutes. I followed the recipe from there. I suggest doubling the sour cream topping."

Fudge Bottomed Chocolate Layer Pie

make-ahead

submitted by: **HersheysKitchens.com**

Prep Time: 30 minutes
Cook Time: 10 minutes
Freeze Time: 2 hours

What Other Cooks Have Done:
"Don't let the marshmallow mixture cool too long. It makes it very hard to stir in the whipped topping."

A chocolate triple play! Top a chocolate pie crust with a layer of dark chocolate and a light, fresh, chocolate marshmallow filling. If you love chocolate, you'd better keep this recipe nearby.

1 cup HERSHEY'S® SPECIAL DARK® Chocolate Chips, divided
2 tablespoons plus ¼ cup milk, divided
1 (6 ounce) packaged chocolate crumb crust
1½ cups miniature marshmallows
1 (8 ounce) container frozen non-dairy whipped topping, thawed and divided
Additional sweetened whipped cream or whipped topping (optional)

1. Place ⅓ cup chocolate chips and 2 tablespoons milk in microwave-safe bowl. Microwave 30 seconds on HIGH (100%); stir. If necessary, microwave in additional 15 second intervals, stirring after each heating, until chips are melted and mixture is smooth when stirred. Spread on bottom of crust. Refrigerate while preparing next step.
2. Place marshmallows, remaining ⅔ cup chocolate chips, and remaining ¼ cup milk in small saucepan. Cook over medium heat, stirring constantly, until marshmallows are melted and mixture is well blended. Transfer to a large bowl; cool completely.
3. Stir 2 cups whipped topping into cooled chocolate mixture; spread 2 cups mixture over chocolate in crust. Blend remaining whipped topping and remaining chocolate mixture; spread over surface of pie.
4. Cover; freeze several hours or until firm. Garnish as desired. Cover; freeze remaining pie. **Yield:** 8 servings.

Per serving: 408 calories, 4g protein, 46g carbohydrate, 25g fat, 0g fiber, 4mg cholesterol, 168mg sodium

Chocolate-Laced Pecan Pie

Two all-time favorites—pecan pie and chocolate—come together in this extrarich pie.

1	(9 inch) unbaked pie shell	½	cup semi-sweet chocolate chips
1	cup light corn syrup		Pecan halves (optional)
⅔	cup white sugar		Semi-sweet chocolate chips,
⅓	cup LAND O'LAKES®		melted (optional)
	Butter, melted	1	cup LAND O'LAKES®
3	eggs		Gourmet Heavy Whipping
½	teaspoon salt		Cream, whipped (optional)
1	cup pecan halves		

1. Preheat oven to 375°F. Place pie shell in a 9 inch pie plate. Crimp or flute edge; set aside.

2. Combine corn syrup, sugar, butter, eggs, and salt in a small bowl. With an electric mixer, beat at medium speed, scraping bowl often, until well mixed. Stir in 1 cup pecans and ½ cup chocolate chips by hand.

3. Pour into prepared pie shell. Cover pie loosely with aluminum foil. Bake in the preheated oven for 30 minutes. Remove aluminum foil; bake for 10 to 15 more minutes or until filling is set. (If browning too quickly, re-cover with aluminum foil.) Cool; refrigerate at least 4 hours or until ready to serve.

4. Dip additional pecan halves halfway into melted chocolate chips, if desired. Cover; refrigerate until set. Garnish pie with dipped pecan halves and serve with whipped cream, if desired. **Yield:** 8 servings.

Per serving: 643 calories, 6g protein, 68g carbohydrate, 42g fat, 3g fiber, 144mg cholesterol, 427mg sodium

holiday fare

submitted by: **Land O'Lakes, Inc.**

Prep Time: 30 minutes
Cook Time: 45 minutes
Chill Time: 4 hours

Test Kitchen Secret:

Melt chocolate chips for garnish in a zip-top plastic bag. Then, if you have chocolate left over after dipping the pecans, snip off a tiny corner of the bag, and drizzle chocolate over the pie for extra garnish.

Hershey's® Chocolate Pie with Chocolate Petal Crust

make-ahead

submitted by: **HersheysKitchens.com**

Prep Time: 30 minutes
Cook Time: 12 minutes
Chill Time: 6 hours

Test Kitchen Secret:
Thaw frozen dough in the refrigerator until it reaches slicing consistency. Bake as directed.

Make a crust out of homemade chocolate cookie dough and fill it with a fluffy chocolate cream for an impressive party pie.

½	cup butter, softened	¼	teaspoon salt
1	cup white sugar	48	HERSHEY'S® Mini Kisses™ Milk Chocolates
1	egg		
1	teaspoon vanilla extract	⅓	cup milk
1¼	cups all-purpose flour	1½	cups miniature marshmallows
½	cup HERSHEY'S® Cocoa	1	cup heavy whipping cream
¾	teaspoon baking soda		

1. Prepare Chocolate Petal Crust: Beat butter, sugar, egg, and vanilla in large bowl until fluffy. Stir together flour, cocoa, baking soda, and salt; beat into butter mixture. Shape soft dough into 2 (7½ inch) logs. Wrap each log in wax paper or plastic wrap; refrigerate several hours or overnight.
2. Preheat oven to 375°F. Grease a 9 inch pie plate.
3. Cut 1 log into ⅛ inch thick slices; place slices, edges touching, on bottom and up sides of prepared pie plate. (Spaces between slices of dough in crust fill in during baking.) Bake in the preheated oven for 8 to 10 minutes. Cool completely. (Remaining roll of dough may be frozen up to 6 weeks for later use.)
4. For the Hershey's® Chocolate Pie: Microwave chocolates and milk in a large microwave-safe bowl on HIGH (100%) 1 minute; stir until well blended. Stir in marshmallows. Microwave 30 seconds; stir. If necessary, microwave in additional 15 second intervals, stirring after each heating, until marshmallows are melted. Cool to room temperature.
5. Beat whipping cream in a medium bowl until stiff; carefully fold into chocolate mixture. Spoon into prepared crust. Refrigerate until firm, about 4 hours. Cover; refrigerate leftover pie. **Yield:** 8 servings.

Per serving: 642 calories, 11g protein, 76g carbohydrate, 34g fat, 6g fiber, 105mg cholesterol, 369mg sodium

Reese's® Frozen Peanut Butter & Milk Chocolate Chip Pecan Pie

Cheesecake and pecan pie lovers alike will croon for this luscious dessert. The fluffy pie filling combines peanut butter, milk chocolate, cream cheese, and toasted pecans into a light frozen favorite.

1 cup chopped pecans
1 tablespoon butter or margarine
1 (11 ounce) package (1¾ cups) REESE'S® Peanut Butter & Milk Chocolate Chips
½ cup milk
2 (3 ounce) packages cream cheese, softened
⅔ cup confectioners' sugar
1 (1.3 ounce) envelope dry whipped topping mix★
1 (6 ounce) packaged crumb crust
Sweetened whipped cream

1. Preheat oven to 325°F. Place pecans and butter in a baking pan; toast in oven about 7 minutes, stirring occasionally, until butter is melted and nuts are coated. Set aside to cool.

2. Meanwhile, place chips and milk in a medium microwave-safe bowl. Microwave on HIGH (100%) 1 minute; stir. If necessary, microwave in additional 15 second intervals, stirring after each heating, just until chips are melted when stirred; cool 10 minutes.

3. With an electric mixer, beat cream cheese and confectioners' sugar until fluffy; blend in chocolate mixture. Prepare whipped topping mix according to package directions; fold into chocolate mixture. Fold in ½ cup toasted pecans; pour into crust. Wrap tightly; freeze 4 to 6 hours or until firm. Garnish with whipped cream and remaining pecans. **Yield:** 6 servings.

★Substitute 2 cups thawed frozen whipped topping, if desired.

Per serving: 855 calories, 14g protein, 73g carbohydrate, 58g fat, 2g fiber, 63mg cholesterol, 402mg sodium

comfort food

submitted by: HersheysKitchens.com

Prep Time: 20 minutes
Cook Time: 8 minutes
Freeze Time: 6 hours

What Other Cooks Have Done:
"I suggest using a 9 inch deep dish crust. The filling was spilling over the sides a bit, so a deep dish would have worked better. This is a great pie to make the day before and let it freeze overnight."

Gone to Heaven Chocolate Pie

make-ahead

submitted by: **HersheysKitchens.com**

Prep Time: 20 minutes
Cook Time: 10 minutes
Chill Time: 2 hours

What Other Cooks Have Done:

"Excellent pie. I used a graham cracker crust, because that's what I had on hand, and it turned out great. It is a very rich pie, so it will serve many."

This pie is so rich, creamy, and delicious it just might be a little taste of heaven!

⅔ cup white sugar	1 (12 ounce) package (2 cups)
⅓ cup cornstarch	HERSHEY'S® SPECIAL
½ teaspoon salt	DARK® Chocolate Chips,
4 egg yolks	divided
3 cups milk	1 (9 inch) pie shell, baked
2 tablespoons butter or	Sweetened whipped cream or
margarine, softened	whipped topping (optional)
1 tablespoon vanilla extract	

1. Stir together sugar, cornstarch, and salt in a 2 quart saucepan. Combine egg yolks and milk. Gradually blend milk mixture into sugar mixture.
2. Cook over medium heat, stirring constantly, until mixture comes to a boil. Boil and stir 1 minute. Remove from heat; stir in butter and vanilla. Add 1¾ cups chocolate chips; stir until chips are melted and mixture is well blended. Pour into cooled pie shell; press plastic wrap onto filling. Cool. Refrigerate several hours or until chilled and firm. Garnish with remaining chocolate chips and whipped cream, if desired. **Yield:** 8 servings.

Per serving: 625 calories, 10g protein, 73g carbohydrate, 35g fat, 1g fiber, 122mg cholesterol, 342mg sodium

Chocolate & Vanilla Swirled Cheesepie

holiday fare

submitted by: **HersheysKitchens.com**

Prep Time: 20 minutes
Cook Time: 36 minutes
Chill Time: 2 hours

What Other Cooks Have Done:

"I garnished mine with raspberry jam. I just heated it in the microwave until warm and drizzled it over the pie. Heaven!"

Ebony and ivory for the taste buds! This quick, easy, and delicious pie swirls the rich flavor of dark chocolate into smooth vanilla cheesecake. Garnish with fresh raspberries and red raspberry jam, if desired.

2 (8 ounce) packages cream	1 (10 inch) packaged crumb crust
cheese, softened	1 cup HERSHEY'S®
½ cup white sugar	SPECIAL DARK®
1 teaspoon vanilla extract	Chocolate Chips
2 eggs	¼ cup milk

1. Preheat oven to 350°F.
2. With an electric mixer, beat cream cheese, sugar, and vanilla until well blended. Add eggs; mix thoroughly. Spread 2 cups batter in crumb crust.
3. Place chocolate chips in a medium microwave-safe bowl. Microwave on HIGH (100%) 1 minute; stir. If necessary, microwave in additional 15 second intervals, stirring after each heating, until chocolate is melted and smooth when stirred. Cool slightly. Add chocolate and milk to remaining batter; blend thoroughly. Drop chocolate batter by tablespoonfuls onto vanilla batter. Gently swirl with knife for marbled effect.
4. Bake in the preheated oven for 30 to 35 minutes or until center is almost set. Cool; refrigerate several hours or overnight. **Yield:** 8 servings.

Per serving: 590 calories, 9g protein, 55g carbohydrate, 39g fat, 1g fiber, 115mg cholesterol, 366mg sodium

Chocolate & Vanilla Swirled Cheesepie

Deep Dark Fudge Topping

The perfect topping to any dessert! Turn ice cream into a chocolate dream with a rich, fudgy topping.

quick & easy

submitted by: HersheysKitchens.com

Prep Time: 5 minutes
Cook Time: 1 minute

Test Kitchen Secret:

Get double the dessert with this topping: Pour a layer of fudge topping over a brownie, then top with a scoop of ice cream and another layer of fudge topping.

1 (12 ounce) package (2 cups) HERSHEY'S® SPECIAL DARK® Chocolate Chips

1 cup whipping cream
1 teaspoon vanilla extract

1. Stir together chocolate chips and whipping cream in a medium microwave-safe bowl. Microwave on HIGH (100%) 1 minute; stir. If necessary, microwave in additional 15 second intervals, stirring after each heating, until chips are melted and mixture is smooth when stirred. Stir in vanilla. Serve warm over ice cream or other desserts. **Yield:** 16 servings.

Per serving: 212 calories, 2g protein, 18g carbohydrate, 16g fat, 0g fiber, 20mg cholesterol, 6mg sodium

Eagle Brand® Hot Fudge Sauce

Velvety hot fudge sauce adds a delightful touch to almost any dessert, from ice cream to fruit.

comfort food

submitted by: Eagle Brand®

Prep Time: 5 minutes
Cook Time: 10 minutes

Test Kitchen Secret:

To reheat sauce, combine desired amount of sauce with small amount of water in a small heavy saucepan. Over low heat, stir constantly until heated through. For spirited flavor, add ⅓ cup flavored liqueur to entire batch of sauce after it has thickened.

1 cup semi-sweet chocolate chips
2 tablespoons butter or margarine
1 (14 ounce) can EAGLE BRAND® Sweetened Condensed Milk (not evaporated milk)

2 tablespoons water
1 teaspoon vanilla extract

1. In a heavy saucepan over medium heat, melt chips, butter, EAGLE BRAND® Milk, and water. Cook, stirring constantly, until thickened, about 5 minutes. Add vanilla. Serve warm over ice cream or as a fruit dipping sauce. Refrigerate leftovers. **Yield:** 12 servings.

Per serving: 189 calories, 3g protein, 27g carbohydrate, 9g fat, 1g fiber, 11mg cholesterol, 64mg sodium

Fudgey Chocolate Fondue

Cake pieces, cookies, marshmallows, cherries, grapes, mandarin orange segments, pineapple chunks, strawberries, and fresh fruit slices are all great dippers.

½	cup butter	½	cup evaporated milk
½	cup HERSHEY'S® Cocoa	1	teaspoon vanilla extract
¾	cup white sugar		

1. Melt butter in a small saucepan over low heat. Remove from heat; immediately stir in cocoa. Add sugar and evaporated milk.
2. Cook over low heat, stirring constantly, until sugar is dissolved and mixture is smooth. Remove from heat; stir in vanilla. Serve warm with assorted fondue dippers. **Yield:** 6 servings.

Per serving: 351 calories, 7g protein, 39g carbohydrate, 19g fat, 6g fiber, 48mg cholesterol, 182mg sodium

party pleaser

submitted by: HersheysKitchens.com

Prep Time: 10 minutes
Cook Time: 10 minutes

What Other Cooks Have Done:
"The chocolate got a little clumpy from the juice of fresh fruits, so the next time I made this, I cleaned the strawberries the day before to give them time to dry and didn't cut them. But it was best with bananas."

Chocolate & Peanut Butter Dipped Apples

Apples coated with chocolate and peanut butter candy coatings are a tasty variation on an old classic.

10	apples, stems removed	¼	cup plus 2 tablespoons shortening, divided
10	wooden ice cream sticks		
1	cup HERSHEY'S® Semi-Sweet Chocolate Chips		
1	(10 ounce) package (1⅔ cups) REESE'S® Peanut Butter Chips, divided		

1. Line a tray with wax paper. Wash apples; dry thoroughly. Insert a wooden stick into each apple; place on prepared tray.
2. Place chocolate chips, ⅔ cup peanut butter chips, and ¼ cup shortening in a medium microwave-safe bowl. Microwave on HIGH (100%) 1 minute; stir. If necessary, microwave in additional 30 second intervals, stirring after each heating, just until chips are melted when stirred. Dip bottom ¾ of each apple into mixture. Twirl and gently shake to remove excess; return to prepared tray.
3. Place remaining peanut butter chips and remaining shortening in a small microwave-safe bowl. Microwave on HIGH 30 seconds; stir. If necessary, microwave on HIGH in additional 15 second intervals, stirring after each heating, just until chips are melted when stirred. Spoon over top section of each apple, allowing to drip down sides. Refrigerate until ready to serve. **Yield:** 10 servings.

Per serving: 431 calories, 7g protein, 51g carbohydrate, 23g fat, 5g fiber, 2mg cholesterol, 61mg sodium

kid-friendly

submitted by: HersheysKitchens.com

Prep Time: 45 minutes
Cook Time: 2 minutes

What Other Cooks Have Done:
"I heated the chocolate on the stove instead of in the microwave. That way I was able to keep the chocolate 'liquid' while dipping all the apples."

Cocoa Cappuccino Mousse

party pleaser

submitted by: HersheysKitchens.com

Prep Time: 20 minutes
Chill Time: 2 hours

What Other Cooks Have Done:
"This stuff is great. I poured it into store-bought cupcake-sized chocolate cups and served it with grated chocolate on top—yum!"

Condensed milk, cocoa, and coffee are cooked together, then folded into whipped cream and chilled in this mocha mousse.

2	teaspoons instant coffee granules	⅓	cup HERSHEY'S® Cocoa
2	teaspoons hot water	3	tablespoons butter
1	(14 ounce) can sweetened condensed milk	2	cups whipping cream, chilled

1. Dissolve coffee granules in hot water. Combine sweetened condensed milk, cocoa, butter, and coffee in a medium saucepan. Cook over low heat, stirring constantly, until butter melts and mixture is smooth. Remove from heat; cool.

2. Beat whipping cream in large bowl until stiff. Gradually fold chocolate mixture into whipped cream. Spoon into dessert dishes. Refrigerate until set, about 2 hours. **Yield:** 8 servings.

Per serving: 445 calories, 8g protein, 34g carbohydrate, 32g fat, 3g fiber, 110mg cholesterol, 130mg sodium

Hershey's® Chocolate Mousse

make-ahead

submitted by: HersheysKitchens.com

Prep Time: 15 minutes
Chill Time: 30 minutes

What Other Cooks Have Done:
"I like to put a generous spoonful of mousse into a glass, add a layer of fresh berries, then add another spoonful of mousse. Just before serving, I top it with whipped cream and chocolate shavings."

Sweetened heavy cream is flavored with cocoa, whipped with gelatin, and chilled for a cool chocolate mousse.

1	teaspoon unflavored gelatin	¼	cup HERSHEY'S® Cocoa
1	tablespoon cold water	1	cup whipping cream, chilled
2	tablespoons boiling water	1	teaspoon vanilla extract
½	cup white sugar		

1. In small cup, sprinkle gelatin over cold water; let stand 1 minute to soften. Add boiling water; stir until gelatin is completely dissolved and mixture is clear. Cool slightly.

2. Stir together sugar and cocoa in a medium bowl; add whipping cream and vanilla. With an electric mixer, beat at medium speed, scraping bottom of bowl occasionally, until mixture is stiff. Pour in gelatin mixture; beat until well blended. Spoon into serving dishes.

3. Refrigerate about 30 minutes before serving. Cover; refrigerate leftover desserts. **Yield:** 4 servings.

Per serving: 372 calories, 6g protein, 35g carbohydrate, 24g fat, 5g fiber, 82mg cholesterol, 26mg sodium

Deep Dark Chocolate Soufflé

You'll fall for this traditional chocolate soufflé served with a scoop of coffee ice cream.

1	tablespoon white sugar	½	cup white sugar	
½	cup HERSHEY'S® Dutch Processed Cocoa	1	teaspoon vanilla extract	
¼	cup all-purpose flour	4	eggs, separated	
¼	cup butter, softened	2	tablespoons white sugar	
1	cup milk	6	scoops coffee ice cream	

1. Preheat oven to 350°F. Butter a 6 cup soufflé dish; coat with 1 tablespoon sugar.
2. Stir together cocoa and flour in a medium bowl. Add butter; blend well. Heat milk in a medium saucepan until very hot. Reduce heat; add cocoa mixture, beating with whisk until smooth and thick. Remove from heat; stir in ½ cup sugar and vanilla. Cool slightly. Add egg yolks, one at a time, beating well after each addition. Cool to room temperature.
3. Beat egg whites in large bowl until foamy; gradually add 2 tablespoons sugar and continue beating until stiff. Stir small amount of beaten egg whites into chocolate mixture; fold chocolate mixture into remaining egg whites. Carefully pour into prepared dish.
4. Bake in the preheated oven for 40 to 45 minutes or until puffed. Serve immediately with scoops of ice cream. **Yield:** 6 servings.

Per serving: 530 calories, 13g protein, 53g carbohydrate, 30g fat, 2g fiber, 279mg cholesterol, 225mg sodium

holiday fare

submitted by: HersheysKitchens.com

Prep Time: 30 minutes
Cook Time: 45 minutes

What Other Cooks Have Done:
"I used fat-free milk and low-fat ice cream. It still turned out great."

Easy Cocoa Ice Cream

This eggless, cooked chocolate ice cream makes enough to serve a crowd.

1	(14 ounce) can sweetened condensed milk	2	cups whipping cream	
⅓	cup HERSHEY'S® Cocoa	1	cup light cream	
		1	tablespoon vanilla extract	

1. In medium saucepan, stir together sweetened condensed milk and cocoa. Cook over low heat, stirring constantly, until mixture is smooth and slightly thickened, about 10 minutes. Remove from heat; cool slightly.
2. Gradually add whipping cream, light cream, and vanilla, beating with whisk until well blended; refrigerate until cold.
3. Place in ice cream freezer container. Freeze according to manufacturer's instructions. **Yield:** 18 servings.

Per serving: 209 calories, 4g protein, 16g carbohydrate, 15g fat, 1g fiber, 52mg cholesterol, 44mg sodium

party pleaser

submitted by: HersheysKitchens.com

Prep Time: 10 minutes
Cook Time: 10 minutes

What Other Cooks Have Done:
"As the ice cream started to get frozen, I added gobs of peanut butter and chopped-up mini Reese's® peanut butter cups. It was truly awesome!"

Jumbo Three-Chip Cookies

Chock-full of chips, these chocolatey cookies are a handful.

comfort food

submitted by: **Nestlé® Toll House®**

Prep Time: 15 minutes
Cook Time: 14 minutes per batch

Test Kitchen Secret:

Chocolate chip cookies are snack classics. Packaged in patterned cellophane bags and tied with colorful ribbon, they make great gifts for any occasion.

4 cups all-purpose flour
1 teaspoon baking powder
1 teaspoon baking soda
1½ cups butter
1¼ cups white sugar
1¼ cups packed brown sugar
2 large eggs
1 tablespoon vanilla extract
1 cup (6 ounces) NESTLÉ® TOLL HOUSE® Milk Chocolate Morsels
1 cup (6 ounces) NESTLÉ® TOLL HOUSE® Semi-Sweet Chocolate Morsels
½ cup NESTLÉ® TOLL HOUSE® Premier White Morsels
1 cup chopped nuts

1. Preheat oven to 375°F.
2. Combine flour, baking powder, and baking soda in medium bowl. Beat butter, white sugar, and brown sugar in large mixer bowl until creamy.

Beat in eggs and vanilla. Gradually beat in flour mixture. Stir in morsels and nuts. Drop dough by level ¼ cup measure 2 inches apart onto ungreased baking sheets.

3. Bake in the preheated oven for 12 to 14 minutes or until light golden brown. Cool on baking sheets for 2 minutes; remove to wire racks to cool completely. **Yield:** 2 dozen.

Per cookie: 379 calories, 5g protein, 46g carbohydrate, 21g fat, 2g fiber, 50mg cholesterol, 200mg sodium

Hershey's® Special Dark® Chocolate Chip Cookies

Can't get enough dark chocolate in your life? Direct from Hershey's® Kitchens comes the delectable cookie sure to satisfy your cravings.

6	tablespoons butter, softened	½	teaspoon baking soda
⅓	cup butter-flavored shortening	½	teaspoon salt
½	cup packed light brown sugar	2	cups HERSHEY'S® SPECIAL DARK® Chocolate Chips
⅓	cup white sugar		
1	egg		
1½	teaspoons vanilla extract	¾	cup chopped nuts (optional)
1¼	cups all-purpose flour		

1. Preheat oven to 350°F.

2. Beat butter and shortening in a large bowl until well blended. Add brown sugar and white sugar; beat thoroughly. Add egg and vanilla, beating until well blended. Combine flour, baking soda, and salt; gradually beat into butter mixture. Stir in chocolate chips and nuts, if desired. Drop by rounded teaspoons onto ungreased baking sheets.

3. Bake in the preheated oven for 10 to 12 minutes or until lightly browned. Cool slightly; remove from baking sheets to wire racks. Cool completely. **Yield:** 3½ dozen.

Per cookie: 136 calories, 2g protein, 14g carbohydrate, 9g fat, 0g fiber, 10mg cholesterol, 62mg sodium

quick & easy

submitted by: HersheysKitchens.com

Prep Time: 15 minutes
Cook Time: 12 minutes per batch

What Other Cooks Have Done:
"I love the deep rich taste of these chocolate chip cookies. Try the recipe with Mexican vanilla extract if you have some."

submitted by: HersheysKitchens.com

Prep Time: 10 minutes
Cook Time: 9 minutes per batch

Test Kitchen Secret:

For ice cream sandwiches: Prepare Reese's® Chewy Chocolate Cookies as directed; cool. Press a small scoop of vanilla ice cream between flat sides of two cookies. Wrap and freeze.

Reese's® Chewy Chocolate Cookies

Chewy chocolate cookies dotted with peanut butter chips, these cookies make great ice cream sandwiches.

2	cups all-purpose flour	2	eggs
¾	cup HERSHEY'S® Cocoa	2	teaspoons vanilla extract
1	teaspoon baking soda	1	(10 ounce) package (1⅔ cups)
½	teaspoon salt		REESE'S® Peanut Butter
1¼	cups butter, softened		Chips
2	cups white sugar		

1. Preheat oven to 350°F. Stir together flour, cocoa, baking soda, and salt; set aside.
2. With an electric mixer, beat butter and sugar until fluffy. Add eggs and vanilla; beat well. Gradually add flour mixture, beating well. Stir in peanut butter chips. Drop by rounded teaspoonfuls onto ungreased baking sheets.
3. Bake in the preheated oven for 8 to 9 minutes. (Do not overbake; cookies will be soft. They will puff while baking and flatten while cooling.) Cool slightly; remove from baking sheets to wire racks. Cool completely. **Yield:** 4½ dozen.

Per cookie: 142 calories, 3g protein, 17g carbohydrate, 7g fat, 2g fiber, 20mg cholesterol, 108mg sodium

submitted by: HersheysKitchens.com

Prep Time: 15 minutes
Cook Time: 12 minutes per batch

What Other Cooks Have Done:

"These cookies are great. I did not add the white sugar. Also, I added dried cranberries instead of the raisins and about ½ cup of chopped pecans."

Oatmeal Cinnamon Chip Cookies

Cinnamon chips are a wonderful surprise in this classic oatmeal favorite.

1	cup butter, softened	2½	cups quick cooking oats
1	cup packed light brown sugar	1	(10 ounce) package (1⅔ cups)
⅓	cup white sugar		HERSHEY'S® Cinnamon
2	eggs		Chips or Semi-Sweet
1½	teaspoons vanilla extract		Chocolate Chips
1½	cups all-purpose flour	¾	cup raisins
1	teaspoon baking soda		

1. Preheat oven to 350°F.
2. Beat butter, brown sugar, and white sugar in bowl until creamy. Add eggs and vanilla; beat well. Combine flour and baking soda; add to butter mixture, beating well. Stir in oats, cinnamon chips, and raisins (batter will be stiff). Drop by heaping teaspoonfuls onto ungreased baking sheets.
3. Bake in the preheated oven 10 to 12 minutes or until lightly browned. Cool 1 minute; remove from baking sheets to wire racks. **Yield:** 4 dozen.

Per cookie: 144 calories, 2g protein, 19g carbohydrate, 7g fat, 1g fiber, 20mg cholesterol, 89mg sodium

Reese's® Chewy Chocolate Cookies

Cocoa-Coconut Oatmeal Nests

quick & easy

submitted by: **HersheysKitchens.com**

Prep Time: 20 minutes
Cook Time: 10 minutes per batch

What Other Cooks Have Done:

"I used two chocolate eggs in each cookie instead of one. They need to be added shortly after the cookies come out of the oven so that the cookies don't break, and so the eggs stick. The cookies were a big hit, and they are especially good warm since the chocolate eggs are melted."

These chocolate oatmeal cookies are sure to become a family favorite! Kids can help place the candy eggs in the cookies.

¾	cup butter, softened	1	teaspoon baking soda
¾	cup white sugar	½	teaspoon salt
¾	cup packed light brown sugar	1	cup MOUNDS® Sweetened Coconut Flakes
2	eggs		
1	teaspoon vanilla extract	1½	cups quick or old fashioned oats
2	cups all-purpose flour		
¼	cup HERSHEY'S® Dutch Processed Cocoa or HERSHEY'S® Cocoa		HERSHEY'S® Candy-Coated Milk Chocolate Eggs (optional)

1. Preheat oven to 350°F.

2. Beat butter, white sugar, and brown sugar in a large bowl until well blended; beat in eggs and vanilla. Stir together flour, cocoa, baking soda, and salt; add to butter mixture, beating until blended. Stir in coconut and oats; drop by heaping teaspoonfuls onto ungreased baking sheets.

3. Bake in the preheated oven for 8 to 10 minutes or until set. Cool slightly; press chocolate egg into center of each cookie, if desired. Remove from baking sheets to wire racks. Cool completely. **Yield:** 4 dozen.

Per cookie: 91 calories, 1g protein, 13g carbohydrate, 4g fat, 1g fiber, 17mg cholesterol, 88mg sodium

Deep Dark Chocolate Cookies

make-ahead

submitted by: **HersheysKitchens.com**

Prep Time: 25 minutes
Cook Time: 7 minutes per batch

What Other Cooks Have Done:

"I only used ¼ cup of cocoa, and I used chocolate chunks instead of chocolate chips. These were a big hit with my family, and I will be making these again!"

These double chocolate chip cookies are perfect for the chocolate lovers in your life.

¾	cup butter, softened	¾	teaspoon baking soda
¾	cup white sugar	½	teaspoon baking powder
½	cup packed light brown sugar	¼	teaspoon salt
1	teaspoon vanilla extract	1	cup HERSHEY'S® Semi-Sweet Chocolate Chips
2	eggs		
1¾	cups all-purpose flour	½	cup chopped walnuts
½	cup HERSHEY'S® Cocoa or HERSHEY'S® Dutch Processed Cocoa		

1. Preheat oven to 375°F.

2. With an electric mixer, beat butter, white sugar, brown sugar, and vanilla at medium speed for about 2 minutes or until creamy. Add eggs; beat well.

3. Stir together flour, cocoa, baking soda, baking powder, and salt; gradually add to butter mixture, beating just until blended. Stir in chocolate chips and nuts. Drop by heaping teaspoonfuls onto ungreased baking sheets.

4. Bake in the preheated oven for 7 minutes or until set. Cool 1 minute; remove from baking sheets to wire racks. Cool completely. **Yield:** 4 dozen.

Per cookie: 113 calories, 2g protein, 14g carbohydrate, 6g fat, 1g fiber, 17mg cholesterol, 68mg sodium

Chocolate Chip Holiday Tea Cakes

For all the chocolate fans out there, this variation of the beloved holiday cookie incorporates chocolate chips inside as well as melted chocolate drizzled on top.

1 cup butter, softened	1 (12 ounce) package (2 cups)
½ cup sifted confectioners' sugar	NESTLÉ® TOLL HOUSE®
1 teaspoon vanilla extract	Semi-Sweet Chocolate
2 cups all-purpose flour	Morsels, divided
⅔ cup finely chopped nuts	

1. Preheat oven to 350°F.

2. With an electric mixer, beat butter and confectioners' sugar until creamy. Beat in vanilla. Gradually beat in flour and nuts. Stir in 1½ cups morsels. Roll dough into 1 inch balls; place on ungreased baking sheets.

3. Bake in the preheated oven for 10 to 12 minutes or until set and light golden brown on bottom. Cool for 2 minutes on baking sheets; remove to wire racks to cool completely.

4. Microwave remaining morsels in an unsealed zip-top plastic bag on HIGH (100%) for 30 seconds; knead bag. Microwave in additional 10 to 15 second intervals, kneading until smooth. Cut tiny corner from bag; squeeze bag to drizzle chocolate over cookies. Refrigerate cookies for about 5 minutes or until chocolate is set. Store at room temperature in airtight containers. **Yield:** 4½ dozen.

Per cookie: 92 calories, 1g protein, 9g carbohydrate, 6g fat, 1g fiber, 9mg cholesterol, 35mg sodium

holiday fare

submitted by: **Nestlé® Toll House®**

Prep Time: 20 minutes
Cook Time: 12 minutes per batch

Test Kitchen Secret:

For a spicier cookie, add 2 to 2½ teaspoons ground cinnamon to the flour before adding to the butter-sugar mixture.

Macaroon Kiss Cookies

holiday fare

submitted by: HersheysKitchens.com

Prep Time: 20 minutes
Cook Time: 12 minutes per batch
Chill Time: 1 hour

What Other Cooks Have Done:

"I make these using a 2 inch cookie scoop, and then I make a large depression in the center of each cookie. I bake them this way and, when cool, place a scoop of ice cream in the depression, and top with hot fudge sauce."

A yummy cookie gets the added treats of coconut flakes and milk chocolate kisses stirred in. Baked to a coconutty classic conclusion!

⅓	cup butter, softened	1¼	cups all-purpose flour
1	(3 ounce) package cream cheese, softened	2	teaspoons baking powder
¾	cup white sugar	¼	teaspoon salt
1	egg yolk	5	cups MOUNDS® Sweetened Coconut Flakes, divided
2	teaspoons almond extract	48	HERSHEY'S® KISSES®
2	teaspoons orange juice		Milk Chocolates, unwrapped

1. Beat butter, cream cheese, and sugar in large bowl until well blended. Add egg yolk, almond extract, and orange juice; beat well. Stir together flour, baking powder, and salt; gradually add to butter mixture, beating until well blended. Stir in 3 cups coconut. Cover; refrigerate 1 hour or until firm enough to handle.

2. Preheat oven to 350°F. Shape dough into 1 inch balls; roll balls in remaining 2 cups coconut. Place on ungreased baking sheets.

3. Bake in the preheated oven for 10 to 12 minutes or until lightly browned. Remove from oven; immediately press chocolate on top of each cookie. Cool 1 minute; carefully remove from baking sheets to wire racks. Cool completely. **Yield:** 4 dozen.

Per cookie: 253 calories, 3g protein, 28g carbohydrate, 15g fat, 2g fiber, 22mg cholesterol, 95mg sodium

Peanut Blossoms

kid-friendly

submitted by: HersheysKitchens.com

Prep Time: 15 minutes
Cook Time: 10 minutes per batch

What Other Cooks Have Done:

"I usually bake the cookies halfway through and then place the chocolate kiss in the center. I place the cookies back in the oven for the last 2 to 3 minutes and the 'kiss' stays in place."

Peanut butter cookies with a chocolate kiss center, these blossoms have big flavor.

48	HERSHEY'S® KISSES® Milk Chocolates	1	egg
½	cup shortening	2	tablespoons milk
¾	cup REESE'S® Creamy or Crunchy Peanut Butter	1	teaspoon vanilla extract
⅓	cup white sugar	1½	cups all-purpose flour
⅓	cup packed light brown sugar	1	teaspoon baking soda
		½	teaspoon salt
		¼	cup white sugar for decoration

1. Preheat oven to 375°F. Remove wrappers from chocolates.

2. Beat shortening and peanut butter in large bowl until well blended. Add ⅓ cup white sugar and brown sugar; beat until light and fluffy. Add egg, milk, and vanilla; beat well. Stir together flour, baking soda, and salt; gradually beat into peanut butter mixture.

3. Shape dough into 1 inch balls. Roll in white sugar; place on ungreased baking sheets.

4. Bake in the preheated oven for 8 to 10 minutes or until lightly browned. Immediately press a chocolate into center of each cookie; cookie will crack around edges. Remove from baking sheets to wire racks. Cool completely. **Yield:** 4 dozen.

Per cookie: 98 calories, 2g protein, 11g carbohydrate, 6g fat, 1g fiber, 6mg cholesterol, 75mg sodium

Forgotten Kiss Cookies

Make these meringue cookies that are light as air and forget about them until the next day. When you bite into one, a marvelous chocolate surprise is in the center.

30	HERSHEY'S® KISSES® Milk Chocolates	⅛	teaspoon salt
2	egg whites	1	teaspoon vanilla extract
⅛	teaspoon cream of tartar	⅔	cup white sugar

1. Preheat oven to 375°F. Grease baking sheet. Remove wrappers from chocolates.

2. With an electric mixer, beat egg whites with cream of tartar, salt, and vanilla in medium bowl until soft peaks form. Gradually add sugar, one tablespoon at a time, beating 4 to 5 minutes or until stiff peaks form. Mixture will be glossy and sugar dissolved.

3. Drop each meringue by half teaspoonfuls onto prepared baking sheet; top with chocolate piece. Cover chocolate with small teaspoon meringue, making certain to completely cover chocolate. Place baking sheet in hot oven. Turn off oven and allow cookies to remain overnight or until oven has cooled completely. **Yield:** 2½ dozen.

Per cookie: 43 calories, 1g protein, 7g carbohydrate, 2g fat, 0g fiber, 1mg cholesterol, 17mg sodium

make-ahead

submitted by: **HersheysKitchens.com**

Prep Time: 20 minutes
Stand Time: at least 6 hours

What Other Cooks Have Done:
"If you are unfamiliar with making meringue, definitely use a mixer. Beat a minute or two on the first part to get the 'soft peaks,' then add the sugar every 20 to 30 seconds. Drop a small ball of meringue (about the size of a large marble) for the kiss to sit on, then cover it over. Boy, did I love this recipe!"

Chocolate-Cherry Thumbprints

Chocolate-Cherry Thumbprints

These cookies are as pretty as they are delicious. Add your mark to them by indenting with your thumb and placing a cherry on top.

1	(12 ounce) package (2 cups) NESTLÉ® TOLL HOUSE® Semi-Sweet Chocolate Morsels, divided	1	teaspoon baking powder	
1¾	cups quick or old fashioned oats	¼	teaspoon salt (optional)	
		¾	cup white sugar	
		⅔	cup butter or margarine, softened	
1½	cups all-purpose flour	2	large eggs	
¼	cup NESTLÉ® TOLL HOUSE® Baking Cocoa	1	teaspoon vanilla extract	
		2	(10 ounce) jars maraschino cherries	

1. Microwave 1 cup morsels in a small microwave-safe bowl on HIGH (100%) for 1 minute; stir. The morsels may retain some of their original shape. If necessary, microwave in additional 10 to 15 second intervals, stirring until smooth. Combine oats, flour, cocoa, baking powder, and salt, if desired, in a medium bowl.

2. With an electric mixer, beat sugar, butter, eggs, and vanilla until smooth. Beat in melted chocolate. Stir in oat mixture. Cover; chill dough for 1 hour.

3. Preheat oven to 350°F. Shape dough into 1 inch balls. Place balls 2 inches apart on ungreased baking sheets. Press centers of balls with thumb. Place maraschino cherry in each center.

4. Bake in the preheated oven for 10 to 12 minutes or until set. Cool on baking sheets for 2 minutes; remove to wire racks to cool completely. Melt remaining morsels; drizzle over cookies. **Yield:** 4 dozen.

Per cookie: 113 calories, 2g protein, 16g carbohydrate, 5g fat, 1g fiber, 16mg cholesterol, 51mg sodium

holiday fare

submitted by: **Nestlé® Toll House®**

Prep Time: 15 minutes
Cook Time: 12 minutes per batch
Chill Time: 1 hour

What Other Cooks Have Done:

"I put the dough in the freezer for a few minutes, and it was much easier to work with. I drizzled white chocolate over the cookies, and they looked very festive for the holidays."

Sweetheart Kisses Cookies

make-ahead

submitted by: **HersheysKitchens.com**

Prep Time: 15 minutes
Cook Time: 10 minutes per batch

Test Kitchen Secret:
For Valentine's Day cookies, add a few drops of red food coloring to the dough and knead gently before rolling out.

Turn your sugar cookies into a romantic gesture with a kiss—a Hershey's® Kiss®, that is!

1	(20 ounce) package sugar cookie dough (purchased or your favorite recipe) HERSHEY'S® Cocoa	48	HERSHEY'S® KISSES® Milk Chocolates, unwrapped and divided
		1	teaspoon shortening

1. Preheat oven to required temperature. Divide dough in half; roll out one half at a time to ¼ inch thickness following package or recipe directions. Cut out with 2 inch heart-shaped cookie cutters; place on ungreased baking sheets.

2. Bake in the preheated oven according to package or recipe directions. Cool completely on wire racks. Sprinkle cookies with cocoa.

3. Place 12 chocolates and shortening in a small microwave-safe bowl. Microwave on HIGH (100%) 1 minute; stir. If necessary, microwave in additional 15 second intervals, stirring after each heating, until chocolates are melted and mixture is smooth when stirred. Drizzle melted chocolate over cookies. Before drizzle sets, place 1 chocolate piece in center of each heart. **Yield:** 3 dozen.

Per cookie: 114 calories, 2g protein, 14g carbohydrate, 6g fat, 1g fiber, 3mg cholesterol, 62mg sodium

Peppermint Brownies

holiday fare

submitted by: **Land O'Lakes, Inc.**

Prep Time: 20 minutes
Cook Time: 35 minutes
Chill Time: 30 minutes

Test Kitchen Secret:
Try using a variety of peppermint candies—red and green make for extra festive brownies.

This rich chocolate brownie has a hint of peppermint.

Brownie

1¼	cups LAND O'LAKES® Butter
6	(1 ounce) squares unsweetened baking chocolate
3	cups white sugar
4	eggs, slightly beaten
½	teaspoon peppermint extract
2½	cups all-purpose flour
½	teaspoon salt

Frosting

1	cup confectioners' sugar
2	tablespoons LAND O'LAKES® Butter, softened*
⅛	teaspoon peppermint extract
1	tablespoon milk, or as needed
¼	cup crushed peppermint candies

1. Preheat oven to 350°F. Grease bottom only of a 9x13 inch pan. Melt 1¼ cups butter and chocolate in a 3 quart saucepan over low heat, stirring occasionally, until smooth. Remove from heat; stir in sugar. Add eggs and ½ teaspoon peppermint extract; beat just until mixed. Stir in flour and salt; mix well.

2. Spread batter into pan. Bake in the preheated oven for 30 to 35 minutes or until brownie just begins to pull away from sides of pan. (Do not overbake.) Cool completely.

3. Combine 1 cup confectioners' sugar, 2 tablespoons butter, and ⅛ teaspoon peppermint extract in a small bowl. With an electric mixer, beat at low speed, gradually adding milk to desired spreading consistency.
4. Drizzle frosting over brownie. Sprinkle with candy; gently press into frosting. Cover; refrigerate to set frosting (30 minutes). Cut into bars.
Yield: 36 servings.
★Substitute LAND O'LAKES® Soft Baking Butter with Canola Oil right from the refrigerator, if desired.

Per serving: 211 calories, 2g protein, 30g carbohydrate, 10g fat, 1g fiber, 43mg cholesterol, 113mg sodium

Deluxe Toll House® Mud Bars

These chewy, chocolate-filled, chocolate-topped bars also have nuts in them. Try them for an afternoon snack.

1⅛	cups all-purpose flour	1	large egg
½	teaspoon baking soda	1	(12 ounce) package (2 cups)
½	teaspoon salt		NESTLÉ® TOLL HOUSE®
¾	cup packed brown sugar		Semi-Sweet Chocolate
½	cup butter, softened		Morsels, divided
1	teaspoon vanilla extract	½	cup chopped walnuts

1. Preheat oven to 375°F. Grease a 9 inch square pan.
2. Combine flour, baking soda, and salt in a small bowl. Beat brown sugar, butter, and vanilla in a large mixer bowl until creamy. Beat in egg; gradually beat in flour mixture. Stir in 1¼ cups morsels and nuts. Spread into prepared baking pan.
3. Bake in the preheated oven for 20 to 23 minutes. Remove pan to wire rack. Sprinkle with remaining morsels. Let stand for 5 minutes or until morsels are shiny; spread evenly. Cool in pan on wire rack; refrigerate for 5 to 10 minutes or until chocolate is set. **Yield:** 36 servings.

Per serving: 115 calories, 2g protein, 14g carbohydrate, 7g fat, 1g fiber, 13mg cholesterol, 79mg sodium

comfort food

submitted by: **Nestlé® Toll House®**

Prep Time: 20 minutes
Cook Time: 23 minutes
Chill Time: 10 minutes

Test Kitchen Secret:

After sitting at room temperature for about 20 minutes, butter should be soft enough. Set it out on the counter while you measure the other ingredients to make the most of your time.

Championship Chocolate Chip Bars

Chocolate chip bars with a rich cookie crust and a chewy chocolate and nut layer on the top.

party pleaser

submitted by: HersheysKitchens.com

Prep Time: 15 minutes
Cook Time: 40 minutes

What Other Cooks Have Done:

"I substituted some butterscotch chips (about ½ cup), and it was very tasty—must have milk close by! Next time, I might bake it a couple of minutes less to soften the crust a little more, but that's personal preference."

1½ cups all-purpose flour
½ cup packed light brown sugar
½ cup cold butter
1 (12 ounce) package (2 cups) HERSHEY'S® Semi-Sweet Chocolate Chips, divided
1 (14 ounce) can sweetened condensed milk
1 egg, beaten
1 teaspoon vanilla extract
1 cup chopped walnuts

1. Preheat oven to 350°F.
2. Stir together flour and brown sugar in a medium bowl; cut in cold butter until crumbly. Stir in ½ cup chocolate chips; press mixture on bottom of ungreased 9x13 inch pan. Bake in the preheated oven for 15 minutes.
3. Meanwhile, combine sweetened condensed milk, egg, and vanilla in large bowl. Stir in remaining 1½ cups chips and nuts. Spread evenly over baked crust. Bake 25 minutes or until golden brown. Cool completely in pan on wire rack. Cut into bars. **Yield:** 36 servings.

Per serving: 187 calories, 3g protein, 23g carbohydrate, 10g fat, 1g fiber, 17mg cholesterol, 43mg sodium

Rich Chocolate Chip Toffee Bars

Chocolate chips and toffee bits melt in your mouth in this delectable cookie creation.

holiday fare

submitted by: HersheysKitchens.com

Prep Time: 20 minutes
Cook Time: 40 minutes

What Other Cooks Have Done:

"Make sure to cut them extra small, because they are so rich. I used Hershey's® Almond Toffee chips and milk chocolate chips instead of semi-sweet. I also used chopped walnuts and pecans, so the recipe ended up having three kinds of nuts. Very yummy!"

2⅓ cups all-purpose flour
⅔ cup packed light brown sugar
¾ cup cold butter
1 egg, lightly beaten
2 cups HERSHEY'S® Semi-Sweet Chocolate Chips, divided
1 cup coarsely chopped nuts
1 (14 ounce) can sweetened condensed milk (not evaporated milk)
1 (10 ounce) package (1¾ cups) SKOR® English Toffee Bits, divided

1. Preheat oven to 350°F. Grease a 9x13 inch pan.
2. Combine flour and brown sugar in a large bowl. Cut in cold butter until mixture resembles coarse crumbs. Add egg; mix well. Stir in 1½ cups chocolate chips and nuts; set aside 1½ cups mixture.
3. Press remaining crumb mixture onto bottom of prepared pan. Bake in the preheated oven for 10 minutes. Pour sweetened condensed milk evenly over hot crust; top with 1½ cups toffee bits. Sprinkle reserved crumb mixture and remaining ½ cup chocolate chips over top.
4. Bake in the preheated oven 25 to 30 minutes or until golden brown. Sprinkle with remaining ¼ cup toffee bits. Cool completely in pan on wire rack. Cut into bars. **Yield:** 48 servings.

Per serving: 210 calories, 3g protein, 25g carbohydrate, 11g fat, 1g fiber, 23mg cholesterol, 103mg sodium

Fudgey Special Dark® Brownies

Change up your brownie routine with a dark chocolate twist. Homemade brownies are perfect for any occasion—the aroma alone will have people running to the kitchen.

¾	cup HERSHEY'S® Cocoa	2	eggs	
½	teaspoon baking soda	1⅓	cups all-purpose flour	
⅔	cup butter or margarine, melted and divided	1	teaspoon vanilla extract	
½	cup boiling water	¼	teaspoon salt	
2	cups white sugar	1	cup HERSHEY'S® SPECIAL DARK® Chocolate Chips	

1. Preheat oven to 350°F. Grease a 9x13 inch pan.
2. Stir together cocoa and baking soda in a large bowl; stir in ⅓ cup butter. Add boiling water; stir until mixture thickens. Stir in sugar, eggs, and remaining ⅓ cup butter; stir until smooth. Add flour, vanilla, and salt; blend completely. Stir in chocolate chips. Pour into prepared pan.
3. Bake in the preheated oven for 35 to 40 minutes or until brownies begin to pull away from sides of pan. Cool completely in pan on a wire rack. Cut into squares. **Yield:** 3 dozen.

Per serving: 152 calories, 3g protein, 22g carbohydrate, 7g fat, 2g fiber, 21mg cholesterol, 73mg sodium

make-ahead

submitted by: HersheysKitchens.com

Prep Time: 15 minutes
Cook Time: 40 minutes

What Other Cooks Have Done:
"I found that the trick to making these turn out scrumptious is to not overbake them. They are very chocolatey, chewy, and moist. They are good even without the chocolate chips."

Chocolate Covered Brownie Bites

Little balls of brownie are dipped in a chocolate glaze to make elegant bite-sized treats. Leave them plain, or decorate with chopped nuts, candy sprinkles, or confectioners' sugar before the chocolate hardens.

1	(19.5 ounce) package brownie mix, any variety	8	ounces semi-sweet baking chocolate
1	(14 ounce) can EAGLE BRAND® Sweetened Condensed Milk (not evaporated milk)	1	teaspoon vanilla extract
		1	teaspoon butter

1. Preheat oven to 350°F. Prepare brownie mix, and bake in the preheated oven per package directions. Remove from oven; while warm, cut the baked brownie into pieces and roll into balls. Cool.
2. In a saucepan over low heat, combine EAGLE BRAND® Milk and chocolate. Stir slowly until chocolate is melted. Add vanilla and butter; mix well. Keeping chocolate mixture warm, dip brownie balls in chocolate until coated. Place on a wire rack and allow excess chocolate to drip off. **Yield:** 30 servings.

Per serving: 161 calories, 2g protein, 26g carbohydrate, 6g fat, 1g fiber, 5mg cholesterol, 74mg sodium

party pleaser

submitted by: Eagle Brand®

Prep Time: 20 minutes
Cook Time: 30 minutes

Test Kitchen Secret:
When melting chocolate, be sure all utensils are very dry. Even a little water will cause chocolate to stiffen and become lumpy.

Reese's® Peanut Butter & Milk Chocolate Chip Brownie Bars

Traditional brownies take on a new dimension when topped with a light and creamy layer of peanut butter and milk chocolate. Top with nuts or melted baking chips for even more flavor.

6 tablespoons butter or margarine, melted	1 (14 ounce) can sweetened condensed milk (not evaporated milk)
1¼ cups white sugar	½ cup REESE'S® Creamy Peanut Butter
2 teaspoons vanilla extract, divided	1 egg
2 eggs	1 (11 ounce) package (1¾ cups) REESE'S® Peanut Butter & Milk Chocolate Chips, divided
1 cup plus 2 tablespoons all-purpose flour	
⅓ cup HERSHEY'S® Cocoa	
½ teaspoon baking powder	¾ teaspoon shortening
½ teaspoon salt	

1. Preheat oven to 350°F. Grease a 9x13 inch pan.

2. Stir together butter, sugar, and 1 teaspoon vanilla in a large bowl. Add 2 eggs; stir until blended. Stir together flour, cocoa, baking powder, and salt. Add to egg mixture, stirring until blended. Spread in prepared pan. Bake in the preheated oven for 20 minutes.

3. Meanwhile, stir together sweetened condensed milk, peanut butter, 1 egg, and remaining 1 teaspoon vanilla. Pour evenly over hot brownie. Reserve 2 tablespoons chips; sprinkle remaining chips over peanut butter mixture. Return to oven; bake 20 to 25 more minutes or until peanut butter layer is set and edges begin to brown. Cool completely in pan on wire rack.

4. Place reserved chips and shortening in small microwave-safe bowl. Microwave on HIGH (100%) 30 seconds; stir. If necessary, microwave in additional 15 second intervals, stirring after each heating, until chips are melted and mixture is smooth when stirred. Drizzle over top of peanut butter layer. When drizzle is firm, cut into bars. Store loosely covered at room temperature. **Yield:** 24 servings.

Per serving: 267 calories, 7g protein, 34g carbohydrate, 12g fat, 2g fiber, 40mg cholesterol, 159mg sodium

Reese's® Peanut Butter & Milk Chocolate Chip Brownie Bars

submitted by: **Nestlé®**

Prep Time: 20 minutes
Cook Time: 10 minutes

What Other Cooks Have Done:

"The only thing I suggest is to melt the chips and marshmallows in a double-boiler before adding them to the sugar mixture. I ended up with random little white morsels that didn't melt—an added bonus for some!"

Maple Walnut Fudge

Sweet, smooth, and scrumptious, this mouth-watering fudge makes great gifts.

1½	cups white sugar	1	(12 ounce) package (2 cups)
1	(5 ounce) can (⅔ cup)		NESTLÉ® TOLL HOUSE®
	NESTLÉ® CARNATION®		Premier White Morsels
	Evaporated Milk	½	cup chopped walnuts
2	tablespoons butter	1½	teaspoons maple-flavored
¼	teaspoon salt		extract
2	cups miniature marshmallows	50	walnut halves or pieces

1. Line a 9x13 inch pan with foil.
2. Combine sugar, evaporated milk, butter, and salt in a medium-sized heavy saucepan. Bring to a rolling boil, stirring constantly, over medium heat. Boil, stirring constantly, for 4½ to 5 minutes. Remove from heat.
3. Stir in marshmallows, morsels, nuts, and maple extract. Stir vigorously for 1 minute or until marshmallows are melted. Pour into prepared baking pan. On top of fudge, place nut halves in rows, spacing about ½ inch apart. Press into fudge; refrigerate until firm. Cut into squares with 1 nut half per square. **Yield:** 50 servings.

Per serving: 100 calories, 1g protein, 13g carbohydrate, 5g fat, 0g fiber, 2mg cholesterol, 32mg sodium

make-ahead

submitted by: **McCormick® & Company**

Prep Time: 10 minutes
Cook Time: 10 minutes
Chill Time: 1 hour

Test Kitchen Secret:

Butter the inside of the saucepan before you begin. This keeps sugar from clinging to the side of the pan and helps prevent fudge from becoming grainy.

Easy Cinnamon Fudge

A hint of cinnamon enhances chocolate in an easy, make-ahead holiday fudge.

1	(16 ounce) box confectioners'	¼	cup milk
	sugar	1½	teaspoons McCORMICK®
½	cup unsweetened cocoa powder		Pure Vanilla Extract
1	teaspoon McCORMICK®	1	cup chopped nuts
	Ground Cinnamon		Whole nuts (optional)
½	cup butter		

1. Line an 8 inch square pan with foil, allowing foil to extend over sides. Butter foil.
2. In a bowl, mix together sugar, cocoa, and cinnamon.
3. In a saucepan, heat butter and milk until butter melts. Remove from heat. Add vanilla. Add sugar mixture. Stir in chopped nuts. Pour into prepared pan. Garnish with whole nuts, if desired. Refrigerate at least 1 hour.
4. Use foil to lift fudge out of pan. Cut into 2 inch squares. Diagonally cut each square in half, making triangles. **Yield:** 32 servings.

Per serving: 110 calories, 1g protein, 16g carbohydrate, 6g fat, 1g fiber, 8mg cholesterol, 31mg sodium

Deep Dark Fudge

Looking for a smooth, rich, and delicious fudge? Your search is over! Marshmallow creme and evaporated milk are the secret ingredients in this flawless fudge!

1½ cups white sugar
1 (7 ounce) jar marshmallow creme
1 (5 ounce) can evaporated milk
¼ cup butter or margarine
1 (12 ounce) package (2 cups) HERSHEY'S® SPECIAL DARK® Chocolate Chips
½ teaspoon vanilla extract

1. Line an 8 or 9 inch square pan with foil. Butter foil.
2. Combine sugar, marshmallow creme, evaporated milk, and butter in a heavy medium saucepan. Cook over medium heat, stirring constantly, to a full boil. Boil, stirring constantly, 5 minutes. Remove from heat; add chocolate chips and vanilla. Stir just until chips are melted; pour into prepared pan. Refrigerate 1 hour or until firm. Cut into squares. Store tightly covered in a cool, dry place. **Yield:** 36 servings.

Per serving: 138 calories, 1g protein, 21g carbohydrate, 6g fat, 0g fiber, 5mg cholesterol, 20mg sodium

comfort food

submitted by: **HersheysKitchens.com**

Prep Time: 10 minutes
Cook Time: 10 minutes
Chill Time: 1 hour

What Other Cooks Have Done:
"This was a hit. However, if you want it thicker, use a quarter less of evaporated milk and you're done. It's the perfect fudge for any occasion!"

Festive Fudge

This sweet, chocolatey fudge is easy to make and is a great addition to party trays.

3 cups semi-sweet chocolate chips
1 (14 ounce) can EAGLE BRAND® Sweetened Condensed Milk (not evaporated milk)
Pinch salt
½ to 1 cup chopped nuts (optional)
1½ teaspoons vanilla extract

1. Line an 8 or 9 inch square pan with foil. Butter foil.
2. In a heavy medium saucepan over low heat, cook chocolate chips with EAGLE BRAND® Milk and salt until chips are melted. Remove from heat; stir in nuts, if desired, and vanilla. Spread evenly into prepared pan.
3. Chill 2 hours or until firm. Turn fudge onto cutting board; peel off foil and cut into squares. Store, covered, in refrigerator. **Yield:** 16 servings.

Per serving: 280 calories, 4g protein, 34g carbohydrate, 17g fat, 2g fiber, 8mg cholesterol, 59mg sodium

kid-friendly

submitted by: **Eagle Brand®**

Prep Time: 10 minutes
Cook Time: 10 minutes
Chill Time: 2 hours

Test Kitchen Secret:
To make Peanut Butter Glazed Fudge, omit nuts. Stir ¾ cup peanut butter chips in with vanilla. Spread in pan and chill as directed. For glaze, in small saucepan, melt ½ cup peanut butter chips with ½ cup whipping cream; stir until thick and smooth. Spread over chilled fudge.

Super-Easy Rocky Road Fudge

Rich and truly divine fudge!

quick & easy

submitted by: **Nestlé® Toll House®**

Prep Time: 15 minutes
Cook Time: 1 minute
Chill Time: 30 minutes

Test Kitchen Secret:
Make fudge on a dry day for best results. If it's a humid day, the candy may have a more sugary texture.

1 (12 ounce) package (2 cups) NESTLÉ® TOLL HOUSE® Semi-Sweet Chocolate Morsels	1 teaspoon vanilla extract
	3 cups miniature marshmallows
	1½ cups coarsely chopped walnuts
1 (14 ounce) can NESTLÉ® CARNATION® Sweetened Condensed Milk	

1. Line a 9x13 inch pan with foil; lightly grease foil.

2. Microwave morsels and sweetened condensed milk in a large microwave-safe bowl on HIGH (100%) 1 minute; stir. Morsels may retain some of their original shape. If necessary, microwave in additional 10 to 15 second intervals, stirring until smooth. Stir in vanilla. Fold in marshmallows and nuts.

3. Press mixture into prepared pan. Refrigerate until ready to serve. Use foil to lift fudge out of pan; remove foil. Cut into pieces. **Yield:** 48 servings.

Per serving: 100 calories, 2g protein, 13g carbohydrate, 5g fat, 1g fiber, 2mg cholesterol, 13mg sodium

Super-Easy Rocky Road Fudge

Double-Decker Fudge

Peanut butter fudge on the bottom and chocolate on top make for doubly delicious fudge.

1	cup REESE'S® Peanut Butter Chips	1	(7 ounce) jar marshmallow creme
1	cup HERSHEY'S® Semi-Sweet Chocolate Chips	¾	cup evaporated milk
2¼	cups white sugar	¼	cup butter
		1	teaspoon vanilla extract

1. Line an 8 inch square pan with foil, extending foil over edges of pan. Measure peanut butter chips into one medium bowl and chocolate chips into a second medium bowl.

2. Combine sugar, marshmallow creme, evaporated milk, and butter in a heavy 3 quart saucepan. Cook over medium heat, stirring constantly, until mixture boils; boil, stirring constantly, 5 minutes. Remove from heat; stir in vanilla. Immediately stir ½ of hot mixture (1½ cups) into peanut butter chips until chips are completely melted; quickly pour into prepared pan. Stir remaining ½ of hot mixture into chocolate chips until chips are completely melted. Quickly spread over top of peanut butter layer.

3. Cool completely. Remove from pan; place on cutting board. Peel off and discard foil; cut fudge into 1 inch squares. Store tightly covered.
Yield: 60 servings.

Per serving: 96 calories, 1g protein, 15g carbohydrate, 3g fat, 0g fiber, 3mg cholesterol, 22mg sodium

make-ahead

submitted by: **HersheysKitchens.com**

Prep Time: 15 minutes
Cook Time: 10 minutes
Cool Time: 1 hour

What Other Cooks Have Done:
"I also sprinkle extra peanut butter and chocolate chips on the fudge when it isn't too hot. This makes it very pretty and adds a nice crunch to the soft fudge."

Special Dark® Fudge Truffles

Coat this rich truffle with your favorite toppings. Be creative—your handmade truffles are sure to impress!

1	(12 ounce) package (2 cups) HERSHEY'S® SPECIAL DARK® Chocolate Chips	Various coatings such as chopped toasted pecans, coconut, confectioners' sugar, cocoa powder, or candy pieces
¾	cup whipping cream	

1. Combine chocolate chips and whipping cream in a medium microwave-safe bowl. Microwave on HIGH (100%) 1 minute; stir. If necessary, microwave in additional 15 second intervals, stirring after each heating, until chips are melted and mixture is smooth when stirred.

2. Refrigerate 3 hours or until firm. Roll mixture into 1 inch balls. Roll each ball in coating. Cover; store in refrigerator. **Yield:** 3 dozen.

Per truffle: 88 calories, 1g protein, 8g carbohydrate, 6g fat, 0g fiber, 7mg cholesterol, 2mg sodium

holiday fare

submitted by: **HersheysKitchens.com**

Prep Time: 10 minutes
Cook Time: 1 minute
Chill Time: 3 hours

Test Kitchen Secret:
If you coat your truffles with confectioners' sugar or cocoa powder, try sifting the coating over the truffles instead of rolling them in it. You'll end up with prettier, less clumped coatings that way.

metric equivalents

The recipes that appear in this cookbook use the standard United States method for measuring liquid and dry or solid ingredients (teaspoons, tablespoons, and cups). The information on this chart is provided to help cooks outside the U.S. successfully use these recipes. All equivalents are approximate.

Equivalents for Different Types of Ingredients

A standard cup measure of a dry or solid ingredient will vary in weight depending on the type of ingredient. A standard cup of liquid is the same volume for any type of liquid. Use the following chart when converting standard cup measures to grams (weight) or milliliters (volume).

Standard Cup	Fine Powder	Grain	Granular	Liquid Solids	Liquid
	(ex. flour)	(ex. rice)	(ex. sugar)	(ex. butter)	(ex. milk)
1	140 g	150 g	190 g	200 g	240 ml
¾	105 g	113 g	143 g	150 g	180 ml
⅔	93 g	100 g	125 g	133 g	160 ml
½	70 g	75 g	95 g	100 g	120 ml
⅓	47 g	50 g	63 g	67 g	80 ml
¼	35 g	38 g	48 g	50 g	60 ml
⅛	18 g	19 g	24 g	25 g	30 ml

Dry Ingredients by Weight

(To convert ounces to grams, multiply the number of ounces by 30.)

1 oz	=	1/16 lb	=	30 g
4 oz	=	¼ lb	=	120 g
8 oz	=	½ lb	=	240 g
12 oz	=	¾ lb	=	360 g
16 oz	=	1 lb	=	480 g

Length

(To convert inches to centimeters, multiply the number of inches by 2.5.)

1 in				=	2.5 cm		
6 in	=	½ ft		=	15 cm		
12 in	=	1 ft		=	30 cm		
36 in	=	3 ft	=	1 yd	=	90 cm		
40 in				=	100 cm	=	1 meter

Liquid Ingredients by Volume

¼ tsp					=	1 ml	
½ tsp					=	2 ml	
1 tsp					=	5 ml	
3 tsp	=	1 tbls		= ½ fl oz	=	15 ml	
	2 tbls	=	⅛ cup	= 1 fl oz	=	30 ml	
	4 tbls	=	¼ cup	= 2 fl oz	=	60 ml	
	5⅓ tbls	=	⅓ cup	= 3 fl oz	=	80 ml	
	8 tbls	=	½ cup	= 4 fl oz	=	120 ml	
	10⅔ tbls	=	⅔ cup	= 5 fl oz	=	160 ml	
	12 tbls	=	¾ cup	= 6 fl oz	=	180 ml	
	16 tbls	=	1 cup	= 8 fl oz	=	240 ml	
	1 pt	=	2 cups	= 16 fl oz	=	480 ml	
	1 qt	=	4 cups	= 32 fl oz	=	960 ml	
				33 fl oz	=	1000 ml	= 1 liter

Cooking/Oven Temperatures

	Fahrenheit	Celsius	Gas Mark
Freeze Water	32° F	0° C	
Room Temperature	68° F	20° C	
Boil Water	212° F	100° C	
Bake	325° F	160° C	3
	350° F	175° C	4
	375° F	190° C	5
	400° F	200° C	6
	425° F	220° C	7
	450° F	230° C	8
Broil			Grill

Recommended Storage Guide

In the Pantry

Baking powder and soda	1 year
Flour, all-purpose	10 to 15 months
Milk, evaporated and	
sweetened condensed	1 year
Mixes	
cake	1 year
pancake	6 months
Peanut butter	6 months
Salt and pepper	18 months
Shortening	8 months
Spices (discard if aroma fades)	
ground	6 months
whole	1 year
Sugar	18 months

In the Refrigerator

Butter and margarine	1 month
Buttermilk	1 to 2 weeks
Eggs (fresh in shell)	3 to 5 weeks
Half-and-half	7 to 10 days
Meat	
casseroles, cooked	3 to 4 days
steaks, chops,	
roasts, uncooked	3 to 5 days
Milk, whole or fat-free	1 week
Poultry, uncooked	1 to 2 days
Sour cream	3 to 4 weeks
Whipping cream	10 days

In the Freezer

Breads	
quick	2 to 3 months
yeast	3 to 6 months
Butter	6 months
Cakes	
cheesecakes and	
pound cakes	2 to 3 months
unfrosted	2 to 5 months
with cooked frosting	*not recommended*
with creamy-type frosting	3 months
Candy and fudge	6 months
Casseroles	1 to 2 months
Cheese	4 months
Cookies	
baked, unfrosted	8 to 12 months
dough	1 month
Eggs (not in shell)	
whites	1 year
yolks	8 months
Ice cream	1 to 3 months
Meat	
cooked	2 to 3 months
ground, uncooked	3 to 4 months
roasts, uncooked	9 months
steaks or chops,	
uncooked	4 to 6 months
Nuts	8 months
Pies	
pastry shell	2 to 3 months
fruit	1 to 2 months
pumpkin	2 to 4 months
custard, cream,	
meringue	*not recommended*
Poultry	
cooked	3 to 4 months
parts, uncooked	9 months
whole, uncooked	12 months
Soups and stews	2 to 3 months

nutritional analysis

Nutrition Analyses Based on Premier Databases

Allrecipes.com is proud to provide ESHA Research's nutrient databases for recipe nutritional analysis. ESHA Research is the premier nutritional analysis provider for the world's nutrition and health industries, having provided nutrient information to health care providers and the world's top food manufacturing firms for more than 16 years. Its nutrient databases total more than 22,000 foods, track 165 nutrient factors, and combine nutrient data from over 1,200 scientific sources of information. For more information about ESHA Research, visit their website at **http://www.esha.com.**

Using Allrecipes.com Information with Care

Allrecipes.com is committed to providing recipe-based nutritional information so that individuals may, by choice or under a doctor's advice, adhere to specific dietary requirements and make healthful recipe choices. The nutritional values that appear in this book and on **Allrecipes.com** nutrition pages are based on individual recipe ingredients. While we have taken the utmost care in providing you with the most accurate nutritional values possible, please note that this information is not intended for medical nutrition therapy. If you are following a strict diet for medical or dietary reasons, it's important that you, first, consult your physician or registered dietitian before planning your meals based on recipes at **Allrecipes.com,** and, second, remain under appropriate medical supervision while using the nutritional information at **Allrecipes.com.**

brand name index

This index lists every recipe by brand name.

recipe title index

This index alphabetically lists every recipe by exact title.

general recipe index

This index lists every recipe by food category and/or ingredient.

favorite recipes journal

Jot down your family's and your favorite recipes for quick and handy reference. And don't forget to include the dishes that draw rave reviews when friends come for dinner.

Recipe	Source/Page	Remarks